THE
HYMNS OF THE ATHARVA-VEDA

THE
HYMNS OF THE ATHARVA-VEDA

Translated
with a Popular Commentary

BY

RALPH T. H. GRIFFITH

VOL. I

GYAN

Published by

GYAN

Gyan Publishing House
5, Ansari Road
Daryaganj, New Delhi-110002
Phone: 011-47034999, 9811692060
E-mail: books@gyanbooks.com

Distribution Network
gyanbooks.com
India, USA, Canada, UK, Australia, France

ISBN : 978-81-212-9944-2 (Set)
ISBN : 978-81-212-9943-5 (PB)
First Published, 1895

2nd Impression 2021

Printed at: Gyan Press, Delhi.

The Hymns of the Atharva-Veda, Vol. I
Author: Ralph T. H. Griffith

THE

HYMNS OF THE ATHARVA-VEDA

TRANSLATED
WITH A POPULAR COMMENTARY

BY

RALPH T. H. GRIFFITH
FORMERLY PRINCIPAL OF BENARES COLLEGE

VOL. I

Benares
PRINTED AND PUBLISHED BY E. J. LAZARUS & Co.
SOLD ALSO BY
LUZAC AND COMPANY, LONDON.

1895

CONTENTS.

PREFACE.

The Atharva-veda is a comparatively late addition to the three ancient Vedas, the Ṛik, Yajus, and Sâman—the Vedas respectively of recited praise, sacrifice, and song or chanted hymn—which formed the foundation of the early religious belief and worship of the Hindus. Unlike these three Vedas, the Atharva-veda derives the name by which it is generally known, not from the nature of its contents but from a personage of indefinitely remote antiquity named Atharvan, who is spoken of in the Ṛigveda as the first priest who 'rubbed Agni forth' or produced fire by attrition, who 'first by sacrifices made the paths' or established ways of communication between men and Gods, and overcame hostile demons by means of the miraculous powers which he had received from heaven. To the descendants of this Atharvan, associated with the Angirases and the Bhṛigus, members of other ancient priestly families often mentioned in the Ṛigveda, the collected hymns—called also the Atharvângirasas and the Bhṛigvangirasas, that is the Songs of the Atharvans and Angirases and the Songs of the Bhṛigus and Angirases, and, in the Gopatha-Brâhmaṇa, the Âtharvaṇa-veda and the Âṅgirasa-veda—were, it is said, originally revealed.

Yet another name of the collection of hymns is Brahma-veda, which is variously explained as (1) the

Veda of the Brahman or chief sacrificial priest whose duty it was to supervise and direct the whole sacrifice and to remedy all faults of omission and commission in its performance, while the other Vedas are respectively those of the Hotar, the Adhvaryu, and the Udgâtar who are regarded as the assistants and inferiors of the Brahman ; (2) as the Knowledge of Prayers (*brahmâṇi*), including benediction, imprecation, spells and charms—the Veda which teaches to appease the Gods and secure their protecting favour, to bless friends, and to curse and destroy human and ghostly enemies, and all noxious creatures ; (3) as the Knowledge or Doctrine of Brahma, the Supreme Self, Soul, or Spirit with which the soul of man is finally redintegrated ; the followers of this Veda asserting its superiority to the three more ancient Vedas on the ground that, while they teach men to fulfil the *dharma* or religious law, the Brahma-veda imparts the sublime and mysterious doctrine which enables those who study it to attain *moksha*, deliverance from further transmigration, and, in the end, complete absorption into the Absolute. The second of these explanations seems, from our point of view, to be the correct one, and the Atharva or Brahma-veda may be regarded as the Veda of Prayers, Charms, and Spells.

I have called the Atharva-veda a comparatively late addition to the three ancient Vedas, of which, it may be observed, one only, the Ṛigveda, is original and historical, the other two being merely liturgical compilations. The Atharva is, like the Ṛik, in the main historical and original, but its contents cannot, as a whole, lay claim to equal antiquity. Professor Whitney says: 'The greater portion of the hymns are plainly shown, both by their language and internal character, to be of much later date than the general contents of the other historic Veda, and even than its tenth book with which they stand nearly connected in import and origin. . . . . . This, however, would not imply that the main body of the Atharva hymns were not already in existence when the compilation of the Ṛik took place. Their character would be ground enough for their rejection and exclusion from the canon until other hands were found to undertake their separate gathering into an independent collection.' Professor Weber also observes: 'The origin of the Atharva-Saṃhitâ dates from the période when Brahmanism had become dominant. It is in other respects perfectly analogous to the Ṛik-Saṃhitâ, and contains the store of song of this Brahmanical epoch. Many of these songs are to be found also in the last, that is the least ancient book of the Ṛik-Saṃhitâ. In the latter they are the latest additions made at the time of its compilation; in the Atharvan they are the proper and natural utterance of the present. The spirit of the two collections is indeed widely different. In the Ṛik there breathes a lively natural feeling, a warm love for nature; while in the Atharvan there prevails, on the contrary, only an anxious dread of her evil spirits and their magical powers. In the Ṛik we find the people in a state of free activity and independence; in the Atharvan we see it bound in the fetters of the hierarchy and superstition.

But the Atharva-Saṃhitâ likewise contains pieces of great antiquity, which may perhaps have belonged more to the people proper, to its lower grades; whereas the songs of the Ṛik appear rather to have been the property of the higher families. It was not without a long struggle that the songs of the Atharvan were permitted to take their place as a fourth Veda. There is no mention made of them in the more ancient portions of the Brâhmaṇas of the Ṛik, Sâman, and Yajus.' Still as Professor Max Müller says, 'the songs known under the name of the Atharvângirasas formed probably an additional part of the sacrifice from a very early time. They were chiefly intended to counteract the influence of any untoward event that might happen during the sacrifice. They also contained imprecations and blessings, and various formulas such as popular superstition would be sure to sanction at all times and in all countries. If once sanctioned, however, these magic verses would grow in importance, nay, the knowledge of the other Vedas would necessarily become useless without the power of remedying accidents, such as could hardly be avoided in so complicated a ceremonial as that of the Brahmans. As that power was believed to reside in the songs of the Atharvângirasas, a knowledge of these songs became necessarily an essential part of the theological knowledge of Ancient India.'*

---

* For further information see von Roth's Litteratur und Geschichte des Weda, pp. 12, 13, and his Abhandlung über den Atharva-veda; Weber's History of Indian Literature (Trübner's Oriental Series), pp. 145—171; Whitney's articles in the Journal of the American Oriental

The Atharva-veda Sanhitâ or Collection is divided into twenty *kâṇḍas*, Books or Sections, containing some seven hundred and sixty hymns and about six thousand verses. In Books I.—VII. the hymns or pieces are arranged according to the number of their verses, without any reference to their subjects or the nature of their contents. The hymns of Book I. contain on an average four verses each; those of Book II. five; those of III. six; those of IV. seven; those of V. from eight to eighteen; those of VI. three; those of VII. many single verses, and upwards to eleven. Books VIII.—XX. contain longer pieces, some of which extend to fifty, sixty, seventy, and even eighty verses. In Books I.—XIII. the contents are of the most heterogeneous description with no attempt at any kind of systematic arrangement of subjects. They consist principally of prayers, formulas, and charms for protection against evil spirits of all sorts and kinds, against sorcerers and sorceresses, diseases, snakes, and other noxious creatures, of benedictions and imprecations, invocations of magical herbs, prayers for children and long life, for general and special protection and prosperity, success in love, trade, and gambling, together with formulas to be employed in all kinds of domestic occurrences. In Books XIV.—XVIII. the subjects are systematically arranged; XIV. treating of marriage ceremonies; XV. of the glorification of the Vrâtya or religious wandering mendicant;

Society, Vol. IV.; Max Müller's Ancient Sanskrit Literature, pp. 445—455; Muir's Original Sanskrit Texts, II. pp. 187—191, and 446—450; and Ludwig's Der Rigveda, III. pp. 28, 29; or Chambers's Encyclopædia; or the Encyclopædia Britannica under Veda.

XVI. and XVII. of certain conjurations; XVIII. of funeral rites and the offering of obsequial cakes to the Manes or spirits of departed ancestors. Book XIX. contains a somewhat miscellaneous collection of supplementary hymns. Book XX. consists—with the exception of what is called the Kuntâpa Section, comprising hymns 127—136—of pieces addressed to Indra and taken entirely from the Ṛigveda. These two Books, which are not noticed in the Atharva-veda Prâtiṣâkhya —a grammatical treatise on the phonetic changes of words in the text—are manifestly a later addition to the Collection. Many of the Atharva hymns reappear in the Ṛigveda, about one-seventh of the Collection, sometimes unchanged and sometimes with important variations, being found in the older compilation. Interspersed in several of the Books are pieces of varying length consisting of curious cosmogonical and mystico-theological speculations which are not without interest as containing the germs of religious and philosophical doctrines afterwards fully developed in the Brâhmaṇas and Upanishads.

In this strange collection of heterogeneous material there is much that is obscure, much that is unintelligible, much that is intolerably tedious, and not a little that is offensive and disgusting to European taste. Yet the spiritual portions of the work have sometimes a strange beauty and grandeur of their own which attracts and fascinates the orthodox Hindu, while the occasional glimpses of light which it throws upon the daily life, the toils and pleasures, the hopes and fears, the joys and sorrows of the average man invests it, I think, for the European reader with greater and more human interest than is possessed by the more ancient Veda. Setting aside the rivalries, wars, and conquests of kings and princes, and the lofty claims and powers of the hierarchy, we may follow the course of the middle-class Âryan's life from the cradle to the funeral pile, and even accompany him to his final home in the world of the Departed. We hear the benedictive charm pronounced over the expectant mother before her child is born, the blessing on the new-born infant, and in due time on the darling's first two teeth. We attend the solemn ceremony in which the youth is invested with his *toga virilis*, the new garment whose assumption signifies his recognition as an adult member of the family with new responsibilities and new duties to perform. As his fancy turns to thoughts of love, we hear him murmuring the charm which shall win him the maiden of his choice, and the lullaby which shall seal every eye but hers in his beloved's house and enable him to visit her without detection or suspicion. We follow him in his formal and somewhat unromantic wooing of a bride through a friend who acts as match-maker; we see the nuptial procession and the bride's introduction to her new home; we hear her benediction on the bridegroom, and the epithalamium pronounced over the wedded pair. The young husband is an agriculturist, and we see him in his field superintending the ploughmen and praying to Indra and Pûshan and the Genii of agriculture to bless their labours. Anon, with propitiatory prayer, he is cutting a new channel to bring the water of the brook to the land which is ready for irrigation ; or he is praying for rain and an abundant crop. Again, when the corn is ripe he is busy among the men who gather in the harvest, invoking the aid of the good-natured goblins—the counterparts of our Robin Goodfellows—, and leaving on the ground some sheaves to remunerate their toil. At sunset he superintends the return of the cows who have been grazing under the protection of the Wind-God in the breezy pastures, and their return under divine guidance, and the re-union of all the members of the household, are celebrated with symbolical mixt oblation, with milk and a brew of grain.

His wealth and family increase in answer to his repeated prayer for children and riches, and a new house must be built on a larger scale. The building is erected under the careful eye of the master and blessed and consecrated with prayers to the Gods and to the Queen of the Home. The mistress of the house brings forth the well-filled pitcher, all present are regaled with 'the stream of molten butter blent with nectar'—which seems to be a euphemistic name for some sort of good liquor—, and the householder enters and takes formal possession of his new dwelling with fire and water, the two most important necessaries of human life. The house, moreover—a wooden building with a thatched roof—has been specially assured against fire by a prayer to Agni the God of that element with the additional security offered by the immediate neighbourhood of a good stream or pool of water.

Such, or something like this, was the ordinary life of the average middle-class agriculturist. A devout believer in the Gods, he did not spend his substance on the performance of costly sacrifices, but was content with simple ceremonies and such humble offerings as he could well afford. His chief care was for the health and well-being of himself, his wife, children, and dependents, for plentiful harvests, and for thriving and multiplying cattle ; and these were the blessings for which he most frequently prayed. His chief troubles were an occasional touch of malarial fever or rheumatism, a late or scanty rain-fall, a storm that lodged his ripe barley, lightning that struck his cattle, and similar mischances caused by the anger of the Gods or the malevolence of demons ; and he was always armed with prayers and spells against the recurrence of such disasters. He was a man of importance in his village, and when he attended the Assembly—which may have been a kind of Municipal Committee or Parish Council—his great ambition was to command respect and attention as a speaker, and with this view he fortified himself with charm and magic herb that inspired eloquence and enabled him to overpower his opponents in debate. His life, on the whole, was somewhat monotonous and dull, but it seems to have suited him as he was continually praying that it might be extended to its full natural duration of a hundred years. At the end of that time, with his sons and his sons' children around him, he was ready to pass away to the felicity that awaited him in the world of the Fathers.

The small merchant or trader lived a less settled

life and saw more of the world than the agriculturist. We see him on the point of starting on a journey for business purposes with his little stock of goods. He first propitiates Indra who is a merchant also, the God who trades and traffics with his worshippers, requiring and receiving prayer and oblations in exchange for the blessings which he sends, and who will now free the travelling merchant's path from wild beasts, robbers, and enemies of every kind. He prays also to many other deities that he may make rich profit and gain a hundred treasures, and commits the care of his children and cattle in his absence to Agni the God of all Âryan men. His ritual is an extensive one as he may be about to journey to all points of the compass, and he must accordingly conciliate all the divine Warders of the heavenly regions. He has to recite some ten hymns of Book VI., invoking the aid of all protecting deities, not forgetting to consult the Weather-Prophet and to obtain from him the promise of auspicious mornings, noons, and nights. He bids an affectionate farewell to the houses of his village, and departs on his way encouraged by the hymn which ensures him a safe and successful journey. In due time he returns having bartered his wares for the treasures of distant places, for bdellium and other fragrant gums and unguents, for Kushṭha and other foreign plants and drugs of healing virtue, for mother-of-pearl, ornaments for the women, and perhaps cloth of finer wool.

The merchant's object in life is gain, and he is not always very scrupulous in his dealings. If he is in debt he would prefer to be freed by the intervention of a God, and not by his own exertions; and he is bold enough even to pray for release from debts which he has incurred without intending to pay them. He is probably the gambler who prays for success in play, and for pardon when he has been guilty of cheating.

We naturally see much less of the life of women in the Atharva-veda, but a fair proportion of the hymns is devoted to them and their interests. We find interspersed among them the love-charms of enamoured maidens, the Bride Oracle or ceremony of finding a husband, the nuptial procession, and the bride's entry into her husband's house as its honoured mistress, the epithalamian benediction, and many spells and charms to ensure her safety and well-being. The mistress of the household had her share of duties, cares, and troubles as well as her quiet joys and pleasures, and she sometimes launches a furious and revengeful imprecation against her unfaithful husband, and with a solemn incantation invokes death and destruction upon her successful rivals.

The text of the Atharva-veda, with 'some amendment of the numerous and obvious false readings of the manuscripts, and some attempts to bring sense out of the utter nonsense which constitutes part of the last two books,' was published at Berlin, in 1856, by Professors Rudolf von Roth and W. D. Whitney. The intention of these distinguished scholars was to prepare and publish a second volume containing complete indexes, notes, and translation. Circumstances have, unfortunately, prevented the full execution of this project; but a most valuable portion of the intended work, Professor Whitney's Index Verborum to the Published Text, appeared in 1881 as Vol. XII. of the Journal of the American Oriental Society.* The Ṣaunakîyâ Chaturâdhyâyikâ, or the Atharva-veda Prâtiṣâkhya, text, translation, and notes, was published by Professor Whitney, in 1862, in Vol. VII. of the same Society. Of the two existing ritual Sûtras of this Veda, an excellent edition of the Kauṣika, with extracts from the commentaries of Dârila and Keṣava, has been brought out, as Vol. XIV. of the Journal of the American Oriental Society, by Professor Maurice Bloomfield; and Dr. Richard Garbe has published a careful edition of the text of the Vaitâna, with critical notes and indexes, followed by a commented translation of the work. An Anukramaṇî or Index to the Atharva-veda is extant. I am indebted to Mr. W. H. Wright, Principal of Queen's College, Benares, and to the Librarian of the Sanskrit College, for the loan of a copy of this work borrowed from a gentleman of Benares.

Portions of a Commentary ascribed—but without sufficient authority—to Sâyaṇa, were discovered, some fourteen years ago, by Râo Bahâdur Shankar Pandurang Pandit, of Bombay, and have been printed, but not

* Since the above was written, Professor Whitney, to the great loss of Sanskrit literature, has passed away to the Fathers. I learn from a notice of his life and labours reprinted from the New York *Nation* that he has left in manuscript nearly ready for the press an annotated translation of the Atharva-veda, which will, I hope, soon be published.

published, in their incomplete state. The Pandit is still waiting—hopelessly, I fear—for the missing portions, of which no trace has as yet been found. I have not succeeded in obtaining the printed sheets, but Professor Whitney who has seen them says (Festgruss an Rudolf von Roth zum Doktor-Jubiläum, 1893, p. 96): 'What there is that is valuable in the Atharva-veda commentary, apart from the various readings, is, on the whole, only what it derives and reports from the auxiliary literature to which we also have access. Independently, and as commentary, I have not found that it anywhere makes important contribution to the understanding of the text.' One Brâhmaṇa, the Gopatha (published in the Bibliotheca Indica, 1870-72), belongs to the Atharva-veda, and its Upanishads, many of which are of comparatively recent date, are said to number one hundred and forty-five.

There is no complete or nearly complete translation of the Atharva-veda in any European language. Professor von Roth has published versions of a few hymns in his History and Literature of the Veda, and elsewhere. Professor Weber has published in Indische Studien, Vols. IV., XIII., and XVII., an excellent translation, with exhaustive notes, of Books I—III., and in Vol. V. the nuptial formulas contained in Book XIV. with a great variety of love-charms and similar formulas from other Books. Mr. Muir has translated some entire hymns and many fragments and detached verses and lines in his Original Sanskrit Texts, especially in the fifth volume of that excellent work. Professor Ludwig has translated—unfortunately without a commentary—about two hundred and thirty of the most important hymns. Dr. Grill in his Hundert Lieder des Atharva-veda has translated and annotated one hundred. M. Victor Henry has published a translation and commentary of Books VII. and XIII. Herr Florenz has published a version of about half of Book VI. Dr. Lucian Scherman has translated and elucidated thirteen of the philosophical hymns, chiefly from Books X., XI., XIII., and XIX., and Professor Maurice Bloomfield has thoroughly discussed and partly translated seven hymns of Books I., II., and VI. in the American Journal of Philology, Vol. VII. 4.

I have not been able to obtain a copy of Herr Florenz's work, but with this exception I have derived the greatest possible benefit and assistance from all the translations and commentaries that I have mentioned, and I readily and thankfully acknowledge my general indebtedness to their authors independently of, and in addition to, special references in my notes and Index of Names, Etc. I need hardly say that the great St. Petersburg Lexicon has been constantly referred to, as well as the dictionaries of Sir M. Monier-Williams and Professor Macdonell, von Roth's edition of the Nirukta, Th. Zachariae's edition of the Anekârthasamgraha, Delbrück's Das Altindische Verbum, and the Vedische Studien of Professors Pischel and Geldner. The Index Verborum edited by Professor Whitney I have found of the very greatest service. Professor Zimmer's Altindisches Leben has also greatly assisted me, and much light has been thrown upon obscure passages by Professor

Bloomfield's edition of the Kauṣika-Sûtra and Dr. Garbe's Vaitâna-Sûtra.

My plan of translation is that previously adopted in my versions of the Hymns of the Ṛigveda and Sâma-veda. While aiming especially at close fidelity to the letter and spirit of the original I have endeavoured to make my translation as readable and intelligible as the nature of subjects and other circumstances permit. I have also attempted to preserve something of the external form of the original hymns by rendering them—in general, so far as I found it possible or expedient—in syllabically commensurate hemistichs and verses. The prevailing metres of the original hymns are Gâyatrî, Anushṭup, Pankti, Trishṭup, and Jagatî, consisting, the first three of three, four, and five octosyllabic Pâdas or divisions, and the last two of four hendecasyllabic and dodecasyllabic Pâdas respectively. In translating the first set I have employed corresponding numbers of the common octosyllabic or dimeter iambic line, and in the second of the ordinary hypercatalectic blank verse line and the Alexandrine. I have not attempted to reproduce the rhythm or tonic metre of the original: such a task, supposing its satisfactory execution to be possible, would require more skill than I possess, and more time and labour than I could spare for the purpose. Moreover, I have found it impossible to carry out universally my general plan of translation. Parts of the Atharva-veda, for instance Book XV. and the greater portion of XVI., are entirely in prose, and hymns, verses, and parts of verses in prose are found in other Books also. 'It is not possible,' as Professor Whitney observes, 'to draw everywhere a sharp line between metrical and non-metrical matter; prose and loose verse slide into one another sometimes in a perplexing manner, or are mixed up in the same stanza.'

I cannot conclude without publicly expressing my deep obligations to Messrs. E. J. Lazarus & Co. of Benares for their spirited liberality in undertaking of their own accord and at their own risk the publication of a costly work which is not likely to be pecuniarily remunerative.

R. T. H. GRIFFITH.

KOTAGIRI, NILGIRI HILLS:
1st November, 1894.

THE

HYMNS OF THE ATHARVA-VEDA.

BOOK THE FIRST.

HYMN I.

Now may Vâchaspati assign to me the strength and powers of Those
Who, wearing every shape and form, the triple seven, are wandering round.

The hymn, which is introductory to the whole Book, is a prayer addressed to Vâchaspati for divine help, favour, and illumination. The metre is Anushṭup, consisting of four equal octosyllabic pâdas, divisions, or quarter-verses. The name means, perhaps, 'the 'After-step,' because each line was stamped regularly after the other, possibly by two choruses, each side taking its turn:' see M. Müller, Vedic Hymns, Part 1. p. xcvi.

1 *Vâchaspati:* or, Lord of Speech; the God or Genius of human life which lasts as long as the power of speech remains in the body. The name occurs in the Ṛigveda, X. 166. 3: 'Press down these men, Vâchaspati, (or, O Lord of Speech) that they may humbly speak to me;' and stanzas 17—19 of Atharva-veda XIII. I are addressed to this God. In Ṛigveda IX. 26. 4 and 101. 5 the name is applied to Soma as the exhilarating drink which makes men eloquent and inspires the song. Vâchaspati is classed in the Nirukta among the deities of the firmament or middle sphere between heaven and earth. His name, being compounded with *páti*, indicates a more recent deification than that of the great Powers of Nature whose presence and superhuman influence were immediately seen and felt.

Those: the Gods in general; or the Maruts or Storm-Gods.

The triple seven: trishaptā́ḥ; a fanciful expression for an indefinite number. So *tríḥ saptá vishpuliṅgakā́*, the three times seven bright

2 Come thou again, Vâchaspati, come with divine intelligence.
Vasoshpati, repose thou here. In me be Knowledge, yea, in me.

3 Here, even here, spread sheltering arms like the two bow-ends strained with cord.
This let Vâchaspati confirm. In me be Knowledge, yea, in me.

4 Vâchaspati hath been invoked: may he invite us in reply.
May we adhere to Sacred Lore. Never may I be reft thereof.

---

sparks of fire; and *tríḥ saptá mayûryàḥ*, the peahens three times seven (Ṛigveda I. 191. 12, 14). In Atharva-veda XIII. 1. 3 the Maruts, who are said to form nine troops of seven each, are called the triple seven, *trishaptấso marutaḥ*, instead of the thrice-three seven; and these powerful deities may be intended here also. Professor Weber would derive the word from the root *sap*, a secondary form of *sach*, to cleave to, to follow, of which *sapta* would be the past participle passive used in the sense of combination, and *trishaptấḥ* might then mean triply combined, 'Gods of three spheres,' the three classes of deities whose spheres of activity are respectively heaven, atmosphere or firmament, and earth. The St. Petersburg Dictionary translates *trishaptấḥ* in this passage by 'zu Dutzenden,' in dozens.

2 *Vasoshpati:* Lord of Treasure, that is, of wealth and food, according to Durga, the Commentator of the Nirukta. Vasoshpati is not mentioned elsewhere in the Veda.

Knowledge: ṣrutám; that which was heard (from the beginning), the Veda, revelation, or sacred knowledge. According to the St. Petersburg Dictionary, 'Gehör,' hearing, is meant. The Nirukta X. 18 has *ní râmaya máyyeva tanúam máma*, 'maintain my self within me,' keep my body and soul together, that I may enjoy the possessions of which thou, Vasoshpati, art the controller.

Book I. has been excellently translated and fully annotated by Weber in Indische Studien, IV. pp. 393—430. Professor Ludwig, also, has translated fifteen of the hymns in Der Rigveda, Vol. III. and Dr. Grill has translated and annotated five.

HYMN II.

WE know the father of the shaft, Parjanya, liberal nourisher,

Know well his mother Pṛithivî, Earth with her manifold designs.

2 Do thou, O Bowstring, bend thyself around us: make my body stone.

Firm in thy strength drive far away malignities and hateful things.

3 When, closely clinging round the wood, the bowstring sings triumph to the swift and whizzing arrow,

Indra, ward off from us the shaft, the missile.

This hymn is a charm against acute diarrhœa or dysentery. The metre is Dvipadâ Trishṭup, consisting of three pâdas or divisions of eleven syllables each, in stanza 3, and Anushṭup in the rest.

1 *Parjanya:* derived probably from an original root *parj*, to sprinkle or moisten, is the rain-cloud and the divine power, or God, that animates it, the generator and nourisher of plants and animal life. Parjanya has been identified with the Lituanian Perkúnas, the God of thunder: see Max Müller, India, What can it Teach us?, pp. 183 sqq. See also The Hymns of the Ṛigveda, General Index, for hymns addressed to this deity. Parjanya is called *the father of the shaft* or arrow, which is to be employed in the charm, on account of the rapid growth, in the rainy season, of the *ṣará* (Saccharum Sara), the reed of which arrows were made, *ṣará* meaning, like the Latin arundo, both reed and arrow.

Pṛithivî: for *pṛithvî*, broad Earth personified as the mother of all beings. *With her manifold designs:* with her countless inventions and productions. According to others *bhû'rivarpasam* means 'many-shaped,' 'presenting many appearances.' Cf. Spenser's 'the dædale earth.'

2 *Bowstring:* which is to be twisted round the patient's body during the recitation of the charm. *Stone:* sound and strong.

3 *The wood:* literally, the tree, meaning the bow. *Indra:* addressed as being the God of battle and the chief tutelary deity of the Âryans.

4 As in its flight the arrow's point hangs between earth and firmament,
So stand this Munja grass between ailment and dysenteric ill!

HYMN III.

We know the father of the shaft, Parjanya strong with hundred powers:
By this may I bring health unto thy body: let the channels pour their burthen freely as of old.

---

4 *Hangs:* literally, stands.

5 *Munja grass: muñja* (Saccharum Munja) is a sort of rush or grass which grows to the height of about ten feet. It is used in basket-work, and the *mekhalâ* or girdle worn by Brâhmans is made from it. It appears from the Kauṣika-Sûtra, XXV. 6, and Dârila's Commentary thereon, that the head of a stalk of Munja grass is to be tied with a cord, then, perhaps, to be suspended from the neck of the patient or to be otherwise attached to his body. As the discharged arrow hangs between heaven and earth, so the grass is to stand between the patient's ailment and *âsrâvá*, diarrhœa in an acute form, or dysentery, that is, to prevent the indisposition from developing into serious disease. The word *âsrâvá*, from *sru*, to flow, + *â*, has been translated differently by Professors Ludwig and Zimmer, but there can be no doubt that Dârila has correctly explained it by *atisâra*, diarrhœa or dysentery. According to the Kauṣika-Sûtra the patient has also to drink a mixture containing earth taken from a field and a lump full of ants, and is to be anointed with sacrificial molten butter, with yet further treatment. See remarks on this hymn by Professor Maurice Bloomfield (to whom we are indebted for an excellent edition of the Kauṣika-Sûtra) in the American Journal of Philology, Vol. VII. pp. 466—469.

The hymn is a charm against constipation and suppression of urine. It closely resembles Hymn II. in its adoption of the formula, We know the father of the shaft; and in the symbolical discharge of the arrow in stanza 9. The metre is Paṅkti, consisting of five octosyllabic pâdas.

1 *Parjanya:* see preceding hymn, note on stanza 1. *By this:* with the aid of this arrow. *Let the channels pour:* my translation of the latter part of this refrain is not literal: In terram dejecta cadant tua cum sonitu *bál*, would, though barbarous, be a closer version: *bál* is an interjection imitative of the sound of a falling substance.

2 We know the father of the shaft, Mitra, the Lord of hundred powers :
By this, etc.

3 We know the father of the shaft, Varuṇa, strong with hundred powers :
By this, etc.

4 We know the father of the shaft, the Moon endowed with hundred powers :
By this, etc.

5 We know the father of the shaft, the Sun endowed with hundred powers :
By this may I bring health unto thy body : let the channels pour their burthen freely as of old.

6 Whate'er hath gathered, as it flowed, in bowels, bladder, or in groins,—
Thus let the conduit, free from check, pour all its burthen as of old.

7 I lay the passage open as one cleaves the dam that bars the lake :
Thus let, etc.

8 Now hath the portal been unclosed as of the sea that holds the flood :
Thus let, etc.

---

2 *Mitra:* the Friend, the gracious God, the Zend Mithra. See Hymns of the Ṛigveda, General Index. Mitra is, perhaps, called *the father of the shaft* because it grows by day over which that deity as a form of the Sun presides.

3 *Varuṇa:* the Coverer or Encompasser; originally the visible starry heaven. Varuṇa's connexion with the shaft or reed is not very obvious. The growth of the future arrow by night, over which Varuṇa presides, may, perhaps, be the ground of relationship.

4 *The Moon:* the influence of the Moon on the sap and growth of plants, of which Soma (another name of the Moon) is the King, is frequently alluded to.

8 *The portal: vastibilám:* literally, the orifice of the bladder.

9 Even as the arrow flies away when loosened from the archer's bow,
Thus let the burthen be discharged from channels that are checked no more.

HYMN IV.

ALONG their paths the Mothers go, sisters of priestly ministrants,
Blending their water with the mead.

2 May yonder Waters near the Sun, or those wherewith the Sun is joined,
Send forth this sacrifice of ours.

3 I call the Waters, Goddesses, hitherward where our cattle drink:
The streams must share the sacrifice.

4 Amrit is in the Waters, in the Waters balm.
Yea, through our praises of the Floods, O horses, be ye fleet and strong, and, O ye kine, be full of strength.

---

9 *The arrow:* here, says the Kauṣika-Sûtra, XXV. 14, *ishum visṛijati*, 'he (the operator) discharges an arrow,' symbolizing thereby the free passage of the loosened contents of the stomach and bladder of the patient. Other operations are to be performed, and a decoction of medicinal herbs is to be administered.

Stanzas 1—3 and the first line of stanza 4 are taken from Ṛigveda I. 23. 16—19, attributed to the Ṛishi Medhâtithi.

1 *The Mothers:* the maternal Waters, the *Âpaḥ* or waters of the firmament regarded as divinities who give and cherish life. *Sisters:* closely connected with the priests who officiate at sacrifices as water is mingled with the ingredients of the Soma libation. *With the mead: mádhunâ; mádhu* meaning sweetness or any sweet or pleasant drink, especially, as here, the expressed juice of the Soma plant.

3 *The streams:* the divine Waters of the ocean of air.

4 *Amrit:* nectar, the drink of the Gods that confers immortality; or immortality itself.

HYMN V.

YE, Waters, truly bring us bliss: so help ye us to strength and power
That we may look on great delight.

2 Here grant to us a share of dew, that most auspicious dew of yours,
Like mothers in their longing love.

3 For you we fain would go to him to whose abode ye send us forth,
And, Waters, give us procreant strength.

4 I pray the Floods to send us balm, those who bear rule o'er precious things,
And have supreme control of men.

In the Ṛigveda the partly-corresponding stanza is in the Pura-ushṇiḥ metre, consisting of three pâdas, the first of which contains twelve, and the second and third eight syllables each. The stanza here has an additional octosyllabic pâda. For the second line of the stanza, as translated above, the reading of the Ṛigveda is: *apắm utá práṣastaye dévâ bhávata vâjínaḥ*: Yea, be ye powerful, ye Gods, to celebrate the Waters' praise. The metre in stanzas 1—3 is Gâyatri, consisting of three octosyllabic pâdas or divisions.

The hymn is taken from Ṛigveda X. 9. 1—3, 5, ascribed to Sindhudvîpa, son of Ambarîsha, or to Triṣiras, son of Tvashṭar. The same stanzas form a hymn of the Sâmaveda (II. IX. II. 10).

1 *Waters*: see the preceding hymn, note on stanza 1. *Great delight*: meaning, according to the Scholiast, perfect knowledge of Brahma.

2 *Dew*: *rásaḥ*; any fluid, here meaning water.

3 The purport of the stanza appears to be:—If you direct us and strengthen us for the work, we are ready and willing to visit any worshipper of yours in whose house we may perform sacrifice in your honour. *Give us procreant strength*: ye give us power to generate, that is, to produce or perform the sacrifice which may be regarded as the offspring of the officiating priests. Professor Grassmann translates the pâda by:—'Ihr Wasser machet kräftig uns.' Ye waters make us powerful. But the force of *jan*—in *janáyatha*, signifying *gen*-eration, procreation, should be preserved. Professor Weber translates the first line differently:—'We bear you thither to the man whose habitation

HYMN VI.

THE Waters be to us for drink, Goddesses, for our aid and bliss:
Let them stream health and wealth to us.

2 Within the Waters—Soma thus hath told me—dwell all balms that heal,
And Agni, he who blesseth all.

3 O Waters, teem with medicine to keep my body safe from harm,
So that I long may see the Sun.

4 The Waters bless us, all that rise in desert lands or marshy pools!
Bless us the Waters dug from earth, bless us the Waters brought in jars, bless us the Waters of the Rains!

---

ye befriend.' Sâyaṇa's authority (Commentary on Sâmaveda II. IX. II. 10. 3) supports this interpretation of *gamâma* as causative = *gamayâma*; but it is not in accordance with Vedic use. Benfey (Die Hymnen des Sâma-Veda) says in note 2, p. 223:—'I now take *aram gam* as meaning to go adorning, to go in order to adorn, to glorify, and accordingly he translates stanza 3 of this Hymn in the Sâma-veda:—'Diesen euren erheben wir, dessen Herrschaft ihr huldreich seid, und machet fruchtbar, Wasser uns:' We glorify this man of yours, the man whose lordship ye befriend, and, Waters, make us rich in fruit. My version of the stanza is based on Ludwig's translation and Commentary (Der Rigveda, I. p. 189, and IV. p. 180).

The first three stanzas of the hymn are to be repeated by Brâhmans at their morning ablutions: see Colebrooke's Essays, I. On the Religious Ceremonies of the Hindus.

Stanzas 1—3 are taken from Ṛigveda X. 9. 4, 6, 7, the two latter being repeated from I. 23. 20, 21, forming a continuation of Hymn IV. of this Book.

2 *Soma:* the God; the juice of the Soma plant personified and regarded as an all-powerful deity. *Agni:* the God of fire. See Hymns of the Ṛigveda, General Index, for both deities. The meaning is that the poet, under the inspiration produced by draughts of Soma juice, has perceived that water possesses healing virtue, and that the waters of the firmament—that is, clouds—contain purifying and health-giving fire or Agni in the shape of lightning.

HYMN VII.

BRING the Kimîdin hither, bring the Yâtudhâna self-declared,
For Agni, God, thou, lauded, hast become the Dasyu's slaughterer.

The hymn is a prayer to Agni and Indra for the detection and destruction of evil spirits. The metre changes in stanza 5 from Anushṭup to Trishṭup which consists of four pâdas of eleven syllables each. M. Müller explains 'its name 'Three-step' by the fact that the three last syllables ⏑ — ⏑, which form the characteristic feature of that metre, and may be called its real vṛitta or turn, were audibly stamped at the end of each turn or strophe:' Vedic Hymns, Part I. p. xcvi. The hendecasyllabic metre in which I render the Trishṭup stanza here and wherever it occurs does not profess to be more than a substitute for the original metre: retaining the number of syllables, it does not attempt to preserve the exact rhythm of the Trishṭup which, I think, is not satisfactorily reproducible in English verse.

1 *The Kimîdin:* one of a class of malignant spirits. According to the Nirukta VI. 11 the word originally means one who goes about crying *Kim idânîm*, Quid nunc? What now? or *Kim idam?* What is this? Literally, a quidnunc; a vile and treacherous spy and informer. *The Yâtudhâna:* one of a class of evil spirits, demons, or sorcerers, explained by Sâyaṇa as Râkshasas, but in the Veda apparently distinct from those violent and voracious ogres. In Ṛigveda VII. 104 and X. 87 there are two long series of imprecations directed against Râkshasas and Yâtudhânas. *The Dasyu's slaughterer:* Dasyus is the general name of a class of powerful superhuman beings hostile to Gods and men, comprising the malignant demons of the air, the withholders of the seasonable rain. Indra as the chief tutelary God of the Âryans is sometimes called—as Agni is here—the slayer of the Dasyu:—'Thou (Indra) from of old wast born to strike the Dasyus dead:' Ṛigveda I. 51. 6. 'He......who slays the Dasyus, He, O men, is Indra:' Ṛigveda II. 12. 10. The name of Dasyus was also sometimes given to the wild indigenous races who opposed the immigration of the Âryans and, later, to all people who did not follow the Vedic ritual or observe the essential Brâhmanical ceremonies.

2 O Jâtavedas, Lord Supreme, controller of our bodies, taste
The butter, Agni, taste the oil: make thou the Yâtudhânas mourn.

3 Let Yâtudhânas mourn, let all greedy Kimîdins weep and wail:
And, Agni, Indra, may ye both accept this sacrifice of ours.

4 May Agni seize upon them first, may strong-armed Indra drive them forth:
Let every wicked sorcerer come hither and say, Here am I.

5 Let us behold thy strength, O Jâtavedas. Viewer of men, tell us the Yâtudhânas.
Burnt by thy heat and making declaration let all approach this sacrifice before thee.

6 O Jâtavedas, seize on them: for our advantage art thou born:
Agni, be thou our messenger and make the Yâtudhânas wail.

7 O Agni, bring thou hitherward the Yâtudhânas bound and chained,
And afterward let Indra tear their heads off with his thunderbolt.

---

2 *Jâtavedas:* the wise, the sapient; a frequently occurring designation of Agni: see Vedische Studien, I. pp. 94, 95. *The butter: âjya*; butter melted or clarified, used for oblations, or for pouring into the holy fire at the sacrifice, or for anointing anything sacrificed; sometimes also oil and milk used instead of clarified butter at a sacrifice. *The oil: taila*; oil expressed from the seeds of the *tila* or sesamum plant (Sesamum Indicum). This oil was not usually offered in oblation; but, besides this special detective sacrifice, it appears to have been sometimes used in sacrifices to the Fathers or Manes: see Atharvaveda XVIII. 4. 32.

The hymn has been translated by Ludwig, Der Rigveda, III. p. 523.

HYMN VIII.

THIS sacrifice shall bring the Yâtudhânas as the flood brings foam:
Here let the doer of this deed, woman or man, acknowledge it.

2 This one hath come confessing all: do ye receive him eagerly.
Master him thou, Bṛihaspati; Agni and Soma, pierce him through.

3 O Soma-drinker, strike and bring the Yâtudhâna's progeny:
Make the confessing sinner's eyes fall from his head, both right and left.

The hymn is a continuation of Hymn VII. The sacrifice has proved effectual (stanza 2), and a Yâtudhâna or sorcerer has been forced to come forward and confess. The metre changes in stanza 4 from Anushṭup to Trishṭup.

1 *This deed:* some act of sorcery. *Woman or man:* sorceress or sorcerer; Yâtudhânî or Yâtudhâna.

2 *Bṛihaspati:* or, O Lord of Prayer. 'Bṛihaspati, alternating with Brahmaṇaspati, is the name of a deity in whom the action of the worshipper upon the gods is personified. He is the suppliant, the priest who intercedes with the gods for men, and protects them against the wicked. Hence he appears as the prototype of the priests and the priestly order, and is also designated as the Puroh ta [High Priest] of the divine community. The essential difference between the original idea represented in this God and those expressed in most of the other and older deities of the Veda consists in the fact that the latter are personifications of various departments of nature, or of physical forces, while the former is the product of moral ideas, and an impersonation of the power of devotion.'—Muir, Original Sanskrit Texts, V. p. 272. For hymns addressed to Bṛihaspati and Brahmaṇaspati, see Hymns of the Ṛigveda, General Index I.

3 *Soma-drinker:* Indra, who is especially the Lord of Soma and the chief drinker of libations made of its juice:—'Known as the Soma-drinker, armed with thunder, who wields the bolt, He, O ye men, is Indra:' Ṛigveda II. 12. 13. This appellation of Indra will be found

4 As thou, O Agni Jâtavedas, knowest the races of these secret greedy beings,
So strengthened by the power of prayer, O Agni, crushing them down a hundred times destroy them.

HYMN IX.

May Indra, Pûshan, Varuṇa, Mitra, Agni, benignant Gods, maintain this man in riches.
May the Âdityas and the Visve Devas set and support him in supremest lustre.

---

in most of the many Ṛigveda Hymns addressed to this deity. *Right and left : páram utá ávaram ;* literally, upper and lower. Weber suggests the possibility of Yâtudhânas being credited with additional eyes.

The hymn has been translated by Ludwig, Der Rigveda, III. p. 523.

The occasion of the hymn is an Abhisheka or inauguration by sprinkling or unction of a Râjâ or King who appears to have been elected from among the members of a princely family. The metre is Trishṭup.

1 *Pûshan :* a God who protects and multiplies cattle and human possessions generally. In character he is a solar deity, and a guide on roads and journeys. As a form of the Sun he beholds the entire universe. The name is derived from *push,* to nourish. For hymns to Pûshan see Hymns of the Ṛigveda, General Index I. p. xxvii. *The Âdityas :* literally, the sons of Aditi, Infinity or Eternity. 'There (in the highest heaven) dwell and reign those gods who bear in common the name of Âdityas. We must, however, if we would discover their earliest character, abandon the conceptions which in a later age, and even in that of the heroic poems, were entertained regarding these deities. According to this conception they were twelve Sun-gods, bearing evident reference to the twelve months. But for the most ancient period we must hold fast the primary signification of their name. They are the inviolable, imperishable, eternal beings. Aditi, eternity or the eternal, is the element which sustains them and is sustained by them......The eternal and inviolable element in which the Âdityas dwell, and which forms their essence, is the celestial light... The Âdityas, the gods of this light, do not therefore by any means coincide with any of the forms in which light is manifested in the

2 May light, O Gods, be under his dominion, Agni, the Sun, all that is bright and golden.
Prostrate beneath our feet his foes and rivals. Uplift him to the loftiest cope of heaven.
3 Through that most mighty prayer, O Jâtavedas, wherewith thou broughtest milk to strengthen Indra,
Even therewith exalt this man, O Agni, and give him highest rank among his kinsmen.
4 I have assumed their sacrifice, O Agni, their hopes, their glory, and their riches' fulness.
Prostrate beneath our feet his foes and rivals. Uplift him to the loftiest cope of heaven.

HYMN X.

THIS Lord is the Gods' ruler; for the wishes of Varuṇa the King must be accomplished.
Therefore, triumphant with the prayer I utter, I rescue this man from the Fierce One's anger.

---

universe. They are neither sun, nor moon, nor stars, nor dawn, but the eternal sustainers of this luminous life, which exists, as it were, behind all these phenomena:' Roth, quoted by Muir, Original Sanskrit Texts, V. p. 56. For hymns addressed to these deities see Hymns of the Ṛigveda, General Index I. p. xxvii. *The Viçve Devas: víçve devấh, víçvedevấh;* the All-Gods, Universal Gods, Collective Gods; all the Gods together. See Hymns of the Ṛigveda, General Index I. p. XXVII.

2 *Loftiest cope of heaven:* highest pitch of earthly happiness.

3 *Thou broughtest milk:* the allusion is obscure. Játavedas, the sapient Agni, appears to have strengthened Indra at some critical time with milk or Soma juice, but the particulars appear to be undiscoverable.

There is a somewhat similar benediction of a newly elected king in Ṛigveda X. 153.

The hymn has been translated by Ludwig, Der Rigveda, III. p. 256.

After intercession with Varuṇa, a priest absolves a sinner who has offended that deity. The metre is Trishṭup in 1, 2, and Anushṭup in 3, 4.

1 *This Lord:* Varuṇa appears as the Asura, divine Being or Lord *par excellence*, the Ahura Mazdâ. 'This god is one of the most interesting creations of the Hindu mind, because though we can still perceive the physical background from which he rises, the vast, starry,

2 Homage be paid, King Varuṇa, to thine anger; for thou, dread God, detectest every falsehood.
I send a thousand others forth together: let this thy servant live a hundred autumns.

3 Whatever falsehood thou hast told, much evil spoken with the tongue,
I liberate thee from the noose of Varuṇa the righteous King.

4 I free thee from Vaiṣvânara, from the great surging flood of sin.
Call thou thy brothers, Awful One! and pay attention to our prayer.

HYMN XI.

VASHAṬ to thee, O Pûshan! At this birth let Aryaman the Sage perform as Hotar-priest.
As one who bears in season let this dame be ready to bring forth her child.

---

brilliant expanse above, his features, more than those of any of the Vedic gods, have become completely transfigured, and he stands before us a god who watches over the world, punishes the evil-doer, and even forgives the sins of those who implore his pardon:' M. Müller, India, What can it Teach us? p. 195.

2 *I send a thousand others forth:* I intercede for this man only. I resign to thee all others to punish as thou wilt.

3 *The noose:* borne by Varuṇa as the moral Governor of the world, to entangle and capture the evil-doer.

4 *Vaiṣvânara:* belonging to, or ruling all men; here meaning Varuṇa. *Call thou thy brothers:* call the other Âdityas that they may see that thou hast pardoned the penitent and restored him to favour.

The hymn has been translated by Ludwig, Der Rigveda, III. p. 445.

The hymn is a charm to be used at child-birth. The details given in stanzas 3—6 are strictly obstetric and not presentable in English: see Appendix. The text appears to be mutilated in some places, and the metre is irregular.

1 *Váshaṭ:* is a sacrificial exclamation uttered by the Hotar or chief priest at the end of the Yâjyâ or sacrificial verse, whereupon the

2 Four are the regions of the sky, and four the regions of the earth:
The Gods have brought the babe; let them prepare the woman for the birth.

HYMN XII.

Born from the womb, brought forth from wind and from the cloud, the first red bull comes onward thundering with the rain.
Our bodies may he spare who, cleaving, goes straight on; he who, a single force, divides himself in three.

---

oblation is cast into the fire by the Adhvaryu, the priest who performs the practical part of the ceremony. O *Pûshan*: addressed as the multiplier and nourisher of human beings: see I. 9. 1. *Aryaman:* meaning the bosom friend, one of the Âdityas who is commonly invoked together with Varuṇa and Mitra: see I. 9. 1. *Hotar-priest:* or Hotar; meaning the Sacrificer (from *hu*, to sacrifice,) or the Invoker (from *hve*, to call); the chief priest who presents the oblation or burnt-offering, or who recites the prayers and invites the Gods to attend the sacrifice.

2 *Have brought the babe:* from those distant regions. Cf. 'Where do you come from, baby, dear? Out of the everywhere into here.'— G. Mac Donald: Baby.

The hymn has been translated by Ludwig, Der Rigveda, III. p. 478.

This hymn has been discussed by Professor Bloomfield (American Journal of Philology, Vol. VII. pp. 469—472), who entitles it a Prayer to Lightning, conceived as the cause of fever, headache, and coughs. It appears to have been placed immediately after Hymn XI. simply because it begins with the word *jarâyujáḥ*, and *jarấyu* is the penultimate word of that hymn. The metre is Jagatî, consisting of four pâdas of twelve syllables each, in 1—3, and Anushṭup in 4.

1 *Born from the womb:* literally, from the placenta; that is, from the womb of the cloud. *Brought forth from wind and from the cloud:* *vâtabhrajâs* emended to *vâtâbhrajâs* by Bloomfield. *The first red bull;* the lightning. According to Weber, puerperal fever is meant:—'A red bull, the first product of the afterbirth, comes on thundering with rain, with glowing breath of wind.'

2 Bending to thee who clingest to each limb with heat, fain would we worship thee with offered sacrifice,
Worship with sacrifice the bends and curves of thee who with a vigorous grasp hast seized on this one's limbs.

3 Do thou release this man from headache, free him from cough which has entered into all his limbs and joints.
May he, the child of cloud, the offspring of the wind, the whizzing lightning, strike the mountains and the trees.

4 Well be it with my upper frame, well be it with my lower parts.
With my four limbs let it be well. Let all my body be in health.

HYMN XIII.

HOMAGE to thee, the Lightning's flash, homage to thee, the Thunder's roar!
Homage to thee, the Stone which thou hurlest against the undevout!

2 Homage to thee, Child of the Flood whence thou collectest fervent heat!
Be gracious to our bodies, give our children happiness and joy.

---

2 *Thee:* Lightning.

In the Anukramaṇî the hymn is designated as a *yakshmanâśanam sûktam*, a hymn which cures consumption. In the Kauśika-Sûtra it is employed as a charm against thunderstorms, and in a performance which is described by the Commentator Dârila as a cure for headache. For further information see Professor Bloomfield's remarks referred to above.

The hymn is a prayer to Lightning personified and deified.

2 *Child of the Flood:* sprung from the waters or watery clouds of the ocean of air. According to others, Child of the Height, that is, the firmament. For an exhaustive discussion of the meaning of *pravát*, see Pischel, Vedische Studien, II. pp. 63—76.

3 Yea, homage be to thee, O Offspring of the Flood!
Homage we pay to thee, the dart and fiery flame:
For well we know thy secret and sublimest home,
where thou as central point art buried in the sea.

4 Thou, Arrow, which the host of Gods created, making it strong and mighty for the shooting,
Be gracious, lauded thus, to our assembly. To thee, that Arrow, be our homage, Goddess!

HYMN XIV.

As from the tree a wreath, have I assumed her fortune and her fame:
Among her kinsfolk long may she dwell, like a mountain broadly-based.

---

3 *In the sea*: in the ocean of air.

4 *The host of Gods*: all the Gods together. *Assembly*: congregation for sacrificial purposes.

Professor Bloomfield has shown (American Journal of Philology Vol. VII. pp. 473—476) by quotations from the Kauṣika-Sûtra that, when that ritual was composed, this hymn was regarded and treated not as a marriage song, as Weber, Ludwig, and Zimmer have interpreted it, but as a woman's incantation against a rival. 'But,' says Professor Bloomfield, 'it seems to me that traces of a more original application are not wanting. The word *pitṛṣu*, translated above doubtingly by 'with her relatives,' means naturally 'among the fathers or manes.' The third stanza of the hymn, considered independently, would be easily explained as one uttered at the funeral of a maiden, and it seems possible that the entire hymn represents similar material somewhat worked over for the occasion.'

1 The woman who employs the incantation speaks:—'I have taken to myself the fortune and fame of my rival as one takes a wreath from a tree: long may she remain unmarried, a fixture in her relatives' house.' Weber, Zimmer, and, apparently, Ludwig assign the stanza to the bridegroom, 'her fortune' meaning the fortune of the bride and *pitṛishu* meaning 'my parents,' or rather 'my kinsfolk.'

2 King Yama, let this maiden be surrendered as a wife
to thee:
Bound let her be meanwhile within her mother's,
brother's, father's house.

3 Queen of thy race is she, O King: to thee do we
deliver her.
Long with her kinsfolk may she sit, until her hair
be white with age.

4 With Asita's and Kaṣyapa's and Gaya's incantation,
thus
As sisters pack within a chest, I bind and tie thy
fortune up.

---

2 The woman devotes her rival hereafter to Yama, King of the Departed. According to Weber, Zimmer, and Ludwig, the stanza is the reply of the bride's relatives to the bridegroom who is addressed as king and *yama*, that is, controller, the word being derived from *yam*, to restrain. According to this interpretation 'her mother's' would be 'thy mother's.'

3 The incantation is continued. *Queen of thy race: kulapấ;* 'guardian of thy house:' Ludwig. 'Thy housekeeper:' Bloomfield. *Her kinsfolk: pitṛishu;* literally, fathers, meaning the father and his brothers or other near relatives. The pronoun not expressed in the text, would be 'thy' according to the interpretation given by Weber, Ludwig, and Zimmer. *Until her hair be white with age:* this is a conjectural rendering, suggested in the St. Petersburg Dictionary and adopted doubtingly by Zimmer, of the probably corrupt *ṣamópyât* of the text. According to Weber *opyât* is the precative from the verb *vap*, to sow, + *ấ*, that is, may she sow or scatter blessings from her head. Ludwig translates similarly.

4 Asita, Kaṣyapa, and Gaya are ancient Ṛishis, the seers or authors of various hymns of the Ṛigveda. *Incantation:* or, prayer. The woman is still the speaker. According to Weber, Ludwig, and Zimmer, the stanza is the bridegroom's reply. Zimmer adds that the *sisters* are those of the bride, who pack her dowry within the chest.

For details of the ceremony which, according to the Kauṣika-Sútra, accompanies the recitation of the hymn, see Bloomfield as quoted above. Zimmer's translation is to be found in his Altindisches Leben, p. 314; and Ludwig's in his Der Rigveda, III. p. 459.

HYMN XV.

LET the streams flow together, let the winds and birds assembled come.
Let this my sacrifice delight them always. I offer it with duly mixt oblation.

2 Come to my call, Blent Offerings, come ye very nigh.
And, singers, do ye strengthen and increase this man.
Hither come every animal: with this man let all wealth abide.

3 All river founts that blend their streams for ever inexhaustible—
With all these confluent streams of mine we make abundant riches flow.

4 All streams of melted butter, and all streams of water and of milk—
With all these confluent streams of mine we make abundant riches flow.

A sacrifice is performed, and prayer is offered for the prosperity of a patron. The metre is mixed. In stanza 1 the first line is Anushṭup and the second Trishṭup. In 2, line 1 is Jagati and line 2 Anushṭup. Stanzas 3 and 4 are Anushṭup.

1 *Them:* the Gods. Weber translates *pradivas*, always, by 'the Eternal Ones':—'May the Eternal Ones accept my sacrifice.' *Duly mixt oblation:* consisting of milk, butter, and the juice of corn (perhaps a sort of beer): see II. 26. 4, 5. Stanzas 1 and 2 occur again with variations in XIX. 1. 1, 2.

2 *This man:* some wealthy householder who pays the expenses of the sacrifice and rewards the officiating priests. *Animal:* domestic animal; cow, horse, goat, sheep.

The Blent Offerings, or Mixt Oblation, are called *saṁsrâvaṇâs*, from *sam*, together, and *sru*, to flow, and every line but one of the stanza contains a word or words of the same derivation.

HYMN XVI.

May potent Agni who destroys the demons bless and shelter us
From greedy fiends who rise in troops at night-time when the moon is dark.

2 Varuṇa's benison hath blessed the lead, and Agni strengthens it.
Indra hath given me the lead: this verily repels the fiends.

3 This overcomes Vishkandha, this drives the voracious fiends away:
By means of this have I o'erthrown all the Piṣâchî's demon brood.

The hymn is a prayer and charm against demons.

1 *The demons:* Yâtus, evil spirits, fiends, or sorcerers who, like the Yâtudhânas (I. VII. 1), assume a variety of shapes and plague and injure men and cattle. *Greedy fiends: atriṇas;* 'tusky fiends:' M. Müller. *At night-time when the moon is dark: amâvâsyâm râtrim;* during the night of new moon, the first night of the first quarter when the moon is invisible.

2 *The lead:* a piece of this metal employed as a charm against demons and sorcery: see Book XII. 2. 1, 19, 20, 53. So in England a horseshoe was in former times generally regarded as a protection against witches, and is still sometimes nailed on or over the door of a house or stable. Iron in other forms also was used as a charm for stables:—'Hang up hooks and shears to scare, Hence the hag that rides the mare Till they be all over wet with the mire and the sweat. This observed, the manes shall be, Of your horses, all knot-free.'—Herrick. Charms and Ceremonies, LXVIII.

3 *Vishkandha:* from *vi,* apart, and *skandha,* shoulder; drawing asunder or racking the shoulders; apparently acute rheumatism in the shoulders and neck. Vishkandha is frequently mentioned in the Atharva-veda, but nowhere clearly defined. The Commentator attributes its attacks to the malice of fiends and evil spirits. *The Piṣâchî's demon brood:* Piṣâchî is the feminine of Piṣâchi (Ṛigveda I. 133. 5), or Piṣâcha, the name of a class of fierce and malignant imps or goblins. Piṣâch in Hindi and Piṣâchi in Tamil are still in common use as general terms for goblins or fiends. The feminine in Hindî is Piṣâchni.

4 If thou destroy a cow of ours, a human being, or a steed,
We pierce thee with this piece of lead so that thou mayst not slay our men.

HYMN XVII.

THOSE maidens there, the veins, who run their course in robes of ruddy hue,
Must now stand quiet, reft of power, like sisters who are brotherless.

2 Stay still, thou upper vein, stay still, thou lower, stay, thou midmost one,
The smallest one of all stands still: let the great vessel e'en be still.

3 Among a thousand vessels charged with blood, among a thousand veins,
Even these the middlemost stand still and their extremities have rest.

4 A mighty rampart built of sand hath circled and encompassed you:
Be still, and quietly take rest.

The hymn has been translated and annotated by Dr. Julius Grill, Hundert Lieder des Atharva-veda, pp. 1, 75.

The hymn is a charm to be employed when venesection is performed.

1 *Brotherless:* unsupported and helpless, when their father is dead, and they have no brother on whom the duty of protecting and finding husbands for them would naturally devolve.

3 *Vessels charged with blood:* see Dr. Wise, Commentary on the Hindu System of Medicine, pp. 63, 64.

4 *Rampart built of sand:* the bandage was probably filled with wet sand to compress and cool the vein.

See Grill, Hundert Lieder des Atharva-veda, pp. 16, 76, and Ludwig, Der Rigveda, III. p. 508.

HYMN XVIII.

WE drive away the Spotted Hag, Misfortune, and Malignity:
All blessings to our children then! We chase Malignity away.

2 Let Savitar, Mitra, Varuṇa, and Aryaman drive away Stinginess from both the hands and feet:
May Favour, granting us her bounties, drive her off. The Gods created Favour for our happiness.

3 Each fearful sign upon thy body, in thyself, each inauspicious mark seen in thy hair, thy face,
All this we drive away and banish with our speech. May Savitar the God graciously further thee.

4 Antelope-foot, and Bullock-tooth, Cow-terrifier, Vapour-form,
The Licker, and the Spotted Hag, all these we drive away from us.

The hymn is a charm to avert evil spirits of misfortune and wickedness, to remove ill-omened personal marks, and to secure prosperity.

The metre is Anushṭup in stanzas 1 (with an irregularity in line 2) and 4, and Jagatî in stanzas 2 and 3.

1 *The Spotted Hag*: or, Lalâmî. *Misfortune*: or, Lakshmî; Fortuna, Fortune; the Goddess of good and ill luck, more usually the former. *Malignity*: or Arâti. *To our children*: Ludwig reads *nír*, out, instead of *prajấyâi*, to our children, which mars the metre: 'Then let all happy things be ours.'

2 *Savitar*: the Sun, especially the morning Sun whose light drives away witches and evil spirits. *Stinginess*: Arâṇi. *From the hands and feet*: on which Arâṇi may have impressed her ill-omened signs. The charm was probably recited over a young child. *Favour*: Anumati; divine Grace, personified as a Goddess representing the Gods' favourable acceptance of worship and oblations.

3 *With our speech*: *vấchâ*; with the voice; with the spell which we utter.

4 *Antelope-foot*: Rishyapadî. *Bullock-tooth*: or, Mighty-tooth; Vṛishadatî. *Cow-terrifier*: Goshedhâ; probably from *go* + *sedhâ*, *sidh*

HYMN XIX.

Let not the piercers find us, nor let those who wound discover us.
O Indra, make the arrows fall, turned far from us, to every side.

2 Turned from us let the arrows fall, those shot and those that will be shot.
Shafts of the Gods and shafts of men, strike and transfix mine enemies!

3 Whoever treateth us as foes, be he our own or strange to us, a kinsman or a foreigner,
May Rudra with his arrows pierce and slay these enemies of mine.

---

meaning to drive away: Cow tailed, according to Weber. *Vapour-form*: Vidhamâ; the exact meaning of the word here is uncertain. The *Licker:* Viledhî. All these are names or epithets of sorceresses, witches, or female fiends of various forms.

Professor Geldner argues with great ingenuity that the subject of the hymn is some semi-domesticated animal, in all probability a house cat, and that the object of the charm is to banish its original wild and fiendish nature, and to retain and improve all its inherent good qualities and make it a friend and a blessing to men: see Vedische Studien, I. pp. 313—315.

The hymn has been translated by Ludwig, Der Rigveda, III. p. 498.

The hymn is a prayer for protection from arrows and for the punishment of enemies in general. The metre is Anushṭup, with an additional pâda in line 1 of stanza 3.

1 *Piercers: vyâdhinas;* hostile archers.

3 *Rudra:* usually derived from *rud*, to howl or roar, the Howler, the Roarer; but more probably from a lost root *rud*, to be red or ruddy, the Red, the Brilliant. Rudra is a God of thunder, storm, and tempest, and the father and leader of the Rudras, Maruts or Storm-Gods. He is represented as a terrible deity whose arrows bring disease or destruction on men and cattle, but is also sometimes addressed as benevolent and auspicious, a healer and a saviour, inasmuch as his

4 The rival and non-rival, he who in his hatred curses us—
May all the deities injure him! My nearest, closest mail is prayer.

HYMN XX.

MAY it glide harmless by in this our sacrifice, O Soma, God! Maruts, be gracious unto us.
Let not disaster, let not malison find us out; let not abominable guiles discover us.

2 Mitra and Varuṇa, ye twain, turn carefully away from us
The deadly dart that flies to-day, the missile of the wicked ones.

---

thunderstorms after long drought purify the air, dispel miasma, and bring health and vigour to everything that has life. 'Far be thy dart that killeth men or cattle: thy bliss be with us, O thou Lord of heroes:' Ṛigveda I. 114. 10. 'Where is that gracious hand of thine, O Rudra, the hand that giveth health and bringeth comfort, Remover of the woe the Gods have sent us? Look thou on me, O mighty, with compassion:' Ṛigveda II. 34. 7. For hymns to Rudra, see Hymns of the Ṛigveda, General Index I.

4 *My nearest, closest mail is prayer:* these words are the conclud ing pâda of Hymn 75, Book VI. of the Ṛigveda, entitled Weapons of War.

The hymn is a prayer, accompanying sacrifice, for protection from enemies. The metre is Jagati in stanza 1, and Anushṭup in the rest of the hymn.

1 *It:* that is, *the deadly dart, vadhás*, of stanza 2. *Soma:* see I. VI. 2. *Maruts:* the sons of Rudra, Gods of the winds and tempests, frequently invoked not only as the senders of storm and rain but as all-powerful protecting deities. 'We invoke with prayer the offspring of Rudra, the brisk, the pure, the worshipful, the active. Cling for happiness-sake to the strong company of the Maruts, the chasers of the sky, the powerful, impetuous:' Ṛigveda I. 64. 12: see M. Müller's Vedic Hymns, Part I. p. 107.

3 Ward off from this side and from that, O Varuṇa, the deadly dart:
Give us thy great protection, turn the lethal weapon far away.

4 A mighty Ruler thus art thou, unconquered, vanquisher of foes,
Even thou whose friend is never slain, whose friend is never overcome.

HYMN XXI.

Lord of the clans, giver of bliss, fiend-slayer, mighty o'er the foe,
May Indra, Soma-drinker, go before us, Bull, who brings us peace.

2 Indra, subdue our enemies, lay low the men who fight with us:
Down into nether darkness send the man who shows us enmity:

---

4 This stanza is taken from Ṛigveda X. 152. 1, a hymn addressed to Indra and ascribed to a Ṛishi Ṣâsa (Ruler) of the family of Bharadvâja.

The hymn is a prayer to Indra for protection from enemies. It is taken, with slight variations, from Ṛigveda X. 152. 2—5, the first stanza of which concludes the preceding hymn XX.

1 *Lord of the clans: viṣā́m pátis;* or Lord of (Aryan) men in general, King = *viṣpátiḥ.* The Ṛigveda has *viṣā́s pátis,* Lord of the clan or tribe. *Fiend-slayer: vṛitrahā́;* slayer of fiends and foes in general, or slayer of Vṛitra the fiend and foe *par excellence,* the Vedic personification of the malignant power which takes possession of the clouds and withholds the seasonable rain. Indra battles with this chief demon of drought, shatters him and his cloud-castles with his thunderbolt and releases the imprisoned waters. *Bull: vṛíshā;* the original meaning of the word was male, masculine, then strong, powerful, then expecially bull, stallion, hero. Sayaṇa explains *vṛíshā* by 'showerer of benefits.' See Vedic Hymns, Part I. pp. 318 sqq.

3 Strike down the fiend, strike down the foes, break thou asunder Vṛitra's jaws.
O Indra, Vṛitra-slayer, quell the wrath of the assailing foe.

4 Turn thou the foeman's thought away, his dart who fain would conquer us:
Grant us thy great protection; keep his deadly weapon far away.

HYMN XXII.

As the Sun rises let thy sore disease and yellowness depart.
We compass and surround thee with the colour of a ruddy ox.

2 With ruddy hues we compass thee that thou mayst live a lengthened life:
So that this man be free from harm, and cast his yellow tint away.

The hymn is a charm against Jaundice.

1 *As the Sun rises:* so, in Ṛigveda I. 50. 11, Sûrya, the Sun, is entreated to remove, as he rises, the sore disease and yellow hue of the afflicted suppliant. *Sore disease: hṛiddyotás;* from *hṛid*, the heart, and *dyut*, to be broken; any severe internal malady. *Yellowness:* yellowish white colour of the skin, and yellowness of the eyes, teeth, and nails, are the most unmistakeable visible signs of pâṇḍu or jaundice which must be the disease intended here. *Ruddy:* see stanzas 2 and 3.

2 *With ruddy hues:* the patient is surrounded with red or ruddy-coloured objects in order to combat the yellow which is symptomatic of the disease: 'should the patient see every thing yellow he will not soon get well:' Wise, Hindu Sysem of Medicine, p. 248. *Cast his yellow tint away: áharito bhúvat;* Weber divides *áhar ito* 'his new life may now begin.'

3 Devatyâs that are red of hue, yea, and the ruddy-coloured kine,
Each several form, each several age,—with these we compass thee about.

4 To parrots and to starlings we transfer thy sickly yellowness:
Now in the yellow-coloured birds we lay this yellowness of thine.

HYMN XXIII.

O Plant, thou sprangest up at night, dusky, dark-coloured, black in hue!
So, Rajanî, re-colour thou these ashy spots, this leprosy.

---

3 *Devatyâs:* the meaning is uncertain. Weber translates, doubtingly, by 'Götterkräfte,' divine powers. The St. Petersburg Dictionary leaves the word unexplained with the remark that animals of some kind must be intended, if the reading is correct. The word does not occur elsewhere.

4 The stanza is taken from Ṛigveda I. 50. 12, and is the second stanza of a *tricha* or triplet, the repetition of which, with due formalities, is considered to be curative of disease. *To parrots and to starlings:* birds with more or less greenish yellow tints or marks. Similarly among the Romans, people with the jaundice were called 'icterici' according to Pliny (H. N. XXX. 11), from the fanciful notion that the disease was cured by looking at the icterus, one of the many varieties of the Sturnidae or starling family. The bird died instead of the patient. *In the yellow-coloured birds: hâridraveshu;* so explained in the St. Petersburg Dictionary. According to Sâyaṇa 'in the Haritâla-trees,' but no tree of that name appears to exist.

The hymn is a charm against Leprosy. Susruta describes seven severe forms of this terrible disease, and mentions eleven slighter varieties: see Wise, Hindu System of Medicine, pp. 258 sqq.

1 *Rajanî:* Rajanî is the name of the Curcuma Longa which may have been one of the plants used in the treatment of leprosy; but the word is probably used here on account of its derivation from *rañj*, to colour: 'So, Colourer, re-colour thou.' 'O du Farbereiche,' 'O thou Colour-rich:' Weber.

2 Expel the leprosy, remove from him the spots and ashy hue:
Let thine own colour come to thee; drive far away the specks of white.

3 Dark is the place of thy repose, dark is the place thou dwellest in:
Dusky and dark, O Plant, art thou: remove from him each speck and spot.

4 I with my spell have chased away the pallid sign of leprosy
Caused by infection, on the skin, sprung from the body, from the bones.

HYMN XXIV.

FIRST, before all, the strong-winged Bird was born; thou wast the gall thereof.
Conquered in fight, the Âsurî took then the shape and form of plants.

---

2 *Let thine own colour come to thee:* addressed to the patient. According to Dr. Grill, the address to the Plant is continued: 'Let the peculiar colour of the disease enter into thee, that is, absorb it, so that the patient may recover.'

4 *Caused by infection:* two varieties of the disease appear to be meant, (1) communicated by contact, breathing the same air, eating with, or wearing the clothes or ornaments of a leper, and (2) caused by the sufferer's own sins, irregularities in eating and fasting, indigestible food, mental agitation, excessive fatigue, etc.

The hymn has been translated by Ludwig, Der Rigveda, III. p. 506, and, with annotations, by Dr. Grill, Hundert Lieder des Atharva-veda, pp. 19, 77.

The hymn is a charm against Leprosy. See I. 23.

1 The first stanza is difficult. Whatever the 'strong-winged Bird' may be, Ṣâmâ the plant to which the charm is addressed is said to have been its gall, probably because both the gall and the Plant were regarded as remedies for leprosy. The Âsuri, the female personification of the fiendish darkness of night, being conquered by the Sun, took

2 The Âsurî made, first of all, this medicine for leprosy, this banisher of leprosy.
She banished leprosy, and gave one general colour to the skin.

3 One-coloured, is thy mother's name, One-coloured is thy father called:
One-colour-maker, Plant! art thou: give thou one colour to this man.

4 Ṣâmâ who gives one general hue was formed and fashioned from the earth:
Further this work efficiently. Restore the colours that were his.

HYMN XXV.

When Agni blazed when he had pierced the Waters, whereat the Law-observers paid him homage,
There, men assever, was thy loftiest birthplace: O Fever, yielding to our prayer avoid us.

---

refuge in the gloom of the forest, and assumed the form of a plant in her offspring, the herb which is addressed: compare, 'O Plant, thou sprangest up at night' (I. 23. 1.). According to Weber the 'strong-winged Bird' is the Sun.

2 *The banisher of leprosy:* this pâda is probably an explanatory gloss. By omitting it and resolving *prathamedáṃ* into *prathamá idáṃ* the regular Anushṭup metre is restored.

3 *One-coloured:* contrasting with the patient's spotted skin.

4 *Ṣâmâ:* the plant to which this name or epithet is given is not identifiable. As an adjective derived from the verb *ṣam* the word would mean 'curative:' 'heilkräftig:' Weber. 'Instead of *ṣâmâ* the Paippalâda recension reads *ṣyâmâ* (the dusky): with which compare I. 23. 1; so also Shankar Pandit according to 2 MSS. Observe also *ṣâmâka* = *ṣyâmâka* in Kauṣika-Sûtra VIII. 11. *ṣyâmâ* is the name of various plants (see St. Petersburg Dictionary, s. v.):' Grill.

The hymn has been translated by Ludwig, Der Rigveda, III. p. 509, and, with annotations, by Dr. Grill, Hundert Lieder, pp. 19. 20, 77, 78.

The hymn is a charm against Fever. The metre is Trishṭup.

1 The meaning of the stanza is that fevers begin to be prevalent

2 If thou be fiery glow, or inflammation, or if thy birthplace call for chips of fuel,
Rack is thy name, God of the sickly yellow! O Fever, yielding to our prayer avoid us.

3 Be thou distress, or agonizing torment, be thou the son King Varuṇa hath begotten,
Rack is thy name, God of the sickly yellow! O Fever, yielding to our prayer avoid us.

---

at the commencement of the annual Rains, when Agni the God of Fire descends in his form of lightning from the Waters of the firmament and falls with the rain into the waters of the earth. *The Law-observers:* the Gods who observe and maintain the everlasting statutes of moral and natural order. The allusion is to the flight of Agni, and his pursuit and discovery by the Gods:—'Him (Agni) the unerring ones (the Gods), observant, found in floods, couched like a lion in his lair:' Ṛigveda III. 9. 4: compare Ṛigveda 1. 45. 1. *O Fever: takmán*, derived from *tak*, to fly at, to pounce upon, meaning that which suddenly seizes, is explained in the St. Petersburg Dictionary as a kind of disease, or probably a whole class of diseases, accompanied by eruptions on the skin. But a comparison of the passages of the Atharvaveda in which the word occurs is sufficient to prove that fever in its many varieties, especially malarial fever, is the disease that is intended. The word does not occur in the Ṛigveda, nor—barring the Kauṣika-Sûtra—is it found in works later than the Atharva-veda. Fever, says Susruta, is the king of diseases. With fever man is born, and with fever he departs from this world. For an exhaustive excursus on Takman, see Grohmann, Medecinisches aus dem Atharva-veda, Indische Studien, IX. pp. 3 81—423, and compare Wise, Hindu System of Medicine, under Fevers (Jwara) pp. 219—233.

Takman, or Fever, is addressed in the hymn as a *devá*, a supernatural being or God, to whose influence the disease may be attributed.

2 *If thy birthplace call for chips of fuel:* if thou be caused by an internal fire which consumes the vital forces, like flame that requires fragments of wood to feed it. *Rack is thy name: hrúḍu*, from *hruḍ*, to draw or contract; cramp or spasm: 'Krampf ist dein name:' Ludwig.

God of the sickly yellow: or, of the yellow colour; a symptom of Paittik Jwara or bilious fever: see Wise, p. 225.

3 *The son King Varuṇa hath begotten:* if thou hast come from the God Varuṇa, sent by him, as the moral Governor of the world, to punish sin.

4 I offer homage to the chilly Fever, to his fierce burning glow I offer homage.
Be adoration paid to Fever coming each other day, the third, or two days running.

HYMN XXVI.

LET that Destructive Weapon be far distant from us, O ye Gods; far be the Stone ye wont to hurl.

2 Our friend be that Celestial Grace, Indra and Bhaga be our friends, and Savitar with splendid wealth.

3 Thou, Offspring of the Waterflood, ye Maruts, with your sun-bright skins, give us protection reaching far.

4 Further us rightly, favour ye our bodies with your gracious love. Give thou our children happiness.

---

4 *Chilly Fever:* coldness of the body and shivering fits are among the symptoms mentioned in the Hindu System of Medicine. The names of the three varieties of intermittent fever mentioned in the second line are, in the text, *anyeyús*, *tritî́yakas* (tertian), and *ubhayadyús* recurring on both, that is, two successive days.

The hymn is a prayer for protection, guidance, and prosperity.

2 *Bhaga:* Baga in Old Persian, Bogŭ in Old Slavonic; Bhaga is the gracious Lord and protector and the bestower of wealth. His name is frequently mentioned in the Ṛigveda with that of Savitar, and he is invoked together with Pûshan and the Âdityas, Mitra, Varuṇa, and Aryaman. See Hymns of the Ṛigveda, General Index II.

3 *Offspring of the Waterflood: pravato napât.* Lightning is so called in I. 13. 2. 3: 'Child of the Flood.' Here Agni is intended, sprung in the form of lightning from the clouds or waters of the firmament: *pravât te agne jánimâ*, 'Agni, thy birth is from the flood:' Ṛigveda X. 142. 2. *With your sun-bright skins:* 'O Maruts, strong and wise, with sun-bright skins:' Ṛigveda VII. 59. 11.

4 *Our bodies:* ourselves, as separate from our children. *Thou:* Agni.

HYMN XXVII.

THERE on the bank those Vipers lie, thrice-seven, having cast their skins:
Now we with their discarded sloughs bind close and cover up the eyes of the malicious highway thief.

2 Far let her go, cutting her way, brandishing, as it were, a club:
Diverted be the new-born's mind: ne'er are the wicked prosperous.

3 Not many have had power enough; the feeble ones have not prevailed,
Like scattered fragments of a reed: ne'er are the wicked prosperous.

4 Go forward, feet, press quickly on, bring to the house of him who pays.
Unconquered and unplundered, let Indrâṇî, foremost, lead the way.

A charm in which snakes' skins are employed.

1 *Vipers:* the Pṛidâku, a venomous snake, adder or viper, is frequently mentioned in the Atharva-veda. *Thrice-seven: trishaptâ's;* indefinitely for a considerable number. According to Weber, 'thrice-coiled:' see I. 1. 1, note. *Bind close:* the sloughs are to make the travellers invisible to robbers. John Aubrey, the English antiquary, who lived in the seventeenth century, recommends the powder obtained from a snake which has been caught at midnight of Midsummer Eve, killed, skinned, and dried in the shade, as a means to procure invisibility.

2 *Let her go:* meaning the mother snake. *Cutting her way:* through her old skin. *A club:* her head, raised for attack. *The new-born's mind:* the attention of the snake who has cast her old skin and got a new one.

3 *Scattered fragments of a reed: veṇóradgâs;* or, 'scattered stalks around a reed.' The word *ádga* is said to mean an oblation of melted butter; or a sacrificial cake.

4 *Go forward, feet:* the speaker of the charm addresses his own feet. He wishes to press on to the house of the man who will pay him for what he brings. *Indrâṇî:* the Consort of Indra. The Goddess will guide him. *Unplundered:* with reference to the charm which the man possesses.

HYMN XXVIII.

God Agni hath come forth to us, fiend-slayer, chaser of disease,
Burning the Yâtudhânas up, Kimîdins, and deceitful ones.

2 Consume the Yâtudhânas, God! meet the Kimîdins with thy flame:
Burn up the Yâtudhânîs as they face thee, thou whose path is black!

3 She who hath cursed us with a curse, or hath conceived a murderous sin;
Or seized our son to take his blood, let her devour the child she bare.

4 Let her, the Yâtudhânî eat son, sister, and her daughter's child.
Now let the twain by turns destroy the wild-haired Yâtudhânîs and crush down Arâyîs to the earth!

HYMN XXIX.

With that victorious Amulet which strengthened Indra's power and might

---

A prayer for the destruction of demons.

1 *Yâtudhânas...Kimîdins:* see I. 7. 1.

2 *Thou whose path is black:* the same epithet, *krishṇávartani*, is given to Agni in the Ṛigveda, VIII. 23. 19.

4 *The twain:* Agni and Indra, or Agni and Soma; both Indra and Soma being associated with Agni as allies in the destruction of demons. *Arâyîs:* Arâyî is originally the personification as a female fiend of the illiberal impiety which refuses to give oblations to the Gods and guerdon to the priests. The word was afterwards used as the designation of a class of malevolent spirits: 'Arâyî, one-eyed, limping hag, fly, ever-screeching! to the hill:' Ṛigveda X. 155. 1.

The hymn, which is a charm to secure the supremacy and success of a dethroned King on his restoration to power, is an adaptation of Hymn X. 174 of the Ṛigveda.

1 *Amulet:* instead of *maṇinâ* the Ṛigveda reading is *havíshâ:* 'With that victorious sacrifice,' an oblation which secures success against one's enemies. *Brahmaṇaspati:* Lord of Prayer: another name of Bṛihaspati: see I. 8. 2, note.

Do thou, O Brahmaṇaspati, increase our strength for kingly sway.

2 Subduing those who rival us, subduing all malignities,
Withstand the man who menaces, and him who seeks to injure us.

3 Soma and Savitar the God have strengthened and exalted thee:
All elements have aided thee, to make thee general conqueror.

4 Slayer of rivals, vanquisher, may that victorious Amulet
Be bound on me for regal sway and conquest of mine enemies.

5 Yon Sun hath mounted up on high, and this my word hath mounted up
That I may smite my foes and be slayer of rivals, rivalless.

6 Destroyer of my rivals, strong, victorious, with royal sway,
May I be ruler of these men, and King and sovran of the folk.

HYMN XXX.

GUARD and protect this man, all Gods and Vasus.
Over him keep ye watch and ward, Âdityas.
Let not death reach him from the hands of brothers,
from hands of aliens, or of human beings.

---

2 This and the following stanza are addressed to the amulet, which reminds one of the old Teutonic Siegerstein or Stone of Victory.

5 The first line is taken, with one variation, from Ṛigveda X. 159. 1. *My word:* the Ṛigveda reading is *mâmakó bhágaḥ*, my happy fate, instead of *mâmakám vácħas*.

The occasion of the hymn is the consecration of a King. Cf. I. 9.

1 *Vasus:* Gods, frequently mentioned with the Âdityas and the Rudras; personifications of the powers of nature, especially of those that are bright and celestial, and sometimes almost synonymous with the Devas.

2 Listen, one-minded, to the word I utter, the sons, O Gods, among you, and the fathers!
I trust this man to all of you: preserve him happily, and to length of days conduct him.

3 All Gods who dwell on earth or in the heavens, in air, within the plants, the beasts, the waters,
Grant this man life to full old age, and let him escape the hundred other ways of dying.

4 You, claiming Anuyâjas or Prayâjas, sharers, or not consumers, of oblation,
You, to whom heaven's five regions are apportioned, I make companions at his sacred sessions.

HYMN XXXI.

Here will we serve with sacrifice the great Controllers of the world,
The four immortal Warders who protect the regions of the sky.

---

3 *Full old age:* extending to at least a hundred years. Prayers for life to last for a hundred winters or autumns are of frequent occurrence in the Ṛigveda: see Hymns of the Ṛigveda, General Index II., under Hundred winters. *The hundred other ways:* see II. 28. 1, and VIII. 2. 27.

4 *Anuyâjas or Prayâjas:* Prayâjas consist of texts and oblations forming part of the introductory ceremony at a Soma sacrifice, and Anuyâjas are the secondary or final offerings: 'Voropfer and Nachopfer:' Weber. *Heaven's five regions:* the regions of the sky are, in the Veda, more usually said to be four or six: see I. 31. 1, 2. *Companions at his sacred sessions: satrasádas;* feast-companions, or assistants at the *sattra* or *satra* (from *sad*, to sit), a long sacrifice, sacrificial session, or Soma ceremony, lasting more than twelve days and conducted by many officiating priests.

The hymn has been translated by Ludwig, Der Rigveda, p. 430.

The hymn is a prayer for protection and general prosperity.

1 *The four immortal Warders:* according to a passage in the Shaḍviṅsa-Brâhmaṇa, Agni is guardian of the east, Yama of the south,

2 Ye, Guardians of the regions, Gods who keep the quarters of the heavens,
Rescue and free us from the bonds of Nirṛiti, from grief and woe!

3 I, free from stiffness, serve thee with oblation, not lame I sacrifice with oil and fatness.
Let the strong Warder God who keeps the regions bring to us hither safety and well-being.

4 Well be it with our mother and our father, well be it with our cows, and beasts, and people.
Ours be all happy fortune, grace, and favour. Long, very long may we behold the sunlight.

HYMN XXXII.

YE people, hear and mark this well: he will pronounce a mighty prayer:
That which gives breathing to the Plants is not on earth nor in the heaven.

Varuṇa of the west, and Soma of the north. According to Manu V. 96, there are eight Lokapâlas or World-protectors who preside over the eight points, cardinal and intermediate, of the compass: these are Indra, Agni, Yama, Sûrya, Varuṇa, Pavana or Vâyu, the God of Wind, Kuvera, the God of Riches, and Soma or Chandra the Moon-God. The word in the text, *âśâpâlâs*, does not occur again in the hymns of the Veda.

2 *Nirṛiti:* Decay or Destruction personified; the Goddess of Misfortune, Death and Corruption.

3 *Free from stiffness......not lame:* in full possession of my bodily powers and active in thy service. *Thee:* Agni, the *strong Warder God* of the next line.

The hymn has been translated by Ludwig, Der Rigveda, III. p. 372.

The hymn is in honour of Heaven and Earth, the Universal Father and Mother. See Max Müller, India, What can it Teach us? pp. 158—162.

1 *He:* the priest. *Will pronounce a mighty prayer:* according to Weber: 'Of mighty Brahman (The Absolute) will he speak.' *The Plants: vîrúdhaḥ;* meaning here especially medicinal herbs.

2 Their station, as of those who rest when weary, is in midmost air:
The base whereon this world is built, the sages know or know it not.

3 What the two trembling hemispheres and ground produced and fashioned forth,
This All, is ever fresh to-day, even as the currents of the sea.

4 This All hath compassed round the one, and on the other lies at rest.
To Earth and all-possessing Heaven mine adoration have I paid.

HYMN XXXIII.

May they, the golden-hued, the bright, the splendid, they wherein Savitar was born and Agni,

---

2 *Their station......is in midmost air:* the Plants, or medicinal herbs, are said (Ṛigveda X. 97. 1) to have been produced 'three ages earlier than the Gods,' *devébhyas triyugám purá*, and in stanza 15 of the same hymn they are called *bṛihaspátiprasûtâs*, commissioned by Bṛihaspati, who is a deity of the middle air and as the Lord of Prayer presides also over *mantras* or spells and charms.

3 *Trembling:* not yet firmly established. *Hemispheres: ródasî;* a dual meaning heaven and earth, without the *antariksha* or intermediate air. *Ground: bhû́mis;* here the land as a portion of the whole earth. Weber gives the word in this place the meaning of air or firmament. *Produced and fashioned forth: nirátakshatam;* the construction of a dual verb with three subjects appears to be somewhat irregular; but *bhû́miçcha* may perhaps be regarded as parenthetical. *This All:* Universal Creation.

4 *The one:* Earth. *The other:* Heaven.

The hymn has been translated by Ludwig, Der Rigveda, III. p. 533.

The hymn is a prayer to the divine Waters (cf. I. 4. 1) for health and happiness.

1 *Savitar,* the Sun, is born in the mists and vapours of the early morning; and *Agni* springs in his form of lightning from the clouds or waters of the sea of air. *Varuṇa:* originally the same as the Greek Ouranos, the visible sky, and afterwards the great God beyond it, the moral Governor of the world. The waters in which he moves are the atmosphere or firmament.

They who took Agni as a germ, fair-coloured, the Waters, bring felicity and bless us!

2 They in the midst whereof King Varuṇa moveth, viewing men's righteous and unrighteous dealing,
They who took Agni as a germ, fair-coloured, those Waters bring felicity and bless us!

3 Whom the Gods make their beverage in heaven, they who wax manifold in air's mid-region,
They who took Agni as a germ, fair-coloured,—those Waters bring felicity and bless us!

4 Ye Waters, with auspicious eye behold me: touch ye my skin with your auspicious body.
May they, the bright and pure, distilling fatness, those Waters, bring felicity and bless us.

HYMN XXXIV.

From honey sprang this Plant to life: with honey now we dig thee up.
Make us as sweet as honey, for from honey hast thou been produced.

2 My tongue hath honey at the tip, and sweetest honey at the root:
Thou yieldest to my wish and will, and shalt be mine and only mine.

---

4 *Distilling fatness: ghṛitaśchútas;* literally, dropping *ghṛita,* melted and clarified butter or oil, used figuratively for fertility and prosperity: 'When I washed my steps with butter, And the rock poured me out rivers of oil:' Job, 29. 6: and 'Thou crownest the year with thy goodness; And thy paths drop fatness:' Psalm LXV. 11.

The hymn is a charm to win and secure a girl's love.

1 *This Plant:* sugar-cane; see stanza 5. *With honey:* with the sweetness which thou containest; or perhaps, as Dr. Grill suggests, with a spade or mattock smeared with honey, which would make the charm more effectual.

3 My coming in is honey-sweet, and honey-sweet my going forth:
My voice and words are sweet: I fain would be like honey in my look.

4 Sweeter am I than honey, yet more full of sweets than licorice:
So mayst thou love me as a branch full of all sweets, and only me.

5 Around thee have I girt a zone of sugar-cane to banish hate,
That thou mayst be in love with me, my darling, never to depart.

HYMN XXXV.

THIS Ornament of Gold which Daksha's children bound, with benevolent thoughts, on Ṣatânîka,
This do I bind on thee for life, for glory, for long life lasting through a hundred autumns.

---

3 *My coming in.........my going forth:* all my doings; my general conduct.

4 *Licorice: madúgha* is an unspecified shrub or plant that yields a sweet juice: see VI. 102. 3 for its employment in combination with other sweet plants.

5 *To banish hate:* and, of course, to inspire love. *My darling, never to depart:* more literally: 'that thou mayst never go away,' or become alienated from me. So in the Eddic Háva-mál, the Lay of the High One, Woden says: 'The seventeenth (song or charm) I know: That the young maid shall never forsake me.'

The second line of the stanza recurs in similar love-songs: see II. 30. 1, and VI. 8. 1—3.

The hymn is one of Dr. Grill's Hundert Lieder.

The hymn is a charm accompanying investiture with an amulet of gold.

1 *Daksha's children: dâkshâyaṇâs;* Daksha is in the Veda a creative power associated with Aditi (Infinity or Eternity), the mother of the

2 This man no fiends may conquer, no Piṣâchas, for this is might of Gods, their primal offspring.
Whoever wears the Gold of Daksha's children hath a long lengthened life among the living.

3 The light, the power, the lustre of the Waters, the strength of Trees, and all their forceful vigour,
We lay on him as powers abide in Indra: so let him wear this Gold and show his valour.

4 With monthly and six-monthly times and seasons, with the full year's sweet essence do we fill thee.
May Indra, Agni, and all Gods together, showing no anger, grant thee what thou wishest.

Âdityas. In post-vedic literature he is generally regarded as the son of Brahmâ, and placed at the head of the Prajâpatis or Lords of Created Beings. The Dâkshâyaṇas, or descendants of Daksha, are mentioned also in the Ṣatapatha-Brâhmaṇa. The investiture of *Ṣatânîka* must be an occurrence of ancient times of which no particulars have been preserved. *A hundred autumns:* regarded as the natural duration of human life; an expression frequently occurring in the Ṛigveda, alternating with 'a hundred winters:' Cf. Isaiah LXV. 20: There shall be no more thence an infant of days, nor an old man that hath not filled his days: for the child shall die a hundred years old.

2 *Piṣâchas:* imps or goblins: see I. 16. 3, note.

Professor Ludwig has translated this hymn, Der Rigveda, III. p. 457.

4 *Six-monthly times: Samâ* meaning a half-year: 'originally, probably, summer (cf. Zend *hama*).'—St. Petersburg Dictionary.

BOOK II.

HYMN I.

VENA beholds That Highest which lies hidden, wherein this All resumes one form and fashion.
Thence Pṛiṣni milked all life that had existence: the hosts that know the light with songs extolled her.

2 Knowing Eternity, may the Gandharva declare to us that highest secret station.
Three steps thereof lie hidden in the darkness: he who knows these shall be the father's father.

The hymn is a glorification of the Prime Cause of all things.

1 *Vena:* Vena, 'the loving Sun' of Rigveda I. 83. 5, *kântaḥ* or 'the beloved,' is said by the Scholiast to be *madhyasthâno devah*, a God of the middle region of the air. He is, apparently, the Sun as he rises in the mists of the morning: see Ṛigveda X. 123. 1. 2. Weber translates Vena by 'der Seher,' the Seer, connecting the word with the Zend root *vaên*, to see. *That Highest:* the Supreme First Cause. *Pṛiṣni:* usually the Speckled Cow, the variegated cloud, regarded as the mother of the Maruts. Here she appears, like the cow Audhumbla of Scandinavian mythology, to represent the creative power of Nature. *All life that had existence: jấyamânâḥ*, the feminine plural stands without a substantive; *prajấḥ*, creatures, may perhaps be understood; or, as Weber suggests, *vrấḥ*, hosts, from the second pâda of the line. *The hosts:* either the beings called into life by this act of Pṛiṣni, or already existing beings produced by an earlier act of creation. So when the foundations of the earth were laid: The morning stars sang together, And all the sons of God shouted for joy.—Job, 38. 7.

2 *The Gandharva:* Vena, the rising Sun. According to Weber, 'the sage.' *Three steps:* according to Mahîdhara, the three *padâni*, steps, or conditions, are production, existence, and disappearance; or the Absolute (Brahma), the Demiurgus or Creator, and the individual soul. Weber suggests that the reference is to the Purusha-Sûkta (Ṛigveda X. 90. 3, 4): 'All creatures are one-fourth of him, three-fourths immortal life in heaven. With three-fourths Purusha went up: one-fourth of him again was here.' *The father's father:* wiser than, and able to instruct, his elders.

3 He is our kinsman, father, and begetter: he knows all beings and all Ordinances.
He only gave the Gods their appellations: all creatures go to him to ask direction.

4 I have gone forth around the earth and heaven, I have approached the first-born Son of Order.
He, putting voice, as 'twere, within the speaker, stands in the world, he, verily is Agni.

5 I round the circumjacent worlds have travelled to see the far-extended thread of Order,
Wherein the Gods, obtaining life eternal, have risen upward to one common birthplace.

HYMN II.

Lord of the World, divine Gandharva, only he should be honoured in the Tribes and worshipped.
Fast with my spell, celestial God, I hold thee. Homage to thee! Thy home is in the heavens.

---

3 *He:* the Almighty Creator. The stanza is taken, with variations, from Ṛigveda X. 82. 3. *To ask direction:* or, for information; to learn who is the Supreme God; or what their several functions and duties are.

4 *Order (ṛita)* is the eternal Law of the Universe, and *the first-born son* thereof is Prajâpati, the Creator, who is in this stanza identified with Agni.

5 *Obtaining life immortal:* Agni alone, it is said, was originally immortal, and the other Gods obtained immortality through him. See Ṛigveda V. 3. 4; VI. 7. 4; VII. 13. 2. According to other texts (Ṛigveda IV. 54, 2, and IX. 106. 8), immortality is conferred on them by Savitar and by Soma. The whole of this Book has been translated, with copious explanatory notes, by Professor Weber, Indische Studien, XIII. pp. 129—216. Sixteen of the hymns have been translated by Professor Ludwig, in Der Rigveda, III., and thirteen by Dr. Grill in his Hundert Lieder des Atharva-veda.

The hymn is a charm to win success in gambling.

1 *Gandharva:* called Viṣvâvasu or Lord of all Wealth in stanza 5, not identified here with the Sun as in II. 1. His especial duty is to guard the heavenly Soma which the Gods obtain through his permission. The glorification of which he is the subject in this gambler's hymn is grossly exaggerated. *The Tribes:* five in number, which constitute the Âryan community.

2 Sky-reaching, like the Sun in brightness, holy,
he who averts from us the Gods' displeasure,
Lord of the World, may the Gandharva bless us,
the friendly God who only must be worshipped.

3 I came, I met these faultless, blameless beings:
among the Apsarases was the Gandharva.
Their home is in the sea—so men have told me,—
whence they come quickly hitherward and vanish.

4 Thou, Cloudy! ye who follow the Gandharva Viṣvâ-
vasu, ye, Starry! Lightning-Flasher!
You, O ye Goddesses, I truly worship.

5 Haunters of darkness, shrill in voice, dice-lovers,
maddeners of the mind—
To these have I paid homage, the Gandharva's wives,
Apsarases.

HYMN III.

THAT little spring of water which is running down-
ward from the hill
I turn to healing balm for thee that thou mayst be
good medicine.

---

3 *Apsarases:* (perhaps from *ap*, water, and *sṛi*, to go) celestial nymphs who dwell among the clouds, the waters of the sea of air, the consorts of the Gandharva or of the class of Gandharvas.

4 *Thou, Cloudy:* six other names of Apsarases are given in Ṛigveda X. 95. 6.

5 *Haunters of darkness:* loving the dark woods when they visit the earth. *Dice-lovers:* This is the point of the hymn. The Gandharva is unduly glorified because he is the consort of the Apsarases; and they are worshipped as being intimately connected with dice and able to influence the gambler's luck. See IV. 38. 1—4; VI. 118. 1; VII. 109. 2, 3. *Maddeners of the mind:* of the gambler.

The hymn contains a charm in which water is used to cure disease.

1 *For thee:* for the mixture which the speaker is preparing, and which the addition of fresh water from the spring will make complete. *That thou mayst be good medicine:* that the whole mixture thus prepared may be thoroughly effectual. Ludwig alters *súbheshajam* to *súbheshajo*, 'that thou mayst have good medicine,' referring *thee* and *thou* to the patient for whose benefit the charm is uttered.

2 Hither and onward! Well! Come on! Among thy hundred remedies
Most excellent of all art thou, curing disease and morbid flow.

3 The Asuras bury deep in earth this mighty thing that healeth wounds.
This is the cure for morbid flow, this driveth malady away.

4 The emmets from the water-flood produce this healing medicine:
This is the cure for morbid flow, this driveth malady away.

5 Mighty is this wound-healing balm: from out the earth was it produced.
This is the cure for morbid flow, this driveth malady away.

6 Bless us the Waters! be the Plants auspicious!
May Indra's thunderbolt drive off the demons. Far from us fall the shafts they shoot against us!

---

2 *Hither............Come on:* the water is addressed. *Thy:* the change of *te* into *me*, my, would make the meaning clearer. *Curing ....morbid flow: anâsrâvám,* literally, without *âsrâvá* or diarrhœa: See I. 2. 4.

3 *The Asuras:* malevolent demons; they are said to have buried water deep in the earth, apparently that men should not profit by it.

4 *The emmets:* 'die Upajikâ:' Grill; 'Die Wassernixen,' nixes, or water-fairies: Weber and Ludwig. 'The *upajî'kās* or *upadî'kás* are a kind of ants who are endowed with the quality of producing water, and that too, beneficent, healing water, wherever they appear, and consequently wherever they are applied:' Bloomfield, American Journal of Philology, VII. p. 483. See also Atharva-veda VI. 100. 2. Termites or white ants appear to be meant, called in Hindi *dîmak* or *diwak*, corrupted from *upajîhvikâ*, an older form of *upajîka* or *upadîka*, and found in the Ṛigveda.

The hymn has been translated by Ludwig, Der Rigveda, III. p. 507, and by Grill with notes, Hundert Lieder, pp. 17, 79.

HYMN IV.

For length of life, for mighty joy, uninjured, ever showing strength
We wear Vishkandha's antidote, the Amulet of Jangiḍa.

2 Amulet of a thousand powers, Jangiḍa save us, all around,
From Jambha, and from Viṣara, Vishkandha, and tormenting pain.

3 This overcomes Vishkandha, this chases the greedy fiends away:
May this our panacea, may Jangiḍa save us from distress.

4 With Jangiḍa that brings delight, Amulet given by the Gods,
We in the conflict overcome Vishkandha and all Râkshasas.

The hymn is a charm to win protection and general prosperity.

1 *Vishkandha's antidote:* Vishkandha was probably rheumatism, and the name of the fiend to whose malignity the disease was attributed: See I. 16. 3. *Jangiḍa:* a plant frequently mentioned in the Atharva-veda as a charm against demons and a specific for various diseases. It appears to have been cultivated (stanza 5), but no description of it has been given, and it cannot now be identified. For its divine effects see XIX. 35. 1—5. The plant seems to have resembled 'that moly That Hermes once to wise Ulysses gave,' (see Homer, Odyssey, X. 305) which according to Dierbach was the Mandrake, and in Theophrastus is the name of a kind of garlic. See Lang's *Custom and Myth* (new edition), pp. 143 sqq.

2 *Jambha:* from *jambh*, to seize with the mouth; a disease, and the name of the fiend that causes it. Weber, citing Kauṣika-Sutra XXXII. 1, *jambhagṛihîtâya stanam prayachhati*, 'he offers the (mother's) breast to the (child) seized by Jambha,' suggests that some infantile disorder, perhaps teething, is intended. *Viṣara:* from *vi* and *ṣṛî*, to split or break in pieces; the name of another fiend and the disease or morbid symptom attributed to him, racking pain or perhaps convulsions. *Tormenting pain:* or violent inflammation, and its originating demon.

4 *Râkshasas:* fierce nocturnal fiends or ogres.

5 May Cannabis and Jangiḍa preserve me from Vishkandha,—that
Brought to us from the forest, this sprung from the saps of husbandry.

6 This Amulet destroys the might of magic and malignity:
So may victorious Jangiḍa prolong the years we have to live.

HYMN V.

INDRA, be gracious, drive thou forth, come, hero, with thy two bay steeds.
Taste the libation, hither, enjoying meath and the hymn, come, fair, to the banquet.

2 O Indra, even as one athirst, fill thee with meath as 'twere from heaven.
Sweet-toned, the raptures of this juice have come to thee as to the light.

---

5 *Cannabis: ṣaṇá;* hemp; Cannabis Sativa. *The saps of husbandry:* the moisture of the cultivated and irrigated soil. The hemp, on the other hand, grows without cultivation.

Indra is invited to come and drink a libation of Soma juice.

1 This stanza and the two that immediately follow it are found, with variations, in Sâmaveda II. iii. i. 22. The metre is somewhat irregular. The stanzas are obscure; and 2 and 3 are characterized by the repetition of *ná*, 'like,' 'as' 'as it were,' which recurs six times. *Two bay steeds:* this is the usual number assigned to Indra in the Ṛigveda; but in one passage (II. 18. 4—6) the worshipper invites the God to come with two, with four, with six, and so on up to a hundred, the progressive multiplication being perhaps intended to indicate the ever increasing rapidity with which the worshipper prays the God to approach. The Scholiast says that by their supernatural power the two horses of Indra multiply themselves indefinitely. *Meath:* the Soma juice.

2 *As one athirst:* literally, like a new (drinker). *Sweet-toned:* accompanied with sweet songs.

3 Swift-conquering Indra, Mitra-like, smote, as a Yati, Vṛitra dead.
Like Bhṛigu he cleft Vala through, and quelled his foes in Soma's rapturous joy.

4 O Indra, let the juices enter thee. Fill full thy belly, sate thee, mighty one! Let the hymn bring thee.
Hear thou my call, accept the song I sing, here, Indra, with thy friends enjoy thyself, to height of rapture.

5 Now will I tell the manly deeds of Indra, the first that he achieved, the thunder-wielder.
He slew the Dragon, then disclosed the waters, and cleft the channels of the mountain torrents.

6 He slew the Dragon lying on the mountain: his heavenly bolt of thunder Tvashṭar fashioned.
Like lowing kine in rapid flow descending the waters glided downward to the ocean.

---

3 *As a Yati:* one of a mythical race of ascetics connected with the Bhṛigus, and said, according to one legend, to have taken part in the creation of the world. The force of the comparison is not very obvious; and perhaps it would be better, as Ludwig suggests, to give *yátiḥ* here the meaning of 'wrestler.' Weber translates it by 'Zaubrer,' magician, enchanter. *Bhṛigu:* a Ṛishi regarded as the ancestor of the ancient race of Bhṛigus who are frequently mentioned in the Ṛigveda in connexion with Agni, and who are specially associated with the Atharva-veda hymns. *Vala:* a demon of drought who steals the cows of the Gods and hides them in a *valá*, enclosure or cave, that is, keeps the seasonable rains imprisoned in dark thick clouds.

5 Stanzas 5—7 are taken from Ṛigveda I. 32. 1—3. *The Dragon:* Ahi, the great serpent, another name of Vṛitra, the chief demon of drought.

6 *The mountain:* the great mountain-like cloud. *Tvashṭar:* the Indian Hephaestus or Vulcanus, the celestial Artificer.

7 Impetuous as a bull he chose the Soma, and quaffed the juices in three sacred beakers.
Maghavan grasped the thunder for his weapon, and smote to death this first-born of the dragons.

HYMN VI.

HALF-YEARS and seasons strengthen thee, O Agni, the years, and all the Verities, and Ṛishis!
Flash forth with thy celestial effulgence: illumine all four regions of the heavens.

2 Kindle thee, Agni, and make this man prosper: rise up erect for high and happy fortune.
Agni, be those uninjured who adore thee, and may thy priests be glorious and no others.

3 These Brâhmans have elected thee, O Agni: be thou propitious in our sacred chamber.
Slayer of rivals, Agni, quell our foemen: watch in our house with care that never ceases.

---

7 *In three sacred beakers: trikadrukeshu;* according to Sâyaṇa, at the three sacrifices called Jyotis, Gauḥ, and Âyus, the first three days of the Abhiplava festival: 'and quaffed in threefold sacrifice the juices.' *Maghavan:* the Bounteous One (Indra).

Indra with his thunderbolt slays the Dragon who obstructs the rain; or shatters the massive clouds that gather at the end of the season of drought, and sends the waters down upon the parched earth. Similarly Apollo, the Sun-God, slew the great serpent Python; and Odin, as God of the Sun or Spring in Northern mythology, slays the serpent who represents the wet and misty winter.

The hymn has been discussed by von Roth in his Abhandlung über den Atharva-veda, pp. 11—14.

The hymn is a prayer to Agni for protection.

1 The poet prays that the Sacrificial Fire, representing Agni on earth, may continually increase in strength and splendour. *Half-years: sámás;* months, according to Mahidhara: days, according to Weber. *Ṛishis:* all the seers or sacred poets to whom the hymns of the Veda have been revealed.

2 *This man:* the institutor of the sacrifice.

3 *Have elected thee:* to be their great Chief Priest. *Sacred chamber:* or, sanctuary; the sacrificial hall or enclosure.

4 Seize, Agni, on thy power and firmly hold it: contend thou with the Friend by way of friendship.
Placed in the centre of our fellows, Agni, flash forth to be invoked by kings around thee.

5 Past those who slay, past enemies, past thoughtless men, past those who hate,—
Yea, Agni, hear us safe past all distresses: give thou us opulence with men about us.

HYMN VII.

HATED by sinners, sprung from Gods, this Plant that turns the curse away
Hath washed from me all curses, as water makes clean from spot and stain.

2 All curses of a rival, each curse of a female relative,
Curse uttered by an angry priest, all these we tread beneath our feet.

3 Spread on the surface of the earth, downward from heaven thy root depends:
With this that hath a thousand joints keep thou us safe on every side.

4 Guard on all sides this woman, guard my children, us, and all our wealth!
Let not malignity o'ercome, nor adversaries conquer us.

---

4 *The Friend:* the God Mitra. *By way of friendship: mitradhā.*
5 The first line of the stanza is in the Anushṭup metre: the rest of the hymn is Trishṭup.

The hymn is a counter-charm against imprecation and malignity.

1 *This Plant:* Darbha or Kuṣa grass (Poa Cynosuroides), much used in sacrificial ceremonies and endowed with various sanctifying qualities.

3 *Downward from heaven:* referring to its divine origin: 'O Plant (Darbha), thy root is in the heavens.' Atharva-veda XIX. 32. 3. *A thousand joints:* Darbha is a grass that spreads rapidly and continually re-roots itself. The multiplicity of joints or roots indicates the far-reaching power of the plant.

5 Upon the curser fall his curse! Dwell we with him whose heart is true!
We split the cruel villain's ribs whose evil eye bewitches us.

HYMN VIII.

TWIN Stars of happy omen, named Releasers, have gone up. May they
Loose, of inherited disease, the uppermost and lowest bond.

2 Vanish this Night, extinct in Dawn! Let those who weave their spells depart.
So let the plague-destroying Plant remove inherited disease.

---

5 *Bewitches us:* dread of the evil eye (chashm-i-bad) is still as prevalent in India, especially among women, as it is, and has been from early times, in Italy—especially in the southern parts—where the reputation of being a jettatore or jettatrice (caster of the evil eye) brings ostracism and social ruin upon people even of the highest rank.

The hymn has been translated by Ludwig, Der Rigveda, III. p. 508, and by Grill, Hundert Lieder, pp. 34, 81.

The hymn is a charm against *kshetriyá*, some hereditary disease, perhaps pulmonary Consumption.

1 *Releasers: vichṛítau;* the ancient name of the lunar asterism called Mûlabarhaṇî or Mûla. *Of inherited disease: kshetriyásya;* the word means originally of, or belonging to, a *kshetra* (Hindi *khet*) a field; and, as a neuter substantive, a chronic, constitutional, or hereditary disease, derived from the mother's body regarded as a productive field. Weber takes the word here to refer to injury of the field or farm; and stanzas 3—5 seem almost to justify his interpretation. An alternative version might be: 'of the spell that binds our field.'

2 *Those who weave their spells:* witches and female fiends. The refrain in this and the following stanzas might be, in accordance with Weber's interpretation: 'May the plague-staying Plant remove the spell that lies upon our field.'

3 With straw of barley tawny-brown in colour with its silvery ears, with stalk and stem of Sesamum—
So let the plague-destroying Plant remove inherited disease.

4 Let homage to thy ploughs be paid, our homage to the pole and yokes.
So let the plague-destroying Plant remove inherited disease.

5 Homage to men with blinking eyes, homage to those who hear and act! To the Field's Lord be homage paid.
So let the plague-destroying Plant remove inherited disease.

HYMN IX.

FREE this man, Daṣavṛiksha! from the demon, from Grâhî who hath seized his joints and members,
And raise him up again, O Tree, into the world of living men.

2 He hath arisen and come once more, rejoined the band of those who live.
May he become the sire of sons, and of all men most fortunate.

---

5 *Men with blinking eyes:* farm-labourers who have worked till they cannot keep their eyes open. Weber suggests that good-natured Kobold-like domestic sprites may be intended. Perhaps they have worked all night; as Milton (L' Allegro) speaks of 'the drudging goblin' who earns his bowl of cream by threshing more corn in one night than ten day-labourers could finish. *The Field's Lord: kshetrapati;* the Genius Loci, the tutelary deity of the field, sometimes said to be Agni, or Rudra: see Ṛigveda IV. 57. 1, 2. The hymn has been translated by Ludwig, Der Rigveda, III. p. 513.

The hymn is a charm to cure dangerous disease.

1 *Daṣavṛiksha:* explained by the Kauṣika-Sûtra and Dârila (XXVII. 5) as an amulet made of ten kinds of holy wood which is to be employed in the process of recovering the patient. *Grâhî:* a female fiend who seizes men and causes death and disease.

2 *He hath arisen:* the effect of the charm being regarded as certain. 'The aorists are prophetic preterits':—Grill.

3 He hath returned to consciousness, rejoined the living's firm abodes,
For hundred leeches are in this, yea, and a thousand healing herbs.

4 The Gods, the Brahman-priests, and plants observed the way to gather thee:
All deities descried the way men gather thee upon the earth.

5 Let him who made it also heal: he, truly, is the deftest leech.
Pure, with a leech he verily shall give thee medicines that heal.

HYMN X.

FROM family sickness, kinsmen's curse, Destruction, from Druh, from Varuṇa's noose I free and save thee.
With spell and prayer I make thee pure and sinless: to thee be both, the Earth and Heaven, auspicious!

---

3 *Hundred leeches are in this:* the amulet possesses the healing power of a hundred physicians and a thousand medicinal herbs.

4 *Brahman-priests:* priests versed in sacred knowledge who supervise and direct the sacrifice.

5 *Him who made it:* probably the God to whom the origin of the amulet, that is, the wood of which it was made, is attributed. *With a leech:* the amulet contains in itself (st. 3) the powers of a hundred physicians and a thousand healing herbs, so the God when he gives it supplies both leech and medicine. The instrumental *bhishájâ*, with a leech, makes the line difficult and obscure. Weber says that it gives no sense, and reads *bhishájâm* instead: 'As purest of physicians it (the amulet) indeed shall give thee (the patient) medicines.'

The hymn is an Absolution and a Benediction, to be used, according to later authorities, in the Birth-ritual or ceremony after the birth of a child, at the first washing of the infant. But this does not appear to be the original object of the hymn.

1 *Family sickness: kshetriyá;* hereditary disease: see II. 8. 1. *Kinsmen's curse:* rivalry and enmity between relatives by blood seem to have been the rule: *bhrâtṛivya*, father's brother's son, cousin, means almost exclusively enemy in the Veda; and *sajâtá* and *sábandhu* frequently imply rivalry as well as consanguinity. *Destruction:* Nirṛiti, the Goddess of Death, Destruction, and Misfortune in general. *Druh:*

2 Gracious to thee be Agni with the Waters, let Soma with the Plants be kind and bless thee.
From family sickness, kinsmen's curse, Destruction, from Druh, from Varuṇa's noose I thus release thee.

3 May kind Wind strengthen thee in air's mid-region, to thee may heaven's four quarters be auspicious.
From family sickness, kinsmen's curse, Destruction, from Druh, from Varuṇa's curse I thus release thee.

4 These Goddesses, four regions of the heavens, on whom the Sun looks kindly, wives of Vâta—
From family sickness, kinsmen's curse, Destruction, from Druh, from Varuṇa's noose I thus release thee.

5 For long life, in the midst of these I set thee. Away pass Nirṛiti, away Consumption!
From family sickness, kinsmen's curse, Destruction, from Druh, from Varuṇa's noose I thus release thee.

6 Thou hast been freed from Phthisis and from trouble, from shame, and from the snare of Druh and Grâhî.
From family sickness, kinsmen's curse, Destruction, from Druh, from Varuṇa's noose I thus release thee.

7 Joy hast thou found, and left ill-will behind thee: thou hast attained the happy world of virtue.

---

the injurer; a female fiend so named: 'May he catch the snares of Druh.' Ṛigveda VII. 59. 8. *Varuṇa's noose:* with which he entangles sinners to destroy them. *Sinless:* meaning, if a new-born child is the subject, free from sin committed by thy parents: 'Let us not suffer for the sin of others:' Ṛigveda VI. 51, 7; 'Loose us from sins committed by our fathers:' Ṛigveda VII. 86. 5.

2 *Plants:* of which the deified Soma is lord and king.

3 *Wind:* Vâyu, the God of Wind, a deity of the middle region of air.

4 *Vâta:* another name of Vâyu; Latin ventus.

5 *Consumption: yákshma:* very frequently mentioned in the Atharva-veda. The cure of this disease is the subject of Hymn CLXI. of Book X. of the Ṛigveda.

6 *Phthisis: yákshma*, again. *Grâhî:* the grasping female fiend who seizes men and kills them: see II. 9. 1.

7 *Joy hast thou found:* the verbs in this line are prophetic preterits: see II. 9. 2, note.

From family sickness, kinsmen's curse, Destruction, from Druh, from Varuṇa's noose I thus release thee.

8 The Gods have freed from sinfulness, redeeming the Sun, the Law from darkness and from Grâhî.
From family sickness, kinsmen's curse, Destruction, from Druh, from Varuṇa's noose I thus release thee.
With spell and prayer I make thee pure and sinless: to thee be both, the Earth and Heaven, auspicious!

HYMN XI.

DART against dart, destroyer of destruction, thou art the missile sent to meet the missile.
Reach thy superior, thou; surpass thine equal.

2 Sraktya art thou, an Amulet art thou, a counter-charm of spells.
Reach thy superior, thou; surpass thine equal.

3 Use spells against the man we hate, against the man who hateth us.
Reach thy superior, thou; surpass thine equal.

4 A prince art thou, giver of speech, thou art our bodies' strong defence.
Reach thy superior, thou; surpass thine equal.

---

8 *Redeeming the Sun, the Law:* as the Gods have rescued the Sun from eclipse and preserved the Order of the Universe from the fiend's attack, so they have absolved thee from sin. The Sun, and the Law, are introduced merely by way of illustration.

The hymn has been thoroughly discussed by Weber, Indische Studien, XIII. pp. 156—163. It has also been translated by Ludwig, Der Rigveda, III. 513.

The subject of the hymn is an Amulet which is to act as a counter-charm against the spells of an enemy.

2 *Sraktya:* one of the *sânta* or holy trees mentioned in a list given in the Kauśika-Sûtra, VIII. 15, and identified by Dârila with the Tilaka which is a tree bearing beautiful flowers. The Amulet that is to ward off witchcraft is made of the wood of this tree: see Bloomfield, American Journal of Philology, VII. 477.

4 *A prince: sûri;* an institutor of sacrifice; a lord or chief. *Giver of speech:* making thy wearer eloquent.

5 Fulgent art thou, and splendid, thou art heavenly lustre, thou art light.
Reach thy superior, thou; surpass thine equal.

HYMN XII.

The spacious Firmament, and Earth and Heaven, the Field's Queen, and the wonderful Wide-Strider,
Yea, the broad middle air which Vâta guardeth, may these now burn with heat while I am burning.

2 Listen to this, ye Gods who merit worship. Hymns here are sung for me by Bharadvâja.
Bound in the noose may he be doomed to trouble whoever mars this that our mind hath purposed.

3 Hear this my call, O Indra, Soma-drinker, as with a burning heart I oft invoke thee.
I smite, as 'twere a tree felled with a hatchet, the man who marreth this my plan and purpose.

The hymn is an appeal to Heaven and Earth and other Powers for sympathy and for vengeance on a malicious adversary who has reviled and obstructed the religious duties of the injured worshipper.

1 *The Field's Queen:* the female deity who is the special guardian of the cultivated land. *Wide-Strider:* Vishṇu, a God of the upper region who as a personification of the Sun traverses the world in three strides, his rising, culmination, and setting: see Ṛigveda I. 154, 155, 156, and VII. 99, 100. *Vâta:* or Vâyu, the God of Wind. *Burn with heat:* sympathize with me in my fiery indignation. Weber and others see here a reference to an ordeal by fire which the Ṛishi undergoes or offers to undergo, and to which the invoked Powers also, as his compurgators, are called upon to submit.

The three worlds, Heaven, Earth, and Firmament, and their three protecting Powers are invoked; but instead of Vâyu himself the Air or Firmament which he governs is again mentioned.

2 *Bharadvâja:* the great Ṛishi of ancient times, celebrated in the Ṛigveda, is supposed to be present and assisting the injured worshipper. *This that our mind hath purposed:* the sacrifice which we intend to perform.

3 *Hatchet:* here again Weber sees an allusion to the heated axe used in the ordeal by fire: but nothing more than an illustration seems to be intended.

4 Together with thrice-eighty Sâma-singers, Angirases, and Vasus, and Âdityas,
May the felicity of the Fathers guard us. I seize that man with fire that Gods have kindled.

5 O Heaven and Earth, regard me with your favour, and, all ye Gods, stand on my side and help me.
Angirases, Fathers worthy of the Soma! woe fall on him who caused the hateful outrage!

6 Whoever either scorns us, O ye Maruts, or blames devotion which we now are paying,
Let his own wicked deeds be fires to burn him. May Heaven consume the man who hates devotion.

7 Thy sevenfold vital breath, thine eight marrows I rend away with prayer.
With Agni as thine envoy, go, prepared, to Yama's dwelling-place.

---

4 *Thrice-eighty Sâma-singers:* or singers of hymns. The meaning is not clear, and Ludwig reads *somapebhiḥ*, Soma-drinkers, instead of *sâmagebhiḥ* which, he says, gives no sense. Weber thinks that the thrice-eighty singers of Sâmans are men, Âdityas, Vasus, Angirases, and Manes who appear at the ordeal as compurgators or witnesses to prove the innocence of the accused, whose importance necessitates the presence of so large a number. The number eighty, Professor Weber observes, frequently occurs in connexion with the Fire-ritual. *Angirases:* regarded as a higher race of beings between Gods and men, the typical first sacrificers, whose ritual is the pattern which later priests must follow. *Fathers:* Manes or Ancestral Spirits; the deified spirits of the ancestors of the Ṛishis, associated with the Gods and exercising superhuman powers: see Hymns of the Ṛigveda, General Index II. *The felicity, ishṭâpûrtám*, of the Fathers, is the reward which they receive in heaven for their sacrifices and pious works on earth. *That man:* the adversary. *With fire:* with fiery indignation.

6 This stanza is taken, with variations, from Ṛigveda VI. 52. 2. It was perhaps spoken by the priest.

7 This stanza and the next are addressed by the complainant to his adversary.

Sevenfold vital breath: drawn through eyes, ears, nostrils, and mouth.

Eight marrows: one in each division of each arm and leg.

8 In Jâtavedas' kindled flame I set the place assigned to thee.
Let fire consume thy body, and thy voice go to the general breath.

HYMN XIII.

Strength-giver, winning lengthened life, O Agni, with face and back shining with molten butter,
Drink thou the butter and fair milk and honey, and, as a sire his sons, keep this man safely.

2 For us surround him, cover him with splendour, give him long life, and death when age removes him.
The garment hath Bṛihaspati presented to Soma, to the King, to wrap about him.

3 Thou for our weal hast clothed thee in the mantle: thou hast become our heifers' guard from witchcraft.
Live thou a hundred full and plenteous autumns, and wrap thee in prosperity of riches.

4 Come hither, stand upon the stone: thy body shall become a stone.
The Universal Gods shall make thy life a hundred autumns long.

---

8 *The general breath*: to the element to which it belongs; like to like.

The hymn has been translated by Ludwig, Der Rigveda, III. p. 445, and translated and thoroughly discussed by Grill, Hundert Lieder, pp. 47, 85—88, and by Weber, Indische Studien, XIII. pp. 164—171.

The subject of the hymn is a youth's investiture with a new garment at a ceremony (*godânam*) performed when he attains the age of sixteen or eighteen years, and shortly before his marriage.

1 *Winning lengthened life*: for the youth.

2 The Gods are addressed, as the imperatives in the first line are plural. The stanza recurs in XIX. 24. 4.

3 Addressed to the youth who has now become an adult member of the family with duties to perform.

4 *Shall become a stone*: firm and strong to endure: cf. I. 2. 2: 'Make my body stone.'

5 So may the Universal Gods protect thee, whom we divest of raiment worn aforetime.
So after thee, well-formed and growing stronger, be born a multitude of thriving brothers.

HYMN XIV.

FORTH from the hall the bold, the sharp, the greedy one, the single-voiced,
Sadânvâs, and all progeny of Chaṇḍa we exterminate.

2 We drive you forth from cattle-shed, from axle, from within the wain,

---

5 *The Universal Gods:* the Viṣve Devâḥ, Viṣvedevas, or All-Gods. *Thriving brothers:* the youth is apparently an only son.

The ceremony, the details of which are given in the Kauṣika-Sûtra, LIII, LIV, reminds one of the Roman youth's assumption of the toga virilis, an occasion which was celebrated with great rejoicings by his friends. The hymn has been translated by Ludwig, Der Rigveda, III. p. 446.

The hymn is a charm to banish evil creatures from the house and homestead.

1 *Forth from the hall: nissâlâm;* according to Sâyaṇa, the name of a Piṣâchî or female goblin. This word and the two following are extremely difficult, and, as they stand in the text, cannot be satisfactorily explained, *The bold: dhṛishṇúm;* a masculine form used apparently for the feminine. *The sharp: dhishâṇam:* the meaning of the word is not clear, and the feminine form is required. Weber reads *dhishâṇâm* accordingly, deriving it from *dhâ*, to hold. *The greedy one: jighatsúam;* from *ghas*, to eat. *The single-toned: ekavâdyâm;* some troublesome creature that utters one constantly repeated sound. Weber suggests that the wood-worm or borer, a most distractingly annoying plague, is meant. *Sadânvâs:* according to the Nirukta, always making a noise (*sadâ*, always, and *nu*, to cry), ever-screeching; or, as Weber, Grassmann, and Grill prefer, demoniacal, fiendish, from *sa*, with, and *dânu* or *dânava*, a demon. *Chaṇḍa:* the fierce one; the name of a chief goblin; perhaps King of the Rats, as conjectured by Weber who thinks, with much probability, that the evil creatures that are to be banished are rats and mice to whom the epithets used will well apply.

Ye daughters of Magundî, we frighten and chase you from our homes.

3 Yonder let the Arâyîs dwell, there where that house is down below.
Let utter indigence and all the Yâtudhânîs settle there.

4 May Bhûtapati drive away, and Indra, the Sadânvâs hence.
Let Indra with his bolt quell those who sit upon our dwelling's floor.

5 Whether ye be of farm and field, or whether ye be sent by men,
Or be ye sprung from Dasyu race, vanish, Sadânvâs, and begone.

6 I have gone round their homes as runs a fleet-foot racer round the post,
And in all races conquered you. Vanish, Sadânvâs, and begone.

HYMN XV.

As Heaven and Earth are not afraid, and never suffer loss or harm,
Even so, my spirit, fear not thou.

---

2 *Magundî*: a female evil spirit not mentioned elsewhere: perhaps the wife of Chaṇḍa and mother of his progeny.

3 *Arâyîs*: female fiends and night-hags: see I. 28. 4. *Down below*: in the darkness of the nether world: or, possibly, the house of an enemy lower down the hill is intended. *Yâtudhânîs*: or, sorceresses, see I. 8. 1.

4 *Bhûtapati*: lord of creatures, especially of ghosts and evil spirits. The name is applied to Rudra, Agni, Bhava, and Ṣarva.

5 *By men*: by human sorcerers. *Sprung from Dasyu race*: originating from, and sent by, fiends.

The hymn has been translated by Ludwig, Der Rigveda, III. p. 522, and, with annotations, by Grill, Hundert Lieder, pp. 1, 89—92.

The hymn is a charm against Fear.

2 As Day and Night are not afraid, nor ever suffer loss or harm,
Even so, my spirit, fear not thou.

3 As Sun and Moon are not afraid, nor ever suffer loss or harm,
Even so, my spirit, fear not thou.

4 As Brâhmanhood and Princely Power fear not, nor suffer loss or harm,
Even so, my spirit, fear not thou.

5 As Truth and Falsehood have no fear, nor ever suffer loss or harm,
Even so, my spirit, fear not thou.

6 As What Hath Been and What Shall Be fear not, nor suffer loss or harm,
Even so, my spirit, fear not thou.

HYMN XVI.

GUARD me from death, Inhaling and Exhaling! All bliss to you!

2 Guard me from overhearing, Earth and Heaven! All hail to you!

3 Do thou, O Sûrya, with thine eye protect me! All hail to thee!

---

4 *Brâhmanhood and Princely Power: bráhma* and *kshatrám;* priests and nobles.

5 *Truth and Falsehood:* Weber reads *ṛitám*, Order, instead of *ánṛitam*, falsehood: 'Falsehood cannot be suitably adduced as an example in such a formula. That would indeed be a sort of sacrilege.' I take the text as I find it, and do not see that it needs alteration.

This non-metrical formula is a prayer for general protection.

1 *Inhaling and Exhaling:* two of the vital airs, Inspiration and Expiration, personified. *All bliss:* or, All hail; *svâhâ;* an auspicious word or benediction used at the end of invocations, like Amen.

3 *Sûrya:* God of the Sun.

4 Agni Vaisvânara, with all Gods preserve me! All hail to thee!

5 Preserve me with all care, O All-Sustainer! All hail to thee!

HYMN XVII.

Power art thou, give me power. All hail!

2 Might art thou, give me might. All hail!

3 Strength art thou, give me strength. All hail!

4 Life art thou, give me life. All hail!

5 Ear art thou, give me hearing! Hail!

6 Eye art thou, give me eyes. All hail!

7 Shield art thou, shield me well. All hail!

HYMN XVIII.

Destruction of the foe art thou, give me the scaring of my foes. All hail!

2 The rival's ruiner art thou, give me to drive my rivals off. All hail!

3 Arâyîs' ruiner art thou, give me to drive Arâyîs off. All hail!

4 Pisâchas' ruiner art thou, give me to drive Pisâchas off. All hail!

5 Sadânvâs' ruiner art thou, give me to drive Sadânvâs off. All hail!

---

4 *Vaisvânara:* belonging to all (Âryan) men; universal; a frequently occurring epithet or appellation of Agni. *With all Gods:* or, with the All-Gods, the Visvedevas or Visve Devas.

5 *All-Sustainer: visvambhara;* Vishnu.

A non-metrical formula addressed to an Amulet.

A non-metrical charm against enemies, goblins, and other evil creatures.

3 *Arâyîs:* female fiends or witches: see I. 28. 4.

4 *Pisâchas:* goblins: see I. 16. 3.

5 *Sadânvâs:* imps, or noisy pests: see II. 14. 1.

HYMN XIX.

BURN thou, O Agni, with that heat of thine against the man who hates us, whom we hate.

2 Flame thou, O Agni, with that flame of thine against the man who hates us, whom we hate.

3 Shine out, O Agni, with that sheen of thine against the man who hates us, whom we hate.

4 Blaze thou, O Agni, with that blaze of thine against the man who hates us, whom we hate.

5 O Agni, with the splendour that is thine darken the man who hates us, whom we hate.

HYMN XXIV.

O ṢERABHAKA, Ṣerabha, back fall your arts of witchery! Back, Kimîdins! let your weapon fall.
Eat your possessor; eat ye him who sent you forth; eat your own flesh.

2 Ṣevṛidhaka, O Ṣevṛidha, back fall your arts of witchery! Back, Kimîdins! let your weapon fall, etc.

A non-metrical charm invoking Agni's aid against an enemy.

Hymns XX—XXIII are exactly similar except that other deities, Vâyu, Sûrya, Chandra or the Moon, and the Waters, are addressed instead of Agni.

A charm against the magic arts of fiends.

1 In this and the three following stanzas four Kimîdins, imps, goblins, or sorcerers (see I. 7. 1.) and in 5—8 four Kimîdinis, or female fiends of the same class, are addressed. *Ṣerabhaka:* the derivation is unknown. According to the St. P. Dictionary, a kind of snake is meant. *Your possessor:* him whose servants ye are; the superior fiend who commands you.

2 *Ṣevṛidhaka: ṣévṛidha*, perhaps a shortened form of *ṣevavṛidha*, means in the five passages of the Ṛigveda in which it occurs, auspicious, bliss-increasing. It may perhaps be used euphemistically here, as Robin Good-fellow is the old name of a 'shrewd and knavish sprite.'

3 O Mroka, Anumroka, back return your arts of witchery! Back, Kimîdins! let your weapon fall, etc.

4 O Sarpa, Anusarpa, back return your arts of witchery! Back, Kimîdins! let your weapon fall, etc.

5 Back fall your witcheries, Jûrṇî! back your weapon, ye Kimîdinîs, etc.

6 Back fall your spells, Upabdi! back your weapon, ye Kimîdinîs, etc.

7 Back fall your witchcrafts, Arjunî! your weapon, ye Kimîdinîs, etc.

8 Back, O Bharûjî! fall your charms, your weapon, ye Kimîdinîs,
Eat your possessor; eat ye him who sent you forth; eat your own flesh.

---

3 *Mroka:* mentioned in V. 31. 9 as a destructive Agni or fire; here, perhaps, representing the burning heat of fever. *Anumroka:* Mroka with the prefix *anu*, with; a slight modification of the name.

4 *Sarpa*, *Anusarpa:* serpent, and serpentine.

5 *Jûrnî:* according to the St. P. Dictionary, a snake that has cast its skin; according to Weber, connected with *jûrṇi*, glowing heat, and meaning fever.

6 *Upabdi:* noise, rattle, clatter. Possibly referring to the chattering of the teeth in cold ague fits.

7 *Arjunî:* white; according to the St. P. Dictionary, a (silvery) snake. Weber thinks that the reference is to the whiteness of the skin in leprosy.

8 *Bharûjî:* according to the St. P. Dictionary, some noxious animal is meant. Weber refers the word to the roots *bhṛij*, *bhrajj*, to fry or roast, and thinks that the burning heat of fever is intended. Professor Weber has carefully discussed all the above-mentioned names in Indische Studien, XIII. pp. 182—186. It is as difficult to ascertain the exact meaning of the words as of the demons' names borrowed by Shakespear from Harsnet, viz. Smulkin, Modo, Mahu, Flibbertigibbet, and Pur.

HYMN XXV.

THE Goddess Pṛiśniparṇî hath blest us, and troubled Nirṛiti.

Fierce crusher of the Kaṇvas she: her have I gained, the mighty one.

2 Victorious in the olden time this Pṛiśniparṇî was brought forth:

With her I cleave, as 'twere a bird's, the head of the Detestables.

4 The hateful fiend who drinks the blood, and him who take away the growth,

The Kaṇva who devours the germ, quell, Pṛiśniparṇî! and destroy.

5 Drive and imprison in a hill these Kaṇvas harassers of life:

Follow them Pṛiśniparṇî, thou Goddess, like fire consuming them.

6 Drive thou away these Kaṇvas, drive the harassers of life afar.

Whither the shades of darkness go, I send the fiends who feed on flesh.

A charm against the fiends who cause abortion.

1 *Pṛiśniparṇî:* (having variegated leaves) Hemionitis Cordifolia, a medicinal plant, a decoction of which is recommended by Suśruta to be taken as a preventive of abortion. The word is given doubtingly by Wise as *Pristapurni*. *Nirṛiti:* the Goddess of Death and Misfortune who rejoices at the destruction of an unborn babe. *Kaṇvas:* a class of evil spirits, mentioned in this place only. In the Ṛigveda the Kaṇvas, descendants of the great Ṛishi Kaṇva, are an illustrious priestly family.

6 *Whither the shades of darkness go:* probably, as Weber suggests, the gloomy depths of the forest. *Feed on flesh:* devour the unborn babe.

The hymn is one of Grill's Hundert Lieder, pp. 20, 92.

HYMN XXVI.

Let them come home, the cattle that have wandered, whom Vâyu hath delighted to attend on,
Whose forms and figures are well known to Tvashṭar. These cows let Savitar drive within this stable.

2 Let the beasts stream together to this cow-pen. Bṛihaspati who knoweth lead them hither!
Let Sinîvâlî guide the foremost homeward. When they have come, Anumati! enclose them.

3 Together stream the cattle! stream together horses and the men!
Hitherward press all growth of grain! I offer sacrifice with mixt oblation.

4 I pour together milk of kine, with butter blending strength and juice.
Well sprinkled be our men, as true to me as cows are to their herd!

5 Hither I bring the milk of cows, hither have brought the juice of corn.
Hitherward have our men been brought, hitherward to this house our wives.

The hymn is a benediction on the cattle as they come home from grazing.

1 *Vâyu:* the God of the wind which refreshes the cattle in their breezy pastures and drives off the flies. *Tvashṭar:* the Artificer of the Gods, regarded as the giver of increase in cattle, his special function in the natural world being the formation of the embryo: 'Tvashṭar the Lord hath made all forms and all the cattle of the field.'—Ṛigveda I. 188. 9. *Savitar:* here the setting Sun.

2 *Bṛihaspati:* as Lord of Prayer including charms. *Sinîvâlî:* a personification of the Night of New Moon: see Weber, Indische Studien, V. pp. 230—232. *Anumati:* here the Night of Full Moon personified.

3 This stanza and the two following form in reality a separate hymn the subject of which is the *saṁsrâvyàm havis* or Mixt Oblation: see I. 15. 1. The fourth pâda of the stanza is hendecasyllabic or Trishṭup instead of the octosyllabic Anushṭup of the rest of the three stanzas.

5 *The juice of corn:* a brew of grain, perhaps, as Weber suggests, a sort of beer. The mixture of ingredients is probably symbolical of the re-union at evening of all the members of the household and the return of the cattle.

The hymn has been translated by Ludwig, Der Rigveda, p. 371, and by Grill, pp. 64, 92.

HYMN XXVII.

Let not the enemy win the cause! Strong and predominant art thou.
Refute mine adversary's speech. Render them dull and flat, O Plant.

2 The strong-winged bird discovered thee, the boar unearthed thee with his snout.
Refute mine adversary's speech. Render them dull and flat, O Plant.

3 Yea, Indra laid thee on his arm, to cast the Asuras to the ground.
Refute mine adversary's speech. Render them dull and flat, O Plant.

4 Indra devoured the Pâṭâ plant that he might lay the Asuras low.
Refute mine adversary's speech. Render them dull and flat, O Plant.

The hymn is a charm against an opponent in debate.

1 *The cause: prâṣim*, debate, from the root *prachh*, to question; not food, from *prâs*, to eat, as Weber and Ludwig have taken it, regarding the hymn as an incantation against robbers, pronounced in order to protect granaries and store-rooms. 'It is rather a charm uttered by an intending disputant before entering upon a debate in the *sabhâ* or *parishad*, the assembly of the village, and addressed to the *pâṭâ*-plant:' see Bloomfield, American Journal of Philology, VII. pp. 479—482, who has discussed the hymn and convincingly established this interpretation by arguments based chiefly on the Kauṣika-Sûtra, XXXVIII. 17 sqq. *Mine adversary's speech:* the speech of each adversary, of all my opponents.

2 *The strong-winged bird:* eagle or falcon. The magic Plant was difficult to discover, requiring the keen sight of a falcon and the sagacity and strength of a wild boar to find and uproot it. Similarly, the magical moly and mandragora or mandrake were 'hard to dig.' See A. Lang's *Custom and Myth*, (New Edition) pp. 143 sqq.

3 *The Asuras:* the demons who fought against the Gods, like the Titans of Grecian mythology.

4 *The Pâṭâ-plant:* probably identical with Pâṭhâ (Clypea Hernandifolia). Like the Scottish rowan, or like St. John's wort, it was potent against fiends.

5 With this I overcome my foes as Indra overcame the wolves.
Refute mine adversary's speech! Render them dull and flat, O Plant.

6 O Rudra, Lord of Healing Balms, dark-crested, skilful in thy work!—
Refute mine adversary's speech. Render them dull and flat, O Plant.

7 Indra, defeat the speech of him who meets us with hostility.
Comfort us with thy power and might. Make me superior in debate.

HYMN XXVIII.

This Child, Old Age! shall grow to meet thee only: none of the hundred other deaths shall harm him.
From trouble caused by friends let Mitra guard him, as a kind mother guards the son she nurses.

2 Mitra or Varuṇa the foe-destroyer, accordant, grant him death in course of nature!
Thus Agni, Hotar-priest, skilled in high statutes, declareth all the deities' generations.

---

5 *With this:* according to Dârila, the speaker chews the root of the plant, and wears a garland made of seven of its leaves. *The wolves: sâlâvṛikân;* according to Sâyaṇa, wild dogs. The word seems to mean any canine animal of prey. Here perhaps fiends who had assumed the shapes of wolves or hyenas are meant.

6 *Lord of Healing Balms:* see I. 19. 3. The verb, Refute, in the second line may perhaps refer to Rudra.

The hymn has been translated by Ludwig, Der Rigveda, III. p. 461, and by Grill, Hundert Lieder, pp. 23, 93.

The hymn is a prayer for long and happy life for a boy.

1 *Hundred other deaths:* cf I. 30. 3. Friends: cf. stanza 3.

2 *Thus Agni:* the benediction seems to have been pronounced at some birth ceremony accompanied with a sacrifice, at which Agni as chief priest is represented as summoning all the Gods to be present.

3 Thou art the Lord of all terrestrial cattle, of cattle born and to be born hereafter.
Let not breath drawn or breath emitted fail him. Let not his friends, let not his foemen slay him.

4 Let Heaven thy father and let Earth thy mother, accordant, give thee death in course of nature,
That thou mayst live on Aditi's bosom, guarded, a hundred winters, through thy respirations.

5 Lead him to life, O Agni, and to splendour, this dear child, Varuṇa! and thou King Mitra!
Give him protection, Aditi! as a mother; All Gods, that his be life of long duration!

HYMN XXIX.

Gods, give him all that earth hath best with bodily strength and happy fate.
Agni and Sûrya grant him life, Bṛihaspati give him eminence!

2 Bestow thou life on him, O Jâtavedas. Store him with future progeny, O Tvashṭar.
Send him, O Savitar, full growth of riches. Let this thy servant live a hundred autumns.

3 May this our prayer bring strength and goodly offspring. Give, both of you one-minded, strength and riches.

---

3 *Thou:* apparently Agni of the preceding stanza. According to Weber, Tvashṭar, Pûshan, or Rudra is intended.

4 *A hundred winters:* regarded as the natural duration of human life: see I. 35. 1.

The hymn has been translated, with annotations, by Grill, Hundert Lieder, pp. 48, 95.

The hymn is a benediction pronounced over a sick man.

2 *Tvashṭar:* whose function is to provide for the increase of the human race.

3 *May this our prayer bring:* there is no verb in the text, and bring, or give, must be supplied. *Both of you:* it is not clear which two of the above-mentioned Gods are intended. *Let him......win:* the verb is not in the text, unless *jáyam* be altered to *jáyat*, which Weber thinks is absolutely necessary.

Let him with might win fields and victory, Indra! setting beneath his feet the rest, his rivals.

4 As Indra's gift, by Varuṇa instructed the fierce one came to us sent by the Maruts.

Let him, O Heaven and Earth, rest in your bosom. Let him not hunger, let him not be thirsty.

5 Ye twain endowed with vigour, grant him vigour. Ye who are rich in milk, give milk to feed him.

These twain have given him vigour, Earth and Heaven, and all the Gods, the Maruts, and the Waters.

6 With health-bestowing drops thine heart I comfort: all-bright again, and undiseased, enjoy them.

Drest in like robes let these two drink the mixture, wearing the Aṣvins' form as an illusion.

7 Erst Indra, wounded, made this strengthening potion, eternal food: thine is it, here presented.

With this live full of vigour through the autumns. Let not thy strength be drained. Leeches have helped thee.

---

4 *The fierce one:* apparently the strong warrior who is now lying sick.

6 *Drops:* there is no substantive in the text, and waters or streams must be supplied. *Let these two drink the mixture:* this appears to refer to a form of procedure like that described in the Kauṣika-Sûtra, XXVII. 8—11. The patient leans upon some healthy man. The mixture (*manthá*, a sort of gruel made of milk and barley-meal) is poured upon the sick man's head, and then offered to the healthy man to whom the thirst of fever is thus transferred, and the patient is relieved. *Aṣvins:* the twin Gods of the dawn. They are also physicians (see Ṛigveda VIII. 18. 8; 22. 10; 75. 1; X. 39. 3), and for this reason probably their characters are assumed by the sick man and his friend.

7 *Wounded:* in some battle with the demons. *The autumns:* the most unhealthy season of the Indian year. *Leeches:* physicians: perhaps with reference to the assumption of the characters of the Aṣvins.

The hymn has been translated by Ludwig, Der Rigveda, p. 493.

HYMN XXX.

As the wind shakes this Tuft of Grass hither and thither on the ground,
So do I stir and shake thy mind, that thou mayst be in love with me, my darling, never to depart.

2 Ye, Asvins, lead together, ye unite and bring the loving pair.
Now have the fortunes of you twain, now have your vows and spirits met.

3 When eagles, calling out aloud, are screaming in the joy of health,
Then to my calling let her come, as to the arrow's neck the shaft.

A charm to win a girl's love.

1 *Tuft of Grass:* here mentioned only by way of illustration. According to the Kausika-Sûtra, XXXV. 21, the procedure to accompany the recitation of the charm is as follows: Between two slips or cuttings taken respectively from a tree (representing the lover) and the creeper that clings round it (signifying the girl), place an arrow (symbolical of Kâma, the Indian Cupid), some Sthakara (probably a fragrant gum or powder), Kushtha (Costus Speciosus, or Arabicus), eyesalve, Madugha (probably licorice), and grass battered by a storm (symbolical of the girl's agitated mind), mix all together with sacrificial butter, and apply: the mode of application is not mentioned; probably the two slips were anointed with it. The second line of the stanza is found also in I. 34. 5, and VI. 8. 1—3.

2 *Ye, Asvins:* in Rigveda X. 85, which describes the wedding of Sûryâ, the daughter of the Sun, regarded as the typical bride, the two Asvins, Gods of the dawn, appear as the groomsmen, the friends of the bridegroom, who had asked and obtained her hand for Soma the Moon-God.

The stanza appears to be spoken by some friend of the lover; the first line being addressed to the Asvins, and the second to the lover and the girl. If *you twain* refers to the Asvins, the meaning can be only: You have done your duty and gained your wishes by making two lovers happy: but this seems forced and unnatural.

3 *As to the arrow's neck the shaft:* straight to her destined husband as the shaft of the arrow is forced into the neck or lower part of the head of the weapon, and fixed firmly there.

4 Let what is inward turn outside, let what is outward be within:
Seize and possess, O Plant, the mind of maidens rich in every charm.

5 Seeking a husband she hath come! and I came longing for a wife:
Even as a loudly-neighing steed my fate and fortune have I met.

HYMN XXXI.

WITH Indra's mighty millstone, that which crushes worms of every sort,
I bray and bruise the worms to bits like vetches on the grinding stone.

2 The Seen and the Invisible, and the Kurûru have I crushed:
Alâṇḍus, and all Chhalunas, we bruise to pieces with our spell.

---

4 *Let what is inward turn outside:* let her mind be thoroughly upset by the tumultuous agitation of love; or with Dr. Grill: let the love that she hides show itself, and let the love that I show find its way into her heart. *O Plant:* the Grass mentioned in stanza 1. *Rich in every charm: viṣvárûpâṇâm;* or, of all shapes and forms.

The hymn has been translated by Ludwig, Der Rigveda, III. p. 517; and by Grill, with annotations, Hundert Lieder, pp. 52, 97.

The hymn is a charm against all sorts of Worms.

1 *Indra's mighty millstone:* a figurative expression meaning (1) the crushing power of Indra (cf. 'Though the stones of God grind slowly, yet they grind exceeding small'), and (2) the priestly spell to which this power has been imparted by the God. In the Ṛigveda (I. 8. 3, and 40. 8) sacrifice employed against enemies is spoken of as a thunderbolt, the special weapon of Indra in his battles with demons, so, similarly, the incantation here is called Indra's millstone which crushes noxious creatures of other kinds.

2 *The Seen and the Invisible:* here the names of two species of worms. The Kurûru, Alâṇḍu, and Chhaluna are also worms of unidentifiable kinds.

3 I kill Alâṇḍus with a mighty weapon: burnt or not burnt they now have lost their vigour.
Left or not left, I with the spell subdue them: let not a single worm remain uninjured.

4 The worm that lives within the ribs, within the bowels, in the head,
Avaskava and Borer, these we bruise to pieces with the spell.

5 Worms that are found on mountains, in the forests, that live in plants, in cattle, in the waters,
Those that have made their way within our bodies,—these I destroy, the worms' whole generation.

HYMN XXXII.

UPRISING let the Sun destroy, and when he sinketh, with his beams
The Worms that live within the cow.

---

3 *With a mighty weapon:* with incantation, which is elsewhere called a *vajra* or thunderbolt: see VI. 134. 1 sqq. and 135. 1. *Burnt or not burnt:* fire appears to be used in the procedure prescribed in the Kauṣika-Sûtra XXVII. 14—18.

4 *Avaskava and Borer*: two other unidentified species of worms which attack the body of man. Of worms, external and internal, there are said to be twenty varieties, each of which has a particular name: see Wise, Hindu System of Medicine, pp, 348—350.

5 The worms that infest the human body having been disposed of, the charm is directed against those which attack trees, plants, and cattle. So, even at the present day, in the rural parishes near Quebec the priests utter incantations over the potato-bugs and grasshoppers. (Harper's New Monthly Magazine, June 1893, p. 106).

The hymn has been translated by Ludwig, Der Rigveda, III. p. 323, and, with annotations, by Grill, Hundert Lieder, pp. 6, 98.

The hymn is a charm against the Worms or Bots which infest cows.

1 According to the Kauṣika-Sûtra, XXVII. 21—24, the ceremony which accompanies the incantation is to be performed at sunrise, noon, and sunset. The sun is considered as especially instrumental in destroying noxious reptiles etc., and in counteracting the operation of poison: see Ṛigveda I. 191. 8, 9. The first *hántu* in line 1, which mars the Anushṭup metre, is merely a gloss and should be eliminated from the text.

2 The four-eyed worm, of every shape, the variegated, and the white—
I break and crush the creature's ribs, and tear away its head besides.

3 Like Atri I destroy you, Worms! in Kaṇva's, Jamadagni's way:
I bray and bruise the creeping things to pieces with Agastya's spell.

4 Slain is the sovran of these Worms, yea, their controlling lord is slain:
Slain is the Worm, his mother slain, brother and sister both are slain.

5 Slain are his ministers, and slain his followers and retinue:
Yea, those that seemed the tiniest things, the Worms have all been put to death.

6 I break in pieces both thy horns wherewith thou pushest here and there:
I cleave and rend the bag which holds the venom which is stored in thee.

---

2 *Four-eyed:* that is, as Dr. Grill explains, marked with a spot above each eye: cf. IV. 20. 7.

3 Atri, Kaṇva, Jamadagni, and Agastya are very celebrated Ṛishis or Seers of the Ṛigveda and regarded as masters of magic arts. Hymn CXCI. of Book I. of the Ṛigveda, the silent repetition of which is said to counteract all venom in reptiles, insects, scorpions, roots, and artificial poisons, is ascribed to Agastya.

4 *Controlling lord: sthapátis;* lord of the district, governor, or chief official.

5 *Ministers: veṣásas;* vassals, according to Hillebrandt.

6 This stanza appears to be addressed to some conspicuously aggressive worm or maggot.

The hymn has been translated by Ludwig, Der Rigveda, III. p. 500, and, with annotations, by Grill, Hundert Lieder, pp. 7, 100.

HYMN XXXIII.

FROM both thy nostrils, from both eyes, from both thine ears, and from thy chin,
Forth from thy brain and tongue I root Consumption seated in thy head.

2 Forth from the neck and from the nape, from dorsal vertebræ and spine,
From arms and shoulder-blades I root Consumption seated in thine arms.

3 Forth from thy heart and from thy lungs, from thy gall-bladder and thy sides,
From kidneys, spleen, and liver thy Consumption we eradicate.

4 From bowels and intestines, from the rectum and the belly, I
Extirpate thy Consumption, from flanks, navel, and mesentery.

5 Forth from thy thighs and from thy knees, heels and the foreparts of thy feet,
Forth from thy loins and hips I draw Consumption settled in thy loins.

6 Forth from thy marrows and thy bones, forth from thy tendons and thy veins
I banish thy Consumption, from thy hands, thy fingers, and thy nails.

7 In every member, every hair, in every joint wherein it lies,
We with the exorcising spell of Kasyapa drive far away Consumption settled in thy skin.

The hymn, which is a charm against Yakshma, Phthisis Pulmonalis or Consumption, is enlarged, with variations, from Ṛigveda X. 163. For an account of the disease and its treatment in India in former times see Wise, Hindu System of Medicine, pp. 321—324.

7 *Kaṣyapa*: a Ṛishi, seer of some hymns of the Ṛigveda, and father of Vivṛihâ to whom the original hymn (Ṛigveda X. 163) is ascribed.

HYMN XXXIV.

MAY this, of all the beasts that Paṣupati rules, Lord of animals, quadruped and biped,
Come, purchased, to the sacrificial portion. May growth of wealth attend the sacrificer.

2 Loosing the seed of future-time existence, give good success, O Gods, to him who worships.
May what is present, duly brought, the victim, go to the deities' belovèd region.

The hymn is a prayer accompanying an animal sacrifice.

1 *This:* the animal selected for sacrifice. *Paṣupati:* Lord of Beasts; usually regarded as a name of the later Rudra. *Quadruped and biped:* a frequently occurring Vedic expression for the people of a household and the domestic and sacrificial animals around them: 'To us and to our cattle may Soma give salutary food, To biped and to quadruped.' ṚV. III. 62. 14. According to the sacrificial ritual there are five *paṣavaḥ* or sacrificial animals, man, horse, ox, sheep, and goat. Man is only a *paṣu,* though the highest, primus inter pares. 'To thee (Bhava) are these five animals *(paṣávaḥ)* allotted, oxen, and sheep, and goats, and men, and horses.' AV. XI. 2. 9. See Zimmer, Altindisches Leben, pp. 72, 73.

The text of the first line of the stanza has apparently no sequence; but the interpretation which, following Weber, I have given, is the only one that will suit. According to Ludwig (Der Rigveda, III. p. 433) the translation would be: 'May Paṣupati, who is Lord and Master of homestead animals, quadruped and biped, Purchased, obtain his sacrificial portion:' which is grammatical but unintelligible.

Purchased: the animal selected for sacrifice was separated from the flock or herd and driven away to feed where it chose. When it was to be sacrificed it was redeemed from the man who had taken possession of it.

2 *Loosing:* liberating; see stanzas 3 and 4. *The seed of future-time existence:* the victim whose sacrifice is to secure future life for the sacrificer. *Duly brought: upā́kṛitam;* the technical term used on such occasions, meaning prepared for the sacred rite and brought to the place of sacrifice. *The victim: ṣaṣamānám;* a euphemistic word for the animal that is to be slaughtered. The victim thus offered to the Gods goes at once to Svarga or heaven, *the deities' belovèd region.* So, at the Horse-sacrifice, the priest addresses the slaughtered animal: 'No; here thou diest not, thou art not injured: by easy paths unto the Gods thou goest.' Ṛigveda I. 162. 21.

3 Those who are looking, deep in meditation, on the bound animal with eye and spirit—
To them, the first, may Agni, God, give freedom, rejoicing in his creatures, Viṣvakarman.

4 Tame animals of every shape, though varied in colour, manifold, alike in nature—
To them, the first, may Vâyu, God, give freedom, Prajâpati rejoicing in his creatures.

5 Let those who know receive before all others the vital breath proceeding from the body.
Go to the sky. Stay there with all thy members. By paths which Gods have travelled go to Svarga.

HYMN XXXV.

We who enjoying it have grown no richer, for whom the sacred altar-fires have sorrowed,
We who compounded with deficient worship,—may Viṣvakarman make our service prosper.

---

3 *Those who are looking:* other animals, relatives and friends of the victim. Agni, or the Sacrificial Fire, is asked to divert and free them from their sad thoughts. *Viṣvakarman:* the Omnific; the Creator of All; here probably an appellative of Agni.

4 *Alike in nature:* all being domestic and sacrificial animals. *Prajâpati:* Lord of Creatures; here probably an appellative of Vâyu.

5 *Those who know:* the Gods in heaven. *Go to the sky:* to Svarga or heaven: see note on stanza 2. According to the Kauṣika-Sûtra XLIV. 15, the victim is slaughtered—its vital breath is stopped—as this stanza is recited.

A hymn of expiation for an imperfectly performed sacrifice.

1 *We:* priests and others complain that through the fault of the institutor of a Soma sacrifice of which they have been partakers they have failed to obtain the benefits which they expected. *Altar-fires: agnáyo dhíshṇyâḥ;* fires lighted on small side altars, usually eight in number. *Sorrowed:* as having been kindled in vain. *Compounded with:* took part in the ill-managed ceremony and so shared the institutor's guilt. *Viṣvakarman:* the Omnific; the Creator of the Universe; the God to whom the expiatory sacrifice is offered. *Our service:* the sacrifice which we are now performing.

2 Ṛishis have called the sacrifice's patron amerced through sin, sorrowing for his offspring.
Those drops of meath whereof he missed enjoyment,—may Viṣvakarman with those drops unite us.

3 Regarding niggard churls as Soma-drinkers, skilful in sacrifice, weak at the meeting,
Whatever sin the captive hath committed, do thou for weal release him, Viṣvakarman!

4 Awful are Ṛishis: unto them be homage, and to their eye and truthfulness of spirit!
Loud homage to Bṛihaspati, O mighty! Homage to thee, O Viṣvakarman! Guard us.

5 The eye of sacrifice, source, and beginning—with voice, ear, spirit unto him I offer.
To this our sacrifice wrought by Viṣvakarman may the Gods come gracious and kindly-hearted.

---

2 *The sacrifice's patron:* The householder who instituted the previous sacrifice, and whose mismanagement has drawn upon him the censure of the Ṛishis or sages. *Sorrowing for his offspring:* who would suffer for the fault of the head of the family. *Meath:* Soma juice; *madhavyân* instead of the meaningless *mathavyân* of the text. *Unite us:* may we be benefited by the Soma libations of the present sacrifice in place of those that were wasted in the former mismanaged ceremony.

3 *Regarding niggard churls as Soma-drinkers:* the institutor of the former sacrifice appears to have admitted illiberal and ungodly persons to the ceremony and allowed them to drink the Soma juice which they were unworthy to touch. Although well versed in the rules of such holy rites, he showed himself weak and infirm in the sacrificial assembly. *The captive:* the guilty institutor of the sacrifice who is brought in bonds (*baddhás*), like a church delinquent in penitential sheet, to obtain absolution by the expiatory ceremony.

4 *Ṛishis:* referring particularly to those who have censured the culprit: see stanza 2.

Bṛihaspati: as Lord of Prayer.

5. *Unto him:* to Viṣvakarman who is the eye of sacrifice, etc.

HYMN XXXVI.

To please us may the suitor come, O Agni, seeking this maid and bringing us good fortune.
Approved by wooers, lovely in assemblies, may she be soon made happy with a husband.

2 As bliss beloved by Soma, dear to Prayer, and stored by Aryaman,
With the God Dhâtar's truthfulness I work the bridal oracle.

3 O Agni, may this woman find a husband. Then verily King Soma makes her happy.
May she bear sons, chief lady of the household, blessèd and bearing rule beside her consort.

The hymn is a charm to secure a husband for a marriageable girl.

1 *The suitor:* the interceder or match-maker whose business is to find a suitable wife for his friend or employer. *O Agni:* addressed as especially connected with marriage, regulating, as the Sun, the proper season for its celebration, and, as the sacrificial fire, the consecrator of the rite: see Ṛigveda I. 66. 4; V. 3, 2; X. 85. 40.

2 *Beloved by Soma:* as Súryâ, the typical bride, was married to Soma, the young maid is regarded as originally belonging to him: see Ṛigveda X. 85. 40. *Dear to Prayer:* or, graced by Brahman, as Weber and Grill interpret. *Stored by Aryaman:* 'Aryaman art thou (Agni) as regardeth maidens' (Ṛigveda V. 3. 2); that is, in connexion with marriage; *aryamán* meaning also a companion, especially a friend who asks a girl in marriage for another. The *bliss* or allotted fate is said by Sâyaṇa to be the young maiden. The stanza is somewhat obscure, and perhaps out of place. Dr. Grill puts it next after stanza 4. *Dhâtar's truthfulness:* Dhâtar is the Establisher or Ordainer, regarded as a separate God, and mentioned here as the Upholder of the sacrament of marriage. *Bridal oracle: pativédanam;* the charm that finds or procures a husband: 'Brautorakel:' Weber.

3 *Chief lady of the household: mahishî*; the technical term for the first married wife; the principal consort of a king. Cf. Ṛigveda X. 85. 26, 27.

4 As this lair, Maghavan! that is fair to look on was dear to wild things as a pleasant dwelling,
So may this woman here be Bhaga's darling, loved by her lord and prizing his affection.

5 Mount up, embark on Bhaga's ship, the full, the inexhaustible,
Thereon bring hitherward to us the lover whom thou fain wouldst wed.

6 Call out to him, O Lord of Wealth! Make thou the lover well-inclined.
Set each on thy right hand who is a lover worthy of her choice.

7 Here is the Bdellium and the gold, the Auksha and the bliss are here:
These bring thee to the husbands, so to find the man whom thou woudst have.

---

4 *This lair:* the hole of some wild animal or perhaps a bird's nest is indicated by way of illustration. *Maghavan:* the Bounteous One, Indra. *Bhaga:* the Dispenser, who brings wealth and happiness, and blesses conjugal love. This God is frequently associated with Indra in prayers for welfare.

5 Addressed to the maiden. *Bhaga's ship:* or the ship of Fortune: with reference probably to some practice by means of which girls endeavoured to discover who should marry them. See Weber, Indische Studien, V. p. 221, for similar customs among the German peasant maidens.

6 *Lord of Wealth:* Indra, the Bounteous One, is probably intended. *On thy right hand:* in the place of honour.

7 *Bdellium:* a costly fragrant gum that exudes from a plant said to be the vine palm (Borassus Flabelliformis). The Sanskrit name of the gum is *gúggulu.* It may have formed part of the girl's dowry, or she may have been anointed and perfumed with it. *The gold:* as dowry or personal ornaments. *The Auksha:* probably a sweet-scented unguent, as Sâyaṇa explains it: see Grill's note. *The bliss:* the charms of the maiden. *To the husbands:* to those who wish to marry thee.

8 May Savitar lead and bring to thee the husband whom thy heart desires.
O Plant, be this thy gift to her!

---

8 *Savitar:* the Sun; regarded as the universal vivifier who will bless the bride: 'Happy is the bride whom the Sun shines on.' The second *nayatu* of the second line is evidently an interpolation; and the last superfluous pâda also seems to be a later addition, as no *Plant* has been mentioned in the preceding stanzas.

The hymn has been translated by Ludwig, Der Rigveda, III. p. 476, and is one of Grill's Hundert Lieder, pp. 55, 102.

BOOK III.

HYMN I.

Let the wise Agni go against our foemen, burning against ill-will and imprecation.
Let him bewilder our opponents' army. Let Jâtavedas smite and make them handless.

2 Mighty are ye for such a deed, O Maruts. Go forward, overcome them and destroy them.
The Vasus slew, and these were left imploring. Wise Agni as our messenger assail them!

3 O Maghavan, O Indra, thou who slayest fiends, and, Agni, thou,
Burn, both of you, against these men, the foeman's host that threatens us.

4 Shot down the slope, with thy two tawny coursers, forth go thy bolt, destroying foes, O Indra!
Slay those who fly, slay those who stand and follow. On every side fulfil these men's intention.

5 Indra, bewilder thou the foemen's army.
With Agni's, Vâta's furious rush drive them away to every side.

The hymn is a prayer or charm to secure the defeat and destruction of enemies in battle.

2 *Maruts:* 'the terrible Storm-gods, literally the Smashers, in whose name the germs of the Italic god of war, Mars, have been discovered.—M. Müller. *The Vasus:* the kind Gods, the Maruts. *These:* the men in whose behalf the hymn is recited, and for whose success prayer and sacrifice were offered to the Gods.

4 *These men's intention:* the hopes and wishes of our own men.

5 The first pâ la is hendecasyllabic, and pâdas 2 and 3 are octosyllabic.

6

6 Let Indra daze their army. Let the Maruts slay it with their might.
Let Agni take their eyes away, and let the conquered host retreat.

HYMN II.

MAY Agni, he who knows, our envoy, meet them, burning against ill-will and imprecation.
May he bewilder our opponents' senses. May Jâtavedas smite and make them handless.

2 This Agni hath bewildered all the senses that were in your hearts:
Now let him blast you from your home, blast you away from every side.

3 Dazing their senses, Indra, come hitherward with the wish and will.
With Agni's, Vâta's furious rush drive them to every side away.

4 Vanish, ye hopes and plans of theirs, be ye confounded, all their thoughts!
Whatever wish is in their heart, do thou expel it utterly.

5 Bewildering the senses of our foemen, seize on their bodies and depart, O Apvâ!

---

6 *Let Indra daze their army:* this and the following hymn are classed in the Kauṣika-Sûtra with *mohanâni*, magical charms for stupefying and bewildering an enemy.

All the hymns of this Book have been translated, with exhaustive annotations, by Professor Weber in Indische Studien, XVII, pp. 179—314; eleven (including this hymn) have been translated by Professor Ludwig in Der Rigveda, III., and seven by Dr. Grill in Hundert Lieder des Atharva-veda. Many passages have been translated and annotated by Professor H. Zimmer in his Altindisches Leben, and several by Dr. John Muir in Original Sanskrit Texts.

The hymn is a *rifaccimento* or another recension of the preceding.

5 *Apvâ:* according to Sâyaṇa, a female deity who presides over sin; according to Mahidhara, sickness or fear. Apparently Apvâ is a personification of colic or dysentery, likely to attack soldiers in the field. *And depart:* or, pass us by, do not attack us. The stanza is taken, with slight variations, from Ṛigveda X. 103. 12.

Go meet them, flame within their hearts and burn them.
Smite thou the foes with darkness and amazement.

6 That army of our enemies, O Maruts, that comes against us with its might, contending—
Meet ye and strike it with unwelcome darkness so that not one of them may know another.

HYMN III.

Loudly he roared. Here let him labour deftly.
Spread, Agni, over spacious earth and heaven.
Let Maruts who possess all treasures yoke thee.
Bring him who reverently paid oblations.

2 Though he be far away, let the red horses bring Indra, bring the sage to us and friendship,
Since with Sautrâmaṇî Gods for him o'erpower Gâyatrî, Bṛihatî, and hymn of praises.

3 King Varuṇa call thee hither from the waters! From hills and mountains Soma call thee hither!

The hymn is a charm for the restoration of an expelled King.

1 *He roared:* the crackling and roaring of Agni the Sacrificial Fire, is a good omen for the success of the ceremony. *Bring him:* addressed to Agni: remember the pious prince and bring him back from exile.

2 *The red horses:* the flames of Agni; *arushâsas* here being an appellative. *Indra:* the King; Indra being the type of regal power. *Sautrâmaṇî:* a special ceremony sacred to Indra as Sutrâman, the Good Protector. *Gods:* priests; cf. Ṛigveda X. 122. 7. *Gâyatrî:* a verse or hymn in the Gâyatrî metre, consisting of three octosyllabic pâdas. *Bṛihatî:* a verse or hymn in the Bṛihatî metre, consisting of thirty-six syllables (8 + 8 + 12 + 8) in four pâdas. The priests by performing the Sautrâmaṇî ceremony for the restoration of the banished King overpower the hymns and prayers of those who favour the enemy who expelled him and would keep him in exile.

3 *From the waters:* Varuṇa, the Encompasser, representing at first the all-embracing heaven that broods over the celestial ocean of air, being especially connected in later times with the terrestrial ocean and the waters of the earth and regarded as their presiding deity: see Muir, Original Sanskrit Texts, V. pp. 74—76. *From hills and mountains:* on which the Soma plant, as yet unidentified, is said to have grown: see Hymns of the Ṛigveda, I. 2. 1, note.

Let Indra call thee hither to these people. Fly hither to these people as a falcon.

4 May the hawk bring the man who must be summoned, from far away, in alien land, an exile.

May both the Aṣvins make thy pathway easy. Come, and unite yourselves with him, ye kinsmen.

5 Let thine opponents call thee back. Thy friends have chosen thee again.

Indra and Agni, all the Gods have kept thy home amid the tribe.

6 He who disputes our calling thee, be he a stranger or akin,

Drive him, O Indra, far away, and do thou bring this man to us.

HYMN IV.

To thee hath come the kingship with its splendour: On! shine as lord, sole ruler of the people.

King! let all regions of the heavens invite thee. Here let men wait on thee and bow before thee.

2 The tribesmen shall elect thee for the kingship, these five celestial regions shall elect thee.

Rest on the height and top of kingly power: thence as a mighty man award us treasures.

---

5 *Thy friends have chosen thee again:* other passages also in the Atharva-veda show that the kingship was sometimes elective: see the following hymn, stanza 2, and V. 19. 15, and VI. 87, 88. Cf. also Ṛigveda X. 173. 1.

The hymn has been translated by Ludwig, Der Rigveda, III. p. 441.

The hymn is a benediction at the election of a King.

1 *On:* I omit *udihi*, rise up, which mars the metre.

2 *Five celestial regions:* the four quarters of the heavens with the addition of the zenith or the nadir; the more usual number is four or six.

3 Kinsmen, inviting thee, shall go to meet thee, with thee go Agni as an active herald.
Let women and their sons be friendly-minded. Thou, mighty one, shalt see abundant tribute.

4 First shall the Asvins, Varuṇa and Mitra, the Universal Gods, and Maruts call thee.
Then turn thy mind to giving gifts of treasure, thence, mighty one, distribute wealth among us.

5 Speed to us hither from the farthest distance. Propitious unto thee be Earth and Heaven.
Even so hath Varuṇa this King asserted, he who himself hath called thee: come thou hither.

6 Pass to the tribes of men O Indra, Indra. Thou with the Varuṇas hast been found accordant.
To his own place this one hath called thee, saying, Let him adore the Gods and guide the clansmen.

7 The Bounteous Paths in sundry forms and places, all in accord, have given thee room and comfort.
Let all of these in concert call thee hither. Live thy tenth decade here, a strong kind ruler.

---

6 *Indra:* the newly-elected king. *The Varuṇas:* apparently meaning the Gods; according to Weber 'the electors,' from *vṛi*, to choose. *This one:* the old king whom the newly-elected prince has succeeded; or, possibly, as Zimmer suggests, Agni, present as the Sacrificial Fire, may be intended.

7 *The Bounteous Paths:* ways to riches, personified as the deities of plenty and prosperity: cf. Ṛigveda V. 51. 14. *Live: vasa*, as suggested in Whitney's Index Verborum, should be read instead of *vaṣa*. *Thy tenth decade:* the last stage of thy full natural life which should extend to a hundred years. The people in Germany have a similar division of human life into ten decades, from childhood up to 'Grace with God:' see Weber, Indische Studien, XVII. p. 193.

The hymn has been translated by Zimmer, Altindisches Leben, p. 164, and by Ludwig, Der Rigveda, III. p. 252.

HYMN V.

THIS Parṇa-Amulet hath come, strong and destroying with its strength my rivals.
The power of the Gods, the plants' sweet essence, may it incite me ceaselessly with vigour.

2 O Parṇa-Amulet, in me set firmly might and opulence.
Within the compass of my rule may I be rooted and supreme.

3 That dear mysterious Amulet which Gods have set within the tree,
May the Gods grant to me to wear together with extended life.

4 As Indra's gift, by Varuṇa instructed, Parṇa hath come, the mighty strength of Soma:
This would I, brightly shining, love and cherish for long life lasting through a hundred autumns.

5 The Parṇa-Charm hath come to me for great security from ill,
That I may be exalted, yea, above the wealth of Aryaman.

The hymn is addressed by a newly-elected King to an Amulet which is to strengthen his position and confirm his authority.

1 *This Parṇa-Amulet:* Parṇa (meaning originally 'feather,' 'feather-like leaf'), in later times generally called Palâśa, is the Butea Frondosa, a beautiful sacred tree with large leaves and fine red flowers. The great ladle with which clarified butter is poured into the fire, and other sacrificial utensils, are made of its wood to which, in the shape of amulets, also the greatest efficacy was ascribed. Professor Weber observes that *parṇa*, feather, is etymologically identical with the German Farn, English fern; cf. the Greek πτέρις, the feathery plant, fern. Fern-seed was supposed to have the power of rendering one who carried it invisible, and the plant was said to be of celestial origin, and able to secure the fulfilment of every wish: see Simrock, Handbuch der Deutschen Mythologie, p. 498. The metre of the first line is irregular, the first pâda being octosyllabic and the second hendecasyllabic.

3 *That dear mysterious Amulet:* meaning the magical virtue possessed by the charm rather than the charm itself, the wearing of which was in the speaker's own power.

6 Sagacious builders of the car, clever and skilful artisans,—
Make all the men on every side, Parṇa, obedient to my will.

7 The kings and makers of the kings, troop-leaders, masters of the horse,—
Make all the men on every side, Parṇa, obedient to my will.

8 Thou, Parṇa, art my body's guard, man kin by birth to me a man.
With splendour of the circling year I bind thee on me, Amulet!

HYMN VI.

Masculine springs from masculine, Aṣvattha grows from Khadira.
May it destroy mine enemies, who hate me and whom I detest.

---

5 *Hath come to me:* or, literally, hath mounted me, that is, probably, been fastened round my neck.

6 *Builders of the car:* the *rathakârah*, wheelwright, carpenter, chariot-maker, was held in high honour in the village community; and as the builder of his war-chariots was on terms of friendly intimacy with the king. He was moreover regarded as the representative of the Ṛibhus, those ancient artificers whose wondrous skill obtained for them a place among the Gods: see Ṛigveda I. 20.

7 *Makers of the kings:* the influential nobles who set the king on his throne. *Masters of the horse: sûtâḥ*; charioteers. In Vedic times these were royal officers of considerable importance, and in the Epic period they were also the heralds of the king.

8 *Parṇa:* Weber takes the word as nominative:—'Thou art my body's feathered guard;' treats it as trisyllabic, and omits *vîro*, man, as a gloss. *Man:* manly, heroic, on account of the magic power which thou possessest, and so akin to me. *With splendour:* by binding thee on, I secure to myself all the splendour of the year.

The hymn is addressed to an Amulet of Aṣvattha wood which is to secure the defeat and destruction of the wearer's enemies.

1 *Aṣvattha (aṣvastha*, standing-place for horses) is the Ficus Religiosa, the Pippal, Peepal, or sacred fig-tree. It is venerated by Hindus, and according to Atharva-veda V. 4. 3 the Gods sit under its shade in the

2 Crush down my foes, Asvattha! Rend, O Burster, those who storm and rage,
With Indra, slayer of the fiends, with Mitra and with Varuṇa.

3 As thou hast rent and torn apart, Asvattha! in the mighty sea,
So rend asunder all those men who hate me and whom I detest.

4 Thou who like some victorious bull displayest thy surpassing might,—
With thee, with thee, Asvattha! we would overcome our enemies.

5 Nirṛiti bind them with the bonds of Death which never may be loosed,
Mine enemies, Asvattha! those who hate me and whom I detest.

6 As thou, Asvattha!, mountest on the trees and overthrowest them,
So do thou break my foeman's head asunder and o'erpower him.

7 Let them drift downward like a boat torn from the rope that fastened it.

---

third heaven. Its seeds germinate in the hollows of other trees, and the new growth, which eventually destroys its foster-mother, is endowed with magical powers somewhat similar to those ascribed to the parasite mistletoe in Europe, especially when it grows on trees, such as the oak and the hazel, which do not usually bear it. The Asvattha generally grows on the Sami (Prosopis Spicigera); in the present instance it springs from the Khadira (Acacia Catechu), and, what is still more surprising, *masculine springs from masculine*, that is, the names of both trees are words of that gender.

2 *O Burster: vaibâdha;* so called because it splits asunder the wood, masonry, or stone in whose crevices its seed has germinated and grown. *With Indra:* in alliance with him.

3 *As thou hast rent:* the Khadira tree. *In the mighty sea:* in the topmost branches that waved in the ocean of air.

5 *Nirṛiti*: the Goddess of Misfortune, Death, and Destruction.

There is no turning back for those whom He who Cleaves hath driven away.

8 With mental power I drive them forth, drive them with intellect and charm.

We banish and expel them with the branch of an Aṣvattha tree.

HYMN VII.

The fleet-foot Roebuck wears upon his head a healing remedy.

Innate disease he drives away to all directions with his horn.

2 With his four feet the vigorous Buck hath bounded in pursuit of thee.

Unbind the chronic sickness, Horn! deeply inwoven in the heart.

3 That which shines yonder, like a roof resting on four walls, down on us,—

Therewith from out thy body we drive all the chronic malady.

---

7 *He who Cleaves:* Aṣvattha, the Burster: see stanza 2.

8 *With the branch:* which was probably waved during the recitation of the charm: see Weber.

The hymn is a charm to drive away hereditary disease.

1 *A healing remedy:* the horn, to be used merely as a charm without reference to the medicinal virtue of the ammonia which it contains. Oil of Hartshorn, Volatile Salt of Hartshorn, and Spirits of Hartshorn, procured by distillation from the antlers of the stag (Cervus Elaphus), were formerly much used in European medicine. *Innate disease: kshetriyá;* perhaps pulmonary consumption: see II. 8. 1.

2 *The vigorous Buck:* the horn representing the animal has attacked thee, that is, the patient's disease.

3 *Like a roof:* 'The animal is compared to a house, its legs are the posts, and its horns the roof':—Grill. According to Weber, the ceremony is performed at night in the open air, and the *roof* is one of the constellations.

4 May those twin stars, auspicious, named Releasers, up in yonder sky,
Loose of the chronic malady the uppermost and lowest bond.

5 Water, indeed, hath power to heal, Water drives malady away.
May water—for it healeth all—free thee from permanent disease.

6 Hath some prepared decoction brought inveterate disease on thee,
I know the balm that healeth it: we drive the malady away.

7 What time the starlight disappears, what time the gleams of Dawn depart,
May evil fortune pass from us, the chronic sickness disappear.

HYMN VIII.

Let Mitra come, arranging, with the Seasons, lulling the Earth to rest with gleams of splendour.
And so let Agni, Varuṇa, and Vâyu make our dominion tranquil and exalted.

2 May Indra, Tvashṭar hear my word with favour, may Dhâtar, Râti, Savitar accept it.
I call the Goddess Aditi, heroes' mother, that I may be the centre of my kinsmen.

---

4 The stanza is almost identical with II. 8. 1.

5 It seems that the patient—probably a child—was bathed at this stage of the ceremony. Dr. Grill refers to Ṛigveda X. 137. 6: 'The waters have a balm for all: let them make medicine for thee.'

7 The ceremony lasts till sunrise, when the patient is supposed to be cured. The hymn is one of Dr. Grill's Hundert Lieder, pp. 8, 105.

The hymn is a charm to secure the submission, love, and fidelity of kinsmen.

1 *Mitra:* the Friend, whose favour is especially necessary in such a case. *Lulling the Earth:* in his character of the Sun and God of Day.

2 *Dhâtar:* the Ordainer: see II. 36. 2. *Râti:* Favour, divine Grace personified: see I. 26. 2. *Heroes' mother:* mother of the Âdityas.

3 Soma I call, and Savitar with homage, and all the Âdityas in the time of contest.
Long may this fire send forth its splendour, lighted by kinsmen uttering no word against me.

4 Here, verily, may you stay: go ye no farther. The strong Herd, Lord of Increase, drive you hither!
To please this man may all the Gods together come unto you and be as dames who love him.

5 We bend together all your minds, your vows and purposes we bend.
We bend together you who stand apart with hopes opposed to ours.

6 I with my spirit seize and hold your spirits. Follow with thought and wish my thoughts and wishes.
I make your hearts the thralls of my dominion: on me attendant come the way I guide you.

HYMN IX.

Heaven is the sire, the mother Earth, of Karṣapha and Viṣapha.
As ye have brought them hither, Gods! so do ye move them hence away.

---

3 *This fire:* the sacrificial fire in which oblations to the invoked deities are offered.

4 *May you stay:* the kinsmen are addressed. *The strong Herd:* Pûshan, the guardian of flocks and herds, and giver of general prosperity. *This man:* the householder who recites the preceding and the following stanzas, this stanza being spoken by one of the officiating priests.

The hymn is a charm against Vishkandha or Rheumatism: see I. 16. 3.

1 Karṣapha and Viṣapha, the latter meaning hoofless, or having distorted hoofs, are said in the S. P. Dictionary to denote two imps or goblins. According to Weber the words are appellatives, the former from *kṛiṣ*, to emaciate, and the latter from *viṣ*, to penetrate, with a suffix *apha* = *abha* used in the formation of the names of some animals (as *vṛishabha*, *ṣalabha*, etc.). The translation would then be: Heaven is the sire, the mother Earth, of that which thins and penetrates (i. e. Vishkandha or Rheumatism). As ye have brought it hither, Gods! so do ye move it hence away.

2 The bands hold fast without a knot: this is the way that Manu used.
I make Vishkandha impotent as one emasculateth bulls.

3 Then to a tawny-coloured string the wise and skilful bind a brush.
Let bandages make impotent the strong and active Kâbava.

4 Ye who move active in your strength like Gods with Asuras' magic powers,—
Even as the monkey scorns the dogs, Bandages! scorn the Kâbava.

5 Yea, I will chide thee to thy shame, I will disgrace the Kâbava.
Under our imprecations ye, like rapid cars, shall pass away.

6 One and one hundred over earth are the Vishkandhas spread abroad.
Before these have they fetched thee forth, Vishkandha-quelling Amulet.

---

2 *The bands:* bandages round the affected parts. *Manu:* the thinker, Man *par excellence,* the progenitor of mankind.

3 *A brush:* with which to produce counter-irritation. I adopt Weber's interpretation of *khṛigala*, which in Ṛigveda II. 39. 4 means apparently a staff or crutch, which would not suit this passage. *Kâbava:* one of the demons of the disease.

4 Instead of *yénâ* a word of one syllable is required by the metre: *yé* should probably be read. *Asuras':* demons'. *The monkey:* when he is safe up a tree.

6 *One and one hundred:* a number frequently used of ill-omened or unpleasant objects; the hundred and one ways of dying have been mentioned before: see I. 30. 3. In AV. V. 30. 16, Takman or Fever is said to have a hundred racking pains. So in Bohemia the popular belief reckoned up a hundred varieties of that disease: see Grohmann, Indische Studien, IX. p. 390. *Before these:* in front of, and to oppose, all these rheumatic pains.

HYMN X.

THE First hath dawned. With Yama may it be a cow to pour forth milk.
May she be rich in milk and stream for us through many a coming year.

2 May she whom Gods accept with joy, Night who approacheth as a cow,
She who is Consort of the Year, bring us abundant happiness.

3 Thou whom with reverence we approach, O Night, as model of the Year,
Vouchsafe us children long to live, bless us with increase of our wealth.

4 This same is she whose light first dawned upon us: she moves established in the midst of others.
Great powers and glories are contained within her: a first-born bride, she conquers and bears children.

5 Loud was the wooden press-gear's ring and rattle, as it made annual oblation ready.
First Ashṭakâ! may we be lords of riches, with goodly children and good men about us.

The hymn is a prayer for a happy New Year.

1 *The First:* an early day of the New Year, regarded as indicative of the fortune of the whole twelvemonth. *With Yama:* may this important day not only illumine us, but send its light even to the realm of Yama, the King of the Departed. *A cow:* the emblem of plenty; giver of abundant blessings. The second line is taken from Ṛigveda IV. 57. 7.

2 *Gods:* probably meaning priests. *Night:* preceding the important day. *Consort of the Year:* see stanza 8.

3 *Model of the Year:* see stanza 1, note.

5 *Wooden press-gear:* literally, wooden press-stones; meaning both the stones and the wooden implements, the pestle and mortar, used for extracting the Soma juice and grinding or pounding the grain required for the sacrifice. *First Ashṭakâ:* an Ashṭakâ is the eighth day after full moon. The first that occurs in the New Year is the occasion which this hymn celebrates.

6 The shrine of Iḷâ flows with oil and fatness: accept, O Jâtavedas, our oblations.
Tame animals of varied form and colour—may all the seven abide with me contented.

7 Come thou to nourish me and make me prosper. Night! may the favour of the Gods attend us.
Filled full, O Ladle, fly thou forth. Completely filled fly back again.
Serving at every sacrifice bring to us food and energy.

8 This Year hath come to us, thy lord and consort, O Ekâshṭakâ.
Vouchsafe us children long to live, bless us with increase of our wealth.

9 The Seasons, and the Seasons' Lords I worship, annual parts and groups,
Half-years, Years, Months, I offer to the Lord of all existing things.

---

6 *The shrine of Iḷâ:* the place of worship and libation personified as a Goddess. *Jâtavedas:* wise Agni. *Tame animals:* representatives of these are brought that they may share the benediction. *All the seven:* ox, horse, sheep, goat, mule, ass, and man; five of which are sacrificial animals: see II. 34. 1.

7 *Ladle:* with which the clarified butter is poured into the sacrificial fire. *Completely filled:* bringing abundant blessings to us in return for our oblation to the Gods.

8 *Ekâshṭakâ:* or First Ashṭakâ; the eighth day after the first full moon of the New Year, regarded, on account of its superior importance, as the Consort of the personified Year.

9 *The Seasons:* the hot weather, the rains, and the cold weather. *The Seasons' Lords:* the genii who preside over those divisions of the year. In Ṛigveda X. 2. 1 Agni is invoked as Lord of Seasons *par excellence.* *The Lord of all existing things:* any one of the great Gods who at the time of worship occupies the foremost place in the thoughts of the worshipper.

10 I offer to the Seasons, to their several groups, to Months, to Years,
Dhâtar, Vidhâtar, Fortune, to the Lord of all existing things.

11 With fatness and libation we sacrifice and adore the Gods.
Wealthy in kine may we retire to rest us in our modest homes.

12 Ekâshṭakâ, burning with zealous fervour, brought forth her babe the great and glorious Indra.
With him the Gods subdued their adversaries: the Lord of Might became the Dasyus' slayer.

13 Indra's and Soma's mother! thou art daughter of Prajâpati.
Satisfy thou our hearts' desires. Gladly accept our sacrifice.

HYMN XI.

For life I set thee free by this oblation both from unmarked decline and from consumption:

---

10 *Dhâtar:* the Ordainer. *Vidhâtar:* the Disposer. *Fortune:* Prosperity, personified.

12 *With religious fervour: tápasâ;* according to Weber, 'seized with the pangs of childbirth.' *Their adversaries:* the Asuras or demons, called also Dasyus, who fought against them.

13 *Indra's and Soma's mother:* the laudation of the personified Ekâshṭakâ or First Ashṭakâ here reaches its climax. 'In stanzas 3 and 8 she was called the Consort of the Year, and here she becomes the mother of two of the chief Gods and daughter of the Father of the Gods:'—Weber. *Prajâpati:* Lord of Creatures, Creator; a Supreme Being above the Vedic Gods and sometimes regarded as their father.

The hymn has been translated by Ludwig, Der Rigveda, III. p. 201.

The hymn is a charm for the recovery of a sick person in extreme danger of death. Stanzas 1—4 are taken, with variations in 3 and 4, from Rigveda X. 161. 1—4, and appear again, without these variations in AV. XX. 96. 6—9.

1 *Unmarked decline:* some insidious disease differing from Râjayakshma or pulmonary consumption. Perhaps, as Prof. Zimmer suggests, hypertrophy may be the complaint intended: see Altindisches Leben, p. 377. *The grasping demon: grâhi,* from *grah,* to seize, a female demon who seizes men and kills them.

Or if the grasping demon have possessed him, free him from her, O Indra, thou and Agni!

2 Be his days ended, be he now departed, be he brought very near to death already,
Out of Destruction's lap again I bring him, save him for life to last a hundred autumns.

3 With sacrifice hundred-eyed and hundred-powered, bringing a hundred lives, have I restored him,
That Indra through the autumns may conduct him safe to the farther shore of all misfortune.

4 Live, waxing in thy strength, a hundred autumns, live through a hundred springs, a hundred winters!
Indra, Agni, Savitar, Bṛihaspati give thee a hundred!
With hundred-lived oblation have I saved him.

5 Breath, Respiration, come to him, as two car-oxen to their stall!
Let all the other deaths, whereof men count a hundred, pass away.

6 Breath, Respiration, stay ye here. Go ye not hence away from him.
Bring, so that he may reach old age, body and members back again.

7 I give thee over to old age, make thee the subject of old age.
Let kindly old age lead thee on. Let all the other deaths, whereof men count a hundred, pass away!

---

2 *A hundred autumns:* autumns representing here, as Prof. Weber remarks, a middle stage between the ancient computation by winters (*hímâs*) and the later reckoning by rainy-seasons (*varshâṇi*), corresponding to the southward advance of the Âryan settlements.

3 *Hundred-powered:* the Ṛigveda has 'hundred-autumned.'

4 *Give thee a hundred:* autumns or years being understood. The third pâda is extravagantly hypermetrical, and cannot be reduced to the Trishṭup standard.

5 *The other deaths:* besides natural death through old age.

8 Old age hath girt thee with its bonds even as they bind a bull with rope.
The death that held thee at thy birth bound with a firmly-knotted noose,
Therefrom, with both the hands of Truth, Bṛihaspati hath loosened thee.

HYMN XII.

Here, even here I fix my firm-set dwelling: flowing with fatness may it stand in safety.
May we approach thee, House! with all our people, unharmed and goodly men, and dwell within thee.

2 Even here, O House, stand thou on firm foundation, wealthy in horses, rich in kine and gladness.
Wealthy in nourishment, in milk and fatness, rise up for great felicity and fortune.

3 A spacious store, O House, art thou, full of clean corn and lofty-roofed.
Let the young calf and little boy approach thee, and milch-kine streaming homeward in the evening.

4 This House may Savitar and Vâyu stablish, Bṛihaspati who knows the way, and Indra.
May the moist Maruts sprinkle it with fatness, and may King Bhaga make our corn-land fruitful.

---

8 *At thy birth:* Prof. Weber is of opinion that the occasion of the hymn is the difficult birth of a child who comes into the world in an apparently dying state.

The hymn is a benediction on the completion of a new house.

1 *Dwelling: ṣấlâm. Fatness: ghṛitâm:* clarified butter, the emblem of abundance and prosperity: see I. 33. 4, note.

3 *Full of clean corn: pûtidhânyâ* being apparently a corrupt reading for *pûtadhânyâ*.

4 *Sprinkle it with fatness:* that is, with fertilizing rain. *Make our corn-land fruitful: ní kṛishim tanotu;* according to Weber 'make our ploughing fruitful,' that is, let our ploughing go deep enough to produce a good harvest; but deep ploughing is not in favour with Indian cultivators even now, and cannot have been necessary or desirable

5 Queen of the Home! thou, sheltering, kindly Goddess, wast stablished by the Gods in the beginning.
Clad in thy robe of grass be friendly-minded, and give us wealth with goodly men about us.

6 Thou Pole, in ordered fashion mount the pillar. Strong, shining forth afar, keep off our foemen.
House! let not those who dwell within thee suffer. Live we, with all our men, a hundred autumns.

7 To this the tender boy hath come, to this the calf with all the beasts,
To this the crock of foaming drink, hither with jars of curdled milk.

8 Bring hitherward, O dame, the well-filled pitcher, the stream of molten butter blent with nectar.
Bedew these drinkers with a draught of Amrit. May all our hopes' fulfilment guard this dwelling.

---

in Vedic times and comparatively virgin soil. The general meaning is clear, but the exact sense in which *ní tanotu* is used is not certain. According to the St. P. Dictionary the compound verb means, to penetrate, to cause to take root.

5 *Queen of the Home:* the female deity who presides over house-building, and who was originally commissioned by the Gods to instruct men in this art. *Robe of grass:* with reference to the thatch on the roof.

6 *Pole:* literally, bamboo; the cross-beam. *The pillar:* probably made of some more durable wood. *Shining forth:* perhaps, because it was smeared with ointment to preserve it from the weather and the attacks of white-ants.

7 *With all the beasts: jágatā́ sahá; jágat* here being used, as it frequently is, in the special sense of domestic animals: see I. 31. 4.

Foaming drink: parisrútas; a beverage prepared from herbs, a sort of beer.

8 *O dame:* the mistress of the newly built house. *Molten butter blent with nectar:* probably, as Weber observes, only euphemistic names for good liquor of some sort. All present seem to have been provided with refreshment as at an English house-warming. *Amrit:* nectar, or any sweet drink. *Hopes' fulfilment: ishṭāpūrtám;* meaning the reward of our pious works.

9 Water that kills Consumption, free from all Consumption, here I bring.
With Agni, the immortal one, I enter and possess the house.

HYMN XIII.

As YE, when Ahi had been slain, flowed forth together with a roar,
So are ye called the Roaring Ones: this, O ye Rivers, is your name.

2 As driven forth by Varuṇa ye swiftly urged your rolling waves,
There Indra reached you as you flowed: hence ye are still the Water-floods.

3 Indra restrained you with his might, Goddesses, as ye glided on
Not in accordance with his will: hence have ye got the name of Streams.

---

9 The householder now enters and takes formal possession of the house with water and fire, the two most important necessaries of human life.

The hymn has been translated by Ludwig, Der Rigveda, p. 463; by Zimmer, Altindisches Leben, p. 150, and by Grill, with annotations, Hundert Lieder, pp. 59, 108.

A hymn on the occasion of cutting a channel for irrigation or to avert a flood.

1 The deified Rivers are addressed. *Ahi:* the Dragon, Vṛitra, the chief demon who keeps the waters of heaven imprisoned in the dark cloud. *The Roaring Ones: nadyàs;* a common name of rivers, derived from the root *nad*, to roar, which appears in *ánadatá*, ye roared, of line 1.

2 *Driven forth by Varuṇa:* so, 'Varuṇa dug the channels for thy forward course, O Sindhu.' Ṛigveda X. 75. 2. *Reached: âpnot. Water-floods: ā́pas;* a play upon the two words which have no etymological connexion.

3 *Restrained: ávîvarata,* from *vṛi. Streams:* literally, water, *vā́r;* another play upon two words of unconnected origin.

4 One only God set foot on you flowing according to your will.
The mighty ones breathed upward fast: hence Water is the name they bear.

5 Water is good, water indeed is fatness. Agni and Soma, truly, both bring water.
May the strong rain of those who scatter sweetness come helpful unto me with breath and vigour.

6 Then verily, I see, yea, also hear them: their sound approaches me, their voice comes hither.
Even then I think I am enjoying Amrit, what time I drink my fill of you, gold coloured!

7 Here, O ye Waters, is your heart. Here is your calf, ye holy ones.
Flow here, just here, O mighty Streams, whither I now am leading you.

---

4 *One only God:* Indra. *The mighty ones:* the Rivers. *Breathed upward; úddnishus;* oppressed by the weight of the God. *Water: udakám;* a play on the *úd* in this word and *úddnishus.*

5 *Water is good:* like Pindar's Ἄριστον μὲν ὕδωρ. *Fatness:* in the shape of fertilizing rain. *Those who scatter sweetness:* the Waters.

6 *Gold-coloured:* gleaming like gold in the sunshine.

7 This stanza contains the practical part of the ceremony, the preceding stanzas being merely introductory. The canal is already cut, and the water of the river is to be admitted. *Here is your heart:* this new channel which the river is to fill is now to be dear to you. *Your calf:* your darling; loved as the calf is by its mother; a common term of endearment. According to the directions given in the Kauṣika-Sûtra XL. 3—6, with the recitation of pâda 1 some gold is deposited; with pâda 2 a frog with rush-like streaks, with a blue and a red thread tied round it, is placed upon the gold; with pâda 3 the frog is covered with an aquatic plant called Avakâ, Ṣevála or Ṣevala (Vallisneria Octandra). The symbolical meaning of each act in this procedure is, Prof. Weber remarks, sufficiently intelligible. All that will be found on the spot in future is figuratively and proleptically represented—the gold-gleaming water with its rushes, its frogs, and its lotus-flowers [Ṣevalas, or aquatic plants].

HYMN XIV.

A Pen wherein to dwell at ease, abundance and prosperity,
Whate'er is called the birth of day, all this do we bestow on you.

2 May Aryaman pour gifts on you, and Pûshan, and Bṛihaspati,
And Indra, winner of the prize. Make ye my riches grow with me.

3 Moving together, free from fear, with plenteous droppings in this pen,
Bearing sweet milk like Soma-juice, come hither free from all disease.

4 Come hither, to this place, O Cows: here thrive as though ye were manured.
Even here increase and multiply: let us be friendly, you and me.

5 Auspicious be this stall to you. Prosper like cultivated rice.
Even here increase and multiply. Myself do we bestow on you.

The hymn is a benediction of the Cattle-pen in which the cows are kept at night.

1 *The birth of day:* born or produced on an auspicious day; all good fortune.

2 *Pour gifts on you:* 'keep you together,' according to Weber. *Of the prize:* booty in battle.

4 *As though ye were manured:* according to Weber, 'wie der mist,' like the cow-dung, which increases rapidly if it be not regularly removed.

5 *Like cultivated rice:* *sârishâkâ* is difficult and perhaps corrupt. *Sâri* may be another form of *sâli*, rice, or, as Weber takes it, the bird Ṣâri or more commonly Ṣârikâ, the Maina (Gracula Religiosa), whose droppings are in accordance with its voracious habits. *Myself do we bestow on you:* that is, I devote myself to your service. Or, with Weber, We bind you closely to myself; that is, by a bond of reciprocal benefits: I feed you well and you are to enrich my land.

6 Follow me, Cows, as master of the cattle. Here may this Cow-pen make you grow and prosper.
Still while we live may we approach you living, ever increasing with the growth of riches.

HYMN XV.

I STIR and animate the merchant Indra: may he approach and be our guide and leader.
Chasing ill-will, wild beast, and highway robber, may he who hath the power give me riches.

2 The many paths which Gods are wont to travel, the paths which go between the earth and heaven,
May they rejoice with me in milk and fatness that I may make rich profit by my purchase.

3 With fuel, Agni! and with butter, longing, mine offering I present for strength and conquest;
With prayer, so far as I have strength, adoring— this holy hymn to gain a hundred treasures.

---

6 *Approach:* the word *úpa-sadema* implying careful attention to the wants of the cows.

The hymn has been translated by Ludwig, Der Rigveda, III. p. 469, and, with annotations, by Grill, Hundert Lieder, pp. 64, 112.

The hymn is a merchant's prayer to Indra, Agni, and other Gods for success in his business.

1 *The merchant Indra:* who deals and traffics with his worshippers, requiring and receiving prayer and oblation in exchange for the blessings which he sends. *Guide and leader:* the merchant being on the point of starting on a journey for business purposes. *Ill-will:* the abstract for the concrete; every enemy. *Wild beast and highway robber:* or, according to Weber, 'wild beast that infests the way.'

2 *May they rejoice with me:* I read *me* instead of *mā́*, as Weber suggests. The meaning is, May the Gods who come from heaven to our sacrifices be pleased with the oblations which I offer to them.

3 The stanza is taken from Ṛigveda III. 18. 3. *This holy hymn:* governed by, I present, in the first line.

4 Pardon this stubbornness of ours, O Agni, the distant pathway which our feet have trodden.
Propitious unto us be sale and barter, may interchange of merchandise enrich me.
Accept, ye twain, accordant, this libation! Prosperous be our ventures and incomings.

5 The wealth wherewith I carry on my traffic, seeking, ye Gods! wealth with the wealth I offer,
May this grow more for me, not less: O Agni, through sacrifice chase those who hinder profit!

6 The wealth wherewith I carry on my traffic, seeking, ye Gods! wealth with the wealth I offer,
Herein may Indra, Savitar, and Soma, Prajâpati, and Agni give me splendour.

7 With reverence we sing thy praise, O Hotar-priest Vaisvânara.
Over our children keep thou watch, over our bodies, kine, and lives.

8 Still to thee ever will we bring oblation, as to a stabled horse, O Jâtavedas.
Joying in food and in the growth of riches may we thy servants, Agni, never suffer.

---

4 The first line of this stanza, borrowed from Ṛigveda I. 31. 16, is superfluous and out of place here. Dr. Grill and Prof. Zimmer leave it untranslated. *Ye twain:* Indra who is addressed in stanza 1, and Agni addressed in 3. *Incomings: útthitam;* explained by the Commentator as *vyavahârâd utpannam lâbhayuktam dhanam:* see Grill's note.

5 *Through sacrifice:* in return for the sacrifice which I offer. *Those:* the text has *devấn*, Gods, which mars the meṭre and is probably a gloss.

6 *Splendour: rúchim;* or, favour; dignity and importance. According to Weber the word here means 'understanding.'

7 *Vaiṣvânara:* dear to all men; an appellative of Agni. This Anushṭup stanza appears to be an interpolation.

8 *As to a stabled horse:* as we carry fodder to a horse that is not turned out to graze. *Jâtavedas:* wise Agni. *Servants: prátiveṣâs;* or, neighbours.

HYMN XVI.

AGNI at dawn, and Indra we invoke at dawn, and Varuṇa and Mitra, and the Asvins twain:
Bhaga at dawn, Pûshan and Brahmaṇaspati, Soma at dawn, and Rudra we invoke at dawn.

2 We call strong Bhaga, conqueror in the morning, the son of Aditi, the great Disposer,
Whom each who deems himself poor, strong and mighty, a king, addresses thus, Grant thou my portion!

3 Bhaga, our guide, Bhaga whose gifts are faithful, favour this hymn and give us wealth, O Bhaga.
Bhaga, augment our store of kine and horses. Bhaga, may we be rich in men and heroes.

According to the Kauṣika-Sûtra this hymn is the beginning of 'the ritual of a travelling merchant when about to start on a trading expedition.' He has also to recite the hymns III. 26 and 27, VI. 1, 3, 4, 5, 6, 7, 59, 93, 107, 128, and IV. 28, with which certain oblations are to be made. See Bloomfield, American Journal of Philology, VII. p. 487.

The hymn has been translated by Ludwig, Der Rigveda, III. p. 215, by Grill, with annotations, Hundert Lieder, pp. 69, 113, and by Zimmer, Altindisches Leben, p. 258.

The hymn is the morning prayer of the great Ṛishi Vasishṭha, taken, with slight variations, from Ṛigveda VII. 41.

1 *At dawn:* prayer and praise in the early morning being most acceptable to the Gods.

2 *Bhaga:* see I. 26. 2. *Conqueror in the morning:* in his character of the early Sun overpowering Ushas or Dawn who in Ṛigveda I. 123. 5 is called his sister. *Disposer:* or, Supporter. *Grant thou my portion:* or, may I receive my share. Weber takes *bhakshi* as the first person singular, Âtmanepada, and the Commentaries make it second person singular, Parasmaipada, of the aorist in each case. The meaning is that everyone, poor and weak, strong and mighty, the king himself, looks to Bhaga as the giver of his allotted fortune.

4 So may felicity be ours at present, and when the Sun advances, and at noontide;
And may we still, O Bounteous One, at sunset be happy in the Gods' protecting favour.

5 May Bhaga verily be bliss-bestower, and through him, Gods! may happiness attend us.
As such with all my might I call and call thee: as such be thou our leader here, O Bhaga.

6 To this our sacrifice may the Dawns incline them, and come to the pure place like Dadhikrâvan.
As strong steeds draw a chariot may they bring me hitherward Bhaga who discovers treasure.

7 May the kind Mornings dawn on us for ever with wealth of kine, of horses, and of heroes,
Streaming with all abundance, pouring fatness. Do ye preserve us evermore with blessings!

---

5 *May Bhaga verily be bliss-bestower: bhágavân;* originally, possessing a happy lot, fortunate, blessed, adorable; now generally meaning Almighty God.

6 *The Dawns:* the lights of morning, personified. *The pure place:* the chamber of sacrifice. *Dadhikrâvan:* or Dadhikrâs, or, in the crude form, Dadhikrâ, is the name of a mythical being often mentioned in the Ṛigveda, and the deified subject of Hymns IV. 38, 39, 40, and VII. 44. He is described as a kind of divine horse, and probably, like Târkshya, is a personification of the morning Sun. Sometimes he is considered as a creation of Heaven and Earth, sometimes of Mitra and Varuṇa, and is invoked in the morning together with Agni, Ushas, and the Asvins. According to Professor Pischel (Vedische Studien, I. 124), Dadhikrâvan may have been originally a most distinguished race-horse, glorified and deified by the exaggerated praises of the bards of a people who were passionately devoted to chariot-racing. *Like Dadhikrâvan* may mean, with the swiftness of the famous mythical horse, the type and model of racers. See Hymns of the Ṛigveda, General Index II.

7 *Do ye preserve us evermore with blessings:* this address to the Gods in general is the conclusion of many Ṛigveda hymns attributed to the Vasishṭhas.

HYMN XVII.

WISE and devoted to the Gods the skilful men bind plough-ropes fast,
And lay the yokes on either side.

2 Lay on the yokes and fasten well the traces: formed is the furrow, sow the seed within it.
Virâj vouchsafe us hearing fraught with plenty! Let the ripe grain come near and near the sickle.

3 The keen-shared plough that bringeth bliss, furnished with traces and with stilts,
Shear out for me a cow, a sheep, a rapid drawer of the car, a blooming woman, plump and strong!

4 May Indra press the furrow down, may Pûshan guard and cherish her.
May she, well stored with milk, yield milk for us through each succeeding year.

The hymn is a farmer's song and prayer to speed the plough.

1 The stanza is taken from Ṛigveda X. 101. 4. *Devoted: sumnayaú* can hardly be the right reading. The Ṛigveda has *sumnayā́*, an instrumental case used adverbially, devoutly; or, through devotion, through fixing their hopes of happiness upon the Gods. *The skilful men:* the ploughmen who understand their work.

2 *Formed is the furrow:* cf. Hymns Ancient and Modern, 383: 'We plough the fields, and scatter The good seed on the land, But it is fed and watered By God's Almighty Hand.'

The stanza is taken, with variations, from Ṛigveda X. 101. 3. *Virấj:* meaning, perhaps, as Prof. Ludwig suggests, Vâk the Goddess of Speech. The Ṛigveda reads *girā́cha,* 'Through song,' or 'by means of our hymn;' and Weber here also translates a conjectural reading *girā́ṃcha,* 'of our prayers or songs.'

3 *Furnished with traces and with stilts: somasā́tsaru;* resolved into *sa-uman* (cf. *uta,* woven or spun, and *umấ,* flax), *sa-tsaru,* with traces, with a handle.—Weber.

4 Indra as the God who sends the necessary rain is prayed to bless the work by cutting the furrow, and Pûshan as the God of Increase is prayed to protect it. *Her:* the furrow personified. *Milk:* meaning plentiful nourishment. The stanza is taken from Ṛigveda IV. 57. 7: its second hemistich, which is a solemn formula, occurs also in Atharva-veda III. 10. 1.

5 Happily let the shares turn up the ploughland, the ploughers happily follow the oxen.
Pleased with our sacrifice, Ṣuna and Sîra! make the plants bring this man abundant produce.

6 Happily work our steers and men! May the plough furrow happily.
Happily be the traces bound. Happily ply the driving-goad.

7 Ṣuna and Sîra, welcome ye this laud, and with the milk that ye have made in heaven
Bedew ye both this earth of ours.

8 Auspicious Sîtâ, come thou near: we venerate and worship thee
That thou mayst bless and prosper us and bring us fruits abundantly.

---

5 Taken from Ṛigveda IV. 57. 8 with variations. *Ṣuna and Sîra:* two deities or deified objects who bless or are closely connected with agriculture. According to Yâska, Ṣuna (the auspicious) is Vâyu, and Sîra (plough) is Âditya or the Sun. The words probably mean, as suggested in the St. P. Dictionary, ploughshare and plough. Prof. Grassmann translates them by 'O Pflug and Lenker,' 'O Plough and Ploughman,' but, 'O Plough aud Ploughshare,' would be a better rendering. *This man:* the owner of the land. The second hemistich of the Ṛigveda stanza is: 'With meath and milk Parjanya make us happy! Grant us prosperity, Ṣuna and Sîra (or O Plough and Ploughshare).'

6 Taken from Ṛigveda IV. 57. 4.

7 Ṛigveda IV. 57. 5.

8 Ṛigveda IV. 57. 6. *Sîtâ:* or, Furrow, personified and addressed as a deity. An elaborate ceremonial, which the recitation of this hymn is to accompany, is prescribed in the Kauṣika-Sûtra: see Weber, Indische Studien, XVII. pp. 256 sqq. In England, Plough-Monday, the first Monday after Twelfth-day, when men returned to the plough at the end of the Christmas holidays, used to be celebrated by the farm-labourers who drew a plough from door to door of the village and solicited 'plough-money' to spend in honour of the day.

9 Loved by the Visvedevas and the Maruts, let Sîtâ be bedewed with oil and honey.
Turn thou to us with wealth of milk, O Sîtâ, in vigorous strength and pouring streams of fatness.

HYMN XVIII.

From out the earth I dig this Plant, an herb of most effectual power,
Wherewith one quells the rival wife and gains the husband for one's self.

2 Auspicious, with expanded leaves, sent by the Gods, victorious Plant,
Drive thou the rival wife away, and make my husband only mine.

3 Indeed he hath not named her name: thou with this husband dalliest not.
Far into distance most remote we drive the rival wife away.

4 Stronger am I, O stronger one, yea, mightier than the mightier;
Beneath me be my rival wife, down, lower than the lowest dames!

---

9 *With oil and honey:* some clarified butter with honey or meath was, it seems, poured into the first furrow to secure a good crop.

The hymn, which is taken, with variations, from Ṛigveda X. 145, is a spell to rid a jealous wife of a more favoured rival.

1 *This Plant:* said to be the Pâṭâ, probably identical with Pâṭhâ (Clypea Hernandifolia), a climbing plant possessing various medicinal properties, and employed for magical purposes: see Atharva-veda II. 27. 4.

2 *Expanded:* or 'erected,' as Weber translates it.

3 *He:* the husband. The Ṛigveda has: 'Her very name I utter not: she takes no pleasure with this man.'

5 I am the conqueror, and thou, thou also art victorious:
As victory attends us both we will subdue my fellow-wife.

6 I've girt thee with the conquering Plant, beneath thee laid the mightiest one.
As a cow hastens to her calf, so let thy spirit speed to me, hasten like water on its way.

HYMN XIX.

QUICKENED is this my priestly rank, quickened is manly strength and force,
Quickened be changeless power, whereof I am the conquering President!

2 I quicken these men's princely sway, the might, the manly strength and force;
I rend away the foemen's arms with this presented sacrifice.

3 Down fall the men, low let them lie, who fight against our mighty prince.
I ruin foemen with my spell, and raise my friends to high estate.

---

6 According to Dârila, with the recitation of the first hemistich leaves of the magical plant are to be placed in the bed of the rival, and not in that of the husband as suggested by Sâyaṇa in his Commentary on the Ṛigveda where the reading is somewhat different. The second hemistich is addressed to the husband.

The hymn is a glorification of the office of Purohita or Household Priest and Counsellor of a King.

1 *Quickened:* or, sharpened, that is, intensified. *Manly strength:* of the people, who constitute the army. *Power:* or, sway; the rule of the second, princely or military class.

3 *Mighty prince:* the rich, powerful, and liberal householder who institutes and pays the expenses of sacrifice: 'our mighty sacrificer:' Weber; 'our Sûri, the Maghavân:' Ludwig.

4 Keener than is the axe's edge, keener than Agni's self are they,
Keener than Indra's bolt are they whose Priest and President am I.

5 The weapons of these men I whet and sharpen, with valiant heroes I increase their kingdom.
Victorious be their power and ever ageless! May all the Gods promote their thoughts and wishes.

6 Let their fierce powers, O Maghavan, be heightened, and upward go the shout of conquering heroes.
Apart and clear, let shout and roar and shriek and lamentation rise!
Let the Gods led by Indra, let the Maruts with our army go.

7 Advance and be victorious, men! Exceeding mighty be your arms!
Smite with sharp-pointed arrows those whose bows are weak. With your strong arms and weapons smite the feeble foe.

8 Loosed from the bowstring fly away, thou Arrow, sharpened by our prayer.
Assail the foemen, vanquish them, conquer each bravest man of theirs, and let not one of them escape.

---

4 *Priest and President: puróhitaḥ;* literally, one set before (praeses), appointed to special functions.

6 *O Maghavan:* mighty or bounteous Indra. *Clear: ketumántaḥ;* according to Weber and Ludwig 'with banners.' *Shout and roar:* of the victors. *Shriek and lamentation:* of the vanquished: cf. Homer, Iliad, IV. 450: ἔνθα δ' ἅμ' οἰμωγή τε καὶ εὐχωλὴ πέλεν ἀνδρῶν ὀλλύντων τε καὶ ὀλλυμένων: 'And then did tumult rise Up to her height; then conquerors' boasts mixed with the conquered's cries:'—Chapman. The Purohita's glorification of his high office has become a war-song with which he inspirits the men who are going forth to battle under his auspicious benediction.

7 The first hemistich is composed of pâdas 1 and 3 of Ṛigveda X. 103. 13.

8 *Our prayer:* or, spell. The stanza is taken, with variations, from Ṛigveda VI. 75. 16.

The hymn has been translated by Ludwig, Der Rigveda, III. p. 234, and by Muir, O. S. Texts, I. p. 283.

HYMN XX.

THIS is thine ordered place of birth whence sprung to life thou shinest forth.
Knowing this, Agni, mount on high and cause our riches to increase.

2 Turn hither, Agni, speak to us, come to us with a friendly mind.
Enrich us, Sovran of the Tribes! Thou art the giver of our wealth.

3 Let Aryaman vouchsafe us wealth, and Bhaga, and Bṛihaspati,
The Goddesses grant wealth to us, Sûnṛitâ, Goddess, give me wealth!

4 We call King Soma to our aid, and Agni with our songs and hymns,
The Âdityas, Vishṇu, Sûrya, and the Brahman-priest Bṛihaspati.

5 Do thou, O Agni, with thy fires strengthen our prayer and sacrifice.
Incite thou us, O God, to give, and send us riches to bestow.

The hymn is a prayer for riches and general prosperity.

1 *This:* the centre of the northern altar or fire-receptacle in the sacrificial court or hall. The first hemistich is taken from Ṛigveda III. 29. 10, the second hemistich of which is: 'Knowing this, Agni, seat thyself, and prosper thou the songs we sing.'

2 *Sovran of the Tribes: viśâm pate;* or, Lord of the people; King of the Âryan settlers. Stanzas 2—7 are taken, with variations, from Ṛigveda X. 141. 1, 2, 3, 6, 4, 5.

3 *The Goddesses:* the consorts of the Gods, Indrâṇî, Agnâyî, Varuṇânî, and other Gnâs or celestial Dames. *Sûnṛitâ:* Pleasantness, Gladness, or Glory, personified as a Goddess.

4 *The Âditya:* Varuṇa, the Âditya *par excellence,* primus inter pares. *The Brahman-priest:* Bṛihaspati, Lord of Prayer, is the Purohita of the Gods and the prototype of the priestly order.

6 Both Indra here and Vâyu we invoke with an auspicious call,
That in assembly all the folk may be benevolent to us, and be inclined to give us gifts.

7 Urge Aryaman to send us gifts, and Indra, and Bṛihaspati,
Vâta, Vishṇu, Sarasvatî, and the strong courser Savitar.

8 Now have we reached the ordering of power, and all these worlds of life are held within it.
Let him who knows urge e'en the churl to bounty. Give wealth to us with all good men about us.

9 May heaven's five spacious regions pour their milk for me with all their might.
May I obtain each wish and hope formed by my spirit and my heart.

10 May speech that winneth cows be mine. With splendour mount thou over me.
May Vâyu hedge me round about. May Pûshan make me prosperous.

---

6 *In assembly:* or, when they meet us; that is, in ordinary intercourse.

7 *Sarasvatî:* a female divinity of the upper region, guardian of the waters, and bestower of fertility; identified also with Vâk the Goddess of Speech.

8 The first hemistich appears to be entirely out of place here. 'The verse in the Yajus-ritual belongs to the so-named vâjaprasavîyâni, which form the kernel of the Vâjapeya-sacrifice, the name of which, in opposition to the explanation given in the Brâhmaṇa itself, appears to me to mean Protection of Power inasmuch as it is a ceremony appointed for the samrâj [lord paramount, or sovereign].'—Weber.

9 *Five spacious regions:* the four quarters of the heavens with the zenith or the nadir. *Milk:* blessings.

10 *Cows:* usually presented to priests by princes and wealthy institutors of sacrifice. *With splendour:* or, with power; addressed to the Sun, the hymn being recited at sunrise.

HYMN XXI.

ALL Fires that are in water and in Vṛitra, all those that man and stones contain within them,
That which hath entered herbs and trees and bushes—to all these Fires be this oblation offered.

2 That which abides in Soma and in cattle, that which lies deep in birds and sylvan creatures,
That which hath entered quadrupeds and bipeds—to all these Fires be this oblation offered.

3 The Fire that rideth by the side of Indra, the God Vaiṣvânara, yea, all-consuming,
Whom, as the victor, I invoke in battles—to all these Fires be this oblation offered.

4 The all-devouring God whom men call Kâma, he whom they call the Giver and Receiver,
Invincible, pervading, wise, and mighty—to all these Fires be this oblation offered.

The hymn, in honour of all varieties of Fire, is especially a charm to appease Agni in his most dreaded form, and to quench the flames of the funeral pile.

1 *In water and in Vṛitra:* existing in the form of lightning in the waters of the air and in the Dragon or great dragonish cloud which, personified as the demon of drought, withholds the seasonable rain. *Man:* contains fire in the shape of the internal heat which is said to effect the digestion of his food, and as the natural vital warmth of the body. *Stones:* contain fire which may be struck out in sparks. *Herbs and trees and bushes:* Agni in the form of lightning enters all plants with the descending rain. The phosphorescence of some species of plants may also be referred to.

2 *In Soma:* as the heating element of the exhilarating beverage. *In cattle:* and the other animals, the fire is the natural heat of their bodies which maintains their strength, swiftness, ferocity and other characteristic qualities.

3 *That rideth by the side of Indra:* the destructive fire of war. *Vaiṣvânara:* Agni as God of all Âryan men, peaceful fire, domestic and sacrificial.

4 *Kâma:* God of wish and desire in general, including love; the inspirer and fulfiller of the wish. See III. 29. 7. Here he is identified with Agni. See Muir, Original Sanskrit Texts, V. p. 403.

5 To thee, strength-giver, glorious, rich in pleasant strains, whom in their minds the thirteen creatures of the world,
And the five sons of man regard as Hotar-priest—to all these Fires be this oblation offered.

6 To him who feeds on ox and cow, sage, bearing Soma on his back,
To all Vaiṣvânara's followers—to these be this oblation paid.

7 All fiery flames that follow after lightning, flashing o'er earth, through firmament and heaven,
All that are in the wind and skyey regions—to all these Fires be this oblation offered.

8 The golden-handed Savitar and Indra, Bṛihaspati, Varuṇa, Mitra, and Agni,
The Angirases we call, the Viṣve Devas: let them appease this Agni, Flesh-devourer.

---

5 *Thirteen creatures of the world:* perhaps all creatures exclusive of men, thirteen being used for a large indefinite number. *Five sons of man:* the eponymi of the five great Âryan tribes and their descendants; the five races, tribes, or peoples frequently mentioned in the Ṛigveda; probably the confederation of the Turvaṣas, Yadus, Anus, Druhyus, and Pûrus. See Hymns of the Ṛigveda, General Index II. under Five races.

6 *Who feeds on ox and cow: ukshânnâya vaṣânnâya:* the first hemistich is taken, with variations, from Ṛigveda VIII. 43. 11, where I have translated these words by 'fed like ox and cow,' a possible rendering which I do not now approve. Sacrifice of oxen and barren cows was not unusual in old Vedic times. *Bearing Soma on his back:* sprinkled with libations of Soma juice. *Vaiṣvânara's followers:* varieties of fire, of which Vaiṣvânara is chief.

8 According to the Kauṣika-Sûtra, with the recitation of this stanza the funeral fire is damped with holy water and extinguished. The preceding stanzas are merely introductory to the practical part.

9 Flesh-eating Agni is appeased, appeased is he who hurteth men.
Now him who burneth every thing, the Flesh-consumer, have I stilled.

10 The mountains where the Soma grows, the waters lying calm and still,
Vâta, Parjanya, Agni's self have made the Flesh-consumer rest.

HYMN XXII.

FAMED be the Elephant's strength, the lofty glory, which out of Aditi's body took existence!
They all have given me this for my possession, even all the Gods and Aditi accordant.

2 On this have Mitra, Varuṇa, Indra, and Rudra fixed their thought.
May those all-fostering deities anoint and balm me with his strength.

3 The strength wherewith the Elephant was dowered, that decks a King among the men, in waters,
Wherewith the Gods at first attained to godhead, O Agni, even with that strength make thou me vigorous to-day.

---

10 *Agni's self:* the fire having done its work and almost burnt itself out, Vâta and Parjanya, or wind and rain, having aided its extinction.

The subject of the hymn is the taming and training of an elephant for the King to ride.

1 *Aditi's body*: Aditi, who appears in the Ṛigveda as mother of the Âdityas, is in later times called Mother of the Gods and Mother of the World. *All the Gods:* 'Without the help of all the Gods and the consent of Aditi it would be impossible to tame so powerful an animal.'—Weber. The King is the speaker.

2 *His strength:* the might of the elephant, tamed with the help of the Gods.

3 *In waters:* when he is sprinkled with the water of consecration. *Attained to godhead:* Agni alone was originally immortal, and the other Gods obtained immortality through him or through Soma. See Ṛigveda V. 3. 4; VI. 7. 4; IX. 106. 8.

4 The lofty strength which sacrifice brings, Jâtavedas! unto thee,
What strength the Sun possesses, all strength of the royal Elephant—such strength vouchsafe to me the pair of Asvins lotus-garlanded!

5 Far as the heavens' four regions spread, far as the eye's most distant ken,
So wide, so vast let power be mine, this vigour of the Elephant.

6 Now hath the Elephant become chief of all pleasant beasts to ride.
With his high fortune and his strength I grace and consecrate myself.

HYMN XXIII.

From thee we banish and expel the cause of thy sterility.
This in another place we lay apart from thee and far removed.

2 As arrow to the quiver, so let a male embryo enter thee.
Then from thy side be born a babe, a ten-month child, thy hero son.

---

5 *Far as the heavens' four regions spread:* let the possession of so mighty an elephant make me supreme ruler over all around me as far as the distant horizon.

The hymn has been translated by Ludwig, Der Rigveda, III. p. 461.

The hymn is a charm to remove sterility, and to assure the birth of male children.

2 *As arrow to the quiver:* according to the Kauṣika-Sûtra an arrow is to be used in the ceremony which the hymn is to accompany.

A ten-month child: born in the tenth lunar month; cf. Ṛigveda V. 78. 8, 9. So also: 'Matri longa decem tulerunt fastidia menses.'—Virgil, Eclogue IV. 61.

3 Bring forth a male, bring forth a son. Another male shall follow him.
The mother shalt thou be of sons born and hereafter to be born.

4 With that auspicious genial flow wherewith steers propagate their kind,
Do thou obtain thyself a son: be thou a fruitful mother-cow.

5 I give thee power to bear a child: within thee pass the germ of life!
Obtain a son, O woman, who shall be a blessing unto thee. Be thou a blessing unto him.

6 May those celestial herbs whose sire was Heaven, the Earth their mother, and their root the ocean,
May those celestial healing Plants assist thee to obtain a son.

HYMN XXIV.

THE plants of earth are rich in milk, and rich in milk is this my word.
So from the rich in milk I bring thousandfold profit hitherward.

2 Him who is rich in milk I know. Abundant hath he made our corn.
The God whose name is Gatherer, him we invoke who dwelleth in his house who sacrifices not.

---

6 *The ocean:* the sea of air. *Celestial herbs:* See Rigveda X. 97. *A son:* 'Nowhere in the Vedic hymns do we find a wish for the birth of a daughter.'—Zimmer.

The hymn has been translated by Ludwig, Der Rigveda, p. 477, and by Zimmer, Altindisches Leben, p. 319.

The hymn is a song of Harvest-Home.

1 *Milk:* here used in its figurative sense of beneficial virtue or blessing. *Word:* or, hymn.

2 *Him who is rich in milk:* that is, in beneficial power; probably a good-natured domestic sprite of the class 'called with us hobgoblins or

3 All the five regions of the heavens, all the five races of mankind,—
As after rain the stream brings drift, let them bring increase hitherward.

4 Open the well with hundred streams, exhaustless, with a thousand streams,
So cause this corn of ours to be exhaustless, with a thousand streams.

5 O Hundred-handed, gather up. O Thousand-handed, pour thou forth.
Bring hither increase of the corn prepared and yet to be prepared.

6 Three sheaves are the Gandharvas' claim, the lady of the house hath four.
We touch thee with the sheaf that is the most abundant of them all.

Robin Goodfellows, that would in those superstitious times grind corn for a mess of milk, cut wood, or do any manner of drudgery work' (Burton's Anatomy of Melancholy, Part I. Sec. 2). Atharva-veda II. 8. 5. *The God:* the superhuman being, the goblin. So Du Cange explains the Low Latin *gobelinus* by a 'daemon qui vulgo Faunus' who was regarded as the protecting deity of agriculture. *Who dwelleth:* who is at present in the house of a godless illiberal churl whom he will be glad to leave.

3 *Five regions:* the four quarters of the heavens with the zenith or the nadir. *Five races of mankind:* the five, that is, all, the great Âryan tribes. See Zimmer, Altindisches Leben, pp. 120, 121. According to Prof. Roth and Prof. Weber, the expression comprehends all human races, the Âryans in the centre and around them all the nations under the four quarters of heaven.

4 *The well:* figuratively or symbolically; the source of plenty.

5 *Hundred-handed* : . . . *Thousand-handed:* two drudging goblins are addressed.

6 Three sheaves of corn are to be left on the ground to remunerate the goblins who are here euphemistically called Gandharvas, a higher and more spiritual class of celestial beings; four are the special perquisite of the mistress; and the best sheaf of all is offered as a sample to the owner of the field. I adopt Weber's translation of *mâtrâ*, sheaves, the word literally signifying measures. Of course the grain would not be measured at the beginning of harvest.

7 Adding and Gathering are thy two attendants,
O Prajâpati.
May they bring hither increase, wealth abundant,
inexhaustible.

HYMN XXV.

Let the Impeller goad thee on. Rest not in peace
upon thy bed.
Terrible is the shaft of Love: therewith I pierce
thee to the heart.

2 That arrow winged with longing thought, its stem
Desire, its neck Resolve,
Let Kâma, having truly aimed, shoot forth and
pierce thee in the heart.

3 The shaft of Kâma, pointed well, that withers and
consumes the spleen,
With hasty feathers, all aglow, therewith I pierce
thee to the heart.

---

7 *Adding and Gathering:* Upohá and Samûhá, names given to the two industrious goblins. *Attendants:* or treasurers; keepers and distributors of thy riches in the shape of corn. *O Prajâpati:* the Protector of Life being closely connected with the harvest which supports it.

The hymn has been translated by Ludwig, Der Rigveda, p. 268.

The hymn is a charm to win a maiden's love.

1 *Impeller:* or, Disturber; Kâma, the God of Love, who is also called, among other names, Madana, the Maddener, and Manmatha, Agitator of the Mind. Weber and Zimmer translate *uttudás* by 'Unruhe,' 'unrest,' 'agitation.'

2 *The spleen:* regarded, with the liver, as the part of the body from which the blood flows, and the seat of the passions and affections.

The hymn has been translated by Muir, Original Sanskrit Texts, V. 407; by Ludwig, Der Rigveda, III. p. 516; by Zimmer, Altindisches Leben, p. 307; and, with annotations, by Grill, Hundert Lieder, pp. 53, 115.

4 Pierced through with fiercely-burning heat, steal to me with thy parching lips,
Gentle and humble, all mine own, devoted, with sweet words of love.

5 Away from mother and from sire I drive thee hither with a whip,
That thou mayst be at my command and yield to every wish of mine.

6 Mitra and Varuṇa, expel all thought and purpose from her heart.
Deprive her of her own free-will and make her subject unto me.

HYMN XXVI.

Ye Gods who dwell within this eastward region, entitled Weapons, Agni forms your arrows.
Be kind and gracious unto us and bless us. To you be reverence, to you be welcome!

2 Ye Gods who dwell within this southward region, entitled Eager, Kâma forms your arrows.
Be kind, etc.

3 Ye Gods who dwell within this westward region, whose name is Radiant, Water forms your arrows.
Be kind, etc.

4 Ye Gods who dwell within this northward region, whose name is Piercers, Vâta forms your arrows.
Be kind, etc.

5 Ye Gods whose home is in this firm-set region—Nilimpas is your name—Plants are your arrows.
Be kind, etc.

The hymn, which is closely connected with hymn XXVII, is a charm to win the favour of the Serpents of all the regions under heaven.

1 *Gods:* the Serpents are addressed as powerful superhuman beings. *Weapons:* or, Heti. *Agni forms your arrows:* or, your arrows are fire.

5 *This firm-set region:* the point directly under the feet, opposite to the zenith. *Nilimpas:* perhaps, smearers, lickers (of themselves).

6 Ye Gods whose home is in this upmost region,
Yearners by name, Bṛihaspati forms your arrows.
Be kind and gracious unto us and bless us. To you be reverence, to you be welcome!

HYMN XXVII.

Agni is regent of the East, its warder is Asita, the Âdityas are the arrows.
Worship to these the regents, these the warders, and to the arrows, yea, to these be worship!
Within your jaws we lay the man who hateṭh us and whom we hate.

2 Indra is regent of the South, its warder Tiraṣchirâji, and the shafts the Fathers.
Worship to these the regents, these the warders, and to the arrows, yea, to these be worship!
Within your jaws we lay the man who hateth us and whom we hate.

3 Of the West region Varuṇa is ruler, Pṛidâku warder, Nourishment the arrows.
Worship, etc.

---

6 *Upmost region:* the highest point of the heaven overhead, the zenith.

The Serpents of the six regions having been conciliated in the preceding hymn, the regents, warders, and arrows of those regions are duly reverenced, and the speaker's enemy is solemnly given over to the Serpents for condign punishment.

1 *Asita:* Black Serpent.

2 *Of the South:* according to Manu V. 96, Yama is the regent of the South. The distribution of the regions is variously given by different authorities. See Atharva-veda 1. 31. 1, note. *Tiraṣchirâji:* the Serpent with transverse streaks. *The Fathers:* Manes, or Ancestral Spirits.

3 *Pṛidâku:* Adder or Viper; frequently mentioned in the Atharva-veda. See I. 27. 1.

4 Soma is ruler of the Western region, Svaja the warder, lightning's flash the arrows.
Worship, etc.

5 Vishṇu is ruler of the firm-set region, Kalmâshagrîva warder, Plants the arrows.
Worship, etc.

6 Bṛihaspati controls the topmost region, Ṣvitra is warder, and the Rain the arrows.
Worship to these the regents, these the warders, and to the arrows, yea, to these be worship!
Within your jaws we lay the man who hateth us and whom we hate.

HYMN XXVIII.

THIS cow was born to bring forth offspring singly, though they created kine of every colour.
When she produces twins in spite of Order, sullen, with groan and grudge she harms the cattle.

---

4 *Svaja:* a variety of Viper. See V. 14. 10, and VI. 56. 2.

5 *Firm-set region:* the nadir. See III. 26. 5. *Kalmâshagrîva:* Spotty-neck.

6 *Topmost region:* the zenith. *Ṣvitra:* White Serpent; an unidentified species.

Professor Weber remarks that no ritual procedure is prescribed in the Kauṣika-Sûtra for this and the preceding hymn; and suggests that they may have found their way into the text after the composition of that work.

The hymn is a charm to change the ill-omened birth of twin calves into a blessing.

1 *They:* the text has *bhûtakṛitaḥ* (Rishis regarded as creators of beings), which is metrically superfluous and almost certainly a gloss. Cows were created of many colours, but were intended to produce only one calf at a birth. When twins are born, a charm is necessary to avert the ill omen; and the Kauṣika-Sûtra prescribes an appropriate ceremony, ending with the bestowal of the peccant cow on the priest. A somewhat similar ceremony is prescribed in the same Ritual when a woman presents her husband with twins. In this case also, it seems, the mother becomes the property of the priest. The same superstition is found at the present time in uncivilized parts of Africa.

2 She brings destruction on the beasts, turned to a flesh-devouring worm.
Yea, give her to the Brahman that she may bring luck and happiness.

3 Be thou auspicious to our folk, bring luck to horses and to kine.
Auspicious unto all this farm, bring luck and happiness to us.

4 Let there be rain and increase here, here be thou most munificent.
Mother of twins, prosper our herd.

5 Where, having left all sickness of their bodies, the pious lead, as friends, their lives of gladness—
Nigh to that world approached the twin calves' mother. Let her not harm our people and our cattle.

6 Where lies the world of those dear friends, the pious, those who have brought due sacrifice to Agni—
Nigh to that world approached the twin calves' mother. Let her not harm our people and our cattle.

At Lutzi, in Mashonaland, 'if a woman gives birth to twins, they are immediately destroyed. This they consider an unnatural freak on the part of a woman, and it is supposed to indicate famine or some other calamity' (The Ruined Cities of Mashonaland, by T. Bent, p. 276).

3 *Farm: kshétrâya;* literally, field.

5 *Nigh to that world:* the home of the Departed. Weber sees here a play on the words *yamínî*, the twin calves' mother, and Yamá (understood) the King of the Dead. The meaning is that the cow nearly died in giving birth to her offspring. Now, as she has been bestowed upon the priest she will be a blessing to us instead of a cause of calamity.

HYMN XXIX.

WHEN yonder kings who sit beside Yama divide among themselves the sixteenth part of hopes fulfilled,
A ram bestowed as sacrifice, white-footed, frees us from the tax.

2 He satisfies each hope and want, prevailing, present and prepared.
The wish-fulfilling ram, bestowed, white-footed, is exhaustless still.

3 He who bestows a white-hooved ram, adequate to the place he holds,
Ascends to the celestial height, the heaven where tribute is not paid to one more mighty by the weak.

4 He who bestows a white-hooved ram, adequate to the place he holds,
Offered with five cakes, lives on that, unwasting, in the Fathers' world.

5 He who bestows a white-hooved ram, adequate to the place he holds,
Offered with five cakes, lives on that, wasteless, while Sun and Moon endure.

The subject of the hymn is immunity from taxation in the next world to be purchased by the performance of a certain sacrifice on earth.

1 New-comers into the next world have to pay one-sixteenth of their *hopes fulfilled*, that is, the reward of their good works on earth, to the assessors of Yama the King of the Departed; but, if they choose, they can compound for this tax before they go thither.

2 *Prevailing:* the ram, like the bull, is an emblem of strength. Indra himself is frequently called the Ram in the Ṛigveda. *Adequate to the place he holds:* 'equivalent to the place in heaven which is assigned to the giver.'—Weber.

6 Like a refreshing draught, like sea, the mighty flood, he faileth not.
Like the two Gods whose home is one, the ram white-footed, faileth not.

7 Whose gift was this, and given to whom? Kâma to Kâma gave the gift.
Kâma is giver, Kâma is receiver. Kâma hath passed into the sea.
Through Kâma do I take thee to myself. O Kâma, this is thine.

8 May Earth receive thee as her own, and this great interspace of air.
Neither in breath and body nor in progeny may this acceptance do me harm.

HYMN XXX.

FREEDOM from hate I bring to you, concord and unanimity.
Love one another as the cow loveth the calf that she hath borne.

---

6 *Two Gods whose home is one:* the Asvins.

7 *Kâma to Kâma gives the gift:* Kâma, Desire, represents both the performer of the sacrifice, who desires a commensurate return, and the God who desires to receive it. 'The infinity of these mutual desires is represented by the immensity of *the sea* in the last pâda.'—Weber. *Through Kâma:* through, or in consequence of the giver's desire the priest accepts the victim for the God.

8 This stanza is addressed to the worshipper by the priest who hints at the risk which he himself runs in accepting for the God an offering which may not give satisfaction, and at the gratitude which his mediation deserves. See Weber, Indische Studien, XVII. pp. 305, 306; and Muir, Original Sanskrit Texts, V. p. 403.

The hymn has been translated by Ludwig, Der Rigveda, III. p. 375.

The hymn is a prayer or charm to secure love and concord in a family.

1 *The cow: aghnyâ*; explained by the Commentators as 'not to be killed;' by the St. Petersburg Dictionary as 'not, or hardly, to be conquered or overcome;' but derived by Weber from *ahan*, day, 'bright-coloured,' like *usra, usrâ, usriya, usriyâ*, steer, cow, ray, morning-light, brightness. Both in the Veda and in classical Sanskrit poetry the cow is the stock example of strong natural affection; *vatsa*, calf, meaning also 'darling' in general. See III. 13. 7.

2 One-minded with his mother let the son be loyal to his sire.
Let the wife, calm and gentle, speak words sweet as honey to her lord.

3 No brother hate his brother, no sister to sister be unkind.
Unanimous, with one intent, speak ye your speech in friendliness.

4 That spell through which Gods sever not, nor ever bear each other hate,
That spell we lay upon your home, a bond of union for the men.

5 Intelligent, submissive, rest united, friendly and kind, bearing the yoke together.
Come, speaking sweetly each one to the other. I make you one-intentioned and one-minded.

6 Let what you drink, your share of food be common: together, with one common bond I bind you.
Serve Agni, gathered round him like the spokes about the chariot nave.

7 With binding charm I make you all united, obeying one sole leader and one-minded.
Even as the Gods who watch and guard the Amrit, at morn and eve may ye be kindly-hearted.

---

6 *Band:* or, strap; the thong with which the yoke is fastened.

7 *The Amrit:* the precious nectar; or, immortality. 'Das Göttliche.'—Weber.

The hymn has been translated by Ludwig, Der Rigveda, III. p. 516; and, with annotations by Grill, Hundert Lieder, pp. 30, 116. Muir has translated stanzas 1—4 in O. S. Texts, V. 439, and Zimmer in Altindisches Leben, p. 316.

HYMN XXXI.

MAY Gods release from failing strength, thou Agni, from malignity!
I free from every evil, from decline: I compass round with life.

2 May Pavamâna free from harm, and Ṣakra from unrighteous deed.
I free from every evil, from decline: I compass round with life.

3 Tame beasts have parted from wild beasts, water and thirst have gone apart.
I free, etc.

4 Parted are heaven and earth, and paths turned to each quarter of the sky.
I free, etc.

5 Tvashṭar prepares the bridal of his daughter; then all this world of life departs and leaves him.
I free, etc.

The hymn is a charm for the recovery of a person who is dangerously ill.

1 *Decline: yákshma;* emaciating disease, phthisis, or pulmonary consumption.

2 *Pavamâna:* the deified Soma, as it flows through the purifying filter. See Ṛigveda or Sâmaveda Index. *Ṣakra:* the Mighty One; Indra.

3 In this and the two following stanzas the speaker gives instances of thorough separation illustrative of the thorough removal of the sick man's disease which the charm is to effect. Tame animals have been reclaimed and thoroughly separated from their wild congeners; heaven and earth, originally in close juxtaposition, have been separated and for ever propped apart (Ṛigveda VI. 8. 3; VIII. 83. 11); Tvashṭar and the world of life to which he gave form have been parted; and so shall it be with the sufferer and his disease.

5 The Ṛigveda, X. 17. 1, has the first hemistich of this stanza with an important variation, *sám eti*, 'comes together,' instead of *ví yâti*, 'goes apart,' '*departs and leaves him.*' Tvashṭar, who is often regarded as the chief agent in natural phenomena and the creator of the first

6 Agni combines the vital airs. The Moon is closely joined with breath.
I free, etc.

7 The Gods have lifted up with breath the Sun whose might is everywhere.
I free, etc.

8 Die not. Live with the breath of those who make and who enjoy long life.
I free, etc.

9 Die not. Stay here. Breathe with the breath of those who draw the vital air.
I free, etc.

10 Rise up with life, conjoined with life. Up, with the sap of growing plants!
I free, etc.

11 We as immortal beings have arisen with Parjanya's rain.
I free from every evil, from decline: I compass round with life.

---

forms of life, appears here to be identified with Prajâpati, the Lord of Creation, and to have prepared to marry his own daughter, which proceeding shocked and alienated the whole world. 'Prajâpati, the Lord of Creation,' says Kumârila, 'is a name of the sun, and he is called so because he protects all creatures His daughter Ushas is the dawn. And when it is said that he was in love with her, this only means that at sunrise, the sun runs after the dawn, the dawn being at the same time called the daughter of the sun, because she rises when he approaches.' See M. Müller's History of Ancient Sanskrit Literature, pp. 529, 530. The legend of Prajâpati and his daughter is related in Ṛigveda X. 61. 5—8. See Muir, Original Sanskrit Texts, IV. pp. 46, 47. Prof. Weber gives, as usual, ample information, regarding the passage in the text, in Indische Studien XVII. pp. 310—313.

6 'As stanzas 1—5 have separation from evil and consumption for their subject, so stanzas 6—10 are concerned with conjunction with vital power especially with the breath of life.'—Weber.

BOOK IV.

HYMN I.

EASTWARD at first the prayer was generated: Vena disclosed bright flashes from the summit,
Disclosed his deepest, nearest revelations, womb of the non-existent and existent.

2 Let this Queen come in front, her Father's daughter, found in the worlds for earliest generation.
For him they set this radiant vault in motion. Let them prepare warm milk for him who first would drink.

This introductory hymn is a *brahmodyam* or enunciation in designedly enigmatical language of cosmogonical and mystico-theological doctrine.

1 Prayer originated in the eastern heaven: when Vena (see II. 1.1), the early Sun, first rose in his glory he poured forth the type of human prayer, his morning song of joy and praise. The Sun is first-born of Heaven and Earth, and his birth is the type of all subsequent generation. *Non-existent:* what does not yet exist, but possesses the possibility of future existence.

2 *This Queen:* Vâk, Speech personified, the Word, the first creation and representative of Spirit, and the means of communication between men and Gods: cf. 'I am the Queen:' Ṛigveda X. 125. 3. *Her Father's daughter:* sprung from Spirit. *For earliest generation:* in Ṛigveda X. 125, 7, 8 Vâk is represented as saying that she brings forth the Father, that is, Heaven the father of all things, and that she holds together all existence. Similarly, the Logos, the Word 'was in the beginning,' and 'all things were made by him.'—St. John, I. 1. *For him:* for Heaven, the deity distinct from the material sky. *They:* the *bhûtakritas* or creators of beings: see III. 28. 1. *Warm milk:* the *gharma* or libation of heated milk, especially offered to the Asvins. *Would drink:* Prof. Ludwig derives *dhâsyáve* here from *dhâ:* 'to him who first wished to create.'

3 He who was born as his all-knowing kinsman declareth all the deities' generations.
He from the midst of prayer his prayer hath taken. On high, below, spread forth his godlike nature.

4 For he, true to the law of Earth and Heaven, established both the mighty worlds securely.
Mighty when born, he propped apart the mighty, the sky, our earthly home, and air's mid-region.

5 He from the depth hath been reborn for ever, Bṛihaspati the world's sole Lord and Ruler.
From light was born the Day with all its lustre: through this let sages live endowed with splendour.

6 The sage and poet verily advanceth the statute of that mighty God primeval.
He was born here with many more beside him: they slumbered when the foremost side was opened.

---

3 *His all-knowing kinsman:* Jâtavedas, the omniscient Agni, sprung like other Gods from Heaven and Earth. *From the midst of prayer:* Agni, identified here with Bṛihaspati, has learnt prayer or devotion from the original prayer mentioned in stanza 1.

4 *He propped apart the mighty:* heaven and earth were originally in close juxtaposition. Agni is here (as in Ṛigveda I. 67. 3) said to have separated them and fixed them in their present position. This action is also ascribed to Indra (Ṛigveda X. 89. 4; 113. 5); to Varuṇa (VII. 86.); to Soma (IX. 101. 15), and to other deities in other passages of the Ṛigveda. This old surviving nature-myth of the original union and subsequent forcible separation of Heaven and Earth is found in Greece, China, and New Zealand, as well as in India. See *Custom and Myth*:—'The Myth of Cronus.'

5 *From the depth:* of the ocean of air, from the womb of the cloud in the shape of lightning. *Bṛihaspati:* identified with Agni.

6 *They slumbered:* all the rest fell asleep, showed no energy, as soon as they were born: the sage (meaning perhaps the Sun) alone remained awake and full of active power.

7 The man who seeks the friend of Gods, Atharvan the father, and Bṛihaspati, with worship,
Crying to him, Be thou all things' creator! the wise God, self-dependent, never injures.

HYMN II.

Giver of breath, giver of strength and vigour, he whose commandment all the Gods acknowledge,
He who is Lord of this, of man and cattle:—What God shall we adore with our oblation?

2 Who by his grandeur hath become sole ruler of all the moving world that breathes and slumbers,
Whose shade is death, whose lustre makes immortal:—What God shall we adore with our oblation?

---

7 *Atharvan:* the ancient priest who is said to have been the first who obtained fire, now associated with the Gods in heaven. *The wise God:* Agni. Skilled in all lore is Agni, he whom erst Atharvan brought to life (Ṛigveda X. 21. 5).

The hymn has been translated by Ludwig, Der Rigveda, III. p. 393.

The hymn, which is taken, with variations, from Ṛigveda X. 121 an address to The Unknown God.

1 *Of this:* world, or creation. *What God: kásmai devā́ya;* cui deo Ka, kaḥ, (quis) Who? that is, the Unknown God, has been applied by Indian Commentators as a name to Prajâpati and to other Gods by a forced interpretation of the interrogative pronoun which recurs in the refrain of each verse of the hymn: Worship we Ka the God with our oblation.

2 *Whose lustre makes immortal:* or, whose shade is life eternal. 'Whose shadow is immortality, whose shadow is death.'—M. Müller. *Chhāyā́* means both 'shadow' and 'reflected light,' 'lustre.' If both senses of the word are intended here the meaning might be: Whose cold shadow (his displeasure, or ignorance of him) is death, while the knowledge of his bright glory makes his worshipper immortal. See M. M. *That breathes and slumbers:* that is, both of Gods and men.

3 To whom both hosts embattled, look with longing, and Heaven and Earth invoke him in their terror;
Whose is this path that measures out the region:—
What God shall we adore with our oblation?

4 Whose is the mighty earth and spacious heaven, and yonder ample firmament between them,
Whose is yon Sun extended in his grandeur:—
What God shall we adore with our oblation?

5 Whose, through his might, are all the Snowy Mountains, and whose, they say is Rasâ in the ocean,
The arms of whom are these celestial quarters:—
What God shall we adore with our oblation?

6 The deathless Waters, born in Law, receiving, protected all the germ in the beginning,—
Waters divine who had the God above them:—
What God shall we adore with our oblation?

7 In the beginning rose Hiraṇyagarbha, even at his birth sole Lord of all creation.
He fixt and firmly stablished earth and heaven:—
What God shall we adore with our oblation?

---

3 *The region:* mid-air.

5 *Rasâ in the ocean:* a mythical river in the sea of air flowing round earth and atmosphere.

6 *Born in Law:* produced in accordance with *ṛitá*, the fixed Order of the Universe. The reference is, not to the waters of the clouds released by Indra, but to the unfathomed depths of water that preceded distinct creation, when 'the earth was without form and void; and darkness was upon the face of the deep. And the Spirit of God moved upon the face of the waters.'—Genesis, I. 2, 3.

7 This is stanza 1 of the Ṛigveda hymn. *Hiraṇyagarbha:* literally 'the gold-germ,' 'the source of golden light,' the Sun-God 'as the great power of the universe, from which all other powers and existences, divine and earthly, are derived, a conception which is the nearest approach to the later mystical conception of Brahmâ, the creator of the world.'—Wallis, Cosmology of the Veda, p. 50.

8 In the beginning, generating offspring, the Waters brought an embryo into being;
And even as it sprang to life it had a covering of gold.

HYMN III.

THREE have gone hence and passed away, the man, the tiger, and the wolf.
Down, verily, the rivers flow, down goeth the celestial Tree, down let our foemen bend and bow.

2 On distant pathway go the wolf, on pathway most remote the thief!
On a far road speed forth the rope with teeth, and the malicious man!

---

8 This stanza is not in the Rigveda. *The embryo* which *had a covering of gold* is the Sun.

The whole hymn should be compared with the Ṛigveda hymn as translated and thoroughly discussed by Prof. Max Müller in his History of Ancient Sanskrit Literature, p. 569, and, later, in Vedic Hymns, Part I. pp. 1—13. The Ṛigveda hymn has also been translated and discussed by Muir, O. S. Texts, IV. pp. 16—18; by Mr. Wallis, Cosmology of the Ṛigveda, p. 50 sqq., and by Prof. Peterson, Hymns from the Ṛigveda. It is, of course, also to be found in all complete translations of the Ṛigveda.

The hymn is a charm against tigers, wolves, thieves, and other noxious creatures.

1 *Have gone hence:* proleptically; the anticipated result of the charm being regarded as actually obtained. *The man:* my human enemy; the thief. *The tiger:* frequently mentioned in the Atharvaveda, but apparently unknown to the seers of the Ṛigveda. *Down goeth the celestial Tree:* the meaning is not clear, and the pâda, which is metrically superfluous, may be an interpolation. Perhaps, as Prof. Ludwig suggests, the reference may be to the Tree which Varuṇa 'sustains erect in the baseless region' (Ṛigveda I. 24. 7), the World-Tree or Tree of Life of the ancient myth, whose roots grow downward from heaven.

2 *The rope with teeth:* the serpent. An Arabic proverb says: He who has been bitten by a serpent dreads a bit of rope.

3 We crush and rend to pieces both thine eyes, O Tiger, and thy jaws, and all thy twenty claws we break.

4 We break and rend the tiger first of creatures that are armed with teeth;
The robber then, and then the snake, the sorcerer, and then the wolf.

5 The thief who cometh near to-day departeth bruised and crushed to bits.
By nearest way let him be gone. Let Indra slay him with his bolt.

6 Let the beast's teeth be broken off, shivered and shattered be his ribs!
Slack be thy bowstring: downward go the wild beast that pursues the hare!

7 Open not what thou hast compressed, close not what thou hast not compressed.
Indra's and Soma's child, thou art Atharvan's tiger-crushing charm.

HYMN IV.

We dig thee from the earth, the Plant which strengthens and exalts the nerves,
The Plant which the Gandharva dug for Varuṇa whose power was lost.

---

6 *Slack be thy bowstring:* a figurative expression for: may thy power of striking thy prey be enfeebled. *The wild beast:* not the tiger, but some smaller rapacious animal.

7 The first hemistich is addressed to the animal: If thy mouth is shut, open it not; if it is open to attack thy prey do not (bite and) close it. Cf. VI. 56. 1.; X. 4. 8. The second hemistich is addressed to the amulet or charm which is to crush the tiger. *Indra's and Soma's child:* probably some poisonous herb, deriving its growth from Soma the King of Plants and its destructive power from the mightiest God Indra. The *tiger-crushing charm* owes its origin to the ancient fire-priest Atharvan, as other charms are ascribed to the Ṛishis Agastya, Asita, Gaya, and Jamadagni. See I. 14. 4; II. 32. 3.

The hymn is a charm to restore virile power.

1 *Whose power was lost:* the legend referred to is not traceable.

2 Let Ushas and let Sûrya rise, let this the speech I utter rise.
Let the strong male Prajâpati arise with manly energy.

HYMN V.

The Bull who hath a thousand horns, who rises up from out the sea,—
By him the strong and mighty one we lull the folk to rest and sleep.

2 Over the surface of the earth there breathes no wind, there looks no eye.
Lull all the women, lull the dogs to sleep, with Indra as thy friend!

3 The women sleeping in the court, lying without, or stretched on beds,
The matrons with their odorous sweets—these, one and all, we lull to sleep.

4 Each moving thing have I secured, have held and hold the eye and breath.
Each limb and member have I seized in the deep darkness of the night.

---

2 *Prajâpati:* Lord of Life; the God who presides over procreation.
For the six remaining stanzas see Appendix.

The hymn is the lullaby or sleep-charm of a lover who is secretly visiting his love.

1 This stanza, and stanzas 3, 5, 6 are taken from Ṛigveda VII. 5. 7, 8, 6, 5. *The Bull who hath a thousand horns:* the sun with his countless rays of light, whose setting brings the time of rest and sleep; or perhaps the starry heaven, as Grassmann translates, is intended; or, according to Aufrecht, the moon. In Ṛigveda I. 154. 6, the 'many-horned and restless oxen' appear to be the stars with their ever twinkling rays, which supports Grassmann's interpretation.

2 *With Indra as thy friend:* the speaker addresses the soporific plant or other charm, strengthened by Indra, which he carries with him.

3 *With their odorous sweets:* wearing garlands of fragrant flowers.

5 The man who sits, the man who walks, whoever stands and clearly sees—
Of these we closely shut the eyes, even as we closely shut this house.

6 Sleep mother, let the father sleep, sleep dog, and master of the home.
Let all her kinsmen sleep, sleep all the people who are round about.

7 With soporific charm, O Sleep, lull thou to slumber all the folk.
Let the rest sleep till break of day, I will remain awake till dawn, like Indra free from scath and harm.

HYMN VI.

THE Brâhman first was brought to life ten-headed and with faces ten.
First drinker of the Soma, he made poison ineffectual.

2 Far as the heavens and earth are spread in compass, far as the Seven Rivers are extended,
So far my spell, the antidote of poison, have I spoken hence.

---

6 *Her: asyai* here = *asyấs*. This pronoun which is the clue to the purpose of the charm is not found in the corresponding stanza of the Ṛigveda hymn, the last four verses (5, 6, 7, 8) of which are, according to Sâyaṇa, to be recited by thieves and house-breakers in pursuit of plunder.

The hymn has been translated, with notes, by Aufrecht in Indische Studien IV. pp. 340 sqq., and by Grill, Hundert Lieder, pp. 51, 118.

The hymn is a charm to make a poisoned arrow harmless.

1 Brâhmans are from their birth endowed with extraordinary and superhuman powers and privileges.

2 *Seven Rivers:* according to Prof. Max Müller, the Indus, the five rivers of the Panjâb (Vitastâ, Asiknî, Parushṇî, Vipâs, Ṣutudrí) and the Sarasvatî. Lassen and Ludwig put the Kubhâ in the place of the last-named. See Zimmer, Altindisches Leben, pp. 3 sqq. *So far:* reaching so far.

3 The strong-winged Bird Garutmân first of all, O Poison, fed on thee:
Thou didst not gripe or make him drunk: aye, thou becamest food for him.

4 Whoever with five fingers hath discharged thee from the crooked bow,
I from the shaft have charmed away the poison of the fastening band.

5 The poison have I charmed away from shaft, cement, and feathered end;
Yea, from the barb, the neck, the horn, the poison have I charmed away.

6 Feeble, O Arrow, is thy shaft, thy poison, too, hath lost its strength.
Made of a worthless tree, thy bow, O feeble one, is impotent.

7 The men who brayed it, smeared it on, they who discharged it, sent it forth,
All these are made emasculate, emasculate the poison-hill.

---

3 *Garutmân:* the celestial Bird; the Sun, who is considered as especially instrumental in counteracting the effects of poison. See Ṛigveda I. 191. 10. There is probably a play on the words *garutmân* and *gṛî*, to swallow.

4 *The fastening band:* which keeps the arrow-head in position.

5 *Cement:* or, perhaps, paint. *The horn:* arrows appear to have been of two kinds, one, the older and less effective, tipped with deer's horn, and the other pointed with *ayas*, bronze or iron. Poisoned arrows, mentioned with approbation in the Ṛigveda (VI. 75. 15), were forbidden to Kshatriyas by the Laws of Manu, that is, the ideal Code of the Mânavas.

7 *Who brayed it:* pounded the leaves and stem of the plant and prepared the poison. *The poison-hill:* the mountain where the plant grew.

8 Thy diggers are emasculate, emasculate, O Plant, art thou.

The rugged mountain that produced this poison is emasculate.

HYMN VII.

So may this water guard us on the bank of Varaṇâvatî.

Therein hath Amrit been infused: with that I ward thy poison off.

2 Weak is the poison of the East, weak is the poison of the North,

So too this poison of the South counts as a cake of curds and meal.

3 When he hath made of thee a cake, broad, steaming, swelling up with fat,

And even in hunger eaten thee, then gripe him not, thou hideous one!

4 Intoxicater! like a shaft we make thy spirit fly away,

Like a pot boiling on the fire, we with our word remove thee hence.

---

8 *O Plant:* the name of the plant from which the poison was extracted is not given. Many of the wild races who inhabit the hills and forests of India poison the arrows with which they kill tigers and other beasts of prey, and they appear to be acquainted with many jungle plants which serve their purpose.

The hymn has been translated by Ludwig, Der Rigveda, III. p. 512.

The hymn is a charm to make a poisonous plant innocuous.

1 In the first hemistich there is a play on the words *vấr*, water, *vârayấtai*, ward off, or guard, and *varaṇấvatyấm*, the locative case of *varaṇấvatî*, which appears to be the name of some river or lake on whose banks the Varaṇa (Crataeva Roxburghii), a plant used in medicine and supposed to possess magical virtues, grows abundantly. The poisonous plant was, it seems, washed in the water of the river and then boiled.

5 We set around thee with the spell as 'twere a gathered armament.
Stay quiet like a rooted tree. Dug up with mattocks, gripe not thou.

6 For coverings men have bartered thee, for skins of deer and woven cloths.
Thou art a thing of sale, O Plant. Dug up with mattocks, gripe not thou!

7 None have attained to those of old, those who wrought holy acts for you.
Let them not harm our heroes here. Therefore I set before you this.

HYMN VIII.

THE Being lays the sap of life in beings: he hath become the sovran Lord of creatures.
Death comes to this man's royal consecration: let him as King own and allow this kingdom.

2 Come forward, turn not back in scorn, strong guardian, slayer of thy foes.
Approach, O gladdener of thy friends. The Gods have blessed and strengthened thee.

---

5 *A gathered armament:* the spell acts like a body of soldiers encompassing the plant and preventing it from doing harm.

6 *For coverings: pavástais;* in Ṛigveda X. 27. 7, the word in the dual means the 'two canopies,' heaven and earth.

7 This stanza, recurring in V. 6. 2, has no meaning here, and is evidently an interpolation.

The hymn has been translated by Ludwig, Der Rigveda, III. p. 201; and, with annotations, by Grill, Hundert Lieder, pp. 28, 121.

The hymn is a benediction pronounced at the consecration of a King.

1 *The Being:* the Divine Being, meaning here the Creator. *Royal consecration:* the Râjasûya was a great sacrifice or religious ceremony performed at the coronation of a supreme sovereign by the King himself and his tributary princes. Mṛityu or the God of Death shows his approval by attending the inauguration of the new King.

2 The King is addressed.

3 All waited on him as he came to meet them. He self-resplendent moves endued with glory.
That is the royal hero's lofty nature: he, manifold, hath gained immortal powers.

4 Stride forth to heaven's broad regions, thou, a tiger on a tiger's skin.
Let all the people long for thee. Let heavenly floods be rich in milk.

5 Heaven's waters joyous in their milk, the waters of middle air, and those that earth containeth—
I with the gathered power and might of all these waters sprinkle thee.

6 The heavenly waters rich in milk have sprinkled thee with power and might
To be the gladdener of thy friends. May Savitar so fashion thee.

7 These, compassing the tiger, rouse the lion to great joy and bliss.
As strong floods purify the standing ocean, so men adorn the leopard in the waters.

---

4 *A tiger:* the type, in the Atharva-veda, of heroic strength and courage. A *tiger's skin:* stepping on a tiger's skin, symbolical of assuming regal powers, was an important part of the ceremony.

5 *Milk:* the blessings which they pour down.

6 *Savitar:* the Sun as the great vivifier and promoter of all growth.

7 *These:* the priests who conduct the ceremony. *The tiger . . . the lion . . . the leopard:* the strong and valiant King. *In the waters:* with which he is sprinkled in the Abhisheka or Sprinkling Ceremony wherewith the King is consecrated.

The hymn has been translated by Ludwig, Der Rigveda, III. p. 458; and by Zimmer, Altindisches Leben, p. 213.

HYMN IX.

APPROACH! thou art the mountain's eye, the living thing that saveth us;
A gift bestowed by all the Gods, yea, the defence that guardeth life.

2 Thou art the safeguard of the men, thou art the safeguard of the kine,
Thou standest ready to protect the horses that are fleet of foot.

3 Thou, also, Salve! art a defence that rends and crushes sorcerers.
Thou knowest, too, of Amrit, thou art the delight of all who live, a jaundice-curing balm art thou.

4 Whomso thou creepest over, Salve! member by member, joint by joint,
From him, like some strong arbiter of strife, thou banishest decline.

5 No imprecation reaches him, no magic, no tormenting fiend,
O Salve, Vishkandha seizes not the man who carries thee about.

6 From lying speech, from evil dream, from wicked act and sinfulness,
From hostile and malignant eye,—from these, O Salve, protect us well.

The hymn is a charm, addressed to a precious Ointment, for protection from all sorts of evil and for the acquisition of wealth.

1 *Eye:* the precious treasure. Instead of *ákaham* of the text, which mars the metre, several MSS. have *akshyam* = *akshium*, 'belonging to the eye,' 'the hill's eye-salve;' but, as Dr. Grill observes, such a limitation is inconsistent with the powers attributed to the ointment, and it would be better to read *akshayám* or *aksharám*, 'the imperishable treasure.'

3 *Jaundice-curing balm: haritabheshajám;* see I. 22.

4 *Decline:* the emaciating disease called Yakshma: see II. 10. 5; 33.

5 *Vishkandha:* rheumatism; see I. 16. 3.

6 *Malignant eye:* see II. 7. 5.

7 I, knowing this, O Salve, will speak the very truth and not a lie:
May I obtain both horse and ox, may I obtain thy life, O man.

8 Three are the slaves that serve the Salve, Fever, Consumption, and the Snake.
Thy father is the loftiest of mountains, named the Triple-peaked.

9 Sprung from the Snowy Mountain's side, this Ointment of the Three-peaked hill
Crushes and rends all sorcerers and every witch and sorceress.

10 If thou art from the Three-peaked hill or hast thy name from Yamunâ,
These names are both auspicious: by these two protect thou us, O Salve!

HYMN X.

Child of the wind and firmament, sprung from the lightning and the light,
May this the gold-born Shell that bears the pearl preserve us from distress.

---

7 The second hemistich, which seems out of place here, is taken, with a variation, from Rigveda X. 97. 4: 'Steed, cow, and garment may I gain, win back thy vital breath, O man:' that is, May I restore thee to life, and receive a horse, etc., as my fee for curing you.

8 *Fever*: see I. 25. 2. *Consumption*: *balâsah*: apparently a kind of *yakshma*; a wasting disease; consumptive expectoration: see Zimmer, Altindisches Leben, p. 385. *Triple-peaked*: *trikakúd*; a high mountain in the Himâlaya; the modern Trikûṭa: see Zimmer A. I. L. p. 30.

10 *Yamunâ*: the river Jamunâ, commonly called Jumna, regarded in mythology as the twin sister of Yama. *Both auspicious*: both mountain and river being endowed with special sanctity.

The hymn has been translated by Ludwig, Der Rigveda, III. p. 507; and by Grill, with annotations, Hundert Lieder, pp. 35, 123.

The hymn is a charm accompanying investiture with a protective amulet of shell.

1 As is usual in addresses to amulets, the origin of the shell is glorified. It was produced from the rain that fell into the sea from the

2 Shell that wast born from out the sea, set at the head of things that shine!
With thee we slay the Râkshasas and overcome voracious fiends.

3 We stay disease and indigence, and chase Sadânvâs with the Shell.
May the all-healing Shell that bears the pearl preserve us from distress.

4 Born in the heaven, sprung from the sea, brought to us hither from the flood,
This gold-born Shell shall be to us an amulet to lengthen life.

5 From ocean sprang the Amulet, from Vṛitra sprang the Lord of Day:
May this protect us round about from shaft of God and Asura.

6 Peerless 'mid golden ornaments art thou: from Soma wast thou born.
Thou gleamest on the quiver, thou art beautiful upon the car: may it prolong our days of life!

---

windy sky, and the iridescent hues of its lining came from the bright flashes of the lightning. *Gold-born:* golden, or excellent by nature. Somewhat similar is the belief mentioned by Dioscorides and Pliny that pearls are formed by drops of rain falling into the oyster-shells when open. The Persians also say that drops of spring rain falling into the pearl-oyster turn into precious pearls.

3 *Sadânvâs:* troublesome noisy pests: see II. 14. 1.

4 *From the flood: sindhutás;* or, from Sindhu, the Indus.

5 *From Vṛitra sprang the Lord of Day:* as the Sun shone out when Vṛitra, the huge cloud, was shattered, so the shell with its bright treasure sprang from the dark depths of the sea. *Asura:* hostile demon.

6 *From Soma wast thou born:* indirectly; libations of Soma juice cause the rain to fall, and the rain produces the shell. *On the car:* in the Ṛigveda the chariot of the Sun is decked with pearl (I. 35. 4); and horses' trappings are sometimes adorned with it (VII. 18. 23, and X. 68. 11). *May it prolong:* this abrupt change of the personal pronoun is not uncommon in the Veda.

7 Bone of the Gods became the pearl's shell-mother: endowed with soul it moveth in the waters.
I bind this on thee for life, strength, and vigour, for long life lasting through a hundred autumns. May the pearl's mother keep and guard thee safely!

HYMN XI.

The Bull supports the wide-spread earth and heaven. The Bull supports the spacious air between them.
The Bull supports the sky's six spacious regions: the universal world hath he pervaded.

2 The Bull is Indra: o'er the beasts he watches. He, Ṣakra, measures out three several pathways.
He, milking out the worlds, the past, the future, discharges all the Gods' eternal duties.

3 Being produced among mankind as Indra, the Caldron works heated and brightly glowing.
Let him not, with good sons, pass off in vapour who hath not eaten of the Ox with knowledge.

---

7 *Bone of the Gods:* another fanciful origin of the shell containing the pearl or, rather, the mother-of-pearl or nacre.

The hymn has been translated by Ludwig, Der Rigveda, III. p. 462; and, with annotations, by Grill, Hundert Lieder, pp. 36, 124.

The hymn is a glorification of the Gharma or Caldron in which the libation of hot milk, offered especially to the Aṣvins, is prepared.

1 *Six spacious regions:* the four quarters of the heavens with the zenith and the nadir.

2 *O'er the beasts:* in the most extended sense of the word, meaning perhaps all animals. *Ṣakra:* or mighty; a common epithet or appellation of Indra. *Three several pathways:* to earth, firmament, and highest heaven.

3 *As Indra:* the Caldron is symbolically called Indra on account of the extraordinary efficacy of the libation which is prepared in it. *With good sons: suprajās;* Ludwig reads *suprayās*, 'an able goer.' *The Ox:* or Bull; here meaning the Caldron or its contents. The hemistich is unintelligible to me.

4 The Ox pours milk out in the world of virtue: in earliest time, he, Pavamâna, swells it.
Parjanya is the stream, Maruts his udder, sacrifice is the milk, the meed his milking.

5 That which not sacrifice nor sacrificer, not giver nor receiver rules and governs,
All-winning, all-supporting, all-effecting,—which of all quadrupeds, tell us! is the Caldron?

6 May we, fame-seekers, reach the world of virtue by service of the Gharma and through fervour,
Whereby the Gods went up to heaven, the centre of life eternal, having left the body.

7 Prajâpati, supreme and sovran ruler, Indra by form and by his shoulder Agni,
Came to Viṣvânara, came to all men's Bullock: he firmly fortified and held securely.

8 The middle of the Bullock's neck, there where the shoulder-bar is placed,
Extends as far to east of him as that is settled to the west.

---

4 *The Ox:* the Caldron. *Pavamâna:* the deified Soma juice as it passes through the purifying filter. *Parjanya:* the deity of the rain-cloud. See I. 2. 1. *The meed:* the honorarium given to the officiating priests by the institutor of a sacrifice. The word (*dákshiṇâ*) means primarily a good cow, the original sacrificial fee.

5 *Of all quadrupeds:* the Caldron had, perhaps, four short legs to support it when placed on the ground. The answer to the question is, the ox.

6 *Service of the Gharma:* the Pravargya ceremony, in which the Gharma or heated libation was offered to the Gods. *Through fervour: tápasâ;* through ardent religious devotion. The Gods are said in other passages to have obtained their immortality through Agni or Soma. See Ṛigveda V. 3. 4; VI. 7. 4; VII. 13. 2; IX. 106. 8.

7 *Shoulder:* his power of bearing; Agni being the general bearer of oblations to the Gods. *Viṣvânara:* the benefactor of all men.

9 He whosoever knows the seven exhaustless pourings of the Ox,
Wins himself offspring and the world: the great Seven Ṛishis know this well.

10 With feet subduing weariness, with legs extracting freshening draughts,
Through toil the plougher and the Ox approach the honeyed beverage.

11 Assigned are these twelve nights, they say, as holy to Prajâpati:
Whoever knows their proper prayer performs the service of the Ox.

12 At evening he is milked, is milked at early morn, is milked at noon.
We know that streams of milk that flow from him are inexhaustible.

HYMN XII.

THOU art the healer, making whole, the healer of the broken bone:
Make thou this whole, Arundhatî!

---

9 *Pourings of the Ox:* meaning, apparently, the libations poured from the Caldron, and the consequent blessings. *Seven Rishis:* Gotama, Bharadvâja, Visvâmitra, Jamadagni, Vasishṭha, Kaṣyapa, and Atri, according to the Ṣatapatha-Brâhmaṇa. Other names are given by other authorities.

10 *The plougher and the Ox:* the priest and the caldron. *Honeyed beverage:* the sweet libation.

12 *Is milked:* the reference is to the three daily sacrifices.

Stanzas 7—12 are purposely obscure, and cannot be intelligibly translated.

The first six stanzas have been translated by Muir, O. S. Texts, V. pp. 399 and 361, and by Ludwig, Der Rigveda, III. p. 534.

The hymn is a charm, addressed to a Plant, to mend a broken bone.

1 *The healer: róhaṇî;* literally, causing to grow (again). *Arundhatî:* a climbing plant, not identified; probably a variety of Convolvulus or bindweed which is to bind fast the injured limb as it binds the tree round which it grows.

2 Whatever bone of thine within thy body hath been wrenched or cracked,
May Dhâtar set it properly, and join together limb by limb.

3 With marrow be thy marrow joined, thy limb united with the limb.
Let what hath fallen of thy flesh, and the bone also, grow again.

4 Let marrow close with marrow, let skin grow united with the skin.
Let blood and bone grow strong in thee, flesh grow together with the flesh.

5 Join thou together hair with hair, join thou together skin with skin.
Let blood and bone grow strong in thee. Unite the broken part, O Plant.

6 Arise, advance, speed forth: the car hath goodly fellies, naves, and wheels.
Stand up erect upon thy feet.

7 If he be torn and shattered, having fallen into a pit, or a cast stone have struck him,
Let the skilled leech join limb with limb, as 'twere the portions of a car.

HYMN XIII.

Gods, raise again the man whom ye, O Gods, have humbled and brought low.

---

2 *Dhâtar*: the God who ordains, establishes, fixes, and preserves.

6 This and the following stanza seem to be out of place here. *The skilled leech*: *ṛibhús*; clever, expert, a skilful workman, meaning here a surgeon. Or the meaning may be: Let him (the God) join limb with limb as joins a smith the portions of a car.

The hymn has been translated by Ludwig, Der Rigveda, III. p. 508; and by Grill, with annotations, Hundert Lieder, pp. 18, 125.

Ye Gods, restore to life again, him, Gods! who hath committed sin.

2 Here these two winds are blowing far as Sindhu from a distant land.
May one breathe energy to thee, the other blow thy fault away.

3 Hither, O Wind, blow healing balm, blow every fault away, thou Wind!
For thou who hast all medicine comest as envoy of the Gods.

4 May the Gods keep and save this man, the Maruts' host deliver him.
All things that be deliver him that he be freed from his offence.

5 I am come nigh to thee with balms to give thee rest and keep thee safe.
I bring thee mighty strength, I drive thy wasting malady away.

6 Felicitous is this my hand, yet more felicitous is this.
This hand contains all healing balms, and this makes whole with gentle touch.

7 The tongue that leads the voice precedes. Then with our tenfold-branching hands,
With these two healers of disease, we stroke thee with a soft caress.

The hymn, taken, with the exception of stanza 6, from Ṛigveda X. 137, is a charm to restore a sick man to health.

1 *Who hath committed sin:* sickness being regarded as the consequence and punishment of sin.

2 *Sindhu:* the Indus.

4 *Offence:* and consequent disease.

5 *Wasting malady:* yakshma, pulmonary consumption.

6 Taken from Ṛigveda X. 60. 12. *More felicitous is this:* my other hand, probably the right. *With gentle touch:* with light friction, laying-on of hands, or hypnotizing passes.

7 *The tongue:* the charm is uttered first, and then the hands are used to relieve the sufferer and to restore him to health.

HYMN XIV.

THE Goat was verily produced from Agni. Through sorrow he beheld, at first, his father.
Through him at first the Gods attained to godhead, and, meet for sacrifices, were exalted.

2 Bearing in hands seethed viands, go with Agni to the cope of heaven.
Reaching the sky that touches heaven, mix with the company of Gods.

3 From earth's high ridge to middle air I mounted, and from mid-air ascended up to heaven.
From the high pitch of heaven's cope I came into the world of light.

4 Mounting the sky they look not round; they rise to heaven through both the worlds,
Sages who paid the sacrifice that pours its streams on every side.

5 First among all the deities, come forward, thou who art eye of Gods and men, O Agni.
Imploring, and accordant with the Bhṛigus, to heaven in safety go the sacrificers!

The hymn is an accompaniment to a sacrifice of a he-goat.

1 The goat as a favourite sacrificial victim is regarded as the offspring of the fire that consumes him and which therefore he looks upon with sorrow. In Ṛigveda I. 162. 4 the goat is called 'the share of Pûshan,' that is, according to Sâyaṇa, of Agni; and in Ṛigveda X. 16. 4 Agni is addressed with the words 'Thy portion is the goat' (differently rendered, however, by Muir and other scholars). *Through him:* through Agni.

2 The institutors of sacrifice are exhorted to win their way to heaven by the performance of religious ceremonies on earth.

3 *Middle air: antáriksham;* or, sky. *Heaven: dívam;* above the sky. *Heaven's cope: divó nā́kas;* a region still higher than the heaven. *The world of light: svarjyótis;* the highest realm of all; the abode of the Sun; the empyrean. See M. Müller, Vedic Hymns, Part I. p. 9; and Zimmer, A. I. Leben, p. 358.

5 *The Bhṛigus:* the descendants of the Ṛishi Bhṛigu, the seer of many of the hymns of the Atharva-veda.

6 With milk and butter I anoint the mighty, celestial Goat, strong-winged, and full of juices.
Through him will we attain the world of virtue, ascending to the loftiest cope, to heaven.

7 Set the Goat's head toward the eastern region, and turn his right side to the southern quarter.
His hinder part turn to the western quarter, and set his left side to the northern region.

8 Set the Goat's backbone upmost in the zenith, and lay his belly downward in the nadir; set his mid-portion in mid-air between them.

9 O'er the dressed Goat lay a dressed skin to robe him prepared, in perfect form, with all his members.
Rise upward to the loftiest vault of heaven: with thy four feet stand firmly in the regions.

HYMN XV.

Let all the misty regions fly together, let all the rain-clouds, sped by wind, assemble.
Let waters satisfy the earth, the voices of the great mist-enveloped Bull who roareth.

2 Let them show forth, the strong, the bounteous Maruts: let plants and shrubs be hung with drops of moisture.
Let floods of rain refresh the ground with gladness, and herbs spring various with each form and colour.

---

6 *Celestial:* regarded as divine as soon as he is selected for sacrifice. *Strong-winged:* prepared to pass rapidly to heaven.

9 In the second hemistich the victim is addressed. The sacrificed animal is immediately transported to heaven. Similarly the Horse is addressed (Rigveda I. 162. 21): 'No, here thou diest not, thou art not injured: by easy paths unto the Gods thou goest.' A detailed account of the Sacrifice of the Goat is given in Atharva-veda IX. 5.

The hymn is a prayer or charm to hasten the coming of the periodical Rains.

1 *Bull:* Parjanya: the God of the thunderous rain-cloud. See I. 2. 1.

3 Cause us who sing to see the gathering vapours: out burst in many a place the rush of waters!
Let floods of rain refresh the ground with gladness; and herbs spring various with each form and colour.

4 Apart, Parjanya! let the troops of Maruts, roaring, swell the song.
Let pouring torrents of the rain that raineth rain upon the earth.

5 Up from the sea lift your dread might, ye Maruts: as light and splendour, send the vapour upward!
Let waters satisfy the earth, the voices of the great mist-enveloped Bull who roareth.

6 Roar, thunder, set the sea in agitation, bedew the ground with thy sweet rain, Parjanya!
Send plenteous showers on him who seeketh shelter, and let the owner of lean kine go homeward.

7 Let the boon Maruts, let the springs and coiling serpents tend you well.
Urged by the Maruts let the clouds pour down their rain upon the earth.

8 Let lightning flash on every side: from all the regions blow the winds!
Urged by the Maruts let the clouds pour down their rain upon the earth.

9 May waters, lightning, cloud, and rain, boon springs and serpents tend you well.
Urged by the Maruts let the clouds pour down their rain upon the earth.

---

4 *Of the rain that raineth rain: varshásya várshato várshantu.*

6 *The owner of lean kine:* who, as grass will immediately spring up, need no longer search for pasture for his cattle.

7 *The springs:* the fountains of heaven. *Coiling serpents: ajagarā́s:* literally, 'goat-swallowers;' pythons; long fantastic-shaped masses of cloud.

10 May he who hath become the plants' high regent, suiting our bodies, Agni of the Waters,
May Jâtavedas send us rain from heaven, Amrit and vital breath to earthly creatures.

11 Sending up waters from the flood and ocean Prajâpati move the sea to agitation!
Forth flow the moisture of the vigorous stallion! With this thy roar of thunder come thou hither,

12 Our Father, Lord divine pouring the torrents. Let the streams breathe, O Varuṇa, of the waters.
Pour the floods down: along the brooks and channels let frogs with speckled arms send out their voices.

13 They who lay quiet for a year, the Brâhmans who fulfil their vows,
The frogs, have lifted up their voice, the voice Parjanya hath inspired.

14 Speak forth a welcome, female frog! Do thou, O frog, accost the rain.
Stretch thy four feet apart, and swim, swim in the middle of the lake.

---

10 *The plants' high regent:* 'He (Agni) ripens plants of every form and nature' (Ṛigveda X. 88. 10). *Of the Waters:* Agni is called *apâm-napât*, Offspring of the Waters, as being born in the shape of lightning from the watery clouds.

11 *The vigorous stallion:* the fertilizing rain-cloud. Similarly: 'Send down for us the rain of heaven, ye Maruts, and let the stallion's streams descend in torrents' (Ṛigveda V. 83. 6). The last pâda of this stanza 11 and the first pâda of that which follows make up the second hemistich of the Ṛigveda stanza referred to, Parjanya being the God addressed.

13 The stanza is taken from Ṛigveda VII. 103. 1. In that hymn the frogs rejoicing in the fall of the periodical Rains after the long drought are represented as Brâhmans busily employed in the performance of religious ceremonies.

15 Khaṇvakhâ, ho! Khaimakhâ, ho! Thou in the middle, Tadurî!
Fathers, enjoy the rain from one who strives to win the Maruts' heart.

16 Lift up the mighty cask and pour down water: let the wind blow, and lightnings flash around us.
Let sacrifice be paid, and, widely scattered, let herbs and plants be full of joy and gladness.

HYMN XVI.

The mighty Ruler of these worlds beholds as though from close at hand
The man who thinks he acts by stealth: all this the Gods perceive and know.

2 If a man stands or walks or moves in secret, goes to his lying-down or his uprising,
What two men whisper as they sit together, King Varuṇa knows: he as the third is present.

3 This earth, too, is King Varuṇa's possession, and the high heaven whose ends are far asunder.
The loins of Varuṇa are both the oceans, and this small drop of water, too, contains him.

---

15 *Khaṇvakhâ, Khaimukhâ* (onomatopoetic words), and *Tadurî* are names of frogs.

16 The first pâda is taken from Ṛigveda V. 83. 8. *Cask:* or, pail; meaning the watery cloud.

The hymn celebrates the omnipresence and omniscience of Varuṇa, the moral Governor of the world; and concludes with an imprecation on an enemy.

2 *His lying-down or his uprising:* cf. 'Thou knowest my downsitting And mine uprising . . . Thou compassest my path And my lying down.'—Psalm 139. 2, 3.

3 *Both the oceans:* the sea of air and the terrestrial ocean; the waters above the firmament and the waters under the firmament.

4 If one should flee afar beyond the heaven, King Varuṇa would still be round about him.
Proceeding hither from the sky his envoys look, thousand-eyed, over the earth beneath them.

5 All this the royal Varuṇa beholdeth, all between heaven and earth and all beyond them.
The twinklings of men's eyelids hath he counted. As one who plays throws dice he settles all things.

6 Those fatal snares of thine which stand extended, threefold, O Varuṇa, seven by seven,
May they all catch the man who tells a falsehood, and pass unharmed the man whose words are truthful.

7 Varuṇa, snare him with a hundred nooses! Man's watcher! let not him who lies escape thee.
There let the villain sit with hanging belly and bandaged like a cask whose hoops are broken.

---

4 *His envoys:* Varuṇa's spies, messengers, or angels are perhaps the other Âdityas. See Ṛigveda I. 25. 13, and VII. 87. 3.

7 *Snare him:* mine enemy. *Like a cask:* swollen with dropsy and bandaged round as a cask or chest is bound with hoops or bands. Dropsy, or some similar disease seems to have been especially regarded as a punishment sent by Varuṇa. So a sufferer addresses Varuṇa (Ṛigveda VII. 89. 2) :—'When . . . I move along, tremulous like a wind-blown skin, Have mercy, spare me, mighty Lord!' See Zimmer, A. I. Leben, p. 392.

I borrow Dr. Muir's translation of Professor Roth's remarks on this hymn :—

'There is no hymn in the whole Vedic literature which expresses the divine omniscience in such forcible terms as this; and yet this beautiful description has been degraded into an introduction to an imprecation. But in this, as in many other passages of this Veda, it is natural to conjecture that existing fragments of older hymns have been used to deck out magical formulas. The first five or even six verses of this hymn might be regarded as a fragment of this sort.'

The hymn has been translated, wholly or in part—stanzas 1—6—, by von Roth, Abhandlung über den Atharva-veda, p. 29; by Muir, O. S. Texts, V. 63; by Kaegi, Der Rigveda, 89; by Max Müller, Chips from a German Workshop, I. 41; by Ludwig, Der Rigveda, III. p. 388; and by Grill, with annotations, Hundert Lieder, pp. 32. 126.

8 Varuṇa sends, and drives away, diseases: Varuṇa is both native and a stranger,
Varuṇa is celestial and is human.

9 I bind and hold thee fast with all these nooses, thou son of such a man and such a mother.
All these do I assign thee as thy portion.

HYMN XVII.

We seize and hold thee, Conquering One! the queen of medicines that heal.
O Plant, I have endowed thee with a hundred powers for every man.

2 Still conquering, banishing the curse, mighty, with thy reverted bloom,
Thee and all Plants have I invoked: Hence let it save us! was my prayer.

3 She who hath cursed us with a curse, or hath conceived a murderous sin,
Or seized our son to take his blood, may she devour the child she bare.

4 What magic they have wrought for thee in dish unbaked or burnt dark-red,
What they have wrought in flesh undressed,—conquer the sorcerers therewith.

5 Ill dream and wretchedness of life, Râkshasa, monster, stingy hags,
All the she-fiends of evil name and voice, we drive away from us.

The hymn is a charm, addressed to a plant endowed with magical virtues, to secure immunity from various kinds of evil, and restoration of health.

1 *Conquering One:* the magical plant is addressed.

2 *With thy reverted bloom:* see stanza 6, note.

3 The stanza is repeated from I. 28. 3.

5 *Stingy hags:* Arâyîs; see I. 28. 4, note.

6 Death caused by famine, caused by thirst, failure of children, loss of kine,
With thee, O Apâmârga, all this ill we cleanse and wipe away.

7 Death caused by thirst, death caused by stress of hunger, loss at play with dice,
All this, O Apâmârga, with thine aid we cleanse and wipe away.

8 The Apâmârga is alone the sovran of all Plants that grow.
With this we wipe away whate'er hath fallen on thee : go in health!

HYMN XVIII.

The moonlight equalleth the sun, night is the rival of the day.
I make effectual power my help : let magic arts be impotent.

2 Gods! if one make and bring a spell on some man's house who knows it not,
Close as the calf that sucks the cow may it revert and cling to him.

---

6 *Apâmârga :* (from *mṛij*, to cleanse or wipe, with *apa + â*) Achyranthes Aspera, a biennial plant frequently used in incantations, in medicine, in washing linen, and in sacrifices, and still believed to have the power of making men proof against the stings of scorpions. It is called also *parâkpushpî*, *pratyakpushpî*, and *pratyakparṇî* from the reverted direction of the growth of its leaves, flowers, and fruit. See IV. 19. 4, 7; VI. 129. 3; and VII. 65. 1.

7 *We cleanse and wipe away : apa mṛijmâhe ;* see note on stanza 6.

8 *On thee ;* some sick man is addressed.

The hymn has been translated by Zimmer, A. I. Leben, p. 66 ; and, with annotations, by Grill, Hundert Lieder, pp. 37, 130.

The hymn is a counter-charm against the magical incantations of others.

1 The meaning is : lighted by this full moon which makes the night as bright as day, I gather a plant whose efficacy is undoubted, which shall counteract the magical practices of malignant fiends and sorcerers.

2 *May it revert :* an allusion to the reverted leaves of the plant used in the incantation : see IV. 17. 6, note.

3 When one puts poison in a dish of unbaked clay to kill a man,
It cracks when set upon the fire with the sharp sound of many stones.

4 Endowed with thousand powers! adjure the bald and those with necks awry.
Back to its author turn the spell like a dear damsel to her friend!

5 I with this Plant have ruined all malignant powers of witchery,
The spell which they have laid upon thy field, thy cattle, or thy men.

6 No power had he who wrought the spell: he hurt his foot, he broke his toe.
His act hath brought us happiness and pain and sorrow to himself.

7 Let Apâmârga sweep away chronic disease and every curse,
Sweep sorceresses clean away, and all malignant stingy hags.

8 Sweep thou away the sorcerers, all stingy fiendish hags away.
All this, O Apâmârga, with thine aid we wipe away from us.

HYMN XIX.

Thou breakest ties of kith and kin, thou causest, too, relationship:

---

4 *Endowed with thousand powers!*: the plant is addressed. *The bald and those with necks awry:* hairless goblins whose heads are twisted round.

7 *Apâmârga:* the magical plant (Achyranthes Aspera): see IV. 17. 6. *Chronic disease; kshetriyá;* see II. 8. 1.

The hymn has been translated, with annotations, by Grill, Hundert Lieder, pp. 25, 131.

The hymn is a charm, like the preceding hymn, to counteract the incantations of enemies, and to secure general protection for the speaker.

1 *Thou:* the plant Apâmârga (see IV. 17. 6) is addressed.

So bruise the sorcerer's offspring, like a reed that groweth in the Rains.

2 Thou hast been blessed with blessing by the Brâhman, Kaṇva Nârshada.
Thou fliest like a flashing dart: there is no fear or danger, Plant! within the limit of thy range.

3 Illumining, as 'twere, with light, thou movest at the head of plants.
The saviour of the simple man art thou, and slayer of the fiends.

4 As once when time began the Gods with thee expelled the Asuras,
Even thence, O Plant, wast thou produced as one who wipes and sweeps away.

5 Thy father's name was Cleaver. Thou with thousand branches cleavest all.
Do thou, turned backward, cleave and rend the man who treateth us as foes.

6 The evil sprang from earth; it mounts to heaven and spreads to vast extent.
Reverted, shaking him with might, thence on its maker let it fall.

---

2 *Kaṇva Nârshada:* a Ṛishi, son of Nṛishad. The celebrated Kaṇva of the Ṛigveda was the son of Ghora. The two name-words, which mar the metre of the hemistich, appear, as Grill observes, to be an interpolated gloss.

4 *Expelled the Asuras:* Indra's victory over the Asuras or hostile demons is attributed to the strengthening power of another plant, Pâṭâ, in II. 27. 4. *One who wipes and sweeps away: apâmârgás;* used here as an appellative.

5 *With thousand branches:* the virtues and powers ascribed to a plant are usually in proportion to the abundance of its roots or branches.

Turned backward: having reverted or retrofracted leaves and flowers: see IV. 17. 6, note.

6 *The evil:* the spell which the charm is to counteract.

7 For thou hast grown reverted, and turned backward also is thy fruit.
Remove all curses far from me, keep most remote the stroke of death.

8 Preserve me with a hundred, yea, protect me with a thousand aids.
May mighty Indra, Lord of Plants! give store of strength and power to thee.

HYMN XX.

It sees in front, it sees behind, it sees afar away, it sees
The sky, the firmament, and earth: all this, O Goddess, it beholds.

2 Through thee, O godlike Plant, may I behold all creatures that exist,
Three several heavens, three several earths, and these six regions one by one.

---

8 *Thousand aids:* with reference to the thousand branches of the plant (stanza 5).

The hymn has been translated, with annotations, by Grill, Hundert Lieder, pp. 34, 132.

The hymn is a charm, addressed to a magical plant, for the acquisition of superhuman powers of sight.

1 *It:* the magical plant. *O Goddess:* the divine plant is directly addressed, and also spoken of in the third person. The plant is said by Dârila to be the *sadampushpâ* (Semperflorens, Ever-blooming) not yet identified. Its virtues resemble those attributed in England to Euphrasy or Eyebright, the plant with which, together with Rue and three drops from the well of Life , the Archangel Michael 'purged the visual nerve' of Adam (Paradise Lost, XI. 414), and enabled him to look into the distant future.

2 *Three several heavens:* the world is divided into earth, sky, and heaven; and each of these, again, is frequently spoken of in the Ṛigveda as threefold. See Wallis, Cosmology of the Ṛigveda, p. 114. *Six regions:* the four quarters of the heavens with the zenith and the nadir.

3 The pupil, verily, art thou of that celestial Eagle's eye.
On earth hast thou alighted as a weary woman seeks her couch.

4 The God who hath a thousand eyes give me this Plant in my right hand!
I look on every one therewith, each Ṣûdra and each Âryan man.

5 Make manifest the forms of things; hide not their essences from sight.
And, thou who hast a thousand eyes, look the Kimîdins in the face.

6 Make me see Yâtudhânas, make thou Yâtudhânîs visible.
Make me see all Piṣâchas. With this prayer, O Plant, I hold thee fast.

7 Thou art the sight of Kaṣyapa and of the hound who hath four eyes.
Make the Piṣâcha manifest as Sûrya when he rides at noon.

---

3 The *celestial Eagle* is Garutmân, the Sun. *Couch: vahyâm* (from *vah*, to carry); originally, a portable bed or litter.

4 *The God who hath a thousand eyes:* Indra; as he is chief Regent of the atmosphere, his countless eyes may be the stars. *Ṣûdra and Âryan:* men of the labouring class, and men of the three higher classes, that is Brâhmans (the priestly caste), Râjanyas or Kshatriyas (the regal and military caste), and Vaiṣyas (husbandmen and tradesmen). The four castes are mentioned only once in the Ṛigveda (X. 90. 12). See Muir, O. S. Texts, II. 368; Ludwig, Der Rigveda, III. 212; Zimmer, Altindisches Leben, pp. 117 sqq., 204, 216, 435.

5 *Kimîdins:* see I. 7. 1.

6 *Yâtudhânas...Yâtudhânîs:* see I. 7. 1; 8. 1. *Piṣâchas:* see I. 16. 3.

7 *Kaṣyapa:* one of a class of semi-divine spirits or genii connected with or regulating the course of the Sun. *Four eyes:* that is, probably, two eyes with a large spot above each. Cf. 'And those two dogs of thine, Yama! the watchers, four-eyed, who look on men and guard the pathway' (Ṛigveda X. 14. 11). The substantive in the text is feminine, *ṣunyấs*, bitch.

8 Kimîdin, Yâtudhâna from their hiding-places have I dragged.
I look on every one with this, Ṣûdra and Âryan man alike.

9 Make that Piṣâcha visible, the fiend who flies in middle air,
The fiend who glides across the sky, and him who deems the earth his help.

HYMN XXI.

The kine have come and brought good fortune: let them rest in the cow-pen and be happy near us.
Here let them stay prolific, many-coloured, and yield through many morns their milk for Indra.

2 Indra aids him who offers sacrifice and praise: he takes not what is his, and gives him more thereto.
Increasing ever more and ever more his wealth, he makes the pious dwell within unbroken bounds.

3 These are ne'er lost, no robber ever injures them: no evil-minded foe attempts to harass them.
The master of the kine lives a long life with these, the Cows whereby he pours his gifts and serves the Gods.

---

8 *With this: téna*, masculine, meaning, not directly the plant, but the God or divine power within it.

9 *Who flies in middle air:* as witches in Europe were popularly believed to do. *Deems the earth his help:* and is satisfied with holes and caverns as hiding-places.

The hymn has been translated by Ludwig, Der Rigveda, III. p. 525, and, with annotations, by Grill, Hundert Lieder, pp. 2, 133.

The hymn, taken with slight variations from Ṛigveda VI. 28. 1—7, is a glorification and benediction addressed to Cows.

3 *These are ne'er lost:* according to Sâyaṇa, the indicative mood here has an imperative force: let them not be lost, let not the robber assail them.

4 The charger with his dusty brow o'ertakes them not, and never to the shambles do they take their way.
These Cows, the cattle of the pious worshipper, roam over wide-spread pasture where no danger is.

5 To me the Cows seem Bhaga, they seem Indra, they seem a portion of the first-poured Soma.
These present Cows, they, O ye men, are Indra. I long for Indra with my heart and spirit.

6 O Cows, ye fatten e'en the worn and wasted, and make the unlovely beautiful to look on.
Prosper my home, ye with auspicious voices! Your power is magnified in our assemblies.

7 In goodly pasturage, bright-hued, prolific, drinking pure water at fair drinking-places,
Never be thief or sinful man your master, and may the dart of Rudra still avoid you!

HYMN XXII.

Exalt and strengthen this my Prince, O Indra. Make him sole lord and leader of the people.
Scatter his foes, deliver all his rivals into his hand in struggles for precedence.

2 Give him a share in village, kine, and horses, and leave his enemy without a portion.

---

4 *The charger......o'ertakes them not:* they are not, or, according to Sâyaṇa, let them not be, carried off in predatory incursions.

5 The owner of the cows regards them as the deities Bhaga and Indra, the representatives of prosperity and power. *They seem a portion:* their milk is as pleasant and efficacious as Soma juice. *They, O ye men, are Indra:* an imitation of the refrain, 'He, O ye men, is Indra' (Ṛigveda II. 12).

7 *Rudra:* see note on I. 19. 3.

The hymn is a benediction on a newly-consecrated King.

1 *Prince: kshatríyam;* ruler, applied in the Ṛigveda to Varuṇa, Mitra, and other Gods; here meaning a Prince or King.

Let him as King be head and chief of Princes. Give up to him, O Indra, every foeman.

3 Let him be treasure-lord of goodly treasures, let him as King be master of the people.
Grant unto him great power and might, O Indra, and strip his enemy of strength and vigour.

4 Like milch-kine yielding milk for warm libations, pour, Heaven and Earth! on him full many a blessing.
May he as King be Indra's well-belovèd, the darling of the kine, the plants, the cattle.

5 I join in league with thee victorious Indra, with whom men conquer and are ne'er defeated.
He shall make thee the folk's sole lord and leader, shall make thee highest of all human rulers.

6 Supreme art thou, beneath thee are thy rivals, and all, O King, who were thine adversaries.
Sole lord and leader and allied with Indra, bring, conqueror, thy foemen's goods and treasures.

7 Consume, with lion aspect, all their hamlets, with tiger aspect, drive away thy foemen.
Sole lord and leader and allied with Indra, seize, conqueror, thine enemies' possessions.

HYMN XXIII.

I FIX my heart on wise and ancient Agni, the Five Tribes' Lord, in many a place enkindled.

---

2 *Of Princes:* members of the same regal family. Cf. 'Give him highest rank among his kinsmen' (I. 9. 3).

5 In this and the two following stanzas the King is addressed.

The hymn has been translated by Ludwig, Der Rigveda, III. 457; by Zimmer, Altindisches Leben, p. 165; and, with annotations, by Grill, Hundert Lieder, pp. 67, 135.

The hymn is a magnification of Agni and a prayer for his protection.

1 *The Five Tribes' Lord:* the special tutelary deity of the Five Âryan Tribes. See II. 2. 1, note.

But, for other opinions regarding the five peoples, races, or tribes, see Muir, O. S. Texts, II. pp. 176 sqq.

We seek him who hath entered all our houses. May he deliver us from grief and trouble.

2 As thou conveyest offerings, Jâtavedas! and fashionest the sacrifice with knowledge,

So bear thou to the Gods the prayer we utter. May he deliver us from grief and trouble.

3 I pray to Agni in each act successful, employed in every sacrifice, the strongest,

Fiend-slayer, served with fatness, strengthening worship. May he deliver us from grief and trouble.

4 We invoke the oblation-bearer, well-born Agni Jâtavedas,

Him, Vaisvânara, almighty. May he set us free from trouble.

5 With whom as friend the Rishis gave their power new splendour, with whom they kept aloof the Asuras' devices,

Agni, with whom Indra subdued the Paṇis. May he deliver us from grief and trouble.

6 Through whom the Gods discovered life eternal, through whom they stored the plants with pleasant juices,

Through whom they brought to men the light of heaven. May he deliver us from grief and trouble.

7 I, suppliant, praise and ever call on Agni, sole Lord of all this world, of all that shineth,

Of what exists and shall exist hereafter. May he deliver us from grief and trouble.

---

5 *The Ṛishis:* ancient saints and sages, bards and seers of the sacred hymns of the Ṛigveda. *Paṇis:* a class of demons of darkness who steal the cows of the Gods and shut them up in caverns, that is, conceal the rays of daylight in dark clouds. See Hymns of the Ṛigveda, General Index II.

6 *Discovered life eternal:* were made immortal. See II. 1. 5. *Stored the plants:* Agni is said to bring all plants to maturity.

HYMN XXIV.

I THINK of Indra, only him for ever, fiend-slayer. May these lauds of mine come near him.
He cometh to the pious offerer's calling. May he deliver us from grief and trouble.

2 Who with strong arms o'ercame his strong opponents, who broke and crushed the power of the demons,
Who won the rivers and the kine in battle. May he deliver us from grief and trouble.

3 Ruler of men, finder of light, the hero: the pressing-stones declare his valour, master
Of sweetest sacrifice with seven Hotars. May he deliver us from grief and trouble.

4 The lord of barren cows and bulls and oxen, finder of light for whom the posts are planted,
For whom the bright juice flows cleansed by devotion. May he deliver us from grief and trouble.

5 Whose favour those desire who offer Soma, whom, arrow-bearer, men invoke in battle,
On whom the hymn depends, in whom is power. May he deliver us from grief and trouble.

6 Who was born, first, for active operation, whose valour as the first hath been awakened,
Who raised his bolt when he encountered Ahi. May he deliver us from grief and trouble.

A hymn of praise and prayer to Indra.

2 *The rivers and the cows:* the imprisoned waters of the air and the rays of daylight for which Indra fought with the fiend Vṛitra or Ahi, that is, the huge mass of cloud that obstructed them.

3 *Pressing-stones:* which extract the juice of the Soma plant, Indra's favourite drink. *With seven Hotars:* performed by the Hotar (see I. 11) and six assistant priests.

4 *The lord of:* to whom are offered. *The posts:* to which sacrificial victims are tied.

6 *Ahi:* the Dragon or Serpent, Vṛitra.

7 Strong Lord, who leadeth hosts to meet for battle, who sendeth riches both of earth and heaven,—
I, suppliant, praise and ever call on Indra. May he deliver us from grief and trouble.

HYMN XXV.

I THINK on Vâyu's and Savitar's holy rites, ye twain who penetrate and guard the living world:
Ye who have come to be this All's pervaders, deliver us, ye two, from grief and trouble.

2 Ye who have counted up the earth's expanses, and in the sky smoothed out the air's mid-region,
Whose going-forth hath ne'er been reached by any, deliver us, ye two, from grief and trouble.

3 Beauteously bright! men rest in thy dominion when thou hast risen up and hastened onward.
Ye, Vâyu, Savitar, preserve all creatures. Deliver us, ye twain, from grief and trouble.

4 Hence, Vâyu, Savitar, drive evil action, chase Ṣimidâ away, drive off the demons.
Ye give us store of energy and power. Deliver us, ye twain, from grief and trouble.

5 Of their own selves let Savitar and Vâyu send favourable strength and wealth and plenty.
Here give us perfect freedom from consumption. Deliver us, ye twain, from grief and trouble.

6 Ye, Savitar and Vâyu, to assist us, enjoy the hymn and the delightful cheerer.
Come hither downward from the stream of blessing. Deliver us, ye twain, from grief and trouble.

A hymn of praise and prayer to Vâyu God of Wind and Savitar the Sun-God.

4 *Ṣimidâ:* apparently a female demon, or a disease attributed to her malevolence. 'May all the rivers keep us free from Ṣimidâ' (Ṛigveda VII. 50. 4).

6 *Cheerer:* the exhilarating Soma juice. *The stream of blessing:* the firmament and heaven whence rain and other blessings flow.

7 Like noblest benisons they have stayed in the God-loving man's abode.
I glorify bright Savitar and Vâyu. Deliver us, ye twain, from grief and trouble.

HYMN XXVI.

O HEAVEN and Earth, I think on you, wise, givers of abundant gifts, ye who through measureless expanses have spread forth.
For ye are seats and homes of goodly treasures. Deliver us, ye twain from grief and trouble.

2 Yea, seats and homes are ye of goodly treasures, grown strong, divine, blessèd, and far-extending.
To me, O Heaven and Earth, be ye auspicious. Deliver us, ye twain, from grief and trouble.

3 I call on you who warm and cause no sorrow, deep, spacious, meet to be adored by poets.
To me, O Heaven and Earth, be ye auspicious. Deliver us, ye twain, from grief and trouble.

4 Ye who maintain Amrit and sacrifices, ye who support rivers and human beings,
To me, O Heaven and Earth, be ye auspicious. Deliver us, ye twain, from grief and trouble.

5 Ye by whom cows and forest trees are cherished, within whose range all creatures are included,
To me, O Heaven and Earth, be ye auspicious. Deliver us, ye twain, from grief and trouble.

6 Ye who delight in nectar and in fatness, ye without whom men have no strength or power,
To me, O Heaven and Earth, be ye auspicious. Deliver us, ye twain, from grief and trouble.

7 The grief that pains me here, whoever caused it, not sent by fate, hath sprung from human action.
I, suppliant, praise Heaven, Earth, and oft invoke them. Deliver us, ye twain, from grief and trouble.

A hymn of praise and prayer to Heaven and Earth, the Parents of all.

4 *Amrit:* here meaning the life-giving rain on which the performance of sacrifices depends.

HYMN XXVII.

I THINK upon the Maruts: may they bless me, may they assist me to this wealth in battle.
I call them like swift well-trained steeds to help us. May they deliver us from grief and trouble.

2 Those who surround the never-failing fountain for ever, and bedew the plants with moisture,
The Maruts, Pṛiṣni's sons, I chiefly honour. May they deliver us from grief and trouble.

3 Bards, who invigorate the milk of milch-kine, the sap of growing plants, the speed of coursers—
To us may the strong Maruts be auspicious. May they deliver us from grief and trouble.

4 They who raised water from the sea to heaven and send it from the sky to earth in showers,
The Maruts who move mighty with their waters, may they deliver us from grief and trouble.

5 They who delight in nectar and in fatness, they who bestow upon us health and vigour,
The Maruts who rain mighty with their waters, may they deliver us from grief and trouble.

6 Whether with stormy might the Maruts stablished this All, or Gods with their celestial power,
Ye, kindly Gods, are able to restore it. May they deliver us from grief and trouble.

7 Potent in battles is the Maruts' army, impetuous train, well-known, exceeding mighty.
I, suppliant, praise and oft invoke the Maruts. May they deliver us from grief and trouble.

A hymn of praise and prayer to the Maruts, the terrible Gods of battle, storm, and tempest, and the gracious senders of the refreshing rain.

2 *Pṛiṣni's sons:* the Maruts are the sons of Rudra and Pṛiṣni, the speckled cloud. See II. 1. 1. *The never-failing fountain:* the rain-cloud.

3 *Bards:* chanters of their thunder-psalm with the music of the winds.

6 *To restore it:* with seasonable rain.

7 *Potent in battles:* see III. 1. 2.

HYMN XXVIII.

I REVERENCE you—mark this—Bhava and Ṣarva, ye under whose control is this that shineth,
Lords of this world both quadruped and biped. Deliver us, ye twain, from grief and trouble.

2 Lords of all near and even of what is distant, famed as the best and skilfullest of archers,
Lords of this world both quadruped and biped, deliver us, ye twain, from grief and trouble.

3 Thousand-eyed foe-destroyers, I invoke you, still praising you the strong, of wide dominion:
Lords of this world both quadruped and biped, deliver us, ye twain, from grief and trouble.

4 Ye who of old wrought many a deed in concert, and showed among mankind unhappy omens;
Lords of this world both quadruped and biped, deliver us, ye twain, from grief and trouble.

5 Ye from the stroke of whose destroying weapon not one among the Gods or men escapeth,
Lords of this world both quadruped and biped, deliver us, ye twain, from grief and trouble.

6 Hurl your bolt, strong Gods, at the Yâtudhâna, him who makes ready roots and deals in magic:
Lords of this world both quadruped and biped, deliver us, ye twain from grief and trouble.

A hymn of praise and prayer to Bhava and Ṣarva, two deities generally mentioned together and more or less connected with Rudra.

1 *This that shineth:* all the radiant world. *Bhava and Ṣarva:* Bhava is sometimes explained as 'the existent,' 'the eternal,' sometimes as 'the producer of everything,' so that according to the latter explanation he is the exact opposite of Ṣarva 'the destroyer:' and possibly the term (Bhava) has been formed with the view of propitiating the terrible god by a favourable name. (Abridged from Muir's translation of a note by Weber: see O. S. Texts, IV. p. 428).

The hymn has been translated by Muir, O. S. Texts, IV. p. 332.

7 Comfort and aid us, ye strong Gods, in battles, at each Kimîdin send your bolt of thunder.
I, suppliant, praise and ever call on Bhava and Ṣarva. Set us free from grief and trouble.

HYMN XXIX.

You twain, O Mitra, Varuṇa, I honour, Law-strengtheners, wise, who drive away oppressors.
Ye who protect the truthful in his battles, deliver us, ye twain, from grief and trouble.

2 Ye the wise Gods who drive away oppressors, ye who protect the truthful in his battles,
Who come, men's guards, to juice pressed forth by Babhru, deliver us, ye twain, from grief and trouble.

A hymn of praise and prayer to Mitra-Varuṇa, or Mitra and Varuṇa as a dual deity (*Mitrâvâruṇau*).

1 *The truthful:* according to the St. P. Dictionary, Satyâvan is a man's name.

2 *Babhru:* a king whom the Asvins assisted in his trouble (Ṛigveda VIII. 22. 10). *Agasti:* more commonly called Agastya, a very celebrated Ṛishi and seer of twenty-five hymns of Book I. of the Ṛigveda. He is one of those indefinable mythic personages who are found in the ancient traditions of many nations, and in whom cosmogonical or astronomical notions are generally figured. Thus it is related of Agastya that the Vindhyan Mountains prostrated themselves before him; and yet the same Agastya is believed to be the regent of the star Canopus. In the Râmâyaṇa he appears as the friend and counsellor of Râma. *Atri:* one of the great Seven Ṛishis, frequently mentioned in the Ṛigveda and said to have been delivered from distress by Indra and by the Asvins (Ṛigveda I. 51. 3, and 112. 7). *Angiras:* one of the Seven Ṛishis and the seer of a number of the Ṛigveda hymns. *Jamadagni:* a celebrated ancient Ṛishi. See II. 32. 3. *Kaṣyapa* also is a well-known Vedic sage, and Vasishṭha is especially famous as the great adversary of Visvâmitra. Of the names which follow, *Saptavadhri* is said (Ṛigveda V. 78. 6) to have been delivered from trouble by the Asvins; *Vadhryaṣva* is mentioned (Ṛigveda VI. 61. 1) as a worshipper of Sarasvatî, and (X. 69.) as a special worshipper and favourite of Agni. The rest are Ṛishis and seers of hymns, of more or less celebrity, and all are mentioned in the Ṛigveda, none being, however, represented as having been especially favoured by Mitra and Varuṇa who in this hymn are glorified as their protectors.

The hymn has been translated by Ludwig, Der Rigveda, III. p. 137.

3 Mitra and Varuṇa who help Agasti, Atri, and Angiras, and Jamadagni,
Ye who help Kaṣyapa, who help Vasishṭha, deliver us, ye twain, from grief and trouble.

4 Mitra and Varuṇa, who help Ṣyâvâṣva, Atri, and Purumîḷha, and Vadhryaṣva,
Ye who help Vimada and Saptavadhri, deliver us, ye twain, from grief and trouble.

5 Ye, Varuṇa, Mitra, who give aid to Kutsa, Gavishṭhira, Bharadvâja, Viṣvâmitra,
Who help Kakshîvan and give aid to Kaṇva, deliver us, ye twain, from grief and trouble.

6 Ye, Mitra, Varuṇa, who help Triṣoka, Medhâtithi, and Uṣanâ son of Kavi,
Ye, Gotama's and Mudgala's protectors, deliver us, ye twain, from grief and trouble.

7 Whose straight-reined car that keeps the track of goodness assails and ruins him who walks perversely—
I, suppliant, praise with constant invocation Mitra and Varuṇa. Save us from affliction.

HYMN XXX.

I TRAVEL with the Rudras and the Vasus, with the Âdityas and All-Gods I wander.
I hold aloft both Varuṇa and Mitra, I hold aloft Indra and both the Aṣvins.

2 I am the Queen, the gatherer-up of treasures, most thoughtful, first of those who merit worship.
The Gods, making me enter many places, in divers spots have set mine habitation.

The hymn, which is taken from Rigveda X. 125, is a glorification of Vâk, Speech personified and deified, the Word, the first creation and representation of Spirit, and the means of communication between men and Gods.

1 Vâk speaks. *Rudras:* the Sons of Rudra, the Maruts or Storm-Gods. *The Vasus:* considered as a separate class, eight deities frequently mentioned in connexion with the Âdityas and the Rudras. *All-Gods:* the Viṣvedevas, here regarded as a separate class.

3 I, verily, myself announce and utter the word that Gods and men alike shall welcome.
I make the man I love exceeding mighty, make him a sage, a Ṛishi, and a Brahman.

4 Through me alone all eat the food that feeds them, each man who sees, breathes, hears the word out-spoken.
They know it not, but yet they dwell beside me. Hear, one and all, the truth as I declare it.

5 I bend the bow for Rudra that his arrow may strike and slay the hater of devotion.
I rouse and order battle for the people, and I have penetrated Earth and Heaven.

6 I cherish and sustain high-swelling Soma, and Tvashṭar I support, Pûshan, and Bhaga.
I load with wealth the zealous sacrificer who pours the juice and offers his oblation.

7 On the world's summit I bring forth the Father: my home is in the waters, in the ocean.
Thence I extend o'er all existing creatures, and touch even yonder heaven with my forehead.

8 I breathe a strong breath like the wind and tempest, the while I hold together all existence.
Beyond this wide earth and beyond the heavens I have become so mighty in my grandeur.

---

7 *The Father:* Dyu or Dyaus = Zeus, Heaven or Sky, produced from Vâk identified with Paramâtmâ, the Supreme and Universal Soul.

Mr. Wallis observes: 'Vâc, 'Speech' is celebrated alone in two whole hymns [of the Ṛigveda], X. 71 and X. 125, of which the former shows that the primary application of the name was to the voice of the hymn, the means of communication between heaven and earth at the sacrifice. The other hymn illustrates the constant assimilation of the varied phenomena of nature to the sacrifice; all that has a voice in nature, the thunder of the storm, the re-awaking of life at dawn, with songs of rejoicing over the new birth of the world, are embodied in this Vâc in the same way as it is said of Bṛihaspati that he embraces all things that are. It is thus another expression for that idea of the unity of the world, which we have seen crowning the mystical speculations of all the more abstract hymns of the collection' (Cosmology of the Ṛigveda, p. 85).

HYMN XXXI.

Borne on with thee, O Manyu girt by Maruts, let our brave men, impetuous, bursting forward,
March on, like flames of fire in form, exulting, with pointed arrows, sharpening their weapons.

2 Flashing like fire, be thou, O conquering Manyu, invoked, O victor, as our army's leader.
Slay thou our foes, distribute their possessions: show forth thy vigour, scatter those who hate us.

3 O Manyu, overcome those who assail us. On breaking, slaying, crushing down the foemen.
They have not hindered thine impetuous vigour: mighty! sole-born! reduce them to subjection.

4 Alone of many thou art worshipped, Manyu: sharpen the spirit of each clan for combat.
With thee to aid, O thou of perfect splendour, we raise the glorious battle-shout for conquest.

5 Unyielding, bringing victory like Indra, O Manyu, be thou here our sovran ruler.
To thy dear name, O victor, we sing praises: we know the spring from which thou art come hither.

6 Twin-born with power, destructive bolt of thunder! the highest conquering might is thine, subduer!
Be friendly to us in thy spirit, Manyu! O much-invoked, in shock of mighty battle!

7 For spoil let Varuṇa and Manyu give us the wealth of both sides gathered and collected;
And let our enemies with stricken spirits, o'erwhelmed with terror, slink away defeated.

The hymn, which is taken from the Ṛigveda (X. 84), is a battle-song addressed to Manyu, Wrath or Warlike Ardour personified and deified.

1 *Like flames of fire in form: agnírûpâḥ;* Homer's δέμας πυρὸς αἰθομενοιο (*Il.* 11. 596).

3 *Sole-born:* having none to rival thee in thine own province.

5 *The spring:* the divine transcendental source.

HYMN XXXII.

HE who hath reverenced thee, Manyu, destructive bolt! breeds for himself forthwith all conquering energy.
Ârya and Dâsa will we conquer with thine aid, with thee the conqueror, with conquest conquest-sped.

2 Manyu was Indra, yea, the God was Manyu; Manyu was Hotar, Varuṇa, Jâtavedas.
The tribes of human lineage worship Manyu. Accordant, with thy fervour, Manyu! guard us.

3 Come hither, Manyu, mightier than the mighty: smite, with thy fervour for ally, our foemen.
Slayer of foes, of Vṛitra, and of Dasyu, bring thou to us all kinds of wealth and treasure.

4 For thou art, Manyu, of surpassing vigour, fierce, queller of the foe, and self-existent,
Shared by all men, victorious, subduer: vouchsafe to us superior strength in battles.

5 I have departed still without a portion, wise God! according to thy will, the mighty.
I, feeble man, was wroth with thee, O Manyu. Come in thy proper form and give us vigour.

6 Come hither, I am all thine own: advancing, turn thou to me, victorious, all-bestowing.
Come to me, Manyu, wielder of the thunder: bethink thee of thy friend, and slay the Dasyus.

The hymn, which is almost identical with Ṛigveda X. 83, is a battle-song addressed to Manyu, personified Wrath, the deity of the preceding hymn.

1 *Dâsa:* a general name applied in the Veda to certain evil beings or demons hostile to Indra and to men. It means also, a savage, a barbarian, as here, one of the original inhabitants of the country opposed to an Âryan immigrant. : In the second hemistich I read *manyúm*, as in the Ṛigveda, instead of *manyur* of the text.

2 *Fervour: tápas;* originally 'heat,' 'burning,' and secondly 'religious austerity,' 'fervid abstraction.'

3 *Dasyu:* fiend, or barbarian.

5 *Without a portion:* without a share in thy favours.

7 Approach, and on our right hand hold thy station, then let us slay a multitude of foemen.
The best of meath I offer to support thee: may we be first to drink thereof in quiet.

HYMN XXXIII.

CHASING our pain with splendid light, O Agni, shine thou wealth on us.
His lustre flash our pain away!

2 For goodly fields, for pleasant homes, for wealth we sacrifice to thee.
His lustre flash our pain away!

3 Best praiser of all these be he, and foremost be our noble chiefs.
His lustre flash our pain away!

4 So that thy worshippers and we, thine, Agni! in our sons may live.
His lustre flash our pain away!

5 As ever-conquering Agni's beams of splendour go to every side,
His lustre flash our pain away!

6 To every side thy face is turned, thou art triumphant everywhere.
His lustre flash our pain away!

7 O thou whose face looks every way, bear off our foes as in a ship.
His lustre flash our pain away!

8 As in a ship across the flood, transport us to felicity.
His lustre flash our pain away!

The hymn, which is almost identical with Ṛigveda I. 97, is a prayer to Agni for protection and general prosperity.

1 *Pain:* suffering inflicted on us by our enemies.

3 *He:* in the original hymn, meaning Kutsa the Ṛishi or seer to whom the hymn is attributed. May he be preëminent among those who celebrate thy praises, and may the chiefs or wealthy householders who have instituted the sacrifice be distinguished among thy worshippers.

8 *Across the flood:* or, over Sindhu, or Indus: As over Sindhu in a ship.

HYMN XXXIV.

THE head of this is prayer, its back the Bṛihat,
Odana's belly is the Vâmadevya;
Its face reality, its sides the metre, Vishṭârî sacrifice produced from fervour.

2 Boneless, cleansed, purified by him who cleanseth, they go resplendent to the world of splendour.
Fire burneth not their organ of enjoyment: much pleasure have they in the world of Svarga.

3 Never doth want or evil fortune visit those who prepare oblation called Vishṭârî.
He goes unto the Gods, he dwells with Yama, he joys among Gandharvas meet for Soma.

4 Yama robs not of generative vigour the men who dress oblation called Vishṭârî.
Borne on his car, a charioteer, he travels: endowed with wings he soars beyond the heavens.

The hymn is a glorification of a certain sacrifice called Vishṭârî, whose chief element is Odana, a mess or broth of mashed rice or other grain cooked with milk.

1 *Of this:* of the Odana. *The Bṛihat:* the name of various Sâmans or songs of praise composed in the Bṛihatî metre which consists of two pâdas of eight syllables each followed by one pâda of twelve and one of eight syllables. *Vâmadevya:* (coming from Vâmadeva the Ṛishi or inspired seer of Book IV. of the Ṛigveda) the name given to various Sâmans. *Vishṭârî:* (meaning 'extensive') the name of the oblation which is the subject of the hymn. In non-sacerdotal language the meaning of the stanza is: Devotion, various songs of praise and the metre in which they are composed, results, and effectiveness are the essential accompaniments of the brew of rice and milk offered in the Vishṭârî sacrifice which is originated by a fervid religious spirit.

2 *By him who cleanseth:* by the purifying Wind. *They:* who offer the Vishṭâri oblation. *Fire:* the flames of the funeral pile. Muir (O. S. Texts, V. p. 307) cites from the Ṣatapatha-Brâhmaṇa, X. 4. 4. 4: 'When a man, knowing this, practises austere fervour, he retains in heaven all his functions, even to that of sexual intercourse.'

3 *He:* the offerer of the oblation. *Gandharvas:* genii who inhabit Svarga or heaven.

5 Strongest is this, performed, of sacrifices : he hath reached heaven who hath prepared Vishṭârî.
The oval-fruited lotus spreads his fibre : there bloom the nenuphar and water-lilies.
Abundant with their overflow of sweetness, these streams shall reach thee in the world of Svarga, whole lakes with lotus-blossom shall approach thee.

6 Full lakes of butter with their banks of honey, flowing with wine, and milk and curds and water—
Abundant with their overflow of sweetness, these streams shall reach thee in the world of Svarga, whole lakes with lotus-blossom shall approach thee.

7 I give four pitchers, in four several places, filled to the brim with milk and curds and water.
Abundant with their overflow of sweetness, these streams shall reach thee in the world of Svarga, whole lakes with lotus-blossom shall approach thee.

8 I part this Odana among the Brâhmans, Vishṭârî, conquering worlds and reaching heaven.
Let me not lose it: swelling by its nature, be it my perfect Cow to grant all wishes!

HYMN XXXV.

ODANA which Prajâpati, the firstborn of Order, dressed with fervour for the Brahman,

---

5 *The oval-fruited :* or *âṇḍîkam* may be a separate plant with egg-shaped fruit or bulbs. Cf. V. 17. 16. *Lotus : kúmudam ;* either the white esculent water-lily or the red lotus whose fruit is also edible. *Nenuphar and water-lilies :* a substitution for the Ṣâlûka, Ṣaphaka, and Mulâlin of the text which seem to be unidentifiable aquatic plants. *Thee :* the offerer of the oblation.

As regards Svarga or heaven and the joys of the departed, see a fuller and more attractive account in Ṛigveda IX. 113. 7—11.

8 *Cow to grant all wishes : dhenúḥ kâmadúghâ ;* the mythical Cow of Plenty, fulfiller of all desires.

The hymn has been translated by Ludwig, Der Rigveda, III. p. 437.

The hymn is a further magnification of the Odana, or oblation of mashed rice and milk (see IV. 34).

1 *Prajâpati :* the Lord of Life; the Creator. *Mṛityu :* the God of Death.

Which guards the worlds from breaking at the centre,—I with this Odana will conquer Mṛityu.

2 Whereby the World-Creators vanquished Mṛityu, that which they found by fervour, toil and trouble,
That which prayer first made ready for the Brahman,—I with this Odana will conquer Mṛityu.

3 That which upholds the Earth, the all-sustainer, that which hath filled air's middle realm with moisture,
Which, raised on high in grandeur, stablished heaven,—I with this Odana will conquer Mṛityu.

4 From which the months with thirty spokes were moulded, from which the twelve-spoked year was formed and fashioned,
Which circling day and night have ne'er o'ertaken,—I with this Odana will conquer Mṛityu.

5 Which hath become breath-giver, life-bestower, to which the worlds flow full of oil and fatness,
To whom belong all the refulgent regions,—I with this Odana will conquer Mṛityu.

6 From which, matured, sprang Amrit into being, which hath become Gâyatrî's lord and ruler,
In which the perfect Vedas have been treasured,—I with this Odana will conquer Mṛityu.

7 I drive away the hostile God-despiser: far off be those who are mine adversaries.
I dress Brahmaudana that winneth all things. May the Gods hear me who believe and trust them.

---

2 *The World-Creators:* see III. 28. 1.

4 *Twelve-spoked year:* cf. Ṛigveda I. 164. 11.

6 *Gâyatrî's lord:* master of the Gâyatrî metre. *Perfect:* or, omniform.

7 *Brahmaudana:* the Odana or mess of rice and milk distributed to Brâhmans, and especially to priests at a sacrifice.

The hymn has been translated by Ludwig, Der Rigveda, III. p. 438.

HYMN XXXVI.

ENDOWED with true strength, let the Bull, Agni Vaiṣvânara, burn them up,
Him who would pain and injure us, him who would treat us as a foe.

2 Him who, unharmed, would injure us, and him who, harmed, would do us harm
I lay between the doubled fangs of Agni, of Vaiṣvânara.

3 Those who, what time the moon is dark, hunt with loud cry and answering shout,
Flesh-eaters, others who would harm,—all these I overcome with might.

4 I conquer the Piṣâchas with my power, and take their wealth away.
All who would injure us I slay. Let mine intention have success.

5 With Gods who flee with him, and match their rapid motion with the Sun,
I with those animals who dwell in rivers and on hills am found.

The hymn is a charm against fiends, human enemies, and troublesome pests.

3 *With loud cry:* *âgaré*, which does not occur elsewhere, is a word of uncertain signification. In the St. Petersburg Dictionary it is suggested that it may stand for *âgâre*, 'in the chamber,' and so Ludwig translates it. Sâyaṇa explains it as meaning 'on the field of battle.' See Grill's note. *Flesh-eaters:* eaters of raw flesh; demons.

4 *Piṣâchas:* goblins, fiends. See I. 16. 3, note.

5 *With Gods:* as Agni: 'Vaiṣvânara hath rivalry with Sûrya' (Rigveda I. 98. 1.); Soma: 'This Pavamâna . . . . mounts up with Sûrya to the sky' (Ṛigveda IX. 27. 5). *With those animals: sáṃ taiḥ paṣúbhiḥ;* this is obscure, and the metre suffers. Grill suggests that instead of *paṣúbhiḥ* some such word as *piṣâchahá*, 'destroyer of Piṣâchas,' should be read: 'With those who dwell in streams and hills I, slayer of the fiends, am found.' Ludwig, retaining *paṣúbhiḥ*, translates 'mit diesen [wie mit] vieh mög ich befunden werden;' 'may I be found with these (as with) cattle.'

6 I trouble the Piṣâchas as the tiger plagues men rich in kine.
They, even as dogs when they have seen a lion, find no hiding-place.

7 Naught with Piṣâchas can I do, with thieves, with roamers of the wood.
Piṣâchas flee and vanish from each village as I enter it.

8 Into whatever village this mine awful power penetrates,
Thence the Piṣâchas flee away, and plot no further mischief there.

9 Those who enrage me with their prate, as flies torment an elephant,
I deem unhappy creatures, like small insects troublesome to man.

10 Destruction seize upon the man, as with a cord they hold a horse,
The fool who is enraged with me! He is not rescued from the noose.

HYMN XXXVII.

With thee, O Plant, in olden time Atharvans smote and slew the fiends.
Kasyapa smote with thee, with thee did Kaṇva and Agastya smite.

---

7 *Thieves . . . roamers of the wood:* the mischievous Piṣâchas are probably meant.

8 *This mine awful power:* which frightens the goblins away.

9 *With their prate:* I adopt the reading *lapitvā́*, suggested by Prof. Whitney in his Index Verborum, instead of *lapitā́*, 'chatterings.'

10 *He is not rescued from the noose:* he shall be caught in the snare of Nirṛiti the Goddess of Misfortune and Destruction.

The hymn has been translated by Ludwig, Der Rigveda, III. p. 526, and, with annotations, by Grill, Hundert Lieder, pp. 3, 136.

The hymn is a spell to drive away Gandharvas and Apsarases.

1 *Atharvans:* the descendants of the great Atharvan, the first Fire-priest. *Kasyapa ... Kaṇva ... Agastya:* see Index.

2 With thee we scare and drive away Gandharvas and Apsarases.
O Ajaşringî, chase the fiends. Cause all to vanish with thy smell.

3 Let the Apsarases, puffed away, go to the river, to the ford,—
Guggulû, Pîlâ, Naladî, Aukshagandhi, Pramandinî.
Ye have become attentive since the Apsarases have past away.

4 Where great trees are, Aşvatthas and Nyagrodhas with their leafy crests,
There where your swings are green and bright, and lutes and cymbals sound in tune,
Ye have become attentive since the Apsarases have past away.

5 Hither hath come this one, the most effectual of herbs and plants.

6 Let Ajaşringî penetrate, Arâţakî with sharpened horn.

7 From the Gandharva, dancing near, the lord of the Apsarases,
Wearing the tuft of hair, I take all manhood and virility.

---

2 *Gandharvas:* see Index. *Apsarases:* see Index. *Ajaşringî:* the name of the plant used in the incantation; literally Goat's Horn, Odina Pinnata.

3 These names are derived from fragrant plants or sweet scents, Guggulû meaning 'Bdellium-scented;' Naladi 'Smelling of Spikenard;' the plants connected with the rest of the names have not been indentified. The names of the six Apsarases mentioned in Ṛigveda X. 95, 6 refer to their looks and habits. *Ye:* the Gandharvas. The charm has now driven the nymphs away.

4 The Aşvattha (see III. 6. 1) is the Holy Fig-tree, Ficus Religiosa; the Nyagrodha is the Indian Fig-tree, Ficus Indica.

6 *Arâţakî:* a name or epithet of Ajaşringî or Goat's Horn.

8 With those dread hundred iron spears, the darts of Indra, let it pierce
The Blyxa-fed Gandharvas, those who bring no sacrificial gift.

9 With those dread hundred golden spears, the darts of Indra, let it pierce
The Blyxa-fed Gandharvas, those who bring no sacrificial gift.

10 O Plant, be thou victorious, crush the Piṣâchas, one and all,
Blyxa-fed, shining in the floods, illumining the selfish ones.

11 Youthful, completely decked with hair, one monkey-like, one like a dog,—
So the Gandharva, putting on a lovely look, pursues a dame.
Him with an efficacious charm we scare and cause to vanish hence.

12 Your wives are the Apsarases, and ye, Gandharvas, are their lords.
Run ye, immortal ones, away: forbear to interfere with men!

---

8 *Iron spears:* the strong thorns or spines of the plant. *Blyxa-fed:* eaters of Avakâ (Blyxa Octandra), a water-plant, called Ṣaivala in later times.

10 *Illumining the selfish ones: jyotayamâmakân*; the meaning is obscure.

11 'The Gandharvas, a class of gods, who are described as hairy, like dogs and monkeys, but as assuming a handsome appearance to seduce the affections of earthly females, are called upon to desist from this unbecoming practice, and not to interfere with mortals, as they have wives of their own, the Apasarases' (Muir, O. S. Texts, V. 309). The Gandharvas here resemble the Fauni and the Satyri of Italy, the latter being represented as woodland genii or deities, ape-like and goat-footed.

HYMN XXXVIII.

HITHER I call the Apsaras, victorious, who plays with skill,

Her who comes freely forth to view, who wins the stakes in games of dice.

2 Hither I call that Apsaras who scatters and who gathers up,

The Apsaras who plays with skill and takes her winnings in the game.

3 Dancing around us with the dice, winning the wager by her play,

May she obtain the stake for us and gain the victory with skill.

May she approach us full of strength: let them not win this wealth of ours.

4 Hither I call that Apsaras, the joyous, the delightful one—

Those nymphs who revel in the dice, who suffer grief and yield to wrath.

5 Who follow in their course the rays of Sûrya, or as a particle of light attend him.

Whose leader from afar, with store of riches, compasses quickly all the worlds and guards them.

Pleased, may he come to this our burnt oblation, together with the Air, enriched with treasure.

The hymn is a charm for success in gambling.

1 *The Apsaras:* the Apsarases are intimately connected with gambling with dice. See II. 2. 5.

5 Stanzas 5—7, differing in metre and unconnected with the object of the charm, are evidently a later addition to the original hymn. They are employed in Kauṣika-Sûtra XXI. 11 as a charm for the protection of cattle. *Who:* apparently the Apsarases as nymphs of the mists of morning. *Leader:* perhaps the Sun.

6 Together with the Air, O rich in treasure, guard here the white cow and the calf, O mighty!
Here are abundant drops for thee, come hither! Here is thy white calf, let thy mind be with us.

7 Together with the Air, O rich in treasure, keep the white calf in safety here, O mighty!
Here is the grass, here is the stall, here do we bind the calf. We are your masters, name by name. All Hail!

HYMN XXXIX.

Agni on earth hath had mine homage. May he bless me.
As I have bowed me down to Agni on the earth, so let the Favouring Graces bow them down to me.

2 Earth is the Cow, her calf is Agni. May she with her calf Agni yield me food, strength, all my wish, life first of all, and offspring, plenty, wealth. All Hail!

3 Vâyu in air hath had mine homage. May he bless me.
As I have bowed me down to Vâyu in the air, so let the Favouring Graces bow them down to me.

4 Air is the Cow, her calf is Vâyu. May she with her calf Vâyu yield me food, strength, all my wish, life first of all, and offspring, plenty, wealth. All Hail!

---

6 *O mighty!*: *vâjin*; according to Ludwig, the horse of the Gandharva is addressed.

7 *Your masters, name by name*: we have power over you (Gandharvas or Apsarases) collectively and severally.

The hymn has been translated by Ludwig, Der Rigveda, III. p. 454; and stanzas 1—4, with annotations, by Grill, Hundert Lieder, pp. 71, 140.

The hymn is a prayer to various deities for health, wealth, and general prosperity.

1 *The Favouring Graces*: the condescending loving-kindnesses of the Gods, personified.

5 The Sun in heaven hath had my homage. May he bless me.
As I have bowed me down unto the Sun in heaven, so let the Favouring Graces bow them down to me.

6 Heaven is the Cow, her calf Âditya. May she yield with her calf the Sun food, strength, and all my wish, life first of all, and offspring, plenty, wealth All Hail!

7 To Chandra in the quarters have I bowed me. May he bless me.
As unto Chandra in the quarters I have bent, so let the Favouring Graces bow them down to me.

8 The quarters are the Cows, their calf is Chandra. May they yield with their calf the Moon food, strength, and all my wish, life first of all, and offspring, plenty, wealth. All Hail!

9 Agni moves having entered into Agni, the Rishis' son, who guards from imprecations.
I offer unto thee with reverent worship. Let me not mar the Gods' appointed service.

10 Skilled in all ways, O God, O Jâtavedas, I offer what is cleansed by heart and spirit
To all thy seven mouths, O Jâtavedas. Do thou accept with pleasure my libation.

HYMN XL.

O Jâtavedas, eastward sacrificers, as foes assail us from the eastern quarter.

---

6 *Âditya :* meaning here the Sun.

7 *Chandra :* the Moon.

9 *Having entered into Agni :* the consecrated fire being taken from the householder's perpetual fire. *The Rishis' son :* first produced on earth by Rishis, as Atharvan, in the olden time. *Seven mouths :* the seven mouths (tongues or flames) of Agni are frequently mentioned in the Rigveda.

The hymn, addressed to Agni Jâtavedas, is a charm directed against rival worshippers.

May they, turned back, be pained for harming Agni.
I drive them backward with mine incantation.

2 O Jâtavedas, southward sacrificers as foes assail us from the southern quarter.
May they, turned back, be pained for harming Yama.
I smite them backward with mine incantation.

3 O Jâtavedas, westward sacrificers as foes assail us from the western quarter.
For harming Varuṇa be they turned and troubled!
I smite them backward with mine incantation.

4 O Jâtavedas, northward sacrificers as foes assail us from the northern quarter.
For harming Soma be they turned and troubled! I smite them backward with mine incantation.

5 O Jâtavedas, nether sacrificers as foes assail us from the stedfast quarter.
For harming Earth let them be turned and troubled.
I smite them backward with mine incantation.

6 Those who pay sacrifice, O Jâtavedas, from air assail us from the midway quarter.
For harming Vâyu be they turned and troubled! I smite them backward with mine incantation.

7 The sacrificers from above assail us, O Jâtavedas, from the lofty quarter.
For wronging Sûrya be they turned and troubled!
I smite them backward with mine incantation.

8 Those from all points assail us, Jâtavedas, who sacrifice from intermediate regions.
For wronging Prayer let them be turned and troubled.
I smite them backward with mine incantation.

---

1 *For harming Agni* : as Regent of the East. The rival and heterodox worshippers are considered to insult and injure the deity who presides over the region of the heaven under which they offer their sacrifices.

5 *Stedfast quarter* : or, region ; the nadir.

6 *Midway* : between heaven and earth.

7 *Lofty quarter* : or, region ; the zenith.

For the Regents or presiding deities of the regions, see note on I. 31. 1.

BOOK V.

HYMN I.

He who with special plans and deathless spirit, waxing, well-born, hath come unto his birth-place,
As he who shines upholds the days, thus Trita, of pure life, bears the Three as their supporter.

2 He who, the first, approached the holy statutes makes, after, many beauteous forms and figures.
Eager to drink, his birth-place first he entered who understands the word when yet unspoken.

This very obscure introductory hymn appears to be a glorification of Trita and Varuṇa.

1 *He who shines:* Sûrya, the Sun-God. *Trita:* a mysterious ancient deity frequently mentioned in the Ṛigveda, principally in connexion with the Maruts, Vâyu, and Indra. His home is in the remotest part of heaven, and he is called Âptya, the Watery, that is, sprung from, or dwelling in, the sea of cloud and vapour. In the Ṛigveda he is identified with the Sacrificial Horse (I. 163. 3); he is said to have 'rent Vṛitra limb from limb' (I. 187. 1), and to have combated and conquered other meteoric demons; as Vâyu or Wind he fans and quickens Agni in the height of heaven (V. 9. 5); he appears to be the celestial purifier of the Soma for Indra (II. 11. 20; IX. 32. 2; 34. 4; 37. 4; 102. 2); and he surrounds the Maruts with the lightning flash and roar (V. 54. 2). Soma identifies Trita sometimes with Vâyu; sometimes with Indra as the pervader of the three worlds; and sometimes with Agni stationed in the three fire-receptacles. See Bergaigne, La Religion Védique, II. pp. 326—330. In this hymn Trita appears as a creative and protecting power. *The Three:* the worlds, earth, middle air, and heaven.

2 *Eager to drink:* or, to form, to create; 'schaffenslustiger.'—Ludwig.

3 He who—the fluid gold, with radiant kinsmen—to fervent glow delivered up thy body,
On him both set names that shall live for ever: to him the regions shall send robes to clothe him.

4 As these have gone to their primeval station, each gaining an imperishable dwelling,
May kissing mothers of the bards' belovèd bring the pole-drawing husband to the sister.

5 By holy wisdom I a sage, Far-Strider! offer to thee this lofty adoration.
This worship both the mighty eddying rivers, coming together to this station, heighten.

6 Seven are the pathways which the wise have fashioned: to one of these may come the troubled mortal.
On sure ground where the ways are parted standeth Life's Pillar in the dwelling of the Highest.

---

3 *He*: Trita, that is, Agni as the Sun, the *fluid gold* whose *kinsmen* are the flashes. *Thy body*: Soma's, according to Ludwig. The meaning of the hemistich is not clear. *Both*: the dual verb has no expressed subject. Heaven and Earth are intended. *Regions*: (*díśaḥ* instead of *víśaḥ*) of the heavens. *Robes*: clouds with which the sun is invested.

4 *These*: Heaven and Earth. *Primeval station*: the position which they have occupied from the earliest time since their separation. See IV. 1. 4. *Kissing mothers*: Heaven and Earth. *Of the bards' belovèd*: *kavíḥ ṣushásya* of the text is absolutely unintelligible and is probably corrupt. Sûrya appears to be meant: 'des von den weisen besungenen [Agni-Surya ?].'—Ludwig. *Pole-drawing husband*: Day. *Sister*: Night.

5 *Far-Strider*: or, having a broad path; Sûrya, the Sun. *Eddying rivers*: here apparently, Heaven and Earth: 'Rodha und Chakrâ [Himmel und Erde].'—Ludwig.

6 The stanza is taken from Ṛigveda X. 5. 6. *Pathways*: *maryā́dāḥ*; long lines or divisions of light. *The wise*: the sages, the Fathers. *The troubled mortal*: the man who is longing for daybreak may approach the pathway of light. Prof. M. Müller translates differently (Vedic Hymns, Part I. p. 253): 'The sages established the seven

7 Working, I go my way with deathless spirit; life, spirit, bodies have gone gladly thither.
Aye, Ṣakra also gives his gift of treasure as when the sacrificer meets with power.

8 Yea, the son asks dominion of his father: this they declared the noblest path to welfare.
Varuṇa, let them see thy revelations: display the wondrous shapes of times to follow.

9 Half with the milk, its other half, thou minglest, and with that half, strong! unbeguiled! increasest.
Let us exalt the gracious friend, the mighty, Varuṇa son of Aditi, strength-giver.
We have told him the marvels sung by poets. The utterance of Heaven and Earth is truthful.

HYMN II.

In all the worlds That was the best and highest whence sprang the Mighty One of splendid valour.
As soon as born he overcomes his foemen, when those rejoice in him who bring him succour.

---

divisions, but mischief befell one of them.' *Where the ways are parted:* where ends the dark road which the Sun travels by night, and the bright path of his daily course begins. *Life's Pillar:* apparently, Agni. The meaning of the whole stanza is uncertain.

7 *Ṣakra:* the mighty Indra. *Meets with power:* obtains the expected reward of his oblations.

9 *Half . . . . thou minglest:* preparest a libation consisting of equal parts of Soma juice and milk. *Gracious: ávim;* 'das schaf,' 'the sheep.'—Ludwig.

The hymn, like the introductory hymn of Book IV., is a *Brahmodyam,* an enunciation in designedly enigmatical language of cosmogonical and mysto-theological doctrine. Translation and explanation can be only conjectural, and some passages do not lend themselves to either. See Ludwig, Der Rigveda, III. p. 394.

The hymn, which is taken, with variations, from Ṛigveda X. 120, ascribed to the Ṛishi Bṛihaddiva, son of Atharvan, is a glorification of Indra.

1 *That:* meaning, according to Sâyaṇa, Brahma the original cause of the Universe. *The Mighty One:* Indra.

2 Grown mighty in his strength, with ample vigour, he as a foe strikes fear into the Dâsa,
Eager to win the breathing and the breathless: All sang thy praise at banquet and oblation.

3 All concentrate on thee their mental vigour what time these, twice or thrice, are thine assistants.
Blend what is sweeter than the sweet with sweetness: win quickly with our meath that meath in battle.

4 If verily in every war the sages joy and exult in thee who winnest treasures,
With mightier power, strong God, extend thy firmness: let not malevolent Kaṣokas harm thee.

5 Proudly we put our trust in thee in battles, when we behold great wealth the prize of combat.
I with my words impel thy weapons onward, and sharpen with my prayer thy vital vigour.

---

2 *Dâsa:* the demon enemies of the Gods. *Eager to win:* Prof. Ludwig makes *sásni* an infinitive. The correct reading is probably *sásnis* as suggested by Prof. Grassmann. *The breathing and the breathless:* the animate and the inanimate world.

3 *Mental vigour: krátum;* 'adoration.'—Wilson. *These:* Soma juices. *Twice or thrice:* with reference, perhaps, to the three daily libations. These invigorate Indra for the performance of his mighty deeds. *What is sweeter:* thine own celestial Soma which is sweeter than that of earth. Sâyaṇa explains the stanza differently:—'To thee all (worshippers) offer adoration, whether those propitiators be two or three. Combine that which is sweeter than the sweet with sweetness, unite that honey with honey.'—Wilson. The 'two or three' are according to Sâyaṇa, the sacrificer and his wife and child, and the second half of the stanza contains a reference to the propagation of children.

4 *Kaṣokas:* a class of demons, according to the St. P. Dictionary. The Ṛigveda has '*Yâtudhânas;*' and Prof. Ludwig suggests that the Atharva-veda hymn was employed as a charm on some special occasion, and Kaṣokas, meaning perhaps people living on the stream Kaṣî, took the place of Yâtudhânas.

6 Thou in that house, the highest or the lowest, which thy protection guards, bestowest riches.
Establish ye the ever-wandering mother, and bring full many deeds to their completion.

7 Praise in the height him who hath many pathways, courageous, strongest, Âptya of the Âptyas.
Through strength he shows himself of ample power: pattern of Pṛithivî, he fights and conquers.

8 Bṛihaddiva, the foremost of light-winners, hath made these holy prayers, this strength for Indra.
Free Lord, he rules the mighty fold of cattle, winning, aglow, even all the billowy waters.

9 Thus hath Bṛihaddiva, the great Atharvan, spoken to Indra as himself in person.
Two sisters free from stain, the Mâtariṣvans, with power impel him onward and exalt him.

---

6 *Establish ye:* apparently the Gods are addressed. *The ever-wandering mother:* the earth before her foundations were fixed. The reading of the Ṛigveda differs:—'Thou stablishest the two much-wandering mothers' (heaven and earth).

7 *Âptya of the Âptyas:* chief of the class of deities called Âptya, dwelling in the waters of the sea of air, and so identified with, or likened to, Trita Âptya. See V. 1. 1. *Pattern of Pṛithivî:* vast and strong as the earth: 'Thou art the counterpart of earth' (Ṛigveda I. 52. 13).

8 *Foremost of light-winners:* according to Sâyaṇa, 'chief of Ṛishis, and enjoyer of heaven, or servant of Âditya, the Sun, Indra.' *He:* Indra. *Fold of cattle:* the realm of the celestial cows or rays of light. *Billowy waters:* of the sea of air.

9 *The great Atharvan:* 'the great priest.'—Grassmann. *As himself:* the priest identifies himself with the God whom he worships. *Two sisters:* Heaven and Earth. *Mâtariṣvans:* Mâtariṣvan in the Ṛigveda is the divine being who brought Agni down from heaven to the Bhṛigus, and is sometimes a mystic name (perhaps, Growing in the mother, the fire-drill) of Agni himself. How the term is applicable to Heaven and Earth is not clear. The Ṛigveda has *svásâraḥ*, sisters, in the plural, explained by Sâyaṇa as 'the sister rivers which abide in the mother *(mâtári)* Earth.'

HYMN III.

Let strength be mine while I invoke thee, Agni! enkindling thee may we support our bodies.
May the four regions bend and bow before me: with thee for guardian may we win the combat.

2 Baffling the rage of our opponents, Agni! guard us as our protector round about us.
Down the steep slope go they who hate us, backward, and let their thought who watch at home be ruined.

3 May all the Gods be on my side in battle, the Maruts led by Indra, Vishṇu, Agni.
Mine be the middle air's extended region, and may the Wind blow favouring these my wishes.

4 For me let them present all mine oblations, and let my mind's intention be accomplished.
May I be guiltless of the least transgression: may all the Gods come hither and protect me.

5 May the Gods grant me riches, may the blessing and invocation of the Gods assist me.
This boon shall the celestial Hotars win us: may we, unwounded, have brave heroes round us.

6 Ye six divine Expanses, give us freedom. Here, all ye Gods, acquit yourselves like heroes.
Let not calamity or curse o'ertake us, nor deeds of wickedness that merit hatred.

The hymn, which is taken, with variations, from Ṛigveda X. 128, ascribed to the Ṛishi Vihavya of the family of Angiras, is a prayer addressed by a King to Agni, Indra, and various other deities for victory in battle, and general protection and prosperity.

1 *The four regions:* the King is about to undertake a *Digvijaya*, the subjugation of the neighbouring countries in all directions.

2 *Down the steep slope:* that leads to destruction.

5 *Celestial Hotars:* the Hotar-priests of the Gods. According to Sâyaṇa, 'my invokers of the Gods.'

6 *Six divine Expanses:* the four cardinal points, and upper and lower spaces or zenith and nadir.

7 Do ye three Goddesses give ample shelter and all success to us ourselves and children.
Let us not lose our children or our bodies: let us not benefit the foe, King Soma!

8 Foodful and much-invoked, at this our calling may the far-reaching Bull grant us wide shelter.
Lord of bay coursers, Indra, bless our children: harm us not, give us not as prey to others.

9 Lord of the world, Creator and Disposer, may the God Savitar who quells assailants,
May the Âdityas, Rudras, both the Asvins, Gods, guard the sacrificer from destruction.

10 Let those who are our foemen stay afar from us: with Indra and with Agni we will drive them off.
The Âdityas and the Rudras, over us on high, have made me strong, a thinker, and a sovran lord.

11 Yea, we call Indra hitherward, the winner of wealth in battle and of kine and horses.
May he mark this our worship when we call him Lord of bay steeds, thou art our friend and comrade.

HYMN IV.

Thou who wast born on mountains, thou most mighty of all plants that grow,
Thou Banisher of Fever, come, Kushṭha! make Fever pass away.

---

7 *Three Goddesses:* Ilâ, Sarasvatî, and Mahî or Bhâratî, personifications of prayer and worship. They are not mentioned in the Ṛigveda hymn.

8 *The far-reaching Bull:* Indra.

11 This stanza is not taken from the Ṛigveda hymn.

The hymn is a charm against Fever and other ailments.

1 *Fever:* see I. 25. *Kushṭha:* a medicinal plant, Costus Speciosus or Arabicus. See VI. 95; 102. 3; XIX. 39.

13

2 Brought from the Snowy Mountain, born on the high hill where eagles breed,
Men seek to buy thee when they hear: for Fever's Banisher they know.

3 In the third heaven above us stands the Aṣvattha tree, the seat of Gods.
There the Gods sought the Kushṭha Plant, embodiment of endless life.

4 There moved through heaven a golden ship, a ship with cordage wrought of gold.
There the Gods won the Kushṭha Plant, the blossom of eternal life.

5 They sailed on pathways paved with gold, the oars they plied were wrought of gold:
All golden were the ships wherein they carried Kushṭha down to earth.

6 O Kushṭha, bring thou hitherward this man of mine, restore his health,
Yea, free him from disease for me.

7 Thou art descended from the Gods, Soma's benignant friend art thou.
Befriend my breath and vital air, be gracious unto this mine eye.

8 Sprung, northward, from the Snowy Hill thou art conveyed to eastern men.
There they deal out among themselves Kushṭha's most noble qualities.

9 Most excellent, indeed, art thou, Kushṭha! most noble is thy sire.

---

3 *Aṣvattha tree:* Ficus Religiosa or Holy Fig-tree; see III. 6. 1, note. The virtues ascribed to Kushṭha are so manifold and mighty that the plant must have a celestial origin. 'The Samoans think that their most valued vegetables were stolen from heaven by a Samoan visitor' (Lang's Custom and Myth).

9 *Thy sire:* Kushṭha's father is said to be Jivala, Vivifier (XIX. 39. 3).

The hymn has been translated with notes by Grill, Hundert Lieder, pp. 9, 141.

Make all Consumption pass away and render Fever powerless.

10 Malady that affects the head, eye-weakness, bodily defect—
All this let Kushṭha heal and cure: aye, godlike is the vigorous power.

HYMN V.

Aryaman is thy grandsire, Night thy mother, and the Cloud thy sire.
Thy name is called Silâchî. Thou, thyself, art sister of the Gods.

2 Whoever drinketh thee hath life: thou savest and protectest man.
As nursing mother of mankind, thou takest all upon thy lap.

3 Thou clingest close to every tree, as a fond damsel clasps her love.
Thy name is called The Conqueror, She who Stands Fast, The Rescuer.

4 Whatever wound the arrow, or the staff, or violence inflicts,
Thereof thou art the remedy: as such restore this man to health.

5 Thou springest from blest Plaxa, or Aṣvattha, Dhava, Khadira,
Parṇa, or blest Nyagrodha, so come thou to us, Arundhatî!

The hymn is a charm, addressed to a Plant, to mend a broken bone.

1 *Silâchî:* more usually called Arundhatî as in stanzas 5 and 9, a medicinal climbing plant formerly applied in cases of severe contusion or fracture. See IV. 12. 1, note. *Sister of the Gods:* see note on V. 4. 3.

5 *Plaxa:* the Waved-leaf Fig-tree, Ficus Infectoria, a large and beautiful tree with small white fruit. *Aṣvattha:* Ficus Religiosa. See III. 6. 1. *Dhava:* a shrub, Grislea Tormentosa. *Khadira:* Acacia Catechu. See III. 6. 1. *Parṇa:* Butea Frondosa. See III. 5. 4. *Nyagrodha:* Ficus Indica. See IV. 37. 4. *Lâkshâ:* meaning apparently a plant on which the cochineal insect which produces the red dye (lâkh, lac) is found.

6 Gold-coloured, bringing happy fate, most lovely, brilliant as the Sun,
Mayst thou, O Healing! come unto the fracture: Healing is thy name.

7 Gold-coloured, bringing happy fate, odorous, hairy-bodied one,
The sister of the Waters art thou, Lâkshâ! and thy soul is Wind.

8 Silâchî is thy name: thy sire, O goat-brown! is a damsel's son.
Thou hast been sprinkled by the mouth of Yama's tawny-coloured horse.

9 Issuing from the horse's blood away she glided to the trees.
Become a wingèd water-brook, and come to us, Arundhatî!

HYMN VI.

Eastward at first the prayer was generated: Vena disclosed bright flashes from the summit,
Disclosed his deepest nearest revelations, womb of the non-existent and existent.

---

8 *Thy sire:* the Cloud. I have translated the text as it stands; but the meaning is not clear. Dr. Grill says, 'I read *kānīnā́ ajábabhruḥ*,' and translates accordingly: 'Silâchî is a damsel's child (daughter of Night), thy father brown-red like the goat.' Zimmer, doubtingly, translates similarly. *Hast been sprinkled by the mouth:* it would be better, perhaps, to read *asnā́*, 'with the blood,' instead of *āsnā́*, 'by the mouth,' as suggested by Prof. Whitney, in his Index Verborum, followed by Dr. Grill who refers to the ancient German custom of sprinkling holy trees with blood. Yama's horse does not appear to be mentioned elsewhere.

9 *Become a wingèd water-brook:* come swiftly as a rapid stream.

The hymn has been translated by Zimmer, A. I. Leben, p. 67; and, with notes, by Grill, Hundert Lieder, pp. 10, 142.

The hymn is mainly a prayer for protection and prosperity.

1 This stanza is repeated from IV. 1. 1.

2 None have attained to those of old, those who wrought holy acts for you.
Let them not harm our heroes here. Therefore I set before you this.

3 Sweet-tongued, exhaustless, they have sent their voices down together in heaven's vault that pours a thousand streams.
His wildly-restless warders never close an eye: in every place the snarers stand to bind men fast.

4 Speed forward, conquering all foes, to win the spoil.
Thou comest on thy haters with a surging sea. Thy name is Fragile. The thirteenth month is Indra's home.

5 Through this now hast thou sent thy gifts. All hail!
With sharpened arms and missiles, kind and friendly, be gracious unto us, Soma and Rudra!

6 Through this hast thou been left in want. All hail!
With sharpened arms and missiles, kind and friendly, be gracious unto us, Soma and Rudra!

7 Through this hast thou committed faults. All hail!
With sharpened arms and missiles, kind and friendly, be gracious unto us, Soma and Rudra!

---

2 Repeated from IV. 7. 7.

3 Taken, with a slight variation, from Ṛigveda IX. 73. 4. *They:* the beams of light which radiate from the Soma juices as they undergo purification. *His warders:* Soma's rays which watch the actions of men, detecting and capturing the wicked like hunters with snares and nooses.

4 The first line is taken from Ṛigveda IX. 110. 1, and is addressed to Soma Pavamâna (the Soma as it is purified) in the original hymn. *Thou . . . . . sea: dvishástádádhyarṇavéṇeyase* seems to be a corruption of *dvishás tarâdhyâ ṛiṇayấ na íyase*, 'As a debt-claimer thou speedest to quell thy foes,' the second hemistich of the same hymn. *Thy name is Fragile:* here the chief subject of the hymn, the thirteenth or intercalary month of the Indian calendar. *Indra's home:* the thirteenth month being created by the Sun or Indra. See XIII. 3. 8.

5 The first line of this, as of each of the two following stanzas, is unintelligible to me.

8 Free us from trouble, free us from dishonour, accept our worship, give us life immortal.

9 O missile of the eye, missile of spirit, thou missile of devotion and of fervour!
Thou art the weapon shot against the weapon. Let those be weaponless who sin against us.

10 Make with thy weapon weaponless, O Agni, all wicked men who deal with us as foemen with eye, with thought, with spirit, or intention.

11 Thou art the house of Indra. I betake me to thee, I enter thee with all my cattle,
With all my people and with all my body, with all my soul, with mine entire possessions.

12 Thou art the guard of Indra. I betake me to thee, etc.

13 Thou art the shield of Indra. I betake me to thee, etc.

14 Indra's protection art thou. I betake me to thee, I enter thee with all my cattle,
With all my people and with all my body, with all my soul, with mine entire possessions.

HYMN VII.

Bring thou to us, bar not the way, Arâti! Stay not the guerdon that is being brought us.
Homage be paid to Failure, to Misfortune, and Malignity.

---

9 The remainder of the hymn is non-metrical.

11 *The house of Indra:* the thirteenth month is the subject of many wildly fanciful speculations in the later Vedic literature. Here the next world appears to be referred to.

The hymn is a charm to deprecate Arâti, or Malignity personified.

1 *Guerdon:* the *dakshiṇâ* or honorarium given to the priests who officiate at a sacrifice. The speaker, who belongs to the sacerdotal class, hopes that his fees may not diminish. See Ṛigveda X. 107, addressed to Dakshiṇâ.

2 The man whom thou preferrest, O Arâti, he who prates to us—
This man of thine, we reverence. Baffle not thou my heart's desire.

3 May our desire which Gods have roused fulfil itself by day and night.
We seek to win Arâti: to Arâti be our homage paid.

4 We, suppliant, call on Bhaga, on Sarasvatî, Anumati.
Pleasant words have I spoken, sweet as honey is, at invocations of the Gods.

5 The portion that I crave with speech intelligent and full of power,
May faith, presented with the gift of tawny Soma, find to-day.

6 Do not thou make our words or wishes fruitless. Let the twain, Indra Agni, bring us treasures.
All, fain to-day to give us gifts, welcome Arâti with your love.

7 Misfortune! go thou far away: we turn thy harmful dart aside.
I know thee well, Arâti! as oppressor, one who penetrates.

8 Oft, coming as a naked girl thou hauntest people in their sleep,
Baffling the thought, Arâti! and the firm intention of a man.

9 To her the mighty, vast in size, who penetrates all points of space,
To her mine homage have I paid, Nirṛiti with her golden hair.

---

4 The second hemistich has four hypermetrical syllables: *mádhumatím*, sweet as honey, may be a gloss that has crept into the text.

8 Cf. Burton's account of succubae (Anatomy of Melancholy, Part 3, Sec. 2).

Nirṛiti: the speaker gives Arâti the name of the far more powerful Goddess of Misfortune, Destruction, and Death.

The hymn has been translated by Ludwig, Der Rigveda, III. p. 305, and, with annotations, by Grill, Hundert Lieder, pp. 39, 145.

10 Auspicious, with her golden hue, pillowed on gold, the mighty one,—
To this Arâti clad in robes of gold mine homage have I paid.

HYMN VIII.

With fuel of Vikaṅkata bring molten butter to the Gods.
O Agni, make them joyful here: let them all come unto my call.

2 O Indra, come unto my call. This will I do. So hear it thou.
Let these exertions for the sake of Indra guide my wish aright.
Therewith, O Jâtavedas, Lord of Bodies! may we win us strength.

3 Whatever plot from yonder, O ye Gods, that godless man would frame,
Let not the Gods come to his call, nor Agni bear his offering up. Come ye, come hither to my call.

4 Run, ye Exertions, farther on. By Indra's order smite and slay.
As a wolf worrieth a sheep, so let not him escape from you while life remains. Stop fast his breath.

5 The Brahman whom those yonder have appointed priest, for injury,
He, Indra! is beneath thy feet. I cast him to the God of Death.

The hymn is a charm for the discomfiture and destruction of hostile priests.

1 *Vikaṅkata:* a thorny tree (Flacourtia Sapida) used as fuel at sacrifices and as the material of the great ladle called *dhruvâ*, and saucers for Soma juice.

4 *Exertions:* the efforts made by the priests to secure the due performance of the sacrifice, personified. *Smite and slay:* the hostile priests.

5 Muir observes (O. S. Texts, I. 289): 'and yet with all this sacredness of his character the priest must be devoted to destruction, if, in the interest of an enemy, he is seeking by his ceremonies to effect the ruin of the worshipper.'

6 If they have issued forth, strongholds of Gods, and made their shield of prayer,
Gaining protection for their lives, protection round about, make all their instigation powerless.

7 Exertions which that man hath made, Exertions which he yet will make—
Turn them, O Indra, back again, O Vṛitra-slayer, back again on him that they may kill that man.

8 As Indra, having seized him, set his foot upon Udvâchana,
Even so for all the coming years I cast those men beneath my feet.

9 Here, Indra Vṛitra-slayer, in thy strength pierce thou their vital parts.
Here, even here, attack them, O Indra. Thine own dear friend am I.
Indra, we closely cling to thee. May we be in thy favouring grace.

HYMN IX.

All hail to Heaven!

2 All hail to Earth!

3 All hail to Air!

4 All hail to Air!

5 All hail to Heaven!

6 All hail to Earth!

---

8 *Udvâchana:* one who screams out; perhaps some demon conquered by Indra. According to the St. Petersburg Dictionary the reading is probably incorrect.

The hymn has been translated by Ludwig, Der Rigveda, III. p. 439.

The hymn is a prayer to Heaven and Earth for protection and assistance.

7 Mine eye is Sûrya and my breath is Vâta, Air is my soul and Pṛithivî my body.
I verily who never have been conquered give up my life to Heaven and Earth for keeping.

8 Exalt my life, my strength, my deed and action; increase my understanding and my vigour.
Be ye my powerful keepers, watch and guard me, ye mistresses of life and life's creators! Dwell ye within me, and forbear to harm me.

HYMN X.

THOU art my wall of stone against the sinner who fights against me from the eastern quarter.
May he encounter it!

2 Thou art my wall of stone against the sinner who fights against me from the southern quarter.
May he encounter it!

3 Thou art my wall of stone against the sinner who fights against me from the western quarter.
May he encounter it!

4 Thou art my wall of stone against the sinner who fights against me from the northern quarter.
May he encounter it!

---

7 *Mine eye is Sûrya:* cf. 'May Sûrya, sovran Lord of eyes, protect me' (V. 24. 9). So Socrates says (Plato, Republic, VI. 18): 'I regard it (the eye) as the most sunlike of all the organs of sensation' (see Muir, O. S. Texts, V. 298). Compare also the Funeral Hymn, Ṛigveda X. 16. 3: 'The sun receive thine eye, the wind thy spirit: go, as thy merit is, to earth or heaven.'

The hymn contains a separate prayer to each of the deities who preside over the regions (see I. 31. 1) for protection from the enemy who threatens the speaker from the quarter under the God's special jurisdiction. The deities are (1) Agni (2) Yama (3) Varuṇa (4) Soma.

1 *May he encounter it:* may the enemy knock his head against that wall.

5 Thou art my wall of stone against the sinner who fights against me from the stedfast region.
May he encounter it!

6 Thou art my wall of stone against the sinner who fights against me from the lofty region!
May he encounter it!

7 Thou art my wall of stone against the sinner who from points intermediate fights against me.
May he encounter it!

8 With Bṛihat I invoke the mind, with Mâtarisvan both the breaths,
The eye from Sûrya, and the ear from Air, the body from the Earth.
We, with Sarasvatî who suits the mind, call Speech to come to us.

HYMN XI.

How, terrible in might, hast thou here spoken to the great God, how to the gold-hued Father?
Thy mind watched, greedy Varuṇa! to recover the brindled cow thou hadst bestowed as guerdon.

---

5 *Stedfast region:* the nadir.

6 Lofty region: the zenith.

8 *Bṛihat:* a Sâman, psalm or sacred song in the Bṛihatî metre. See III. 3. 2. *Mâtarisvan:* here apparently meaning Vâta or Wind. *Both the breaths:* inspiration and expiration. *The eye from Sûrya:* see V. 9. 7. *Air:* as the conductor of sound. *Earth:* see V. 9. 7. *Who suits the mind:* being the wise Goddess of eloquence and learning. *Speech:* Vâk, speech personified and deified. See IV. 1. 2.

This curious hymn contains a dialogue between the primeval priest Atharvan and Varuṇa about the possession of a wonderful brindled cow. The God has bestowed the cow upon the priest, and now retracts his gift. Atharvan remonstrates.

1 Atharvan speaks. *Spoken:* declared thy promise to give me the cow. *The great God:* Heaven. *The gold-hued Father:* the Sun.

2 Not through desire do I revoke my present: I bring this brindled cow to contemplate her.
Now by what lore, by what inherent nature, knowest thou all things that exist, Atharvan?

3 Truly I am profound in wisdom, truly I know by nature all existing creatures.
No Dâsa by his greatness, not an Ârya, may violate the law that I will stablish.

4 None, self-dependent Varuṇa! existeth wiser than thou or sager by his wisdom.
Thou knowest well all these created beings: even the man of wondrous powers fears thee.

5 O self-dependent Varuṇa, wise director, thou knowest verily all generations.
What is, unerring one! beyond this region? What more remote than that which is most distant?

6 One thing there is beyond this air, and something beyond that one, most hard to reach, remotest.
I, Varuṇa, who know, to thee declare it. Let churls be mighty in the lower regions. Let Dâsas sink into the earth beneath them.

7 Many reproaches, Varuṇa, dost thou utter against the misers who revoke their presents.
Be not thou added to that crowd of niggards: let not men call thee an illiberal giver.

---

2 Varuṇa replies. *To contemplate her:* or, to count her with the rest of the herd.

3 In this and the two following stanzas Atharvan speaks.

6 Varuṇa replies. Beyond the air is heaven, and beyond that is infinity. But the question and answer are obscurely worded. Muir translates the question and answer differently: 'What other thing is beyond this atmosphere? and what is nearer than that remotest thing, O thou unerring? There is one thing beyond this atmosphere; and on this side of that one there is that which is near though inaccessible.' *I, Varuṇa:* the nominative, as required by the context. The text has Varuṇa in the vocative.

7 Atharvan speaks.

8 Let not men call me an illiberal giver. I give thee back the brindled cow, O singer.
Attend, in every place where men inhabit, with all thy powers, the hymn that tells my praises.

9 Let hymns of praise ascend to thee, uplifted in every place of human habitation.
But give me now the gift thou hast not given. Thou art my friend for ever firm and faithful.

10 One origin, Varuṇa! one bond unites us: I know the nature of that common kinship.
I give thee now the gift that I retracted. I am thy friend for ever firm and faithful.

11 God, giving life unto the god who lauds me, Sage strengthener of the sage who sings my praises.
Thou, self-dependent Varuṇa! hast begotten the kinsman of the Gods, our sire Atharvan.
On him bestow most highly-lauded riches. Thou art our friend, high over all, our kinsman.

HYMN XII.

THOU in the house of man this day enkindled worshippest Gods as God, O Jâtavedas.

---

8 Varuṇa speaks. *Vikshú* should be read instead of *dikshú* in this and in the following stanza.

9 Atharvan speaks this stanza and the first hemistich of 10. *Ever firm and faithful: saptápadas;* literally 'having taken seven steps' by which an alliance or a marriage is confirmed.

10 *One origin:* the ancient Ṛishis frequently assert their kinship with the Gods, as sons of Dyaus or Father Heaven. Varuṇa speaks the second hemistich and the first of the following stanza.

11 *Unto the god:* the priest Atharvan. The second and third lines are spoken by the poet of the hymn.

The hymn has been translated by Muir, O. S. Texts, I. 396. See also Roth, Abhandlung über den Atharva Veda, p. 9.

This hymn, which is one of the Âpris or Propitiatory Hymns, consisting of invocations of a series of deified objects said to be forms of Agni, is taken from Rigveda X. 110, ascribed to the Ṛishi Jamadagni, son of Bhṛigu, or to Bhṛigu's son Râma who is generally called Paraṣurâma.

Observant, bright as Mitra, bring them hither. Thou art a sapient and foreknowing envoy.

2 Tanûnapât, fair-tongued! with sweet meath balming the paths and ways of Order, make them pleasant.
Bear to the Gods our sacrifice, exalting with holy thoughts our hymns of praise and worship.

3 Invoked, deserving prayer and adoration, O Agni, come accordant with the Vasus.
Thou art, O youthful Lord, the Gods' Invoker, so, best of sacrificers, bring them quickly.

4 By rule the Sacred Grass is scattered eastward, a robe to clothe this earth when dawns are breaking.
Widely it spreads around and far extended, fair for the Gods and bringing peace and freedom.

5 Let the expansive Doors be widely opened, like wives who deck their beauty for their husbands.
Lofty, celestial, all-impelling Portals, admit the Gods and give them easy entrance!

6 Pouring sweet dews let holy Night and Morning, each close to each, be seated at their station,—
Lofty, celestial Dames with gold to deck them, assuming all their fair and radiant beauty.

---

2 *Tanûnapât:* or, Son of Thyself; a frequently recurring name of Agni, so called because fire is sometimes self-generated, as in the lightning, or produced by attrition, and not necessarily derived from other fire. Other fanciful derivations of the word are given. *Order:* sacrifice ordained by divine law.

3 *Vasus:* Gods. *Youthful:* continually reproduced by the fire-drill.

4 *Sacred Grass: barhis*; generally kuşa grass, strewn on the place of sacrifice, especially on the Vedi or altar, and forming a layer on which the offerings are placed, and a seat for the sacrificers and the Gods who are present at the ceremony. Here the Sacred Grass is personified and deified.

5 *Doors:* of the sacrificial chamber, representing the portals of the eastern heaven.

7 Come the first two celestial sweet-voiced Hotars, arranging sacrifice for man to worship,
As singers who inspire us in assemblies, showing the eastern light with their direction!

8 Let Bhâratî come quickly to our worship and Ilâ showing like a human being.
So let Sarasvatî and both her fellows, deft Goddesses, on this fair grass be seated.

9 Hotar more skilled in sacrifice, bring hither with speed to-day God Tvashṭar, thou who knowest,
Even him who formed these two, the Earth and Heaven, the Parents, with their forms, and every creature.

10 Bring thou to our oblations which thou balmest the companies of Gods in ordered season.
Agni, Vanaspati, the Immolator sweeten our offered gifts with meath and butter!

11 Agni as soon as he was born made ready the sacrifice and was the Gods' preceder.
May the Gods eat our offering consecrated according to this true Priest's voice and guidance.

---

7 *Hotars:* perhaps Agni and Varuṇa.

8 *Bhâratî* (called also Mahî), *Ilâ*, and *Sarasvatî* are Goddesses who preside over sacred speech, prayer and praise.

9 *Hotar more skilled:* Agni, superior in sacrificial knowledge and skill to all human priests. *Tvashṭar:* the divine artificer. See II. 5. 6.

10 *Vanaspati:* literally, Lord of the Wood; here meaning the sacrificial post, which is enumerated among the Âprî deities or deified objects, and regarded as a form of Agni.

Other Âprî hymns, generally addressed to the same deities or deified objects, are Ṛigveda I. 13, 142, 188; II. 3; III. 4; V. 5; VII. 2; IX. 5.

HYMN XIII.

VARUṆA, Sage of heaven, hath given me the gift: with spells of mighty power I draw thy poison out.

Dug up, not dug, adherent, I have seized it fast: low hath thy venom sunk like water in the sands.

2 All the non-fluid portion of thy venom, I receive in these.

I take thy middlemost, thy highest, lowest juice: may it be spent and lost by reason of thy fear.

3 Strong is my cry like thunder with the rainy cloud: with powerful incantation let thy strength be stayed.

I, with the men to aid, have seized that juice of his; as light from out the gloom, let Sûrya rise on high.

4 I with this eye destroy thine eye, and with this poison conquer thine.

Live not, O Snake, but die the death: back go thy venom on thyself.

5 Listen to me, Black Snakes and hateful creatures, Lurker-in-Grass, Karait, and Brown, and Spotty,

Approach not near the house my friend inhabits: give warning, and rest quiet with your poison.

The hymn is a charm against snakes.

1 *Thy poison:* a snake is addressed.

2 *In these:* there is no clue to the feminine substantive: perhaps some herbs are intended.

3 The text of the second pâda of the first hemistich is corrupt, and my translation thereof is only a makeshift.

5 *Karait: kairâta*, the name of a variety of snake, means 'found among the Kirâtas,' one of the barbarous tribes who inhabit woods and mountains and live by hunting (the Kirrhadae of Arrian). The Karait is one of the most deadly of Indian Thanatophidia. *The house my friend inhabits:* a conjectural version, *stâmdnam* of the text being a *vox nihili*.

6 Even as the cord that strings the bow, I slacken, as it were, the cars
Of the All-conquering serpent's wrath, of the fierce rage of Black, and Brown, Taimâta, and Apodaka.

7 And Âligî and Viligî, their father and the mother too,—
What will ye do? Your venomed sap, we know, is utterly powerless.

8 Daughter of Urugûlâ, she-fiend whom the black-skinned mother bare—
All female serpents' poison who crept swiftly near is impotent.

9 Dwelling beside the mountain's slope, the quick-eared porcupine exclaimed:
Of all these she-snakes homed in earth the poison is most powerless.

10 Tâbuva or not Tâbuva, thou verily art not Tâbuva: poison is killed by Tâbuva.
Tastuva or not Tastuva, thou verily art not Tastuva: poison is killed by Tastuva.

---

6 *All-conquering (sâtrâsâhâ), Taimâta,* and *Apodaka* (waterless, non-aquatic) are unidentifiable varieties of snakes.

7 *Âligî and Viligî:* not identified.

8 *Urugûlâ:* the meaning of the word, and the snake indicated are not known.

9 *The quick-eared porcupine:* whose quills moreover protect her from the attacks of snakes. Cf: 'Forth issuing from the mountain's side the mungoose (the deadly enemy of snakes) spake these words and said: The scorpion's venom hath no strength: Scorpion, thy venom is but weak' (Rigveda I. 191. 16).

10 *Tâbuva* and *Tastuva* are supposed antidotes that render snakes' poison ineffectual. Snake-charmers at the present day exhibit stones which they say have the power of drawing the poison out of a wound inflicted by a snake. In England, formerly, Brazil Wood was held to be a certain preventive of snake-bites.

HYMN XIV.

AN eagle found thee: with his snout a wild boar dug thee from the earth.
Harm thou, O Plant, the mischievous, and drive the sorcerer away.

2 Beat thou the Yâtudhânas back, drive thou away the sorcerer;
And chase afar, O Plant, the man who fain would do us injury.

3 As 'twere a strip cut round from skin of a white-footed antelope,
Bind, like a golden chain, O God, his witchcraft on the sorcerer.

4 Take thou his sorcery by the hand, and to the sorcerer lead it back.
Lay it before him, face to face, that it may kill the sorcerer.

5 Back on the wizard fall his craft, upon the curser light his curse!
Let witchcraft, like a well-naved car, roll back upon the sorcerer.

6 Whoso, for other's harm hath dealt—woman or man—in magic arts,
To him we lead the sorcery back, even as a courser with a rope.

7 Now whether thou hast been prepared by Gods or been prepared by men,
We, with our Indra at our side to aid us, lead thee back again.

The hymn is a charm against witchcraft.

1 *An eagle found thee:* the efficacy of magical plants depends in a great measure, upon the difficulty of procuring them. See Lang (Custom and Myth, pp. 149 sqq. 'Moly and Mandragora'). See also AV. II. 27. 2.

4 *Thou:* O Plant.

7 *Thou:* the Spell cast by the enemy.

8 Agni, victorious in fight, subdue the armies of our foes!
Back on the sorcerer we cast his sorcery, and beat it home.

9 Thou who hast piercing weapons, pierce him who hath wrought it; conquer him.
We do not sharpen thee to slay the man who hath not practised it.

10 Go as a son goes to his sire: bite as a trampled viper bites.
As one who flies from bonds, go back, O Witchcraft, to the sorcerer.

11 Even as the timid antelope or hind from her assailant flees,
So swiftly let the sorcery o'ertake and reach the sorcerer.

12 Straighter than any arrow let it fly against him, Heaven and Earth!
So let that witchcraft seize again the wizard like a beast of chase.

13 Let it go contrary like flame, like water following its course.
Let witchcraft, like a well-naved car, roll back upon the sorcerer.

HYMN XV.

PLANT! I have those who shall avert the threatened danger, ten and one.
O sacred Plant, produced aright! make sweetness, sweet thyself, for me.

---

10 *As one who flies from bonds:* or, if *bándhum*, the alteration suggested in the St. Petersburg Dictionary, be read instead of *bandhám:* As, to his friend, the fugitive, back, Witchcraft, to the sorcerer!

The hymn has been translated and annotated by Grill, Hundert Lieder, pp. 26, 147.

2 Twenty and two, O Plant, have I who shall avert the threatened ill.
O sacred Plant, produced aright! make sweetness, sweet thyself, for me.

HYMN XVI.

Bull! if thou art the single bull, beget. Thou hast no vital sap.

HYMN XVII.

These first, the boundless Sea, and Mâtarisvan, fierce-glowing Fire, the Strong, the Bliss-bestower,
And heavenly Floods, first-born by holy Order, exclaimed against the outrage on a Brahman.

2 King Soma first of all, without reluctance, made restitution of the Brahman's consort.
Mitra and Varuṇa were the inviters: Agni as Hotar took her hand and led her.

Stanzas 3—11 of the hymn, which is a charm for general prosperity, are exactly the same with the exception of the numbers which increase by eleven in each stanza (thirty and three, forty and four, and so on) up to one hundred and ten in stanza 10, stanza 11 concluding with one thousand and one hundred.

The hymn, which is a charm for the increase and prosperity of cattle, contains ten other similar lines, the only difference being that in the place of *ekavṛisháh*, single bull, *dvivṛisháh*, double bull, or, worth two bulls, *trivṛisháh*, triple bull, or, worth three bulls, and so on, follow in regular order up to *ekâdaṣah*, eleven-fold, in stanza 11, in which *ápodakah*, waterless, stands instead of the *arasáh*, sapless, of the preceding lines.

The subject of the hymn, parts of which are taken from Ṛigveda X. 109, is the abduction by a Kshatriya of a Brahman's wife, and her subsequent restoration to her husband. The Ṛigveda hymn contains only seven stanzas, concluding with stanza 11 of the Atharva-veda hymn.

1 *Sea:* the ocean of air. *Mâtarisvan:* probably Wind. *Fire:* Agni. *The Strong:* Indra. *Bliss-bestower:* Soma. *Outrage on a Brahman:* 'Brahmâ's sin,' according to Sâyaṇa. See note on stanza 5.

2 *Were the inviters:* acted as interceders, or match-makers, at the renewed marriage.

3 The man, her pledge, must by the hand be taken when he hath cried, She is a Brahman's consort.
She stayed not for a herald to conduct her: thus is the kingdom of a ruler guarded.

4 She whom they call the star with loosened tresses, descending as misfortune on the village,
The Brahman's consort, she disturbs the kingdom where hath appeared the hare with fiery flashing.

5 Active in duty serves the Brahmachârî: he is a member of the Gods' own body.
Through him Bṛihaspati obtained his consort, as the Gods gained the ladle brought by Soma.

6 Thus spake of her those Gods of old, Seven Ṛishis, who sate them down to their austere devotion:
Dire is a Brahman's wife led home by others: in the supremest heaven she plants confusion.

---

3 *Her pledge*: her sponsor. *Thus*: by observing justice and causing the abducted wife to be restored. These three stanzas correspond, with slight variations, to stanzas 1—3 of the Ṛigveda hymn.

4 The real cause of the misfortune attributed to meteoric influence is some disrespect shown to a Brahman's wife. *Hare with fiery flashing*: some meteoric phenomenon.

5 Ṛigveda X. 109. 5. *Brahmachârî*: a youth in the first stage of a Brâhman's religious life; a religious student. *Bṛihaspati*: that is, the injured Brahman; Bṛihaspati representing the sacerdotal class. *The ladle*: *juhûm*, which Prof. Ludwig takes to be the lady's name: 'Juhû, O Gods, conducted home by Soma.' The meaning is obscure. A legend quoted by Sâyaṇa says that Juhû or Vâk, the wife of Bṛihaspati who is identified with Brahmâ, had been deserted by her husband. The Gods then consulted together as to the means of expiating his sin, and restored her to him. The legend has evidently grown out of the misunderstanding of the ancient hymn.

6 Stanza 4 of the Ṛigveda hymn. *Seven Ṛishis*: celebrated saints, sages, and inspired seers of ancient times, Bharadvâja, Kaṣyapa, Gotama, Atri, Vasishṭha, Viṣvâmitra, and Jamadagni.

7 When infants die, untimely born, when herds of cattle waste away,
When heroes strike each other dead, the Brahman's wife destroyeth them.

8 Even if ten former husbands—none a Brâhman—had espoused a dame,
And then a Brahman took her hand, he is her husband, only he.

9 Not Vaiṣya, not Râjanya, no, the Brâhman is indeed her lord:
This Sûrya in his course proclaims to the Five Races of mankind.

10 So then the Gods restored her, so men gave the woman back again.
Princes who kept their promises restored the Brahman's wedded wife.

11 Having restored the Brahman's wife, and freed them, with Gods' aid, from sin,
They shared the fulness of the earth and won themselves extended sway.

12 No lovely wife who brings her dower in hundreds rests upon his bed,

---

8 *Râjanya:* man of the military and princely class = Kshatriya.

10 Stanza 6 of the Ṛigveda hymn.

11 Stanza 7 of the Ṛigveda hymn.

Mr. Muir observes at the end of his translation of the non-Ṛigveda portion of the hymn (O. S. Texts, I. p. 281): 'This hymn appears to show that, however extravagant the pretensions of the Brāhmans were in other respects, they had, even at the comparatively late period when it was composed, but little regard to the purity of the sacerdotal blood, as they . . . . were in the habit of forming unions with the widows of Rājanyas or Vaiśyas, even if they did not even take possession of the wives of such men while they were alive.'

The hymn has been translated also by Zimmer, Altindisches Leben, p. 197, and by Ludwig, Der Rigveda, III. p. 446.

Within whose kingdom is detained, through want of sense, a Brahman's dame.

13 No broad-browed calf with wide-set ears is ever in his homestead born,
Within whose kingdom is detained, through want of sense, a Brahman's dame.

14 No steward, golden-necklaced, goes before the meat-trays of the man
Within whose kingdom is detained, through want of sense, a Brahman's dame.

15 No black-eared courser, white of hue, moves proudly, harnessed to his car,
In whose dominion is detained, through want of sense, a Brahman's dame.

16 No lily grows with oval bulbs, no lotus-pool is in his field,
In whose dominion is detained, through senseless love, a Brahman's dame.

17 The men whose task it is to milk drain not the brindled cow for him
In whose dominion is detained, through senseless love, a Brahman's dame.

18 His milch-cow doth not profit one, his draught-ox masters not the yoke
Wherever, severed from his wife, a Brahman spends the mournful night.

HYMN XVIII.

The Gods, O Prince, have not bestowed this cow on thee to eat thereof.
Seek not, Râjanya, to devour the Brahman's cow which none may eat.

The hymn declares the wickedness and ruinous consequences of oppressing and robbing Brâhmans.

2 A base Râjanya, spoiled at dice, and ruined by himself, may eat
The Brâhman's cow, and think, To-day, and not tomorrow, let me live!

3 The Brâhman's cow is like a snake, charged with dire poison, clothed with skin.
Râjanya! bitter to the taste is she, and none may eat of her.

4 She takes away his strength, she mars his splendour, she ruins everything like fire enkindled.
That man drinks poison of the deadly serpent who counts the Brâhman as mere food to feed him.

5 Whoever smites him, deeming him a weakling—blasphemer, coveting his wealth through folly—
Indra sets fire alight within his bosom. He who acts thus is loathed by Earth and Heaven.

6 No Brâhman must be injured, safe as fire from him who loves himself.
For Soma is akin to him and Indra guards him from the curse.

7 The fool who eats the Brahmans' food and thinks it pleasant to the taste,
Eats, but can ne'er digest, the cow that bristles with a hundred barbs.

8 His voice an arrow's neck, his tongue a bowstring, his windpipes fire-enveloped heads of arrows,
With these the Brahman pierces through blasphemers, with God-sped bows that quell the hearts within them.

9 Keen arrows have the Brâhmans, armed with missiles: the shaft, when they discharge it, never faileth.
Pursuing him with fiery zeal and anger, they pierce the foeman even from a distance.

---

4 *Deadly serpent:* the Taimâta, mentioned in V. 13. 6.

10 They who, themselves ten hundred, were the rulers of a thousand men,
The Vaitahavyas, were destroyed for that they ate a Brâhman's cow.

11 The cow, indeed, when she was slain o'erthrew those Vaitahavyas, who
Cooked the last she-goat that remained of Kesaraprâbandhâ's flock.

12 One and a hundred were the folk, those whom the Earth shook off from her:
When they had wronged the Brâhman race they perished inconceivably.

13 Among mankind the Gods' despiser moveth: he hath drunk poison, naught but bone is left him.
Who wrongs the kinsman of the Gods, the Brâhman, gains not the sphere to which the Fathers travelled.

14 Agni, in sooth, is called our guide, Soma is called our next of kin.
Indra quells him who curses us. Sages know well that this is so.

---

10 *Vaitahavyas:* a tribe or people in the north; literally, descendants or people of Vîtahavya. A Ṛishi of this name appears to be mentioned in Ṛigveda VI. 15, a hymn ascribed to him by Sâyaṇa. The Vaitahavyas are mentioned in the Anuṣâsana Parva of the Mahâbhârata, 1952—1977, where they are said to have been defeated and slain in battle.

11 *Kesaraprâbandhâ:* I can find no other mention of this woman.

12 *One and a hundred:* 'an unlucky number (used with reference to phases of disease, modes of death, and the like), cf. III. 9. 6; VIII, 2. 27.'—Grill's note on VII. 115. 3. *The Earth shook off:* in horror at their wickedness. Cf. Job, 38. 12: 'Hast thou commanded the morning . . . . And caused the dayspring to know his place; That it might take hold of the ends of the earth, That the wicked might be shaken out of it?'

The hymn has been translated by Muir, O. S. Texts, I. 285 (2nd edition); by Ludwig, Der Ṛigveda, III. p. 447; with annotations, by Grill, Hundert Lieder, pp. 41, 148; and by Zimmer, A. I. Leben, p. 199.

15 Prince! like a poisoned arrow, like a deadly snake, O lord of kine!
Dire is the Brâhman's arrow: he pierces his enemies therewith.

HYMN XIX.

The sons of Vîtahavya, the Sṛiñjayas, waxed exceeding strong.
They well-nigh touched the heavens, but they wronged Bhṛigu and were overthrown.

2 When men pierced Bṛihatsâman through, the Brâhman, son of Angiras,
The ram with teeth in both his jaws, the sheep, devoured their progeny.

3 If men have spat upon, or shot their rheum upon a Brâhman, they
Sit in the middle of a stream running with blood, devouring hair.

4 While yet the Brahman's cow which men are dressing quivers in her throes,
She mars the kingdom's splendour: there no vigorous hero springs to life.

5 Terrible is her cutting-up: her bitter flesh is cast away,
And it is counted sin among the Fathers if her milk is drunk.

The subject of the hymn is the wickedness and the ruinous consequences of oppressing, robbing, or insulting a Brahman.

1 *Vîtahavya:* see V. 18. 1. *Sṛiñjayas:* a people in the north. See Zimmer, A. I. Leben, p. 132. *Bhṛigu:* see II. 5. 3. The story of the overthrow of the Vaitahavyas is told in the Mahâbhârata, Anuṣâsana Parva, 1952—1977, but Bhṛigu is there said to have given refuge to the King Vitahavya after his defeat.

2 *Bṛihatsâman:* the name of this descendant of the ancient Ṛishi Angiras does not recur in the Veda, and his story is not mentioned elsewhere.

3 *They sit:* after death, in the infernal regions.

6 If any King who deems himself mighty would eat a Brâhman up,
Rent and disrupted is that realm wherein a Brâhman is oppressed.

7 She grows eight-footed, and four-eyed, four-eared, four-jawed, two-faced, two-tongued,
And shatters down the kingdom of the man who doth the Brâhman wrong.

8 As water swamps a leaky ship so ruin overflows that realm.
Misfortune smites the realm wherein a Brâhman suffers scath and harm.

9 The very trees repel the man, and drive him from their sheltering shade,
Whoever claims, O Nârada, the treasure that a Brâhman owns.

10 That wealth, King Varuṇa hath said, is poison by the Gods prepared.
None hath kept watch to guard his realm who hath devoured a Brâhman's cow.

11 Those nine-and-ninety people whom Earth shook and cast away from her,
When they had wronged the Brâhman race were ruined inconceivably.

12 Oppressor of the Brahmans! thus the Gods have spoken and declared,

---

7 *She*: the cow.

9 *Nârada*: a *devarshi* or saint of the celestial class who often comes down to earth to report what is going on in heaven and return with his account of what is being done on earth. His name is introduced to make the warning more solemn and impressive.

11 *Those nine-and-ninety*: cf. V. 18. 12, where they are said to have been a hundred and one.

The step-effacing wisp they bind upon the dead shall be thy couch.

13 Oppressor of the Brahmans! tears wept by the man who suffers wrong,
These are the share of water which the Gods have destined to be thine.

14 The share of water which the Gods have destined to be thine, is that,
Oppressor of the priest! wherewith men lave the corpse and wet the beard.

15 The rain of Mitra-Varuṇa falls not on him who wrongs the priest.
To him no counsel brings success: he wins no friend to do his will.

HYMN XX.

FORMED out of wood, compact with straps of leather, loud is the War-drum as he plays the hero.
Whetting thy voice and vanquishing opponents, roar at them like a lion fain to conquer!

2 The fastened frame hath roared as 'twere a lion, like a bull bellowing to meet the heifer.

---

12 *The step-effacing wisp:* obliterating the footsteps of the dead on his journey to the other world, so that Death may not reach the surviving kinsmen by the same path. Muir translates *kūḍ̣ham* (wisp) by 'cloth,' Ludwig, Zimmer, and Hillebrandt by 'fessel,' 'fetter,' and Roth and Grill by 'Büschel' 'tuft' or 'wisp.' See Grill's note.

14 *The beard:* to be shaved off before cremation.

The hymn has been translated by Ludwig, Der Rigveda, III. p. 451; by Zimmer, A. I. L. p. 201; by Grill, with annotations, Hundert Lieder, pp. 43, 150; and by Muir, O. S. Texts, I. 286, who observes: 'The attention of the reader is directed to the intensity of contempt and abhorrence which is sought to be conveyed by the coarse imagery contained in verses 3, and 12—14.'

The hymn, addressed to the War-drum, is a charm to secure victory in a coming battle. Compare Ṛigveda VI. 47. 29—31.

Thou art a bull, thine enemies are weaklings: thine is the foe-subduing strength of Indra.

3 Like a bull marked by strength among the cattle, roar seeking kine and gathering up the booty.
Pierce through our adversaries' heart with sorrow, and let our routed foes desert their hamlets.

4 Victorious in the battle, loudly roaring, seizing what may be seized, look all around thee.
Utter, O Drum, thy heavenly voice with triumph. Bring, as a priest, our enemies' possessions.

5 Hearing the Drum's far-reaching voice resounding, let the foe's dame, waked by the roar, afflicted,
Grasping her son, run forward in her terror amid the conflict of the deadly weapons.

6 Thou, first of all, O Drum, thy voice shalt utter: over the ridge of earth speak forth exultant.
Crunching with might the army of the foemen, declare thy message pleasantly and clearly.

7 Loud be thy roar between the earth and heaven. Swift let thy sounds go forth in all directions.
Neigh at them, thunder, set in opposition, song-maker, good ally that friends may conquer.

8 He shall send forth his voice whom art hath fashioned. Make thou the weapons of our warriors bristle.
With Indra for ally call out our heroes, and with thy friends scatter and chase the foemen.

9 Resonant, roaring, with thy powerful weapons, warning, and heard by troops in many places,
Knowing all rules and winning us advantage, deal fame to many where two kings are fighting.

---

4 *As a priest:* skilled in the use of incantations.

9 *All rules:* of warfare.

10 Bent on advantage, mightier, gaining treasures, victor in war, the spell hath made thee keener.
As, in the press, the stone to stalks of Soma, thus, Drum! go dancing to our foes' possessions.

11 Foe-conqueror, victor, vanquishing opponents, seeker of booty, mastering, destroying,
Speak out as a skilled speaker tells his counsel, speak strength to us that we may win the battle.

12 Shaker of things unshaken, readiest comer to battles; conquering foes, resistless leader,
Guarded by Indra, watching our assemblies, go quickly, breaker of their hearts who hate us.

HYMN XXI.

Speak to our enemies, O Drum, discouragement and wild dismay.
We bring upon our foemen fear and discord and discomfiture. Drum! drive these enemies away.

2 When sacrificial butter hath been offered, let our foemen flee
Through consternation, terrified, trembling in mind and eye and heart.

3 Wrought out of wood, compact with straps of leather, dear to all the clan,
Bedewed with sacrificial oil, speak terror to our enemies.

4 As the wild creatures of the wood flee in their terror from a man,
Even so do thou, O Drum, roar out against our foes to frighten them, and then bewilder thou their thoughts.

---

12 *Watching our assemblies:* favourably regarding our gatherings for sacrificial purposes.

The hymn has been translated by Ludwig, Der Rigveda, III. p. 460, and, with annotations by Grill, Hundert Lieder, pp. 68, 153.

The hymn, addressed to the personified War-drum (cf. V. 20.) and various deities, is a charm to secure victory in battle.

5 As, when the wolf approaches, goats and sheep run sorely terrified,
Even so do thou, O Drum, roar out against our foes to frighten them, and then bewilder thou their thoughts.

6 As birds of air, day after day, fly in wild terror from the hawk, as from a roaring lion's voice,
Even so do thou, O Drum, roar out against our foes to frighten them, and then bewilder thou their thoughts.

7 May all the deities whose might controls the fortune of the fray
Frighten away our enemies with Drum and skin of antelope.

8 Let those our enemies who go yonder in their battalions shake
In fear at shadows and the sounds of feet which Indra sporteth with.

9 To all the quarters of the sky let clang of bowstrings and our Drums
Cry out to hosts of foes that go discomfited in serried ranks.

10 Âditya, take their sight away! Follow them close, ye motes of light.
Let them cleave fast to foot-bound hosts when strength of arm hath past away.

11 Do ye, O mighty Maruts, sons of Pṛiṣni, crush down, with Indra for ally, our foemen.
King Soma, Varuṇa, great God and sovran, Indra too, aye, Death,—

12 May these embattled Gods, brilliant as Sûrya—All hail!—one-minded, conquer those who hate us.

---

10 *Âditya:* O Sun. *Let them cleave fast:* I can get no intelligible meaning out of the *patsaṅgînîḥ* of this *pâda*. 'Fusz-schlingen [patsaṅginî?] sollen [an ihnen] haften,' 'let foot-snares cling to them.'—Ludwig.

The hymn has been translated by Ludwig, Der Rigveda, III. p. 374.

HYMN XXII.

HENCE, filled with holy strength let Agni, Soma, and Varuṇa, the Press-stone, and the Altar,
And Grass, and glowing Fuel banish Fever. Let hateful things stay at a distance yonder.

2 And thou thyself who makest all men yellow, consuming them with burning heat like Agni,
Thou, Fever! then be weak and ineffective. Pass hence into the realms below or vanish.

3 Endowed with universal power! send Fever downward, far away,
The spotty, like red-coloured dust, sprung from a spotty ancestor.

4 When I have paid obeisance to Fever I send him downward forth.
So let Ṣakambhara's boxer go again to the Mahâvṛishas.

5 His mansions are the Mûjavans, and the Mahâvṛishas his home.
Thou, Fever, ever since thy birth hast lived among the Bahlikas.

6 Fever, snake, limbless one, speak out! Keep thyself far away from us.
Seek thou a wanton Dâsî girl and strike her with thy thunderbolt.

The hymn is a charm against Fever.

1 *Grass:* the Sacred Grass strewn in the sacrificial court or chamber. See V. 12. 4. *Fever: takmán:* meaning especially malarial fever. See. I. 25. 1.

3 *Endowed with universal power:* the wonderful plant Kushṭha (Costus Speciosus, or Arabicus), is addressed.

4 *Ṣakambhara's boxer:* Fever. Ṣakambhara (Dung-bringer) appears to be the name of one of the demons of disease.

5 *Mûjavans:* apparently a hill tribe in the north-west of India. *Mahâvṛishas:* a people in the same region. *Bahlikas:* a Bactrian race, the people of Balkh. See Muir, O. S. Texts, II, 351.

7 Go, Fever, to the Mûjavans, or, farther, to the Bahlikas.
Seek a lascivious Ṣûdra girl and seem to shake her through and through.

8 Go hence and eat thy kinsmen the Mahâvṛishas and Mûjavans.
These or those foreign regions we proclaim to Fever for his home.

9 In a strange land thou joyest not: subdued, thou wilt be kind to us.
Fever is eager to depart, and to the Bahlikas will go.

10 Since thou now cold, now burning hot, with cough besides, hast made us shake,
Terrible, Fever, are thy darts: forbear to injure us with these.

11 Take none of these to be thy friends, Cough, or Consumption, or Decline:
Never come thence again to us! O Fever, thus I counsel thee.

12 Go, Fever, with Consumption, thy brother, and with thy sister, Cough,
And with thy nephew Herpes, go away unto that alien folk.

13 Chase Fever whether cold or hot, brought by the summer or the rains,
Tertian, intermittent, or autumnal, or continual.

14 We to Gandhâris, Mûjavans, to Angas and to Magadhas
Hand over Fever as it were a servant and a thing of price.

---

12 *Herpes: pâmán.*

14 *Gandhâris:* the country of Gandhâra is placed by Lassen to the west of the Indus, and to the south of the Kophen or Kâbul river. King Darius in a rock-inscription mentions the Ga(n)dâra together with the Hi(n)du as people subject to him, and the Gandarii, together with the Parthians, Khorasmians, Sogdians, and Dadikae, are

HYMN XXIII.

I HAVE called Heaven and Earth to aid, have called divine Sarasvatī,
Indra and Agni have I called: Let these destroy the worm, I prayed.
2 O Indra, Lord of Treasures, kill the worms that prey upon this boy.
All the malignant spirits have been smitten by my potent spell.
3 We utterly destroy the worm, the worm that creeps around the eyes,
The worm that crawls about the nose, the worm that gets between the teeth.
4 Two of like colour, two unlike, two coloured black, two coloured red,
The tawny and the tawny-eared, Vulture and Wolf, all these are killed.
5 Worms that are white about the sides, those that are black with black-hued arms,
All that show various tints and hues, these worms we utterly destroy.

---

said by Herodotus to have formed part of the army of Xerxes. The name of the country is preserved in the modern Kandahar. See Muir O. S. Texts, II. 342, and Zimmer, Altindisches Leben, p. 30. 'The Angas and Magadhas are tribes living in South Behar, and the country bordering it on the west. We have thus in this verse two nations situated to the north-west, and two to the south-east, whom we may suppose, from the maledictions pronounced on them, to have been hostile or alien tribes, who lived on the borders of Brahmanical India, and to have been beyond its boundaries at the time this incantation was composed' (Roth, Lit. and Hist. of the Veda, p. 42, quoted by Muir, O. S. T., II. 352).

The hymn has been translated by Ludwig, Der Rigveda, III. p. 510, and, with annotations, by Grill, Hundert Lieder, pp. 12, 154.

The hymn, which is very similar to II. 32, is a charm for the destruction of parasitic worms.

6 Eastward the Sun is mounting, seen of all, destroying things unseen,
Crushing and killing all the worms invisible and visible.

7 Let the Yevâshas, Kaskashas, Ejatkas, Sipavitnukas,
Let both the worm that we can see, and that we see not, be destroyed.

8 Slain the Yevâsha of the worms, slain too is the Nadaniman.
I have reduced them all to dust like vetches with the pounding-stone.

9 The worm Sâranga, white of hue, three-headed, with a triple hump,—
I split and tear his ribs away, I wrench off every head he has.

10 I kill you, worms, as Atri, as Kaṇva and Jamadagni killed.
I crush the worms to pieces with a spell that erst Agastya used.

11 The King of worms hath been destroyed, he who was lord of these is slain.
Slain is the worm whose mother, whose brother and sister have been slain.

12 Destroyed are his dependants, those who dwell around him are destroyed,
And all the worms that seem to be the little ones are done to death.

13 Of every worm and insect, of the female and the male alike,
I crush the head to pieces with a stone and burn the face with fire.

---

6 An adaptation of Ṛigveda I. 191. 8: 'Slayer of things unseen, the Sun, beheld of all mounts, eastward, up, Consuming all that are not seen, and evil spirits of the night (Yâtudhânis).'

7 *Yevâshas:* this word and those that follow are names of varieties of vermin or noxious insects that cannot be identified.

10 Cf. II. 32. 3.

The hymn has been translated by Ludwig, Der Rigveda, III. p. 501.

HYMN XXIV.

SAVITAR, Lord of furthering aids, protect me, in this my prayer, in this mine act, in this my sacerdotal charge, in this performance, in this thought, in this my plan and wish, in this my calling on the Gods! All hail!

2 May Agni, Lord of forest trees, protect me, in, etc.

3 May Heaven and Earth, the Queens of bounties, save me.

4 May Varuṇa, the Lord of waters, save me.

5 May Mitra-Varuṇa, Lords of rain, preserve me.

6 Lords of the mountains, may the Maruts save me.

7 May Soma, Lord of plants and herbs, protect me.

8 May Vâyu, Lord of middle air, protect me.

9 May Sûrya, sovran Lord of eyes, protect me.

10 May the Moon, Lord of constellations, save me.

11 May Indra who is Lord of heaven protect me.

12 The Maruts' father, Lord of cattle, save me.

13 May Mṛityu, Lord of living creatures, save me.

14 May Yama, Regent of the Fathers, save me.

15 May the Forefathers of old time protect me.

The hymn is the prayer of a priest for protection and effectual aid in the discharge of his sacerdotal duties. The refrain of stanza 1 is repeated in every stanza.

6 *Mountains:* or, great clouds; *párvata* (knotty, consisting of rugged masses) having both these meanings in the Veda.

12 *The Maruts' father:* Rudra. See. I. 19. 3.

13 *Mṛityu:* God of Death.

14 *Yama:* King of the Departed.

15—17 'When His Majesty [the Emperor of Japan] promulgated the Constitution he did "humbly and solemnly swear to the Imperial Founder of Our House and to Our other Imperial Ancestors," and did "now reverently make Our prayer to Them and to Our Illustrious Father, and implore the help of Their Sacred Spirits."'—Henry Norman, The Real Japan.

16 May Fathers of succeeding ages save me.

17 Next may the Fathers of our fathers save me, in this my prayer, in this mine act, in this my sacerdotal charge, in this performance, in this thought, in this my plan and wish, in this my calling on the Gods! All hail!

HYMN XXV.

Let the man, sower of the germ, lay, as a feather on a shaft,
Limb drawn from limb, whate'er is culled from cloud and from the womb of heaven.

2 Even as this broad earth received the germ of all the things that be,
Thus within thee I lay the germ. I call thee, Earth, to strengthen it.

3 O Sinîvâlî, set the germ, set thou the germ, Sarasvatî!
In thee let both the Asvins, crowned with lotuses, bestow the germ.

4 Let Mitra-Varuṇa and God Bṛihaspati lay the germ in thee.
Indra and Agni lay the germ, Dhâtar bestow the germ in thee.

The hymn is a charm to accompany the Garbhâdhâna ceremony to ensure or facilitate and bless conception.

1 *From cloud:* 'out of the mountain.'—Ludwig. In I. 11. 2, the Gods are said to bring the embryo from all the regions of the sky and earth.

3 *Sinîvâlî:* the Goddess of the day of new moon, and also of fecundity and easy birth, like the Latin Goddess Lucina (lucna, luna, the Moon). Râkâ, the Goddess presiding over the actual day of full moon, and Gungû identified by Sâyaṇa with Kuhû, another Goddess presiding over the day of conjunction when the moon rises invisible, also appear to be associated with childbirth. So in old Eddic poetry, the Norns are called the midwives of mankind. The stanza is taken from Ṛigveda X. 184. 2.

5 Let Vishṇu form and mould the womb, let Tvashṭar duly shape the forms,
Prajâpati infuse the stream, and Dhâtar lay for thee the germ.

6 Drink thou the procreative draught well-known to Varuṇa the King,
Known to divine Sarasvatî, and Indra slayer of the foe.

7 Thou art the germ of plants and herbs, thou art the germ of forest trees,
The germ of each existing thing, so here, O Agni, lay the germ.

8 Rise up, put forth thy manly strength, and lay the germ within the womb.
A bull art thou with vigorous strength: for progeny we bring thee near.

9 Prepare thee, Bârhatsâmâ, let the germ be laid within thy side.
The Soma-drinking Gods have given a son to thee, thy son and mine.

10 O Dhâtar, thou Disposer, lay within the body of this dame
A male germ with the noblest form, for her, in the tenth month, to bear.

11 Tvashṭar, celestial artist, lay within the body of this dame
A male germ with the noblest form for her in the tenth month to bear.

---

5 Taken from Ṛigveda X. 184. 1.

7 This and the following stanza are addressed to Agni who is regarded as the special giver of children. See Ṛigveda I. 66. 4; 68. 4; III. 1. 23.

9 *Bârhatsâmâ*: (from *bṛihat-sâman*) the name of the woman who is the subject of the hymn; daughter of Bṛihatsâman.

The hymn has been translated and explained by Weber, Indische Studien, V. p. 227, and translated by Ludwig, Der Rigveda, III. p. 478.

12 Savitar, vivifier, lay within the body of this dame
A male germ with the noblest form for her in the tenth month to bear.

13 O Lord of Life, Prajâpati, within this woman's body lay
A male germ with the noblest form for her in the tenth month to bear.

HYMN XXVI.

In sacrifice for you may sapient Agni—All hail!—use Yajus texts and fuel.

2 May Savitar the God—All hail!—foreknowing, chief in this sacrifice, employ them.

3 In this great rite—All hail!—may sapient Indra use lauds, rejoicings, well-yoked coursers.

4 Bring Praishas in the rite—All hail!—and Nivids, learnèd, connected, with the Consorts.

5 As a dame brings her son—All hail!—O Maruts, connected, in the rite bring measures.

6 Here Aditi is come—All hail!—preparing the rite with grass and lustral waters.

7 Let Vishṇu in this rite in varied manner—All hail! use well-yoked steeds, his fervours.

The hymn is a bidding prayer, inviting the Gods' presence and assistance at a sacrifice.

1 *Yajus texts:* sacrificial formulas, as opposed to *ṛichas*, recited hymns, and *sâmans*, chanted psalms.

3 *Lauds, rejoicings:* joyous recitations of praise. *Well-yoked coursers:* a figurative expression for the well-adapted parts of the ceremony which the deity contributes and directs.

4 *Praishas:* liturgical exhortations or invitations. *Nivids:* invocations of the Gods, inserted in certain parts of the liturgy. *The Consorts:* of the Gods. See note on III. 20. 3.

5 *Maruts:* addressed as singers, chanters of their thunder-psalm. *Measures: chhândâṅsi;* sacred or magical hymns, differing from *ṛich*, *sâman*, and *yajus*.

8 Let Tvashṭar in this rite in varied manner—All hail!—use forms, his well-yoked coursers.

9 Let Bhaga in this rite use prayers, foreknowing—All hail! for this use well-yoked coursers.

10 Let Soma in this rite in varied manner—All hail!—use milk-streams, well-yoked coursers.

11 Let Indra in this rite in varied manner—All hail!—use powers, his well-yoked coursers.

12 Hitherward come ye with the prayer, O Aṣvins, exalting sacrifice with cry of Vashaṭ!
Bṛihaspati!—All hail!—with prayer come hither. Here is the rite, here heaven for him who worships.

HYMN XXVII.

UPLIFTED be this sacrificer's fuel: lofty and brilliant be the flames of Agni!
Splendidly bright, fair-faced, with all his offspring, Tanûnapât the Asura, many-handed.

2 God among Gods, the God bedews the paths with fatness and with mead.

3 With store of mead to sacrifice comes Agni, comes Narâsansa Agni, friendly-minded, comes Savitar, righteous God who brings all blessings.

---

8 *Forms:* Tvashṭar being the great artificer, creator of all forms of life.

11 *Powers:* Indra's heroic might.

12 *Vashaṭ:* the sacrificial exclamation, when the oblation is cast into the fire. See I. 11. 1.

Bṛihaspati: Lord of Prayer. See I. 8. 2.

The hymn has been translated by Ludwig, Der Rigveda, III. p. 27.

An Âprî or Propitiatory hymn addressed to a series of deities or deified objects.

1 *With all his offspring:* other fires. 'The other fires are verily thy branches.'—Ṛigveda I. 59. 1. *Tanûnapât:* Son of Thyself, self-generated. See V. 12. 2. *Asura:* Lord divine.

3 *Narâsansa:* Praise of Men; a name or epithet of Agni in Âprî hymns.

4 Hither he comes with power and fatness also, the luminous, implored with adoration.

5 At holy rites and offerings Agni loveth the scoops: let this man worship Agni's greatness.

6 He is the furtherer at glad oblations: there stood the Vasus and the treasure-givers.

7 Ever the Doors divine, and all protect this worshipper's holy work.

8 Far-reaching, ruling by the Law of Agni,
May Dawn and Night, the holy, speeding near us, aid this our sacrificial ceremony.

9 Celestial Hotars, with the tongues of Agni praise and extol our lofty ceremony, so that our sacrifice be well conducted!

10 Three Goddesses upon this grass be seated, Iḍâ, Sarasvatî, Mahî, and Bhâratî adored with praise.

11 This our nutritious genial flow, God Tvashṭar! and growth of wealth, pour down on this man's kindred.

12 Vanaspati, rejoicing, of thyself send God-ward! Let Agni, Immolator, sweeten our libation.

---

4 *The luminous: vâhnis:* or, the priest; or, the furtherer (of oblations). See M. Müller, Vedic Hymns, Part I. pp. 37 sqq.

5 *The scoops:* or ladles, used for pouring the butter on the sacrificial fire. *This man:* the institutor of the sacrifice.

6 *Vasus and the treasure-givers:* the Gods who enrich the men who worship them.

7 *Doors divine:* of the sacrificial court or chamber. See V. 12. 5. *And all:* there is no substantive. *Devâḥ*, Gods, is probably understood.

8 *Dawn and Night:* personified as Goddesses.

9 *Celestial Hotars:* priests of the Gods. See V. 12. 7., where two only are invoked.

10 *Iḍâ, Sarasvatî, Mahî:* Goddesses who preside over prayer and praise. See V. 12. 8. Iḍâ is the same as Iḷâ. *Bhâratî* is said to be another name of Mahî.

12 *Vanaspati:* the sacrificial post, regarded as a form of Agni. See V. 12. 10. *Send God-ward:* convey our offerings to the Gods in heaven.

13 Pay sacrifice to Indra, Jâtavedas Agni, with Hail!
Let all the Gods accept the gifts we offer.

HYMN XXVIII.

For lengthened life, to last through hundred autumns, they equalize with nine the nine spirations.
Three in gold, three in silver, three in iron by heat are stablished in their several places.

2 May Agni, Sun, and Moon, and Earth, and Waters, Sky, Air, the Quarters and the Points between them,
And Parts of Years accordant with the Seasons by this three-threaded Amulet preserve me.

3 In the three-threaded Charm rest triple fulness! Let Pûshan cover it with milk and butter.
Here rest abundant store of food and people, may ample store of cattle rest within it.

4 Enrich this charm, Âdityas, with your treasure; magnify this, when magnified, O Agni.
Endow it with heroic strength, O Indra: therein be lodged a triple power of increase.

---

13 *Hail!*: *svâhâ*; the sacrificial exclamation which consecrates the offering, regarded also as an Âprî deity and a form of Agni.

The hymn has been translated by Ludwig, Der Rigveda, III. p. 434.

The hymn is a charm, accompanying investiture with an Amulet, to ensure general protection and prosperity for the wearer.

1 *Nine spirations*: the vital airs (cf. our vapours, spirits) are usually enumerated as three or five; or, with the other vital organs, six, seven, nine (as here) or ten, or thirteen. The amulet consists of three strands or threads, one of gold, one of silver, and one of iron, each of which contains three protective powers, that is, one for each of the vital airs on which the life of the wearer depends. *By heat*: through the fervour of the priest who prepared the charm; or, possibly through the fire that was used in melting the metals.

5 With gold let Earth protect thee, and with iron, accordant, all-sustaining Agni save thee!
And in accordance with the plants may silver, regarding thee with favour, grant thee vigour.

6 This gold, born threefold at its first production, grew the one thing that Agni loved most dearly: it fell away, one part of injured Soma.
One part they call seed of the sapient Waters. This gold bring thee long life when triply threaded!

7 Three lives of Jamadagni, thrice the vital force of Kaṣyapa,
Three sights of immortality, three lives have I prepared for thee.

8 When with the three-stringed charm came three strong eagles, sharing the Sacred Syllable and mighty,
With immortality they drove off Mṛityu, obscuring and concealing all distresses.

9 The golden guard thee from the sky, the silvern guard thee from the air,
The iron guard thee from the earth! This man hath reached the forts of Gods.

10 May these three castles of the Gods keep thee secure on every side.
Endowed with strength, possessing these, be thou the master of thy foes.

11 The God who first bound on in the beginning the deities' immortal golden castle,—
Him I salute with ten extended fingers. Blest be the three-stringed charm I bind upon thee.

---

5 Addressed to the person who is to wear the amulet.

6 *One part of injured Soma:* meaning, apparently, that originally it came partly from the Moon (Soma) when eclipsed.

8 *Sacred Syllable:* the mystical syllable Om. *With immortality:* or with Amrit, the drink of Gods, the Water of Life, which confers immortality. The meaning is not clear. The priest is ascribing a mysterious origin and supernatural powers to the amulet. *Mṛityu:* Death; the God of Death.

12 Aryaman be thy binder-on, and Pûshan and Bṛihaspati:
Whatever name the brood of day possess, therewith we fasten thee.

13 With Seasons and with Lengths of Time, for vigour and extended life,
With all the splendour of the Sun we fasten thee about the neck.

14 Drawn forth from butter and with meath besprinkled, firm as the earth, unshakable, triumphant,
Breaking down foes and casting them beneath me, be fastened on me for exalted fortune!

HYMN XXIX.

Made ready in the east drive forth, take notice of what is happening here, omniscient Agni!
Thou bringest medicine and healest sickness: through thee may we win horses, kine, and people.

2 Accordant with all Gods, O Jâtavedas Agni perform this work as we beseech thee,
That this defence of his may fall, whoever hath caused us pain, whoever hath consumed us.

3 Unanimous, with all the Gods together, so do this thing O Agni Jâtavedas, that this defence of his may fall and fail him.

4 Pierce both his eyes, pierce thou the heart within him, crush thou his teeth and cleave his tongue asunder.
Rend thou, most youthful Agni, that Piṣâcha whoso amid them all of this hath eaten.

---

12 *The brood of day:* auspicious things, produced in the sunlight as opposed to ill-omened creatures of night and darkness.

14 Spoken by the recipient of the amulet.

The hymn has been translated by Ludwig, Der Rigveda, III. p. 387. See also Zimmer, Altindisches Leben, pp. 53, 56.

The hymn is a charm for the destruction of Piṣâchas.

1 *In the east:* the region of the heavens over which Agni presides.

5 Whatever of his body hath been taken, plundered, borne off, or eaten by Piṣâchas,
This, Agni, knowing it, again bring hither! We give back flesh and spirit to his body.

6 If some Piṣâcha in my food raw, ready, thoroughly cooked, or, spotty, hath deceived me,
Let the Piṣâchas with their lives and offspring atone for this, and let this man be healthy.

7 If one hath cheated me in milk or porridge, in food from grain or plants that need no culture,
Let the Piṣâchas, etc.

8 If one, flesh-eater, in a draught of water have wronged me lying in the bed of goblins,
Let the Piṣâchas, etc.

9 If one, flesh-eater, in the day or night-time have wronged me lying in the bed of goblins,
Let the Piṣâchas, etc.

10 O Agni Jâtavedas, slay the bloody Piṣâcha, flesh-devourer, mind-destroyer.
Strong Indra strike him with his bolt of thunder, courageous Soma cut his head to pieces!

11 Thou, Agni, ever slayest Yâtudhânas, the fiends have never conquered thee in battles.
Consume thou from the root the flesh-devourers, let none of them escape thy heavenly weapon.

12 Collect, O Jâtavedas, what hath been removed and borne away.
Let this man's members grow, let him swell like the tendril of a plant.

---

5 *Of this:* of the body of this sick man, whose emaciation is attributed to the diabolical arts of Piṣâchas.

8 *Lying on the bed of goblins: ṣáyânam,* lying, agrees with *mâ,* me. Ludwig suggests that *ṣáyânas* should be read, to agree with *kravyất,* flesh-eater, which would be more intelligible and appropriate.

12 *What hath been removed:* all the flesh that the sick man has lost.

13 Like as the Soma's tendril, thus, O Jâtavedas, let him swell.
Let him live, Agni! Make him fat, free from consumption, full of sap.

14 Here, Agni, is the fuel, here are logs that crush Pisâchas down.
O Jâtavedas, willingly accept them and be pleased therewith.

15 Accept, O Agni, with thy flame the billets of Târshṭâgha wood.
Let the flesh-eater who would take the flesh of this man lose his form.

HYMN XXX.

From thy vicinity I call, from near, from far, from nigh at hand.
Stay here: depart not: follow not the Fathers of the olden time. I bind thy vital spirit fast.

---

15 *Târshṭâgha wood:* the word does not occur again in the hymns; and the tree, probably called Tṛishṭâgha, which supplied the fuel, cannot be identified. Târshṭâgha fuel is mentioned in the Kauṣika-Sûtra, XXV. 27. *Lose his form:* and so be annihilated.

This invocation of Agni to counteract and destroy the malevolent fiends who sapped men's strength and took their lives is a far more sensible proceeding than the European belief, countenanced by the law and generally prevalent even at the beginning of last century, which attributed any insidious and unaccountable illness to the malevolent machinations and noxious charms of witches, who were usually poor old women with wrinkled faces, hairy lips, squinting eyes, squeaking voices, and scolding tongues. 'Dr. Sprenger, in his *Life of Mohammed*, computes the entire number of persons who have been burned as witches during the Christian epoch at *nine millions*.'—Chambers's Encyclopædia.—Witchcraft.

The hymn has been translated by Ludwig, Der Rigveda, III. p. 526.

The hymn is a charm to restore to life and health a man who is dangerously ill.

2 If any man, a stranger or akin, hath cast a spell on thee,
I with my voice to thee declare thy freedom and release therefrom.

3 If in thy folly thou hast lied or cursed a woman or a man,
I with my voice declare to thee thy freedom and release therefrom.

4 If thou art lying there because of mother's or of father's sin,
I with my voice declare to thee thy freedom and release therefrom.

5 Accept the healing medicine, the balm thy mother and thy sire,
Thy sister and thy brother bring. I make thee live through lengthened years.

6 O man, stay here among us; stay with all thy spirit: follow not
Yama's two messengers. Approach the castles where the living dwell.

---

4 *Because of mother's or of father's sin:* so in the Ṛigveda: 'Let us not suffer for the sin of others' (VI. 51. 7); and 'Loose us from sins committed by our fathers' (VII. 86. 5). Compare also Taittirîya-Brâhmaṇa III. 7. 12. 3 cited by Muir: 'May Agni free me from any sin which my mother or my father committed when I was a babe unborn;' and 'And his disciples asked him, saying, Master, who did sin, this man, or his parents, that he was born blind?' (St. John IX. 2). Disease, if not caused by some malevolent demon, was generally regarded as the punishment of sin against Gods or men.

6 *Yama's two messengers:* 'And those two dogs of thine, Yama! the watchers, four-eyed, who look on men and guard the pathway .... Dark-hued, insatiate, with distended nostrils, Yama's two envoys roam among the people' (Ṛigveda X. 14. 11, 12). See also Atharva-veda VIII 1. 9; 2. 11; 8. 10. In England there is a somewhat similar popular belief. 'In Yorkshire, the Kirk-Grim [Church-spectre] is usually a huge black dog with eyes like saucers, and is called a padfoot. It generally frequents the church lanes; and he who sees it knows that he must die within the year.'—S. Baring-Gould, Strange Survivals, p. 16.

7 Come back as thou art called to come, knowing the outlet of the path,
And the approach and its ascent, the way of every living man.

8 Be not alarmed: thou wilt not die. I give thee lengthened years of life.
Forth from thy members have I charmed Decline that caused the fever there.

9 Gone is the pain that racked thee, gone thy fever, gone thy heart's disease.
Consumption, conquered by my voice, hath, like a hawk, fled far away.

10 Two sages, Sense and Vigilance, the sleepless and the watchful one,
These, the protectors of thy life, shall be awake both day and night.

11 This Agni must be waited on. Here let the Sun mount up for thee.
Rise from deep death and come away, yea, from black darkness rise thou up!

12 Homage be paid to Yama, and to Mṛityu, and to the Fathers, and to those who guide us!
I honour first, for this man's preservation, that Agni who well knoweth how to save him.

13 Let breath and mind return to him, let sight and vigour come again.
Let all his body be restored and firmly stand upon its feet.

14 Provide this man with breath and sight, O Agni, and with his body and his strength unite him.
Thou knowest Amrit: let him not go hence, nor dwell in house of clay.

---

10 *Sense and Vigilance:* 'Alert and Watchful.'—Muir.

14 *Thou knowest Amrit:* 'thou hast the knowledge of immortality.'—Muir.

15 Let not thine inward breathing fail, let not thine outward breath be lost.
Let Sûrya who is Lord Supreme raise thee from death with beams of light.

16 Tied, tremulously moving, here the tongue is speaking in the mouth.
With thee I charmed Decline away and Fever's hundred agonies.

17 This living world, unconquered of the Gods, is most beloved of all.
To whatsoever death thou wast destined when thou wast born, O man,
This death and we call after thee. Die not before decrepit age!

HYMN XXXI.

The spell that they have cast for thee on unbaked dish or mingled meal,
The witchcraft wrought on undressed meat, this I strike back again on them.

2 The spell that they have cast for thee on jungle-cock, goat, hornèd ram,

---

16 *Fever's hundred agonies:* so in Bohemian popular belief there were originally a hundred varieties of fever. See Grohmann, Medicinisches aus dem Atharva-Veda, Indische Studien, IX. p. 390.

17 Life is sweet; and you must not die before your time, before the natural termination of your life in extreme old age.

The hymn has been translated by Muir, O. S. Texts, V. 440, and by Ludwig, Der Rigveda, III. 494.

The hymn is a counter-charm to secure protection from all kinds of spells and incantations of an enemy.

2 *Hornèd ram: kurîrîṇi;* literally, (the animal) decorated with the *kurîra*, a kind of head-dress for women. According to Zimmer, some domestic bird, like the cock, the crested bird, must be meant. Coming between *goat* and *ewe*, I think *ram* is the most suitable meaning, his horns representing the *kurîra* with the nature of which we are not acquainted. Or *kurîrîṇi* may be an epithet of *ajé*, as Prof. Geldner explains: 'or hornèd goat.' See Vedische Studien, Part I. p. 130.

The witchcraft wrought upon thy ewe, this I strike back again on them.

3 The spell that they have cast upon thy beast that hath uncloven hooves,
The ass with teeth in both his jaws, this I strike back again on them.

4 The secret spell upon thy plants Amûlâ or Narâchî, spell
That they have cast upon thy field, this I strike back again on them.

5 The spell that wicked men have cast on thine original household-fire,
And on thy sacrificial hall, this I strike back again on them.

6 The spell that they have cast upon thy public room, thy gambling-board,
Spell they have cast upon thy dice, this I strike back again on them.

7 The spell that they have cast upon thine army or thy shafts and arms,
Spell they have cast upon the drum, this I throw back again on them.

8 Charm they have laid within thy well or buried in the burning-ground,
Charm they have laid within thy home, this I throw back again on them.

9 The spell that they have wrought for thee in flickering fire of human bones,—
Mroka, consuming, cannibal, this I throw back again on them.

---

4 *Amûlâ:* the Methonica Superba; a species of lily. *Narâchî:* some unidentified plant.

5 *Household fire:* Gârhapatya (agni); the western sacred fire maintained by every master of a house.

9 *Mroka:* Agni in his most dreaded form; the fire of the funeral pile.

10 He brought this by no proper path, by the right path we drive it back.
The fool in folly brought it to those who observe established bounds.

11 No power had he who wrought the spell: he hurt his foot, he broke his toe.
Unlucky for his wealthy lords, he hath wrought happiness for us.

12 May Indra slay with mighty bolt, may Agni with his missile pierce
The sorcerer who brings the curse, who deals with roots and secret spells.

---

10 *He:* the hostile enchanter, whose incantations have been improperly conducted, and launched against honest men who are proof against them.

11 Cf. IV. 18. 6. *His wealthy lords:* the rich men who hired his services who has cursed us in vain.

BOOK VI.

HYMN I.

Sing, Âtharvaṇa, at eve, sing loudly, bring a splendid present: hymn God Savitar with praises.

2 Yea, praise him whose home is in the river, Son of Truth, the youthful, gracious friend whose word is guileless.

3 Savitar our God shall send us many everlasting treasures, that both paths may well be travelled.

HYMN II.

For Indra, ministering priests! run ye and press the Soma juice,
That he may hear his praiser's word, and this my call.

2 Thou into whom the drops find way as sap pours life into a tree,
Drive off in thine abundant might our demon foes.

3 For Indra, thunder-armed, who drinks the Soma press the Soma out:
He, youthful, conqueror, and Lord, is praised by all.

A hymn of praise to Savitar.

1 *Âtharvaṇa:* descendant of the great Ṛishi Atharvan; Atharva-priest. The Âdhvaryu addresses the Udgâtar or Chanting Priest.

2 *River:* the sea of air; the heavens. *Youthful:* ever young and strong.

3 *Savitar . . . shall send: savitá́ sâvishat;* a frequently recurring play upon the two words, both from the root *sû* to set in motion, vivify, produce. *That both paths:* of the rising and declining Sun; *srutî* being read, as suggested in the St. P. Dictionary, instead of the manifestly corrupt *sushtutî*, eulogies.

A hymn in praise of Indra.

HYMN III.

GUARD us the Maruts! Guard us well, O Indra, Pûshan, Aditi.
Guard us, O Waters' Child, and Rivers Seven. May Vishṇu guard us, and the Sky.

2 May Heaven and Earth take care of us for victory, may Pressing-Stone and Soma save us from distress.
Sarasvatî, auspicious Goddess, guard us well: preserve us Agni and his kind protecting powers.

3 Preserve us both the Asvins, Gods and Lords of Light, and let the Dawns and Night bring us deliverance.
The Waters' Child protect our house from every harm. Do thou, God Tvashṭar, make us strong for health and wealth.

HYMN IV.

MAY Tvashṭar, Brahmaṇaspati, Parjanya hear my holy prayer.
May Aditi with all her sons, the brothers, guard us, invincible, protecting power.

2 May Aṅsa, Bhaga, Varuṇa, and Mitra, Aryaman, Aditi, and Maruts guard us.
May we be freed from that oppressor's hatred. May he keep off that foeman who is near us.

A hymn to various deities for protection and prosperity.

1 *Waters' Child:* a frequently occurring appellation of Agni, born in the form of lightning from the watery clouds of the firmament. *Rivers Seven:* the Indus, the Five Rivers of the Panjâb, and either the Sarasvatî or the Kubhâ. See IV. 6. 2.

A hymn to various deities for protection.

1 *Parjanya:* God of the rain-cloud. See I. 2. 1. *Aditi with all her sons:* see note on I. 9. 1.

2 *Aṅsa:* one of the Âdityas. *He:* any one or each of the friendly Gods.

3 May both the Asvins further our devotion. With ceaseless care deliver us, Wide-Ranger! O Father Heaven, keep from us all misfortunes.

HYMN V.

Agni, adored with sacred oil, lift up this man to high estate.
Endow him with full store of strength and make him rich in progeny.

2 Advance him, Indra! Let him be ruler of all akin to him.
Grant him sufficiency of wealth: guide him to life and length of days.

3 Prosper this man, O Agni, in whose house we offer sacrifice.
May Soma bless him, and the God here present, Brahmaṇaspati.

HYMN VI.

The godless man whoever plots against us, Brahmaṇaspati,
Thou shalt give up as prey to me the worshipper who pour the juice.

2 If, Soma, any spiteful man hath aimed at us whose thoughts are kind,
Smite with thy bolt upon his face: he, crushed to pieces, vanisheth.

---

3 *Wide-Ranger;* far-reaching Heaven. *Father Heaven: dyaushpitar* = Zeu pater, Jupiter.

A prayer to Agni and Indra for the well-being of a princely patron.

3 *Here present:* Brahmaṇaspati being sometimes identified with Agni who is present as the sacrificial fire.

The hymn has been translated by Ludwig, Der Rigveda, III. p. 431.

A hymn for protection from wicked men.

2 *With thy bolt:* more usually the weapon of Indra.

3 Soma, whoever troubleth us, be he a stranger or akin,
Deprive him of the strength he hath: slay him thyself like mighty Dyaus!

HYMN VII.

SOMA! what pathway Aditi and the three guileless Mitras use, come thou with help to us thereby.

2 Thereby thou, conquering Soma, wilt give Asuras to be our prey, thereby be ye our advocates.

3 Whereby ye Gods repelled and stayed the powers of the Asuras, thereby give shelter unto us.

HYMN VIII.

LIKE as the creeper throws her arms on every side around the tree,
So hold thou me in thine embrace that thou mayst be in love with me, my darling, never to depart.

2 As, when he mounts, the eagle strikes his pinions downward on the earth,
So do I strike thy spirit down that thou mayst be in love with me, my darling, never to depart.

---

3 *Dyaus:* Heaven; 'the bright sky itself, the old Dyaus, worshipped as we know by the Âryas before they broke up into separate peoples and languages, and surviving in Greece as Zeus, in Italy as Jupiter, Heaven-father, and among the Teutonic tribes as *Tŷr* and *Tiu*.'—M. Müller, India, What can it Teach us? p. 194.

The hymn has been translated by Ludwig, Der Rigveda, III. p. 430.

A prayer to Soma and other Gods for help and protection.

1 *Three guileless Mitras:* Mitra and the two other Âdityas, Varuṇa and Aryaman, who are usually associated with him.

A charm to win a maiden's love.

1 *Creeper: libujâ;* probably, woodbine. See Rigveda X. 10. 13. The refrain of the three stanzas occurs also in I. 34. 5, and II. 30. 1. The more literal translation is: That thou mayst nevermore depart, or, be estranged.

The hymn has been translated and explained by Weber, Indische Studien, V. 261 sqq.; and by Grill, Hundert Lieder, pp. 54, 158.

3 As in his rapid course the Sun encompasses the heaven and earth,
So do I compass round thy mind that thou mayst be in love with me, my darling, never to depart.

HYMN IX.

DESIRE my body, love my feet, love thou mine eyes, and love my legs.
Let both thine eyes and hair, fond girl! be dried and parched through love of me.

2 I make thee hang upon mine arm, I make thee lie upon my heart.
Thou yieldest to my wish, that thou mayst be submissive to my will.

3 May they whose kisses are a bond, a love-charm laid within the heart,
Mothers of butter, may the cows incline that maid to love of me.

HYMN X.

ALL HAIL for hearing to the Earth, to Trees, to Agni, sovran Lord!

2 All hail for breath to Air, for powers of life to Vâyu, sovran Lord!

The hymn is a charm to win a maiden's love.

1 *Fond girl!:* said proleptically.

2 *I make:* the wish is regarded as already obtained.

3 *Whose kisses are a bond:* whose caresses make their calves love them. The cows, 'the milky mothers,' the patterns of strong affection, are to soften the maiden's heart and fill it with a portion of their own passionate love. See Weber, Indische Studien, V. p. 264.

A thanksgiving for life, hearing, and sight.

1 *Earth:* perhaps as being a good conductor of sound, and so connected with hearing. *Sovran Lord:* of trees and plants, the most important productions of the earth.

2 *Vâyu:* as God of Wind and the air which supports life.

3 All hail for vision to the Stars, to Heaven, to Sûrya, sovran Lord!

HYMN XI.

ASVATTHA on the Ṣamî-tree. There a male birth is certified.

There is the finding of a son: this bring we to the women-folk.

2 The father sows the genial seed, the woman tends and fosters it.

This is the finding of a son: thus hath Prajâpati declared.

3 Prajâpati, Anumati, Sinîvâlî have ordered it.

Elsewhere may he effect the birth of maids, but here prepare a boy.

HYMN XII.

I, AS the Sun goes round the heaven, have travelled round the Serpents' race.

I ward thy poison off, as Night parts all else living from the Sun.

---

3 *Stars:* the eyes of heaven. *Sûrya:* as the God of light. Cf. 'May Sûrya, sovran Lord of eyes, protect me' (V. 24. 9.)

An epithalamian charm to ensure the birth of a boy.

1 The production of fire by means of the drill, the upper part of which is made of Aṣvattha, and the lower part or receptacle of Ṣamî wood, represents the union of man and wife. Moreover, the Aṣvattha, which has a masculine name, springing from, and growing on, the feminine Ṣamî-tree, is typical of the male child in due time to be born. See III. 6. 1.

2 *Prajâpati:* Lord of Life, whose favouring aid is invoked on these occasions. See Ṛigveda X. 184. 1, and Atharva-veda V. 25. 13.

3 *Anumati* and *Sinîvâlî* (see V. 25. 3) are deities presiding over different phases of the moon and associated with conception and child-birth. See Weber, Indische Studien, V. pp. 228 sqq.

The hymn has been translated and elucidated by Weber, Indische Studien, V. p. 264. See also Ludwig, Der Rigveda, III. p. 477.

A charm against venomous serpents.

2 With this, discovered in the days of old by Brahmans, Ṛishis, Gods,
With this I ward thy poison off, thou Biter! formed and forming now.

3 With mead I mingle flowing streams: the hills and mountains shall be mead,
Parushṇî and Ṣîpâlâ mead. May it be well with mouth and heart.

HYMN XIII.

Worship to weapons of the Gods! worship to weapons of the Kings!
Then worship to the people's arms! worship, O Death, be paid to thee!

2 Let worship be to thy defence and to thine accusation paid.
Death! be this worship paid to thy good-will and thy malevolence!

3 Worship to thy physicians, to thy sorcerers be worship paid!
Death! let this reverence be done unto thy Brâhmans and thy roots.

---

2 *With this:* drug or charm, understood.

3 *Parushṇî:* one of the rivers of the Panjâb, now called the Râvî. *Ṣîpâlâ:* a stream full of the aquatic plant Ṣipâla, Ṣaivala, or Avakâ (Blyxa Octandra).

A hymn of homage to Death.

1 *Gods:* priests, whose weapons are religious fervour, and the power of blessing and cursing. *The people's:* belonging to the Vaisyas, the men who constitute the third class or caste of the community, agriculturists and tradesmen.

2 *Defence* and . . . *accusation:* all that is said in thy favour and against thee.

3 *Roots:* used in incantations to destroy enemies.

HYMN XIV.

Remove thou all Decline that lurks within the members and the joints,
The firmly-settled heart-disease that racks the bones and rends the limbs.

2 From the consumptive man I pluck Decline as 'twere a severed part.
I cut the bond that fetters him, even as a root of cucumber.

3 Begone, Consumption, hence away, like a young foal that runs at speed.
Then, not pernicious to our men, flee, yearly visitant like grass!

HYMN XV.

Most excellent of all the plants art thou: thy vassals are the trees.
Let him be subject to our power, the man who seeks to injure us.

2 Whoever seeks to injure us, with kinsmen or no kin to aid,
May I be uppermost of all, even as this Plant is queen of trees.

A charm against Consumption.

1 *Decline: baläsam;* the gradual wasting away that frequently follows Takman or malarial fever. See Zimmer, A. I. Leben, 386, 387. The stanza is addressed to some medicinal plant.

2 *As'twere a severed part: mushkarám yáthâ;* sicut testiculum.

3 *Yearly visitant like grass:* usually prevalent in the rainy season when grass suddenly springs up in the greatest abundance.

A charm for power and preëminence.

2 *This Plant:* the Talâṣâ of stanza 3, an unidentified shrub or tree; *vetasî,* ratan, according to Keṣava.

3 *Soma:* this famous plant has remained unidentified till recently (see Max Müller, Biographies of Words, Appendix III., quoted in The Hymns of the Ṛigveda, Vol. I. p. 3). 'Dr. Aitchison has lately stated that Soma must be the *Ephedra pachyclade,* which in the Hari-rud valley is said to bear the name of *hum, huma,* and *yahma.* This

3 As Soma hath been made the best of all oblations 'mid the plants,
So, as Talâṣâ is the queen of trees, may I be chief of all.

HYMN XVI.

O Âbayu, non-Âbayu, dire is thy juice, O Âbayu: we eat the gruel made of thee.

2 Vihalha is thy father's name, thy mother's is Madâvatî.
Yea, verily thou art not he, thou who hast well protected liḟe.

3 Go thou to rest, Tauvilikâ! This noisy cry hath sunk to rest.
Go hence, depart, Nirâla, thou! the tawny and the tawny-eared.

---

supposition is confirmed by Dr. Joseph Bornmüller, a botanist long resident in Kerman, who identifies the Soma plant with some kind of Ephedra, probably *Ephedra distachya*, but who remarks that different varieties of Ephedra are to be found from Siberia to the Iberian peninsula, so that we must give up the hope of determining the original home of the Aryas by means of the habitat of the Soma plant' (Quarterly Review, No. 354, October 1894, p. 455).

Apparently a medicinal charm.

1 *Âbayu:* a non-identified plant. It seems to have been poisonous in its natural condition, but medicinal when cooked and properly prepared. *Non-Âbayu:* no longer retaining thy poisonous properties.

2 *Vihalha* and *Madâvatî* appear to be unidentified plants. *Thou art not he:* thou art no longer the poisonous plant thou wast.

3 *Tauvilikâ:* some kind of animal or plant. *Nirâla:* said to be a kind of fish.

The fourth verse, consisting of one line, is untranslatable: Thou art Alasâlâ in front, thou art Silanjâlâ (a weed growing in corn) behind: Nilagalasâlâ (probably a weed of similar kind).

HYMN XVII.

EVEN as this mighty Earth conceived the germ of all the things that be,
So may the germ of life be laid in thee that thou mayst bear a son.

2 Even as this mighty Earth hath borne and bears the stately forest trees,
So may the germ of life be borne in thee that thou mayst bear a son.

3 Even as this mighty Earth hath borne and bears the mountains and the hills,
So may the germ of life be borne in thee that thou mayst bear a son.

Even as this mighty Earth supports the moving world that dwells thereon,
So may the germ of life be borne in thee that thou mayst bear a son.

HYMN XVIII.

THE first approach of Jealousy, and that which followeth the first,
The pain, the fire that burns within thy heart we quench and drive away.

2 Even as the earth is dead to sense, yea, more unconscious than the dead,
Even as a corpse's spirit is the spirit of the jealous man.

A charm to ensure conception and the birth of a son.

1 *Earth:* the Mother of all: Heaven and Earth, Ouranos and Gaia, being regarded as the Universal Parents. So in the Genesis of the New Zealanders: 'The Heavens which are above us and the Earth which lies beneath us, are the progenitors of men, and the origin of all things.'—Max Müller, India, What can it Teach us? p. 154.

The hymn has been translated by Ludwig, Der Rigveda, III. p. 477.

A charm to banish Jealousy.

2 *Dead to sense:* cf. 'bruta tellus' (Horace, Odes I. 34. 9).

3 The thought that harbours in thy heart, the fluttering doubt that dwells therein,
Yea, all thy jealousy, like heat born of the dance, I banish thence.

HYMN XIX.

Let the Gods purify me, let men purify me with a prayer.
Cleanse me all creatures that exist! may Pavamâna make me pure.
2 May Pavamâna make me pure for wisdom and for power and life, and unassailed security.
3 God Savitar, by both of these, filter and pressing out the juice, purify us that we may see.

HYMN XX.

He goes away as 'twere from this fierce burning fire, inebriated and lamenting he departs.
Let him, the lawless, seek another and not us. Worship be paid to Fever armed with fiery heat.
2 To Rudra and to Fever be our worship paid: worship be paid to Varuṇa the splendid King!
Worship to Dyaus, to Earth, worship be paid to Plants!

---

3 *Like heat born of the dance:* or, if *dṛiter*, as suggested in the St. P. Dictionary and adopted by Weber, be read instead of *nṛiter*, 'like breath from leathern bag.'

The hymn has been translated by Ludwig, Der Rigveda, III. p. 514, by Weber, Indische Studien, V. p. 235, and by Grill, Hundert Lieder, pp. 28, 159.

A prayer for purification.

1 *Pavamâna:* the deified Soma juice as it is clarified by passing through the filter.

The hymn has been translated by Ludwig, Der Rigveda, III. p. 431.

A charm against Fever.

1 *He:* Fever personified.

2 *Rudra:* as sender of disease and death. See I. 19. 3. *Fever:* see I. 25. 1. *Dyaus:* Heaven.

3 Thou who, aglow with heat, makest all bodies green,
to thee, red, brown, I bow, the Fever of the wood.

HYMN XXI.

Of all the three terrestrial realms the ground is verily the best.
I from the skin that covers these gather a healing medicine.

2 Thou art the best of medicines, most excellent of Plants art thou,
As Soma 'mid the wandering stars, as Varuṇa among the Gods.

3 Endowed with wealth, denying not, give freely fain to give your gifts!
Ye stay the hair from falling off: ye strengthen and increase its growth.

HYMN XXII.

Dark the descent; the strong-winged birds are golden: they fly aloft to heaven, enrobed in waters.
They have come hither from the seat of Order, and inundated earth with streams of fatness.

---

3 *Green:* or yellow. See I. 25. 3, where Fever is called 'God of the sickly yellow.'

Of the wood: especially prevalent in densely wooded districts.

The hymn has been translated by Ludwig, Der Rigveda, III. p. 511.

A charm to strengthen hair and promote its growth.

1 *Three terrestrial realms:* the world is divided into heaven, firmament, and earth, and each of these, again, is sometimes spoken of as threefold. Cf. Ṛigveda IV. 53. 5, and VII. 87. 5. *The skin that covers these:* the surface of the ground; the skin on which the plants grow as hair grows on the skin of the head.

2 *Soma:* the Moon.

3 *Ye stay the hair from falling off:* the plants endowed with these virtues are left unnamed.

The hymn has been translated, with notes, by Grill, pp. 50, 160.

A hymn to the Maruts or Storm-Gods.

1 This stanza, which recurs in IX. 10. 22, is taken from Ṛigveda I. 16. 47. *Strong-winged birds:* here the Maruts.

2 Ye make floods rich in milk, make plants propitious, what time ye stir, O golden-breasted Maruts!
Pour down your showers of vigorous strength and favour there where ye sprinkle mead, O Maruts, heroes!

3 O Maruts, send ye down, streaming with water, rain which, may, filling all the sloping valleys,
Leap like a bold girl in a man's embraces, or like a matron tumbled by her husband.

HYMN XXIII.

Here flow the restless ones, they flow unceasing through the day and night.
Most excellently wise I call the Goddess Waters hitherward.

2 Let the deft Waters, summoned, give permission that we bear them off,
And quickly set us on our way.

3 Let all the people celebrate the rite of Savitar the God.
Sweet unto us be Waters, Plants propitious!

---

2 *Golden-breasted:* wearing ornaments of gold on their breasts, the lightning flashing from the stormy clouds. Cf. Ṛigveda II. 34. 2; V. 55. 1; 57. 5.

3 This stanza contains two difficult words, *gláhā* and *érum*, in the second line. See Prof. Pischel's explanation, Vedische Studien, I. pp. 82—85.

Stanzas 1 and 2 have been translated by Ludwig, Der Rigveda, III. p. 463.

A hymn to the Waters.

2 *Bear them off:* fetching the water required for sacrificial purposes was part of the religious service, and accompanied with duly prescribed ceremonies preceded by a prayer to the Goddesses for their assent.

HYMN XXIV.

FORTH from the Hills of Snow they stream, and meet in Sindhu here or there.
To me the sacred Waters gave the balm that heals the heart's disease.

2 Whatever rupture I have had that injured eyes or heels or toes,
All this the Waters, skilfullest physicians, shall make well again.

3 All Rivers who have Sindhu for your Lady, Sindhu for your Queen,
Give us the balm that heals this ill: this boon let us enjoy from you.

HYMN XXV.

MAY all the five-and-fifty which meet round the tendons of the neck
Depart and vanish hence away like plaguing insects' buzz and hum!

2 Those seventy-and-seven which meet round the upper vertebræ,
Let them all vanish hence away like plaguing insects' buzz and hum!

A hymn to the Rivers.

1 *Sindhu:* the Indus.

2 *Skilfullest physicians:* cf. I. 6. 2, 3, and III. 7. 5.

3 *For your Lady:* Sindhu or the deity of the river is sometimes feminine in the Veda.

The hymn has been translated, with notes, by Grill, Hundert Lieder, pp. 13, 161.

A charm against Apachitas, pustules or scrofulous swellings. See Bloomfield, Kauṣika-Sûtra, p. XLIV. Dr. Wise (Hindu System of Medicine) says: 'When many small tumours like plums appear in the axilla, neck, back, and groins, they are produced by diseased fat, and phlegm. They suppurate slowly, and continue to appear and suppurate for a long period, when it is called *Apachi*.' Cf. AV. VI. 83; VII. 74. 1, 2; 76. 1, 2.

3 Those nine-and-ninety which, combined, attack the shoulder round about,
Let them all vanish hence away like plaguing insects' buzz and hum!

HYMN XXVI.

Let me go free, O Misery: do thou, the mighty, pity us.
Set me uninjured in the world of happiness, O Misery.
2 From thee, from thee who fliest not from us, O Misery, we fly.
Then at the turning of the paths let Misery fall on someone else.
3 May the immortal, thousand-eyed, dwell otherwhere apart from us.
Let him afflict the man we hate: smite only him who is our foe.

HYMN XXVII.

Gods! whatsoe'er the Dove came hither seeking, sent to us as the envoy of Destruction,
For that let us sing hymns and make atonement. Well be it with our quadrupeds and bipeds!
2 Auspicious be the Dove that hath been sent us, a harmless bird, O Gods, that seeks our dwelling!
May Agni, Sage, be pleased with our oblation, and may the missile borne on wings avoid us.

A hymn to Affliction.

1 *O Misery*: *pâpman*; meaning both sin and distress.

A charm to avert threatened misfortune.

1 The hymn, taken from Ṛigveda X. 165, is ascribed to the Ṛishi Kapota (Pigeon or Dove) son of Nirṛiti or Destruction. A dove, regarded as an ill-omened bird and the messenger of Death, has flown into the house, and the Gods are entreated to turn the inauspicious visit to a blessing.

In England the dove who 'returning bore the mark of earth restored to the long labouring ark' (see Genesis 8. 11), is regarded as 'the very blessed spirit of peace' and love.

3 Let not the arrow that hath wings distract us. Beside the fire-place, on the hearth it settles.
May it bring welfare to our men and cattle: here let the Dove, ye Gods, forbear to harm us.

HYMN XXVIII.

Drive forth the Dove, chase it with holy verses: rejoicing bring we hither food and cattle,
Obliterating traces of misfortune. Most fleet may it fly forth and leave us vigour.

2 These men have strengthened Agni's might, these men have brought the kine to us.
They have sung glory to the Gods. Who is the man that conquers them?

3 Be reverence paid to him who, while exploring the path for many, first approached the river,
Lord of this world of quadrupeds and bipeds: to him be reverence paid, to Death, to Yama!

HYMN XXIX.

On those men yonder fall the wingèd missile: the screeching of the Owl is ineffective,
And that the Dove beside the fire hath settled.

A charm to avert threatened misfortune. See VI. 27. 1, and Ṛigveda X. 165. 5.

2 *These men*: the priests.

3 *The river*: which separates the world of life from the home of the dead. 'Yama first found for us the road to travel: this pasture never can be taken from us. Men born on earth tread their own paths that lead them whither our ancient Fathers have departed' (Ṛigveda X. 14. 2). Compare Atharva-veda XVIII. 3. 13, and Muir, O. S. Texts, V. 288 sqq.

A charm to avert threatened misfortune.

1 Pàdas 2 and 3 are taken from Ṛigveda X. 165. 4. *Ineffective*: on us.

2 Thine envoys who came hither, O Destruction, sent or not sent by thee unto our dwelling,
The Dove and Owl, effectless be their visit!

3 Oft may it fly to us to save our heroes from slaughter, oft perch here to bring fair offspring.
Turn thee and send thy voice afar: cry to the region far away;
That I may see thee in the home of Yama reft of all thy power, that I may see thee impotent.

HYMN XXX.

OVER a magic stone, beside Sarasvatî, the Gods ploughed in this barley that was blent with mead.
Lord of the plough was Indra, strong with hundred powers: the ploughers were the Maruts, they who give rich gifts.

2 Thy joy in hair that falleth or is scattered, wherewith thou subjectest a man to laughter—
To other trees, far from thee will I drive it. Grow up, thou Ṣamî, with a hundred branches.

3 Auspicious, bearing mighty leaves, holy one, nurtured by the rain,
Even as a mother to her sons, be gracious, Ṣamî, to our hair.

---

3 *Oft may it fly to us:* may the ill-omened bird become an auspicious visitant. *Of Yama:* the King of the Departed who sent thee forth.

A charm to promote the growth of hair.

1 *This barley:* used in the sacrifice.

2 *Ṣamî:* Prosopis Spicigera or Acacia Suma, regarded as a holy tree as its wood was used to form part of the drill by which the sacrificial fire was kindled. *With a hundred branches:* and so symbolical of an abundant crop of hair.

The hymn has been translated by Ludwig, Der Rigveda, III. p. 511. See also Zimmer, Altindisches Leben, pp. 59, 274.

HYMN XXXI.

THIS spotted Bull hath come and sat before his mother in the east,
Advancing to his father Heaven.

2 As expiration from his breath his radiance penetrates within. The Bull shines out through all the sky.

3 He rules supreme through thirty realms—One winged with song hath made him mount—
Throughout the days at break of morn.

HYMN XXXII.

WITH butter, in his hall where fire is burning, perform that sacrifice which quells the goblins.
Burn from afar against the demons. Agni! Afflict not in thy fury us who praise thee.

2 Let Rudra break your necks, O ye Piṣâchas, and split your ribs asunder, Yâtudhânas!
Here, Mitra-Varuṇa! may we dwell safely: with splendour drive the greedy demons backward.
Let them not find a surety or a refuge, but torn away go down to Death together.

A hymn to Sûrya the Sun-God, taken with variations from Ṛigveda X. 189.

1 *This spotted Bull:* the Sun. *His mother:* Earth, or Dawn.

3 *Thirty realms:* all the divisions of the world. *One winged with song:* perhaps Agni, whose flames ascend amid the hymns of the priests. The reading of the Ṛigveda is: *vấk pataṅgấya dhîyate*, Song is bestowed upon the Bird, that is, on the Sun whose morning song represents prayer. See Ludwig, Der Rigveda, IV. p. 159.

A charm against fiends and goblins.

1 *Goblins:* Yâtudhânas; see I. 7. 1. *Demons:* Râkshasas; fierce nocturnal fiends or ogres.

2 *Piṣâchas:* malignant imps; see I. 16. 3, note. *Mitra-Varuṇa:* the two Gods addressed as a dual deity, *mitrâvaruṇau*. *Greedy demons: atriṇas;* or 'tusky fiends,' as Prof. Max Müller renders the word.

HYMN XXXIII.

He who controls this air and men who aid his strength, and wood, and heaven, the lofty seat which Indra loves.

2 The bold whose overpowering might the boldest never hath defied,—
Fortress-like, unassailable is Indra's wrath, and fame, and force.

3 May he bestow on us that wealth, far-spreading, bright with yellow hue.
Indra is mightiest Lord among the folk.

HYMN XXXIV.

Send forth thy voice to Agni, to the manly hero of our homes,
So may he bear us past our foes.

2 That Agni who with sharpened flame of fire consumes the Râkshasas,
So may he bear us past our foes.

3 He who from distance far remote shineth across the tracts of land,
May he transport us past our foes.

4 He who beholds all creatures, who observes them with a careful eye,
May he transport us past our foes.

5 That brilliant Agni who was born beyond this region of the air,
May he transport us past our foes!

A hymn to Indra for the gift of riches. In stanzas 1 and 2 the phraseology is obscure and the construction loose, and the correctness of the text is not free from suspicion.

In stanza 2, line 2 I have adopted Prof. Geldner's explanation of *vyáthiḥ*, wrath, and *purā́*, fortress, as a secondary form of *púr*. See Vedische Studien, II. p. 29.

A hymn to Agni for protection from enemies.

HYMN XXXV.

FORTH from the distance far away Vaiṣvânara come to succour us! Agni approach our eulogies!

2 Vaiṣvânara with friendly thoughts hath come to this our sacrifice, Agni who saves from woe, to lauds.

3 Vaiṣvânara hath formed the hymn and laud of the Angirases. To these may he bring glorious light.

HYMN XXXVI.

HOLY Vaiṣvânara we seek, the Lord of light and endless life, the burning One who fadeth not.

2 He hath directed all things; he sends forth the Seasons in his might, furthering sacrifice's power.

3 Agni Kâma in other homes shines forth the sole imperial Lord of all that is and is to be.

HYMN XXXVII.

HITHERWARD, having yoked his steeds, came Imprecation, thousand-eyed,

Seeking my curser, as a wolf the home of one who owneth sheep.

A hymn to Agni Vaiṣvânara, the God of all Âryan men.

3 *Angirases:* descendants of the famous Ṛishi Angiras, the priests who by using the magical formulas of the Atharva-veda protect the sacrifice from the effects of inauspicious accidents. *These:* the officiating priests and the institutor of the sacrifice.

A hymn in honour of Agni Vaiṣvânara.

2 *He hath directed all things:* the deity who is the object of worship being at the time of adoration regarded as the supreme God.

3 *Agni Kâma:* the two Gods being identified here as in III. 21. 4. See Muir, O. S. Texts, V. p. 403, and Weber, Indische Studien, V. pp. 225, 226.

A charm to divert Imprecation.

The hymn has been translated, with notes, by Grill, Hundert Lieder, pp. 25, 161.

2 Avoid us, Imprecation! as consuming fire avoids the lake.
Smite thou the man who curses us, as the sky's lightning strikes the tree.

3 Who curses us, himself uncursed, or, cursed, who curses us again,
Him cast I as a sop to Death, as to a dog one throws a bone.

HYMN XXXVIII.

WHAT energy the lion hath, the tiger, adder, and burning fire, Brâhman, or Sûrya,
And the blest Goddess who gave birth to Indra, come unto us conjoined with strength and vigour!

2 All energy of elephant and panther, all energy of gold, men, kine, and waters,
And the blest Goddess who gave birth to Indra come unto us conjoined with strength and vigour.

3 Might in car, axles, in the strong bull's courage, in Varuṇa's breath, in Vâta, in Parjanya,
In Warrior, in the war-drum stretched for battle, in the man's roar and in the horse's mettle,
May the blest Goddess who gave birth to Indra come unto us conjoined with strength and vigour.

HYMN XXXIX.

LET sacrifice, like fame, thrive sped by Indra, inspired, well-ordered, with a thousand powers.
To highest rank raise me who bring oblation, me who move forth to far-extended vision.

A prayer for surpassing strength and energy.

1 *The blest Goddess:* Aditi.

3 *In Warrior:* in Râjanya or Kshatriya, one of the military and princely class. *War-drum:* see V. 20.

The hymn has been translated by Ludwig, Der Rigveda, III. p. 240.

A priest's prayer for power and glory.

1 *Raise me:* the sacrifice is addressed. *Far-extended vision:* meaning, life of long duration.

2 We will pay sacrifice and serve with worship our glorious Indra, famous for his glories.
Give thou us sway which Indra hath promoted, and in this boon of thine may we be famous.

3 Indra was glorious at his birth; Agni, Soma were born renowned.
And glorious am I, the most illustrious of all that is.

HYMN XL.

Here may we dwell, O Heaven and Earth, in safety. May Savitar and Soma send us safety.
Our safety be the wide air: ours be safety through the oblation of the Seven Ṛishis.

2 May the Four Quarters give this hamlet power: Savitar favour us and make us happy!
May Indra make us free from foes and danger: may wrath of Kings be turned to other places.

3 Make thou us free from enemies both from below and from above.
O Indra, give us perfect peace, peace from behind and from before.

HYMN XLI.

For mind, for intellect, for thought, for purpose, for intelligence,
For sense, for hearing, and for sight, let us adore with sacrifice.

---

3 *Glorious am I:* the prayer is regarded as already fulfilled.

The hymn has been translated by Ludwig, Der Rigveda, III. p. 240.

A prayer for peace and security.

1 *Seven Ṛishis:* see IV. 11. 9.

A prayer for protection, long life, and various blessings.

2 For expiration, vital air, and breath that amply nourishes,
Let us with sacrifice adore Sarasvatî whose reach is wide.

3 Let not the Ṛishis, the divine, forsake us, our own, our very selves, our lives' protectors.
Do ye, immortal, still attend us mortals, and give us vital power to live the longer.

HYMN XLII.

I LOOSE the anger from thy heart as 'twere the bowstring from a bow,
That we, one-minded now, may walk together as familiar friends.

2 Together let us walk as friends: thy wrathful feeling I remove.
Beneath a heavy stone we cast thy wrath away and bury it.

3 I trample on thine anger thus, I tread it down with heel and toe:
So dost thou yield thee to my will, to speak no more rebelliously.

HYMN XLIII.

FOR stranger and for friend alike this Darbha-grass removeth wrath.
Soother of Anger is it called because it calms the angry man.

A charm to effect a reconciliation between estranged friends.

2 *Beneath a heavy stone:* the symbolical action somewhat resembles the North-American Indians' custom of 'burying the hatchet' as a sign and pledge of peace.

The hymn has been translated by Ludwig, Der Rigveda, III. p. 515, and, with notes, by Grill, Hundert Lieder, pp. 29, 162.

A charm to effect the reconciliation of estranged friends.

1 *Darbha:* see II. 7. 1.

2 This Plant that hath abundant roots spreads to the place where waters meet.
Soother of Anger is the name of Darbha-grass that springs from earth.

3 We draw thine obstinacy forth, set in thy mouth and in thy jaw:
So dost thou yield thee to my will, to speak no more rebelliously.

HYMN XLIV.

FIRM stood the heaven, firm stood the earth, firm stood this universal world.
Firm stood the trees that sleep erect: let this thy malady be still.

2 Of all thy hundred remedies, a thousand remedies combined,
This is the surest cure for flux, most excellent to heal disease.

3 Thou art the stream that Rudra pours, the closest kin of Amrita.
Thy name is called Vishâṇakâ: thou sprangest from the Fathers' root, removing illness caused by wind.

---

3 *Obstinacy:* the rebellious and provoking words that thou hast spoken.

The hymn has been translated, with notes, by Grill, Hundert Lieder pp. 30, 162.

A charm to remove disease.

1 *Firm stood the heaven:* when it had been separated from the earth and established in its present place. See IV. 1. 4.

2 *Flux:* *âsrâvá;* see I. 2. 4.

3 *Vishâṇakâ:* an unidentified plant or tree. *From the Fathers root:* thou camest originally from the saints in heaven. *Removing illness caused by wind:* *vâtikṛitanâśanī;* *wind* meaning one of the bodily humours. The disease is probably rheumatism, called *bât* in Hindî, explained in Mathurâ Prasâda Misra's Trilingual Dictionary by *vâtarog, vâyurog,* and other words signifying wind-disease and wind. Zimmer (Altindisches Leben, p. 389) explains differently.

The hymn has been translated by Ludwig, Der Rigveda, III. p. 509.

HYMN XLV.

Sin of the Mind, avaunt! begone! Why sayest thou what none should say?

Go hence away, I love thee not. Go to the forests and the trees. My heart is in our homes and cows.

2 Whatever wrong we have committed, sleeping or waking, by ill-wish, dislike, or slander,

All these offences, which deserve displeasure, may Agni take from us and keep them distant.

3 Indra and Brahmaṇaspati! whatever foolish deed we plan,

May provident Âṅgirasa preserve us from the sin and woe.

HYMN XLVI.

Thou, neither quick nor dead, O Sleep, art fraught with Amrit of the Gods.

Thy name is Araru: thy sire is Yama; Varuṇânî bare thee.

2 We know thy birth, O Sleep, thou art son of the sisters of the Gods: the minister of Yama thou, thou art Antaka, thou art Death.

So well we know thee who thou art. Sleep, guard us from the evil dream.

A prayer for preservation from mental sin and promptings to do wrong.

3 *Âṅgirasa:* descended from the ancient Ṛishi Angiras, a priest after the order of Angiras, especially a name of Bṛihaspati or Brahmaṇaspati. According to Prof. Ludwig, Agni is meant. See Der Rigveda, III. p. 443, where the hymn is translated.

Stanzas 2 and 3 are taken, with variants, from Ṛigveda X. 164. 3, 4.

A charm against evil dreams.

1 *Araru:* an enemy, as being akin to Death. *Varuṇânî:* Consort of Varuṇa.

2 *Antaka:* the Finisher.

3 As men discharge a debt, as they pay up an eighth and half-an-eighth,
So the whole evil dream do we pay and assign unto our foe.

HYMN XLVII.

Dear to all men, all-prosperer, all-creating, may Agni, guard us at the morn's libation.
May he, the brightly pure one, give us riches: may we have life, enjoying food together.

2 At this our second offering may Indra, Maruts, and Viṣve Devas never fail us.
Still may the favour of the Gods be with us, blest with long life and speaking words that please them.

3 We pour this third libation of the Sages who fashioned forth the cup in proper order.
Winners of heaven, may they, Sudhanvan's children, lead our fair sacrifice to happy fortune.

---

3 The stanza is an imitation of Ṛigveda VIII. 47. 17: 'As we collect (or, discharge) the utmost debt, even the eighth and sixteenth part, So unto Âptya (Trita Âptya, a mythical being residing in the remotest part of heaven, to whom it was customary to wish away and consign any threatened calamity) we consign together all the evil dream.'

The hymn has been translated by Ludwig, Der Rigveda, III. p. 498.

A hymn to accompany the three daily libations.

1 *Dear to all men:* or, Vaiṣvânara.

2 *Second offering:* at mid-day.

3 *The Sages*: the Ṛibhus, the three sons of Sudhanvan who is said to have been a descendant of Angiras. They were named severally Ṛibhu, Vibhvan, and Vâja, and styled collectively Ṛibhus from the name of the eldest. 'Through their assiduous performance of good works they obtained divinity, and became entitled to receive praise and adoration. They are supposed to dwell in the solar sphere, and there is an indistinct identification of them with the rays of the sun: but, whether typical or not, they prove the admission, at an early date, of the doctrine, that men might become divinities.'—Wilson. The Ṛibhus are said to have made four sacrificial cups out of the single chalice that had been fabricated by Tvashṭar, signifying, perhaps, that some innovation in sacrificial procedure was attributed to them. See Ṛigveda I. 20, and 161.

HYMN XLVIII.

THOU art the Hawk, Gâyatrî's lord: I hold thee fast. Happily bear me to the goal of this my sacrifice. All hail!

2 Thou art the Ṛibhu, lord of Jagatî: I hold thee fast. Happily bear me to the goal of this my sacrifice. All hail!

3 Thou art the Bull, the Trishṭup's lord: I hold thee fast. Happily bear me to the goal of this my sacrifice. All hail!

A non-metrical hymn of sacrificial formulas used at the three daily libations or Soma-pressings.

1 *The Hawk:* this verse is addressed at the morning libation to Agni who from his rapid motion in his form of lightning is called the hawk: cf. 'I have begotten this new hymn for Agni, falcon of the sky' (Ṛigveda VII. 15. 4). In the myth of the rape of the celestial Soma by the falcon—one of the favourite subjects of the Vedic poets (see Ṛigveda I. 80. 2; 93. 6; III. 43. 7; IV. 26. 4—7; 27. 3, 4; IX. 72. 3)—the falcon represents Agni who in the form of lightning penetrates the laden thunder-clouds and carries off their heavenly treasure, the ambrosial, life-giving rain. *Gâyatrî's lord:* Agni being identified with the Gâyatrî metre in which his praises are sung, and which is the prominent metre in invocations addressed to him at the morning libation.

2 *The Ṛibhu:* the representative of the three Ṛibhus (see VI. 47. 3), to whom this verse is addressed at the evening libation. *Jagatî:* this being the chief metre employed at the evening libation.

3 *The Bull:* the Mighty One, Indra, to whom the verse is addressed at the mid-day libation. Cf. 'Thine, only thine, is the noonday libation' (Ṛigveda IV. 35. 7).

The hymn has been thoroughly discussed by Prof. Bloomfield in his article entitled The Myth of Soma and the Eagle, in the Festgrüss an Rudolph von Roth zum Doktor-Jubiläum, 24 August, 1893.

HYMN XLIX.

O Agni, in thy body man hath never found a wounded part.
The Ape devours the arrow's shaft as a cow eats her afterbirth.

2 Thou like a fleece contractest and expandest thee what time the upper stone and that below devour.
Closely compressing head with head and breast with breast he crunches up the tendrils with his yellow jaws.

3 The Eagles have sent forth their voice aloud to heaven: in the sky's vault the dark impetuous ones have danced.
When they come downward to repair the lower stone, they, dwellers with the Sun, have gained abundant seed.

HYMN L.

Destroy the rat, the mole, the boring beetle, cut off their heads and crush their ribs, O Asvins.

A hymn in honour of Agni.

1 *The Ape: kapíḥ;* 'der braune,' the brown.—Ludwig. *The arrow's shaft:* the reed of which the arrow is made. There seems to be a play on the word *téjanam* which means both inflammation and reed. As the monkey is not injured by the reed or possible arrow-shaft which he chews, so nimble fire only absorbs additional heat. According to an Indian lexicographer *kapiḥ* is a name of the Sun.

2 *The upper stone: uttaradrá* (—dru?—Whitney's Index). The reading appears to be corrupt.

3 *The Eagles:* the stanza is taken, with variants, from Ṛigveda X. 94. 5 where *the Eagles* are the rapidly-moving stones which press out the Soma-juice. The meaning here may perhaps be: The mighty, roaring flames of Agni rise on high, dark clouds gather and are tossed about in the upper air, and finally descend in the shape of fertilizing rain. *The lower stone:* perhaps the earth. The stanza is very obscure.

The hymn has been translated by Ludwig, Der Rigveda, III. p. 432.

A charm for the destruction of vermin.

1 *The boring beetle: tardám* (from tṛid, to cut through, or bore); 'borer,' getreide-wurm?: Ludwig. According to the St. Petersburg Dictionary some bird (cf. Latin turdus, a thrush) is meant.

Bind fast their mouths; let them not eat our barley: so guard, ye twain, our growing corn from danger.

2 Ho! boring beetle, ho! thou worm, ho! noxious grub and grasshopper!

As a priest leaves the unfinished sacrifice, go hence devouring not, injuring not this corn.

3 Hearken to me, lord of the female borer, lord of the female grub! ye rough-toothed vermin!

Whate'er ye be, dwelling in woods, and piercing, we crush and mangle all those piercing insects.

HYMN LI.

Cleansed by the filter of the Wind comes Soma past all our enemies, meet friend of Indra.

2 May the maternal Waters make us ready: cleanse us with fatness they who cleanse with fatness!

The Goddesses bear off each blot and tarnish: I come forth from the waters cleansed and stainless.

3 O Varuṇa, whatever the offence may be, the sin which men commit against the heavenly folk—

When, through our want of thought we violate thy laws, punish us not, O God, for that iniquity.

HYMN LII.

Slaying the Râkshasas, the Sun mounts upward in the front of heaven,

Âditya, from the mountains, seen of all, destroying things unseen.

A prayer for purification and forgiveness of sins.

3 *Varuṇa:* addressed as the moral Governor of the world. The stanza is taken, with a slight variant, from Ṛigveda VII. 89. 5.

A charm against noxious reptiles and insects.

1 The stanza is made up of fragments of Ṛigveda I. 191. 8, 9.

2 The kine had settled in their pen, wild animals had sought their lairs;
The wavelets of the brooks had passed away, and were beheld no more.

3 I have brought Kaṇva's famous Plant, life-giving, and itself inspired,
The medicine that healeth all: may it suppress my hidden foes.

HYMN LIII.

May Heaven and Earth, wise pair, may lofty Ṣukra grant me this thing by reason of the guerdon.
May Agni, Soma mark through this libation: may Vâyu, Savitar, and Bhaga guard us.

2 Again return to us our breath and spirit, again come back to us our life and vision!
Vaisvânara, unscathed, our bodies' guardian, stand between us and every woe and danger!

3 We are again united with our bodies, with happy mind, with spirit, strength, and splendour.
May Tvashṭar here make room for us, and freedom, and smooth whate'er is injured in our bodies.

---

2 The stanza is taken, with variations, from stanza 4 of the same hymn, the Ṛigveda reading being *ketávo jánânâm*, the lights of men, instead of *ûrmáyo nadînâm*, the wavelets of the brooks. The poet means that he has been bitten or stung by some venomous creature since sunset, and that now with the help of the rising sun and a magical plant he will destroy the unseen enemies who attacked him.

3 *Kaṇva* has been mentioned before (II. 32. 3), together with Atri, Agastya, and Jamadagni, as a celebrated Ṛishi regarded as a master of magic arts.

A prayer for recovery and preservation of health and security.

1 *Ṣukra:* the bright and pure; Soma. *Guerdon:* the honorarium given to the officiating priests.

The hymn has been translated by Ludwig, Der Rigveda, III. p. 506.

HYMN LIV.

I WIN the love of Indra that his friend may reach yet higher state.
Increase, as rain the grass, this man's dominion and his lofty fame.

2 Confirm the princely power in him, Agni and Soma! grant him wealth.
In all the circuit of his rule make him yet higher for your friend.

3 The man who shows us enmity, whether a stranger or akin,
Thou wilt give up entire to me who sacrifice and press the juice.

HYMN LV.

OF all the many God-frequented pathways that traverse realms between the earth and heaven,
Consign me, all ye Gods, to that which leadeth to perfect and inviolable safety.

2 Maintain us in well-being Summer, Winter, Dew-time, and Spring, Autumn, and Rainy Season.
Give us our share of cattle and of children. May we enjoy your unassailed protection.

3 Pay to the Year your lofty adoration, to the first Year, the second, and the present.
May we abide in the auspicious favour and gracious love of these who claim our worship.

A benediction on a newly elected King.

1 *Increase:* Indra is addressed.

2 *For your friend:* for Indra's sake.

A prayer for general protection and prosperity.

2 *Dew-time:* *śiśirah;* the cool season or first spring, comprising the months Mâgha and Phâlguna, from the middle of January to the middle of March.

3 *The first Year, the second, and the present:* making up the cycle of three lunar years at the end of which an intercalary month was added. See Zimmer, Altindisches Leben, p. 370.

The hymn has been translated by Ludwig, Der Rigveda, III. p. 218.

HYMN LVI.

LET not the serpent slay us, O Gods, with our children and our folk.
Let it not close the opened mouth nor open that which now is closed.

2 Be worship paid unto the black, worship to that with stripes across!
To the brown viper reverence, reverence to the demon brood!

3 I close together fangs with fang, I close together jaws with jaw.
I close together tongue with tongue, I close together mouth with mouth.

HYMN LVII.

THIS is a medicine indeed, Rudra's own medicine is this,
Wherewith he warns the arrow off, one-shafted, with a hundred tips.

2 Besprinkle it with anodyne, bedew it with relieving balm:
Strong, soothing is the medicine: bless us therewith that we may live.

3 Let it be health and joy to us. Let nothing vex or injure us.
Down with the wound! Let all to us be balm, the whole be medicine.

A charm against snakes.

2 *The black:* Asita. *With stripes across:* Tiraschirâji. See III. 27. 2. *Viper:* Svaja; meaning according to an Indian Commentator 'self-produced:' perhaps = Latin vipera, i. e. vivipara, producing its young alive, or from the root *svaj*, to twist or cling round.

The hymn has been translated by Ludwig, Der Rigveda, III. p. 502, and, with annotations, by Grill, Hundert Lieder, pp. 5, 162.

A charm for a wound or bruise.

1 *Rudra's own medicine:* Rudra being the healer as well as the inflicter of wounds and diseases. See I. 19. 3.

3 *Down with the wound!:* so (Rigveda VIII. 20. 26) 'Cast, Maruts! to the ground our sick man's malady: replace the dislocated limb.'

HYMN LVIII.

May Indra Maghavan give me name and glory. May Heaven and Earth, this couple, make me famous.

May Savitar the deity make me honoured. Here may the man who gives the guerdon love me.

2 Indra from Heaven and Earth receiveth glory, among the plants the Waters have their glory;

Even so may we be glorious 'mid all the Universal Gods.

3 Indra and Agni were renowned, famous was Soma at his birth;

So too am I illustrious, most glorious of all that is.

HYMN LIX.

First, O Arundhatî, protect our oxen and our milky kine:

Protect each one that is infirm, each quadruped that yields no milk.

2 Let the Plant give us sheltering aid, Arundhatî allied with Gods;

Avert Consumption from our men and make our cow-pen rich in milk.

3 I welcome the auspicious Plant, life-giving, wearing every hue.

Far from our cattle may it turn the deadly dart which Rudra casts.

A priest's prayer for power and glory.

1 *The man who gives the guerdon:* the institutor of the sacrifice who pays the expenses and rewards the priests.

3 This stanza is repeated from VI. 39. 3.

A charm to protect cattle and men.

1 *Arundhatî:* a medicinal climbing plant, called also Silâchî. See IV. 12. 1; V. 5. 5.

3 *Rudra:* see I. 19. 3.

According to the Kauṣika-Sûtra L. 13, the hymn is 'part of the ritual of a travelling merchant when about to start on a trading expedition.' See III. 15, and Bloomfield, American Journal of Philology, VII. 487.

HYMN LX.

WITH forelock loosened o'er his brow here comes the wooer of the bride,
Seeking a husband for this maid, a wife for this unmarried man.

2 Wooer! this girl hath toiled in vain, going to others' marriages.
Now to her wedding, verily, wooer! another maid shall come.

3 Dhâtar upholds the spacious earth, upholds the sky, upholds the Sun.
Dhâtar bestow upon this maid a husband suited to her wish!

HYMN LXI.

THE Waters send me what is sweet and pleasant, Sûra bring all I need for light and vision!
The deities, and all of pious nature, and Savitar the God afford me freedom!

2 I set the heaven and the earth asunder, I brought all seven seasons into being.
My word is truth, what I deny is falsehood, above celestial Vâk, above the nations.

The subject of the hymn is the Wooing of a Bride.

1 *The wooer: aryamá;* the interceder or match-maker whose business is to find a suitable wife for his friend or employer. See II. 36. 1.

3 *Dhâtar:* here regarded as the Upholder of the sacrament of marriage. See II. 36. 2.

The hymn has been translated and annotated by Weber, Indische Studien, V. pp. 236—238, and by Grill, Hundert Lieder, pp. 56, 164. Zimmer also has translated it in Altindisches Leben, p 306.

A prayer for prosperity and greatness.

1 *Freedom: vyáchas;* literally, expansion, amplitude, ample room.

2 This and the following stanza must be taken to signify hyperbolically the possession of infinite power. *Seven seasons:* the six pairs of months and the thirteenth or intercalary month. Six seasons only are known by name: see VI. 55, 2.

3 I gave existence to the earth and heaven, I made the seasons and the seven rivers.
My word is truth, what I deny is falsehood, I who rejoice in Agni's, Soma's friendship.

HYMN LXII.

CLEANSE us Vaisvânara with rays of splendour! With breath and clouds let quickening Vâyu cleanse us,
And, rich in milky rain, let Earth and Heaven, worshipful, holy, cleanse us with their water.

2 Lay hold on Sûnṛitâ whose forms and regions have fair smooth backs, her who is all men's treasure.
Through her may we, in sacrificial banquets singing her glory, be the lords of riches.

3 For splendour, seize on her whom all men worship, becoming pure yourselves, and bright, and brilliant.
Here, through our prayer, rejoicing in the banquet, long may we look upon the Sun ascending.

HYMN LXIII.

THAT collar round thy neck, not to be loosened, which Nirṛiti the Goddess bound and fastened,
I loose for thy long life and strength and vigour. Eat, liberated, food that brings no sorrow.

2 To thee, sharp-pointed Nirṛiti, be homage! Loose thou the binding fetters wrought of iron.
To me, in truth, again doth Yama give thee. To him, to Yama, yea, to Death, be homage!

A prayer for purification and riches.

2 *Sûnṛitâ:* Excellence, Pleasantness, Gladness, or Glory, personified. The etymology and the exact meaning are uncertain. Here, in connexion with Agni and Vâyu, the meaning 'Dawn' (see M. Müller, Vedic Hymns, I. p. 446) would be suitable.

The subject is the symbolical liberation of a victim from the sacrificial stake representing the recovery of a sick man from a dangerous illness.

3 Compassed by death which comes in thousand manners, here art thou fastened to the iron pillar.
Unanimous with Yama and the Fathers, make this man rise and reach the loftiest heaven.

4 Thou, mighty Agni, good and true, gatherest up all precious things.
Bring us all treasures as thou art enkindled at libation's place.

HYMN LXIV.

Agree and be united: let your minds be all of one accord,
Even as the Gods of ancient days, unanimous, await their share.

2 The rede is common, common the assembly, common the law, so be their thoughts united.
I offer up your general oblation: together entertain one common purpose.

3 One and the same be your resolve, be all your hearts in harmony:
One and the same be all your minds that all may happily consent.

---

3 *Loftiest heaven:* the summit of human felicity. See I. 9. 2.

4 The stanza is taken from Rigveda X. 191. 1. *At libation's place:* in the sanctuary where libations are offered.

The hymn has been translated by Ludwig, Der Rigveda, III. p. 433.

A hymn to promote Agreement or Unanimity in an assembly.

1 *Agree and be united:* the Ṛigveda has 'Assemble, speak together.'

2 *Common the assembly:* this *sámitis* appears to have been a general assembly of the people on some important occasion, such as the election of a king.

The hymn, which is taken, with variants, from Ṛigveda X. 191. 2—4, has been translated, with notes, by Grill, Hundert Lieder, pp. 30, 164, and by Ludwig, Der Rigveda, III. p. 372.

HYMN LXV.

THE angry spirit hath relaxed: loose are the arms that act with mind.
Do thou, destroyer, overcome and drive these foemen's might away, and then bring opulence to us.

2 The shaft for handless fiends which, Gods! ye cast against the handless ones,—
With this, in shape of sacrifice, I rend the arms of enemies.

3 Indra made first for Asuras the shaft designed for handless foes:
Victorious shall my heroes be with Indra as their constant friend.

HYMN LXVI.

HANDLESS be every foeman who assaileth, they who with missiles come to fight against us!
Dash them together with great slaughter, Indra! and let their robber chief run pierced with arrows.

2 Ye who run hither bending bows, brandishing swords and casting darts,
Handless be ye, O enemies! Let Indra mangle you to-day.

3 Handless be these our enemies! We enervate their languid limbs.
So let us part among ourselves, in hundreds, Indra! all their wealth.

A sacrificial charm against enemies.

1 *Destroyer: párâṣara;* Indra, conqueror and destroyer of Asuras who fought against the Gods, and of the demons who harass men.

2 *Handless:* who fight without human hands and arms. The magical missile employed against these demons is called *nairhastám* intended for *nirhasta*, or handless, fiends. Cf. III. 1. 1, 2. 1.

The hymn has been translated by Ludwig, Der Rigveda, III. p. 372.

A charm for the destruction and plunder of enemies.

Translated by Ludwig, Der Rigveda, III. p. 372.

HYMN LXVII.

INDRA and Pûshan have gone forth along the ways on every side.
To-day those hosts of enemies must flee bewildered far away.

2 Ye foes, come hitherward dismayed like serpents when their heads are gone.
Let Indra slay each bravest one of you whom Agni hath confused.

3 Gird thou a bullock's hide on these, make those as timid as the deer.
Let the foe flee away, and let his kine come hitherward to us.

HYMN LXVIII.

SAVITAR hath come hither with the razor: come thou, O Vâyu, with the heated water.
One-minded let Âdityas, Rudras, Vasus moisten the hair: shave, ye who know King Soma.

2 Let Aditi shave the beard, and let the Waters bathe it with their strength:
Prajâpati restore his health for sight and days of lengthened life!

3 The razor used by Savitar, for shaving, who knoweth Varuṇa and royal Soma,—
Even with this shave ye this man, O Brahman. Let him be rich in horses, kine, and children.

A charm for the destruction and plunder of enemies.

3 *Gird thou a bullock's hide on these:* make our men invulnerable. Translated by Ludwig, Der Rigveda, III. p. 372.

A charm to accompany the shaving of the beard.

1 The formal shaving may be part of the Godânavidhi, the ceremony of anointing part of the head of a youth when he has attained the age of sixteen or eighteen years (see II. 13); or it may be connected with the Dikshâ, the religious ceremony of initiation or Confirmation. In this case the operation appears to be performed on a sick man (stanza 2) to expedite his restoration to health.

Translated by Ludwig, Der Rigveda, III. p. 430.

HYMN LXIX.

MINE be the glory in the hill, in vales, in cattle, and in gold,
Mine be the sweetness that is found in nectar and in flowing wine!

2 With your delicious honey balm me, Asvins, Lords of splendid light!
That clear and resonant may be the voice I utter to mankind.

3 In me be strength, in me be fame, in me the power of sacrifice:
Prajâpati establish this in me as firm as light in heaven!

HYMN LXX.

As wine associates with flesh, as dice attend the gaming-board,
As an enamoured man's desire is firmly set upon a dame,
So let thy heart and soul, O Cow, be firmly set upon thy calf.

2 As the male elephant pursues with eager step his female's track,
As an enamoured man's desire is firmly set upon a dame,
So let thy heart and soul, O Cow, be firmly set upon thy calf.

3 Close as the felly and the spoke, fixt as the wheel-rim on the nave,
As an enamoured man's desire is firmly set upon a dame,
So let thy heart and soul, O Cow, be firmly set upon thy calf.

A priest's prayer for power and glory.

A benediction on cow and calf.
Translated and annotated by Grill, Hundert Lieder, pp. 66, 165.

HYMN LXXI.

WHAT food I eat of varied form and nature, food whether gold, or horse, sheep, goat, or bullock,
Whatever gift I have received, may Agni the Hotar make it sacrifice well-offered.

2 Whatever, sacrificed or not, hath reached me, bestowed by men and sanctioned by the Fathers,
Whereby my heart seems to leap up, may Agni the Hotar make that sacrifice well-offered.

3 What food I eat unjustly, Gods! or, doubtful between bestowing and refusing, swallow,
Through greatness of Vaiṣvânara the mighty may that same food be sweet to me and blessèd!

HYMN LXXII.

SEE APPENDIX.

HYMN LXXIII.

LET Varuṇa come hither, Soma, Agni, Bṛihaspati come hither with the Vasus!
Unanimous, ye kinsmen, come united, come to the glory of this mighty guardian.

2 The inclination which your hearts have harboured, the purpose which hath occupied your spirits,
This I annul with sacrifice and butter. In me be your sweet resting-place, O kinsmen.

3 Stand even here: forsake me not. Before us may Pûshan make your path unfit to travel.
Vâstoshpati incessantly recall you! In me be your sweet resting-place, O kinsmen!

A priest's benediction after eating.

1 *Make it sacrifice:* make it benefit me as a duly performed sacrifice would do.

A charm pronounced by a King to confirm the fidelity of discontented kinsmen.

1 *This mighty guardian:* meaning himself.

2 *The inclination:* to desert me.

3 *Vâstoshpati:* Lord of the Home. Sometimes a name of Indra.

HYMN LXXIV.

CLOSE gathered be your bodies: be your minds and vows in unison!
Here present Brahmaṇaspati and Bhaga have assembled you.

2 Let there be union of your minds, let there be union of your hearts:
All that is troubled in your lot with this I mend and harmonize.

3 As, free from jealousy, the strong Âdityas have been the Vasus' and the Rudras' fellows,
So free from jealousy, Lord of Three Titles! cause thou these people here to be one-minded.

HYMN LXXV.

FORTH from his dwelling drive that man, the foeman who assaileth us:
Through the Expellent sacrifice hath Indra rent and mangled him.

2 Indra, Foe-Slayer, drive him forth into the distance most remote,
Whence never more shall he return in all the years that are to come.

3 To the three distances, beyond mankind's Five Races, let him go,

---

A charm pronounced by a King to secure the unanimity and fidelity of his people.

2 *With this:* sacrifice.

3 *Lord of Three Titles:* probably Agni, who is called also Vaiśvânara and Jâtavedas.

A charm to effect the removal of an enemy.

1 *Expellent sacrifice; nairbâdhyam (haviḥ)*; an oblation to secure expulsion.

3 *Three distances:* beyond earth, firmament, and heaven. *Three skies:* see IV. 20. 1.

Translated by Ludwig, Der Rigveda, III. p. 373, and by Grill, Hundert Lieder, pp. 22, 165.

Beyond the three skies let him go, whence he shall never come again
In all the years that are to be, long as the Sun is in the heaven.

HYMN LXXVI.

Those who are sitting round this babe prepare him to be looked upon.
Let Agni thoroughly inflamed with all his tongues rise from his heart.

2 For length of life I use the name of Agni the Consuming God,
Whose smoke the sage who knows the truth beholds proceeding from his mouth.

3 The man who knows his fuel laid in order by the Kshatriya
Sets not his foot upon the steep declivity that leads to Death.

4 Those who encompass slay him not: he goes not near his lurking foes—
The Kshatriya who, knowing well, takes Agni's name for length of life.

HYMN LXXVII.

Firm stands the heaven, firm stands the earth, firm stands this universal world,
Firm stand the rooted mountains. I have put the horses in the stall.

A benediction pronounced over a new-born child of the Kshatriya or military and royal class.

Translated by Ludwig, Der Rigveda, III. p. 459.

A charm to bring the cattle home.

1 *Have put*: *atishṭhipam*; from *sthâ*, to stand: literally, have caused to stand.

2 I call the Herdsman, him who knows the way to drive the cattle forth,
Who knows the way to drive them home, to drive them back and drive them in.

3 O Jâtavedas, turn them back: a hundred homeward ways be thine!
Thou hast a thousand avenues: by these restore our kine to us.

HYMN LXXVIII.

LET this man be again bedewed with this presented sacrifice,
And comfort with the sap of life the bride whom they have brought to him.

2 With life's sap let him comfort her, and raise her high with princely sway.
In wealth that hath a thousand powers, this pair be inexhaustible!

3 Tvashṭar formed her to be thy dame, Tvashṭar made thee to be her lord.
Long life let Tvashṭar give you both. Let Tvashṭar give a thousand lives.

---

2 *The Herdsman:* Agni. The stanza is taken, with variations, from Ṛigveda X. 19. 4.

Translated by Ludwig, Der Rigveda, III. p. 468.

A nuptial benediction.

1 *Be again bedewed:* refreshed and made stronger than before. *With this presented sacrifice:* or, with this oblation for success. 'Mit diesem bhûtam haviḥ.'—Ludwig. 'Durch diese kräft'ge Darbringung,' through this powerful offering.—Weber. See Grill's note.

3 *Tvashṭar:* who develops the embryo, shapes all forms, and creates husband and wife for each other.

Translated by Weber, Indische Studien, V. p. 238, by Ludwig, Der Rigveda, III. p. 371, and by Grill, Hundert Lieder, pp. 57, 166.

HYMN LXXIX.

MAY this our Lord of Cloudy Sky, bedewed with liquid drops, preserve unequalled riches in our homes.

2 Lord of the Cloudy Sky, bestow vigour and strength on our abodes. Let wealth and treasure come to us.

3 Thou, God bedewed with drops, art Lord of infinite prosperity.
Grant us thereof, give us thereof: may we enjoy this boon of thine.

HYMN LXXX.

HE flieth in the firmament observing all the things that be:
We with this offering will adore the greatness of the Heavenly Hound.

2 The three, the Kâlakâñjas, set aloft in heaven as they were Gods—
All these I call to be our help and keep this man secure from harm.

3 In waters is thy birth, in heaven thy station, thy majesty on earth and in the ocean.
We with this offering will adore the greatness of the Heavenly Hound.

A prayer for prosperity.

1 *Lord of Cloudy Sky:* Parjanya, God of the rain-cloud, on whose favour the growth of grass and grain depends. See I. 2. 1.

A prayer for help and protection.

1 *The Heavenly Hound:* some conspicuous star, perhaps the Dog-star, Sirius, which was called *κύων* by the Greeks and Canis or Canicula by the Latins, both words being closely connected with the Sanskrit *ṣvân.*

2 *Kâlakâñjas:* meaning originally, black-spotted; stars of some unidentifiable constellation.

3 *Thy birth:* the origin of the Heavenly Hound. So with the Greeks Sirius was said to have been the dog of the great hunter Orion, and the Latin Canis or Canicula was the dog of Erigone translated with its mistress to the sky.

Translated by Ludwig, Der Rigveda, III. p. 373.

HYMN LXXXI.

THOU art a grasper, holding fast both hands: thou drivest fiends away.

A holder both of progeny and riches hath this Ring become.

2 Prepare accordantly, O Ring, the mother for the infant's birth.

On the right way bring forth the boy. Make him come hither. I am here.

3 The Amulet which Aditi wore when desirous of a son,

Tvashṭar hath bound upon this dame and said, Be mother of a boy.

HYMN LXXXII.

I CALL the name of him who comes, hath come, and still draws nigh to us.

Foe-slaying Indra's name I love, the Vasus' friend with hundred powers.

2 Thus Bhaga spake to me: Let him bring thee a consort by the path

Whereon the Asvins brought the bride Sûryâ the child of Savitar.

A charm to facilitate child-birth.

1 *Holding fast both hands:* the ring or bracelet was apparently placed first on one hand or arm and then on the other; or there were two connected rings, regarded as one amulet. See Kauṣika-Sûtra XXXV. 11.

Translated by Weber, Indische Studien, V. p. 239, by Ludwig, Der Rigveda, III. p. 477.

A charm to win a bride.

1 *Of him:* of Indra who is always ready to come and help us.

The Vasus' friend: whose associates are the Vasus, sometimes the Gods in general, sometimes a special class of deities. See I. 30. 1.

2 *Whereon the Aṣvins brought the bride:* see II. 30. 2, and Rigveda X. 85, which contains a full account of Sûryâ's wedding.

3 Great, Indra, is that hook of thine, bestowing treasure, wrought of gold:
Therewith, O Lord of Might, bestow a wife on me who long to wed.

HYMN LXXXIII.

HENCE, Sores and Pustules, fly away even as the eagle from his home.
Let Sûrya bring a remedy, the Moon shine forth and banish you.

2 One bright with variegated tints, one white, one black, a couple red:—
The names of all have I declared. Begone, and injure not our men.

3 Hence, childless, shall the Pustule flee, granddaughter of the dusky one.
The Boil shall fly away from us, the morbid growth shall vanish hence.
Taste, happy in thy mind, thine own oblation, as I with Svâhâ with my heart present it.

---

3 *That hook*: cf. 'Long be thy grasping-hook wherewith thou givest ample wealth to him Who sheds the juice and worships thee' (Ṛigveda VIII. 17. 10); the expression being borrowed from the employment of a hook to draw down the high branches of a fruit-tree.

Translated by Ludwig, Der Rigveda, III. 470, and with notes, by Weber, Indische Studien, V. p. 239—241, and Grill, Hundert Lieder, pp. 57, 167.

A charm against sores and pustules.

1 *Hence, Sores and Pustules*: *ápachitas*; see VI. 25. 1.

3 *Boil*: *glaúḥ*; explained in the St. Petersburg Dictionary as a round lump, a wen-like excrescence (perhaps related to *globus* and *glomus*). *Morbid growth*: *galuntáḥ*; an unknown word, not explained in the St. Petersburg Dictionary, meaning, apparently, a tumour of some kind. *Thine own oblation*: offered for the express purpose of removing thee. *Svâhâ*: the exclamation, All hail!

Translated by Ludwig, Der Rigveda, III. p. 500.

HYMN LXXXIV.

Thou in whose dread mouth I present oblation, that these bound victims may obtain their freedom,
The people deem that thou art Earth: I know thee thoroughly, and I say thou art Destruction.

2 Be thou enriched, O Welfare, with oblations, here, among us is thine allotted portion.
Free—Hail to thee!—from sin those here and yonder.

3 Do thou, Destruction, thus, without a rival, release us from the iron bonds that bind us.
To me doth Yama verily restore thee. To him, to Yama, yea, to Death be worship!

4 Thou hast been fastened to an iron pillar, here compassed with a thousand deaths around thee.
In full accord with Yama and the Fathers, send this man upward to the loftiest heaven.

HYMN LXXXV.

Let Varaṇa the heavenly tree here present keep disease away.
The Gods have driven off Decline that entered and possessed this man.

A charm to accompany the symbolical loosing of sacrificial victims.

1 *Earth:* one meaning of the word *nirṛitiḥ*, Destruction or Death, being the bottom or lower parts of the earth.

2 *O Welfare:* apparently an euphemistic expression for Destruction, as the Greek Eumenides, Gracious Goddesses, was for the Furies. Prof. Ludwig reads *bhúme*, O Earth, instead of the *bhûte*, O Welfare, of the text.

3 *The iron bonds:* of sin. *Thee:* some man who has been dangerously ill.

4 This stanza is repeated from VI. 63. 3.

Translated by Ludwig, Der Rigveda, III. p. 444.

A charm against Consumption or Decline.

1 *Varaṇa:* the tree Crataeva Roxburghii, found in all parts of India, used in medicine and supposed to possess magical virtues. See X. 3.

2 We with the speech of Indra and of Mitra and of Varuṇa,
We with the speech of all the Gods will drive Decline away from thee.

3 Even as Vṛitra checked and stayed these waters flowing every way,
With Agni, God of all mankind. I check and banish thy Decline.

HYMN LXXXVI.

THIS is the Lord of Indra, this the Lord of Heaven, the Lord of Earth,
The Lord of all existing things: the one and only Lord be thou.

2 The Sea is regent of the floods, Agni is ruler of the land,
The Moon is regent of the stars: the one and only Lord be thou.

3 Thou art the King of Asuras, the crown and summit of mankind:
Thou art the partner of the Gods: the one and only Lord be thou.

HYMN LXXXVII.

HERE art thou: I have chosen thee. Stand stedfast and immovable.
Let all the clans desire thee: let not thy kingdom fall away.

A glorification of a newly consecrated King.

3 *Asuras:* earthly lords.

Translated by Ludwig, Der Rigveda, III. p. 241.

A benediction addressed to a newly elected King.

The hymn is taken, with slight variations, from Ṛigveda X. 173. 1—3.

2 Be even here: fall not away: be like a mountain unremoved.
Stand stedfast here like Indra's self, and hold the kingship in thy grasp.

3 This man hath Indra stablished, made secure by constant sacrifice.
Soma, and Brahmaṇaspati here present bless and comfort him!

HYMN LXXXVIII.

Firm is the sky, firm is the earth, and firm is all this living world;
Firm are these mountains on their base, and stedfast is this King of men.

2 Stedfast may Varuṇa the King, stedfast the God Bṛihaspati,
Stedfast may Indra, stedfast, too, may Agni keep thy stedfast reign.

3 Firm, never to be shaken, crush thy foemen, under thy feet lay those who strive against thee.
One-minded, true to thee be all the regions: faithful to thee, the firm, be this assembly!

HYMN LXXXIX.

This strength that Soma hath bestowed, the head of her who gladdeneth,—
With that which thence hath been produced we make thy spirit sorrowful.

A benediction addressed to a newly elected King. Stanzas 1 and 2 are taken from Ṛigveda X. 173. 4, 5.

A charm to win a maiden's love.

1 *Soma:* as Lord of Plants. *Of her who gladdeneth:* *preṇyáḥ* is apparently the genitive case of *preṇī* the feminine of *preṇi* which is found in the Ṛigveda, (I. 112. 10) with the meaning of 'loving,' 'friendly,' derived from *prī*, to please or gladden. Preṇī then may mean some plant that possesses the power of awaking love, like

2 We make thy spirit sorrowful, we fill thy mind with pain and grief.
As smoke accompanies the wind, so let thy fancy follow me.

3 May Varuṇa and Mitra, may Sarasvatî the Goddess, may
The centre of the earth, and both her limits bring thee close to me.

HYMN XC.

The shaft that Rudra hath shot forth against thy members and thy heart,
Here do we draw from thee to-day, and turn it hence to every side.

2 From all the hundred vessels spread throughout the members of thy frame,
From all those vessels and canals we call the poisonous matter forth.

3 Worship to thee, the archer, and, O Rudra, to thy levelled shaft!
Yea, worship to thine arrow when it left the bow, and when it fell!

Satyrion, Vervain, Basil, Mallow, and others in Europe. The head of the Preṇí was perhaps dried and powdered and administered in food, or in some other way employed in the incantation.

Translated by Weber, Indische Studien, V. p. 242.

A charm to cure a man who has been poisoned.

1 *Rudra:* the terrible God whose shafts bring death or disease on men and cattle. In this case the body of the sufferer has been poisoned.

2 *Hundred vessels: ṣatám dhamánayaḥ;* all the countless vessels and nerves by means of which the different functions of the body are performed. See Wise, Hindu System of Medicine, pp. 63, 64.

The hymn has been translated by Grill, Hundert Lieder, pp. 14, 168.

HYMN XCI.

They made this barley ready with a team of eight, a team of six.
With this I drive to westward, far away, thy bodily disease.

2 Vâta breathes downward from above, and downward Sûrya sends his heat;
Downward is drawn the milch-cow's milk: so downward go thy malady!

3 The Waters verily bring health, the Waters drive disease away.
The Waters cure all malady: may they bring medicine for thee.

HYMN XCII.

Be fleet as wind, Strong Steed, when thou art harnessed; go forth as swift as thought at Indra's sending.
Let the possessors of all wealth, the Maruts, yoke thee, and Tvashṭar in thy feet lay swiftness.

2 That speed, that lies concealed in thee, O Charger, speed granted to the hawk or wind that wandered,—
Therewith, Strong Steed, saving in shock of battle, endowed with might by might win thou the contest.

A charm against disease.

1 *They made this barley ready:* prepared the ground by ploughing for the growth of the grain used in the incantation. The number of oxen employed has increased the efficacy of the corn.

3 *The Waters cure all malady:* cf. III. 7. 5. So Pastor Kneipp, the famous Bavarian water-doctor, maintains that what cannot be cured by water is altogether incurable. Water is the panacea. Hydropathy is the one saving principle which can be applied in every case.

Translated by Grill, Hundert Lieder, pp. 14, 168.

A charm to strengthen and inspirit a War-horse.

3 Bearing thy body, Charger, may thy body run blessing us and winning thee protection.
May he, unswerving, to uphold the mighty, stablish his lustre as a God in heaven.

HYMN XCIII.

YAMA, Death direly fatal, the Destroyer, with his black crest, Ṣarva the tawny archer,
And all the Gods uprisen with their army, may these on every side avoid our heroes.

2 With mind, burnt-offerings, butter, and libation, to royal Bhava and the archer Ṣarva,
To these the worshipful I pay my worship: may they turn elsewhere things with deadly venom.

3 Save us, All-Gods and all-possessing Maruts, from murderous stroke and things that slay with poison.
Pure is the might of Varuṇa, Agni, Soma. May Vâta's and Parjanya's favour bless us.

HYMN XCIV.

WE bend your minds in union, bend in harmony your hopes and plans:
You there, who turn to sundered ways, we bend and bow in unison.

---

3 This stanza is taken, with variants, from Ṛigveda X. 56. 2, a funeral hymn, and is there addressed to the spirit of the departed, Vâjin (strong, strong steed, charger or racer) being either the dead man's name or meaning 'hero.' The second line is obscure.

Translated by Ludwig, Der Rigveda, III. p. 459.

A prayer for protection from poison.

1 *Yama:* the King of the Departed, distinguished from Death the Destroyer. *Ṣarva:* a deity, generally mentioned together with Bhava (see IV. 28. 1). His name does not occur in the Ṛigveda.

2 *Bhava:* a deity attending on Rudra: in later mythology a name or form of Ṣiva whose consort is the awful Goddess Bhavâní.

A charm to reconcile a King's discontented people.

Translated by Ludwig, Der Rigveda, III. p. 514.

2 I with my spirit make your spirits captive: these with their thoughts follow my thought and wishes.
I make your hearts submissive to mine order: closely attending go where I precede you.

3 I have invoked both Heaven and Earth, invoked divine Sarasvatî,
Indra and Agni have I called: Sarasvatî, so may we thrive!

HYMN XCV.

In the third heaven above us stands the Aşvattha tree, the seat of Gods.
There the Gods gained the Kushṭha plant, embodiment of endless life.

2 There moved through heaven a golden ship, a ship with cordage wrought of gold.
There Gods obtained the Kushṭha plant, the flower of immortality.

3 Thou art the infant of the plants, the infant of the Snowy Hills:
The germ of every thing that is: free this my friend from his disease.

HYMN XCVI.

The many plants of hundred shapes and forms that Soma rules as King,
Commanded by Bṛihaspati, deliver us from grief and woe!

A charm to remove disease.

1 This and the following stanza are repeated from V. 4. 3, 4.

A prayer for deliverance from sin and sorrow.

1 *Commanded:* or, commissioned, or, engendered. The line is taken from Ṛigveda X. 97. 15.

2 Let them release me from the curse and from the noose of Varuṇa,
Free me from Yama's fetter, and from every sin against the Gods!

3 From every fault in look, in word, in spirit that we, awake or sleeping, have committed,
May Soma, with his godlike nature, cleanse us.

HYMN XCVII.

THE sacrifice is victor, Agni victor, victorious is Soma, Indra conquers:
So will we bring oblation unto Agni, this sacrifice that I may win all battles.

2 Praise to you, Mitra-Varuṇa, hymn-singers! Here swell with meath dominion blest with children.
Far into distant regions drive Destruction, and even from committed sin absolve us.

3 In this strong hero be ye glad and joyful: cleave ye to him even as ye cleave to Indra,
Victorious, kine-winner, thunder-wielder, who quells a host and with his might destroys it.

---

2 Taken, with a variant, from Ṛigveda X. 97. 16.

Translated by Ludwig, Der Rigveda, III. p. 506, and by Grill, Hundert Lieder, pp. 38, 168.

A prayer for the success and prosperity of a King.

1 This stanza is spoken by the institutor of the sacrifice for success in war.

2 This and the following stanza are spoken by the officiating priest. *Praise: svadhā́*; here a sacrificial exclamation, like Svâhâ = All hail!

3 Addressed to the King's subjects.

Translated by Ludwig, Der Rigveda, III. p. 460.

HYMN XCVIII.

INDRA be victor, never to be vanquished, to reign among the Kings as sovran ruler!
Here be thou meet for praise and supplication, to be revered and waited on and worshipped.

2 Thou fain for glory, an imperial ruler, hast won dominion over men, O Indra.
Of these celestial tribes be thou the sovran: long-lasting be thy sway and undecaying!

3 Thou governest the north and eastern regions, Indra! fiend-slayer! thou destroyest foemen.
Thou hast won all, far as the rivers wander. Bull, called to help, on our right hand thou goest.

HYMN XCIX.

INDRA, before affliction comes, I call thee from the wide expanse.
The mighty guardian, born alone, wearer of many names, I call.

2 Whatever deadly missile launched to-day flies forth to slaughter us,
We take both arms of Indra to encompass us on every side.

3 We draw about us both the arms of Indra, our deliverer. May they protect us thoroughly.
O Savitar, thou God, O royal Soma, make thou me pious-minded for my welfare.

A hymn of praise to Indra.

2 *These celestial tribes:* the heavenly Gods.

3 *Bull:* or, Strong.

A hymn for protection in battle.

1 *Born alone:* peerless from thy birth.

3 *Make thou:* each of you separately.

Translated by Grill, Hundert Lieder, pp. 18, 168.

HYMN C.

THE Gods and Sûrya gave the gift, the Earth and Heaven bestowed the boon.
The three Sarasvatîs in full accord bestowed the antidote.

2 That water, Upajîkâs! which Gods poured for you on thirsty land,
With that same water sent by Gods, drive ye away this poison here.

3 The daughter of the Asuras art thou, and sister of the Gods.
Thou who hast sprung from heaven and earth hast robbed the poison of its power.

HYMN CI.

SEE APPENDIX.

A charm against poison.

1 *Three Sarasvatîs:* the multiplication is analogous to that of the three heavens and three earths. See IV. 20. 2.

2 *Upajîkâs:* termites or white ants. See note on II. 3. 2. 'Whence do these Ants get their moisture? Our house was built on a hard ferruginous conglomerate, in order to be out of the way of the White Ants, but they came despite the precaution, and not only were they in this sultry weather able individually to moisten soil to the consistency of mortar for the formation of galleries . . . . but when their inner chambers were laid open, these were also surprisingly humid; yet there was no dew, and the house being placed on a rock they could have no subterranean passage to the bed of the river, which ran about three hundred yards below the hill. Can it be that they have the power of combining the oxygen and hydrogen of their vegetable food by vital force [so] as to form water?' (Quoted from Dr. Livingstone's well-known work by the Rev. J. G. Wood, "Strange Dwellings," p. 280.)

3 Addressed to some magical herb, probably Arundhatî or Silâchî which is called *sister of the Gods* in V. 5. 1. *Asuras:* divine beings; Gods.

Translated by Ludwig, Der Rigveda, III. p. 511.

HYMN CII.

EVEN as this ox, O Asvins, steps and turns together with his mate,
So let thy fancy turn itself, come nearer, and unite with me.

2 I, as the shaft-horse draws the mare beside him, draw thee to myself.
Like grass that storm and wind have rent, so be thy mind attached to me!

3 Swiftly from Bhaga's hands I bear away a love-compelling charm
Of ointment and of sugar-cane, of Spikenard and the Kushṭha plant.

HYMN CIII.

BṚIHASPATI and Savitar prepare a rope to bind you fast!
Let Bhaga, Mitra, Aryaman, and both the Asvins make the bond.

2 I bind together all of them, the first, the last, the middlemost.
Indra hath girded these with cord: bind them together, Agni, thou!

A charm to win a maiden's love.

1 The Asvins are addressed as having been the first teachers of ploughing (Ṛigveda I. 117. 21), and also perhaps as groomsmen and conductors of the bride at Sûryâ's wedding (Ṛigveda X. 85. 8, 9). The second line is addressed to the absent maiden.

2 *Grass: tṛiṇam* (Whitney's Index Verborum) instead of *tṛiṇma* of the text. Cf. II. 30. 1.

3 *Bhaga's hands:* Bhaga being a deity who presides over love and marriage.

Translated by Weber, Indische Studien, V. 243, and by Grill, Hundert Lieder, pp. 54, 169.

A charm to check the approach of a hostile army.

Translated by Ludwig, Der Rigveda, III. p. 518.

3 Those yonder who approach to fight, with banners raised along their ranks,
Indra hath girded these with cord: bind them together, Agni, thou!

HYMN CIV.

We bind our foemen with a bond that binds them close and holds them fast.
Their breath and respiration I dissever, and their lives from life.

2 This bond, made keen by Indra, I have formed with heat of holy zeal.
Securely bind our enemies, O Agni, who are standing here.

3 Indra and Agni bind them fast, Soma the King, and both the Friends!
May Indra, girt by Maruts, make a bond to bind our enemies.

HYMN CV.

Rapidly as the fancy flies forth with conceptions of the mind,
So following the fancy's flight, O Cough, flee rapidly away.

2 Rapidly as an arrow flies away with keenly-sharpened point,
So swiftly flee away, O Cough, over the region of the earth!

3 Rapidly as the beams of light, the rays of Sûrya, fly away,
So, Cough! fly rapidly away over the current of the sea!

A charm to check the approach of a hostile army.

3 *Both the Friends:* Mitra and Varuṇa.

Translated by Ludwig, Der Rigveda, III. 518.

A charm to cure Cough.

Translated by Ludwig, Der Rigveda, III. p. 510.

HYMN CVI.

Let flowery Dûrvâ grass grow up about thine exit and approach.
There let a spring of water rise, or lake with blooming lotuses.

2 This is the place where waters meet, here is the gathering of the flood.
Our home is set amid the lake: turn thou thy jaws away from it.

3 O House, we compass thee about with coolness to envelop thee.
Cool as a lake be thou to us. Let Agni bring us healing balm!

HYMN CVII.

Entrust me, Viṣvajit, to Trâyamâṇâ.
Guard, Trâyamâṇâ, all our men, guard all our wealth of quadrupeds.

2 To Viṣvajit entrust me, Trâyamâṇâ.
O Viṣvajit, guard all our men, etc.

3 To Viṣvajit entrust me, O Kalyâṇî.
Guard, O Kalyâṇî, all our men, etc.

A charm to protect a house from fire.

1 *Dûrvâ grass:* Panicum Dactylon; a creeping grass with 'flower-bearing branches erect. By far the most common and useful grass in India. It grows everywhere abundantly, and flowers all the year.'—Roxburgh. In Hindûstâṇî it is called *dûb*. The speaker is addressing his house.

2 *Thou:* Agni or Fire is addressed. The hymn may be compared with Ṛigveda X. 142. 6—8.

Translated by Grill, Hundert Lieder, pp. 63, 170.

A charm to protect men and cattle.

1 *Viṣvajit:* All-subduing; an epithet of Indra; also the name of an *ekâha* or one-day sacrifice performed in the course of the *gavâmayana*, a *sattra* (see I. 30. 4) or prolonged Soma sacrifice lasting a whole year. *Trâyamâṇâ:* Protectress; the name of a medicinal plant.

3 *Kalyâṇî:* Propitious one; the name of a leguminous shrub, Glycine Debilis.

4 To Sarvavid entrust me, O Kalyâṇî.
O Sarvavid, guard all our men, guard all our wealth of quadrupeds.

HYMN CVIII.

Intelligence, come first to us with store of horses and of kine!
Thou with the rays of Sûrya art our worshipful and holy one.

2 The first, devout Intelligence, lauded by sages, sped by prayer,
Trusted by Brahmachârîs, for the favour of the Gods I call.

3 That excellent Intelligence which Ṛibhus know, and Asuras,
Intelligence which sages know, we cause to enter into me.

4 Do thou, O Agni, make me wise this day with that Intelligence
Which the creative Ṛishis, which the men endowed with wisdom knew.

5 Intelligence at eve, at morn, Intelligence at noon of day,
With the Sun's beams, and by our speech we plant in us Intelligence.

---

4 *Sarvavid:* Omniscient; an epithet of Agni.

A prayer for wisdom.

2 *Brahmachârîs:* religious students.

3 *Ṛibhus:* who were deified on account of their artistic skill. See III. 5. 6, note. *Asuras:* divine beings.

4 *Creative Ṛishis:* *ṛishayo bhûtakṛitaḥ;* see III. 28. 1. and IV. 35. 2.

5 *Speech:* or prayer.

HYMN CIX.

The Berry heals the missile's rent, it heals the deeply-piercing wound.
The Gods prepared and fashioned it. This hath sufficient power for life.

2 When from their origin they came, the Berries spake among themselves:
The man whom we shall find alive shall never suffer injury.

3 Asuras buried thee in earth: the Gods again uplifted thee,
Healer of sickness caused by wounds and healer of the missile's rent.

HYMN CX.

Yea, ancient, meet for praise at sacrifices, ever and now thou sittest down as Hotar.
And now, O Agni, make thy person friendly, and win felicity for us by worship.

2 'Neath Jyaishṭhaghnî and Yama's Two Releasers this child was born: preserve him from uprooting.
He shall conduct him safe past all misfortunes to lengthened life that lasts a hundred autumns.

A charm to heal punctured wounds.

1 *The Berry: pippalî;* the fruit of the Asvattha, Pippal or Peepul, the Ficus Religiosa, or Holy Fig-tree. See III. 6. 1.

2 *From their origin:* from the hands of their Creator. *Whom we shall find alive:* to whom we are brought before his life is extinct.

3 *Asuras:* fiends. *Buried thee:* to prevent thee from saving human life. Cf. II. 3. 3.

Translated by Ludwig, Der Rigveda, III. 509, and by Zimmer, Altindisches Leben, p. 389.

A benediction on a new-born child.

2 *Jyaisṭhaghnî:* or Jyeshṭhaghnî: the sixteenth lunar mansion, called Jyeshṭhâ in XIX. 7. 3. *Yama's Two Releasers:* two auspicious stars whose rising releases from Death and disease; Vichṛitau. See II. 8. 1. *From uprooting: mûlabárhaṇât;* a play upon the word, the asterism being called also Mûlabarhaṇî. *He:* Agni.

3 Born on the Tiger's day was he, a hero, the Constellations' child, born brave and manly.
Let him not wound, when grown in strength, his father, nor disregard his mother, her who bare him.

HYMN CXI.

Unbind and loose for me this man, O Agni, who bound and well restrained is chattering folly.
Afterward he will offer thee thy portion when he hath been delivered from his madness.

2 Let Agni gently soothe thy mind when fierce excitement troubles it.
Well-skilled I make a medicine that thou no longer mayst be mad.

3 Insane through sin against the Gods, or maddened by a demon's power—
Well-skilled I make a medicine to free thee from insanity.

4 May the Apsarases release, Indra and Bhaga let thee go.
May all the Gods deliver thee that thou no longer mayst be mad.

HYMN CXII.

Let not this one, O Agni, wound the highest of these: preserve thou him from utter ruin.

---

3 *Tiger's day:* the tiger being in the Atharva-veda the type of valour.
Translated by Ludwig Der Rigveda, III. p. 431.

A charm to cure insanity.

4 *Apsarases:* who as Goddesses of gambling, 'dice-lovers, maddeners of the mind' (II. 2. 5), may have caused the insanity.

Translated by Zimmer, Altindisches Leben, p. 393, and by Grill, Hundert Lieder, pp. 21, 170.

A health-charm for man, woman, and son.

1 *This one: ayám*, this, hic, stands without a substantive. Dr. Grill suggests that *iyám*, haec, this (she-fiend), should be read. *The highest:* the father, the chief of the household. *The she-fiend: Gráhi.* See II. 9. 1.

Knowing the way do thou untie the nooses of the she-fiend: let all the Gods approve thee.

2 Rend thou the bonds of these asunder, Agni! the threefold noose whereby the three were fastened.

Knowing the way untie the she-fiend's nooses: free all, the son, the father, and the mother.

3 The elder brother's bonds, still left unwedded, fettered in every limb and bound securely,

Loose these, for they are bonds for loosing: Pûshan, turn woes away upon the babe-destroyer.

HYMN CXIII.

This sin the Gods wiped off and laid on Trita, and Trita wiped it off on human beings.

Thence if the female fiend hath made thee captive, the Gods by prayer shall banish her and free thee.

2 Enter the particles of light and vapours, go to the rising fogs or mists, O Evil!

Hence! vanish in the foams of rivers. Pûshan, wipe woes away upon the babe-destroyer!

3 Stored in twelve separate places lies what Trita hath wiped away, the sins of human beings.

Thence if the female fiend hath made thee captive, the Gods by prayer shall banish her and free thee.

---

2 *Of these:* father, mother, and son.

3 *Pûshan:* as the God who cherishes and multiplies life. *Babe-destroyer:* the fiend who kills the unborn babe. See II. 25. 4.

Translated by Ludwig, Der Rigveda, III. p. 469, and by Grill, Hundert Lieder, pp. 15, 171.

A charm to banish the fiend Grâhî.

1 *Trita:* the mysterious being to whom unpleasant things are consigned. See V. 1. 1.

3 Trita's repository may be compared to Milton's limbo (Paradise Lost, III. 490) into which follies and vanities 'upwhirled aloft Fly o'er the backside of the world far off.'

Translated by Ludwig, Der Rigveda, III. p. 444, and by Grill, Hundert Lieder, pp. 15, 171.

HYMN CXIV.

WHATEVER God-provoking wrong we priests have done, O Deities,
Therefrom do ye deliver us, Âdityas! by the right of Law.

2 Here set us free, O holy ones, Âdityas, by the right of Law,
When striving, bringing sacrifice, we failed to offer it aright.

3 With ladle full of fatness we, worshippers, pouring holy oil,
Striving, have failed, O all ye Gods, against our will, to offer it.

HYMN CXV.

WHATEVER wrong we wittingly or in our ignorance have done,
Do ye deliver us therefrom, O all ye Gods, of one accord.

2 If I, a sinner, when awake or sleeping have committed sin,
Free me therefrom as from a stake, from present and from future guilt.

3 As one unfastened from a stake, or cleansed by bathing after toil,
As butter which the sieve hath cleansed, so all shall purge me from the sin.

A prayer asking pardon for faults and errors in the performance of sacrifice.

1 *We priests: devā́sas* instead of *dévā́sas* of the text; literally, we gods. See III. 3. 2; 10. 2.

3 *To offer it:* in the proper manner.

Translated by Ludwig, Der Rigveda, III. 443, and by Grill, H. L. pp. 45, 172.

A prayer asking pardon for sin.

Translated by Ludwig, Der Rigveda, III. p. 443, and by Grill H. L., pp. 46, 172.

HYMN CXVI.

THE wealth which husbandmen aforetime, digging, like men who find their food with knowledge, buried,
This to the King, Vivasvân's son, I offer. Sweet be our food and fit for sacrificing!

2 May he, Vaivasvata, prepare our portion. May he whose share is mead with mead besprinkle
Our sin in hasty mood against our mother, or guilt whereby a sire is wronged and angered.

3 Whether this sin into our heart hath entered regarding mother, father, son or brother,
Auspicious be to us the zeal and spirit of all the fathers who are here among us.

HYMN CXVII.

THAT which I eat, a debt which still is owing, the tribute due to Yama, which supports me,
Thereby may I be free from debt, O Agni. Thou knowest how to rend all bonds asunder.

2 Still dwelling here we give again this present; we send it forth, the living from the living.
Throwing away the grain whence I have eaten, thereby shall I be free from debt, O Agni.

3 May we be free in this world and that yonder, in the third world may we be unindebted.
May we, debt-free, abide in all the pathways, in all the worlds which Gods and Fathers visit.

A prayer for pardon of sin against mother, father, son, or brother.

1 *Wealth:* in the shape of seed-corn. *Vivasvân's son:* Yama, King of the Departed, son of Vivasvân or the Sun.

2 *Vaivasvata:* son of Vivasvân.

Translated by Ludwig, Der Rigveda, III. p. 443.

A prayer for freedom from Debt.

1 *Due to Yama:* see VI. 116. 1.

3 *In the third world:* in heaven. *Unindebted:* free from the tax which new-comers have to pay. See III. 29. 1.

Translated by Ludwig, Der Rigveda, III. p. 444.

HYMN CXVIII.

If we have sinned with both our hands, desiring to take the host of dice for our possession,
May both Apsarases to-day forgive us that debt, the fiercely-conquering, fiercely-looking.

2 Stern viewers of their sins who rule the people, forgive us what hath happened as we gambled.
Not urging us to pay the debt we owed him, he with a cord hath gone to Yama's kingdom.

3 My creditor, the man whose wife I visit, he, Gods! whom I approach with supplication,—
Let not these men dominate me in speaking. Mind this, ye two Apsarases, Gods' Consorts!

HYMN CXIX.

The debt which I incur, not gaming, Agni! and, not intending to repay, acknowledge,
That may Vaiṣvânara, the best, our sovran, carry away into the world of virtue.

2 I cause Vaiṣvânara to know, confessing the debt whose payment to the Gods is promised.
He knows to tear asunder all these nooses: so may we dwell with him the gentle-minded.

3 Vaiṣvânara the Purifier purge me when I oppose their hope and break my promise,
Unknowing in my heart. With supplication, whatever guilt there is in that, I banish.

A prayer asking forgiveness of cheating at play.

1 *Fiercely-conquering, fiercely-looking:* according to Muir (O. S. Texts, V. 430) Ugrajit and Ugrampaṣyâ are the names of the two Apsarases.

2 *With a cord:* to keep us bound as debtors in the other world.

3 *Gods' Consorts:* wives of the celestial Gandharvas. See II. 2. 3, note.

Translated by Ludwig, Der Rigveda, III. p. 455.

A prayer for release from debts incurred without intention of payment.

1 *Into the world of virtue:* not imputing my action to me as a fault.

2 *Nooses:* bonds of debt.

3 *Their hopes:* my creditors' hopes of payment.

Translated by Ludwig, Der Rigveda, III. p. 442.

HYMN CXX.

If we have injured Air, or Earth, or Heaven, if we have wronged our Mother or our Father,
May Agni Gârhapatya here absolve us, and bear us up into the world of virtue.

2 Earth is our Mother, Aditi our birth-place: our brother Air save us from imprecation!
Dyaus, Father, save us, from the world of Fathers! My world not lost, may I approach my kindred.

3 There where our virtuous friends, who left behind them their bodily infirmities, are happy,
Free from distortion of the limbs and lameness, may we behold, in heaven, our sons and parents.

HYMN CXXI.

Spreading them out, untie the snares that hold us, Varuṇa's bonds, the upper and the lower.
Drive from us evil dream, drive off misfortune; then let us go into the world of virtue.

2 If thou art bound with cord, or tied to timber, fixt in the earth, or by a word imprisoned,
Our Agni Gârhapatya here shall free thee, and lead thee up into the world of virtue.

A prayer for forgiveness of sins and for felicity hereafter.

1 *Agni Gârhapatya:* the sacred fire perpetually maintained by a householder (*gṛihapati*), received from his father and transmitted to his son.

2 *My world:* my home in heaven.

3 Compare III. 28. 5. sqq.

Translated by Ludwig, Der Rigveda, III. p. 442, and by Grill, Hundert Lieder, 72, 123. See also Muir, O. S. Texts, V. pp. 41, 299, 306.

A prayer for felicity in the other world.

1 *Untie:* addressed to Agni Gârhapatya, the deity of the householder's sacred fire.

3 The two auspicious stars whose name is called Releasers have gone up.
Send Amrit hither, let it come freeing the captive from his bonds!

4 Open thyself, make room: from bonds thou shalt release the prisoner.
Freed, like an infant newly born, dwell in all pathways where thou wilt.

HYMN CXXII.

THIS portion I who understand deliver to Viṣvakarman first-born son of Order.
So may we follow to the end, unbroken, beyond old age, the thread which we have given.

2 This long-drawn thread some follow who have offered in ordered course oblation to the Fathers:
Some, offering and giving to the friendless, if they can give: herein they find their heaven.

3 Stand on my side and range yourselves in order, ye two! The faithful reach this world of Svarga.
When your dressed food hath been bestowed on Agni, to guard it, wife and husband, come together!

4 Dwelling with zeal I mount in spirit after the lofty sacrifice as it departeth.

---

3 *Releasers:* see II. 8. 1.

4 In the first line Amrit, the Water of Life, is addressed, and in the second the person who is to be benefited.

Translated by Ludwig, Der Rigveda, III. p 442.

A prayer for felicity in the other world.

1 *Viṣvakarman:* the Omnific; the architect of the universe, a deity closely resembling Prajâpati the Lord of Life and often not distinguished from him. *The thread which we have given:* the thread of life which we hand on to our children. 'Let not my thread, while I weave song, be severed, nor my work's sum, before the time, be shattered' (Ṛigveda II. 28. 5).

3 *Ye two:* the institutor of the sacrifice and his wife.

4 *After the lofty sacrifice:* sacrifices go to heaven, and are stored up there to await and reward their performer on his arrival. Cf. Ṛigveda X. 14. 8, and Atharva-veda VI. 123, 2; XI. 1. 36; XVIII. 2. 30.

Agni, may we, beyond decay, invited, in the third heaven, feast and enjoy the banquet.

5 These women here, cleansed, purified, and holy, I place at rest, singly, in hands of Brahmans.

May Indra, Marut-girt, grant me the blessing I long for as I pour you this libation.

HYMN CXXIII.

YE who are present, unto you I offer this treasure brought to us by Jâtavedas.

Happily will the sacrificer follow: do ye acknowledge him in highest heaven.

2 Do ye acknowledge him in highest heaven: ye know the world here present in assembly.

In peace will he who sacrifices follow: show him the joy which comes from pious actions.

3 Gods are the Fathers, and the Fathers Gods. I am the very man I am.

4 I cook, I give, I offer up oblation. From what I gave let me not be disparted.

5 O King, take thou thy stand in heaven, there also let that gift be placed.

Recognize, King, the gift which we have given, and be gracious, God!

---

5 *You:* Viṣvakarman, Agni, and Indra.

Translated by Ludwig, Der Rigveda, III. p. 432.

A prayer for felicity in heaven.

1 *Ye who are present:* Gods who attend the sacrifice. *Follow:* to heaven, and enjoy the reward of his sacrifice there. See VI. 122. 4.

2 *The joy which comes from pious actions: ishṭâpûrtám*; see II. 12. 4. note.

5 *O King:* Yama as King of the Departed.

HYMN CXXIV.

From the high firmament, yea, out of heaven a water-drop with dew on me hath fallen.
I, Agni! share the merit of the pious, with vigour, milk, and hymns and sacrifices.

2 It is a fruit if any tree hath dropped it, a breath, if from the sky it hath descended.
Where it hath touched my body or my garment, thence may the Waters drive Destruction backward.

3 It is a fragrant ointment, happy fortune, sheen all of gold, yea, purified from blemish.
Spread over us are all purifications. Death and Malignity shall not subdue us.

HYMN CXXV.

Mayst thou, O Tree, be firm indeed in body, our friend that furthers us, a goodly hero.
Put forth thy strength, compact with thongs of leather, and let thy rider win all spoils of battle.

2 Its mighty strength was borrowed from the heaven and earth: its conquering force was brought from sovrans of the wood.
Honour with sacrifice the Car like Indra's bolt, the Car girt round with straps, the vigour of the floods.

3 Thou bolt of Indra, vanguard of the Maruts, close knit to Varuṇa and child of Mitra,—
As such, accepting gifts which here we offer, receive, O godlike Chariot, these oblations.

An Omen from the sky.

Translated by Ludwig, Der Rigveda, III. p. 498.

Glorification of a War-chariot.

1 The hymn is taken from Ṛigveda VI. 47. 26—28. *O Tree: vánaspate;* literally, lord of the wood: the chariot.

Translated by Ludwig, Der Rigveda, III. p. 459.

HYMN CXXVI.

SEND forth thy voice aloud through earth and heaven, and let the world in all its breadth regard thee.
O Drum, accordant with the Gods and Indra, drive thou afar, yea, very far, our foemen.

2 Thunder out strength and fill us full of vigour, yea, thunder forth and drive away misfortunes.
Drive hence, O Drum, drive thou away mischances. Thou art the fist of Indra, show thy firmness.

3 Conquer those yonder and let these be victors. Let the Drum speak aloud as battle's signal.
Let our men, winged with horses, fly together. Let our car-warriors, Indra! be triumphant.

HYMN CXXVII.

OF abscess, of decline, of inflammation of the eyes, O Plant,
Of penetrating pain, thou Herb, let not a particle remain.

2 Those nerves of thine, Consumption! which stand closely hidden in thy groin—
I know the balm for that disease: the magic cure is Ṣîpudru.

Glorification of the War-drum.

1 The hymn is taken, with variants, from Ṛigveda VI. 47. 29—31.

3 *Those*: the enemy. *These*: our own men.

A charm to banish various diseases.

1 *Abscess*: *vidradhá*; probably the same as *bidradhi*; 'internal abscesses of the abdomen.'—Wise, Hindu System of Medicine, p. 210. *Decline*: *baláśa*; see IV. 9. 8. *Inflammation of the eyes*: *lóhita*. *Penetrating pain*: *visályaka*.

2 The sick man is addressed, the apostrophe to personified Consumption being parenthetical. *Ṣîpudru*: apparently some unknown tree or plant. The word does not occur elsewhere.

3 We draw from thee the piercing pain that penetrates and racks thy limbs,
That pierces ears, that pierces eyes, the abscess, and the heart's disease.
Downward and far away from thee we banish that unknown decline.

HYMN CXXVIII.

WHAT time the heavenly bodies chose the Weather Prophet as their King,
They brought him favouring weather, and, Let this be his domain, they said.

2 May we have weather fair at noon, may we have weather fair at eve,
Fair weather when the morning breaks, fair weather when the night is come.

3 Fair weather to the day and night, and to the stars and sun and moon,
Give favourable weather thou, King, Weather Prophet, unto us.

---

3 *Unknown decline: ajñâtayakshmá*; see III. 11. 1.

The hymn, with exception of the last line which appears to be a later addition, has been translated, with much information regarding the diseases mentioned, in Altindisches Leben, p. 386.

A prayer for Fair Weather.

1 *The heavenly bodies: nákshatrâṇi*; the stars and constellations regarded as the controllers of the weather. The moon is, even now, similarly regarded by some people. *The Weather Prophet: ṣakadhûmam*; literally 'him of the dung-smoke,' one who foretells the weather by the way in which smoke rises from a fire of cow-dung. The Ṣakadhûma was an old Brâhman, who, as supposed to have the power of foretelling the weather, was naturally regarded as its controller.

The hymn is prescribed in the Kauṣika-Sûtra, XXX. 13, as part of the ritual of a merchant when about to start on an expedition. It has been translated and thoroughly discussed by Prof. Bloomfield (American Journal of Philology, VII. pp. 484—488). See also Weber, Omina et Portenta, p. 363, and Zimmer, Altindisches Leben, p. 353.

4 Be worship ever paid to thee, O Weather Prophet, King of Stars,
Who gavest us good weather in the evening and by night and day!

HYMN CXXIX.

WITH fortune of the Sisu tree—with Indra as my friend to aid—
I give myself a happy fate. Fly and begone, Malignities!

2 That splendour and felicity wherewith thou hast excelled the trees—
Give me therewith a happy fate. Fly and begone, Malignities!

3 Blind fortune, with reverted leaves that is deposited in trees—
Give me therewith a happy fate. Fly and begone, Malignities.

HYMN CXXX.

THIS is the Apsarases' love-spell, the conquering resistless ones'.
Send the spell forth, ye Deities! Let him consume with love of me.

A charm to obtain success and happiness.

1 *Sisu:* Dalbergia Sisu; commonly spelt Sissoo: a stately timber tree common in Bengal and Northern India. For rapid growth, beauty, and usefulness few trees can be compared with it.

3 *With reverted leaves:* referring to the plant called Apâmârga. See IV. 19.

A woman's love-charm.

1 *The conquering resistless ones': rathajítâm râthajiteyînâm*; the words are hardly explicable. See Grill, who reads instead *arthajítâm arthajitînâm*, and translates 'Der altgewohnt ausrichtigen.'

Translated by Weber, Indische Studien, V. p. 244, by Ludwig, Der Rigveda, III. p. 515, and by Grill, Hundert Lieder, pp. 58, 174.

2 I pray, may he remember me, think of me, loving and beloved.
Send forth the spell, ye Deities! Let him consume with love of me.

3 That he may think of me, that I may never, never think of him,
Send forth the spell, ye Deities! Let him consume with love of me.

4 Madden him, Maruts, madden him. Madden him, madden him, O Air.
Madden him, Agni, madden him. Let him consume with love of me.

HYMN CXXXI.

DOWN upon thee, from head to foot, I draw the pangs of longing love.
Send forth the charm, ye Deities! Let him consume with love of me.

2 Assent to this, O Heavenly Grace! Celestial Purpose, guide it well!
Send forth the charm, ye Deities! Let him consume with love of me.

3 If thou shouldst run three leagues away, five leagues, a horse's daily stage,
Thence thou shalt come to me again and be the father of our sons.

A woman's love-charm.

2 *Heavenly Grace:* Anumati; Favour of the Gods. See I. 18. 2, note. *Celestial Purpose:* Âkûti; Plan or Intention, personified as a Goddess.

3 *Leagues:* the *yójanam*, sometimes regarded as a distance of four or five miles, is more correctly estimated at four *kroṣas* or *kos*, or about eight miles.

Translated by Weber, Indische Studien, V. p. 244, and by Grill, Hundert Lieder, pp. 58, 175.

HYMN CXXXII.

The Philter, burning with the pangs of yearning love, which Gods have poured within the bosom of the floods,
That spell for thee I heat by Varuṇa's decree.

2 The charm which, burning with the pangs of love, the General Gods have poured within the bosom of the floods,
That spell for thee I heat by Varuṇa's decree.

3 The Philter, burning with the pangs of longing, which Indrâṇî hath effused within the waters' depth,
That spell for thee I heat by Varuṇa's decree.

4 The charm, aglow with longing, which Indra and Agni have effused within the bosom of the floods,
That spell for thee I heat by Varuṇa's decree.

5 The charm aglow with longing which Mitra and Varuṇa have poured within the bosom of the floods,
That spell for thee I heat by Varuṇa's decree.

HYMN CXXXIII.

By the direction of that God we journey, he will seek means to save and he will free us;
The God who hath engirt us with this Girdle, he who hath fastened it, and made us ready.

2 Thou, weapon of the Ṛishis, art adored and served with sacrifice.
First tasting of the votive milk, Zone, be a hero-slayer thou!

A woman's love-charm.

2 *General Gods:* the Viṣve Devas or All-Gods,

Translated by Weber, Indische Studien, V. p. 245.

The hymn is a glorification of the sacred Girdle.

1 *Journey:* pursue our course through life.

3 As I am now Death's Brahmachârî claiming out of the living world a man for Yama,
So with Austerity and Prayer and Fervour I bind this Girdle round the man before me.

4 She hath become, Faith's daughter, sprung from Fervour, the sister of the world-creating Ṛishis;
As such, O Girdle, give us thought and wisdom, give us religious zeal and mental vigour.

5 Thou whom primeval Ṛishis girt about them, they who made the world,
As such do thou encircle me, O Girdle, for long days of life.

HYMN CXXXIV.

THIS Thunderbolt shall take its fill of Order, scare life away and overthrow the kingdom,
Tear necks in pieces, rend the napes asunder, even as the Lord of Might the neck of Vṛitra.

2 Down, down beneath the conquerors, let him not rise, concealed in earth, but lie down-smitten with the bolt.

3 Seek out the fierce oppressor, yea, strike only the oppressor dead.
Down on the fierce oppressor's head strike at full length, O Thunderbolt!

---

3 *Death's Brahmachârî*: a religious student endowed with power by Mṛityu, the God of Death.

4 *She*: the girdle. *World-creating Ṛishis*: see III. 28. 1; IV. 1. 2.

Translated by Ludwig, Der Rigveda, III. p. 432.

A priest's prayer for power to punish wrong-doers.

1 *This Thunderbolt*: this sacrifice, which when employed against enemies is as powerful a weapon as the bolt of Indra. So Milton speaks of 'sermons, prayers, and fulminations.' and George Herbert calls Prayer 'reversèd thunder.' *Lord of Might*: Indra.

2 *Him*: the wicked man.

Translated by Ludwig, Der Rigveda, III. p. 448.

HYMN CXXXV.

WHATE'ER I eat I turn to strength, and thus I grasp the Thunderbolt,
Rending the shoulders of that man as Indra shattered Vṛitra's neck.
2 I drink together what I drink, even as the sea that swallows all.
Drinking the life-breath of that man, we drink that man and swallow him.
3 Whate'er I eat I swallow up, even as the sea that swallows all.
Swallowing that man's vital breath, we swallow him completely up.

HYMN CXXXVI.

BORN from the bosom of wide Earth the Goddess, godlike Plant, art thou:
So we, Nitatnī! dig thee up to strengthen and fix fast the hair.
2 Make the old firm, make new hair spring, lengthen what has already grown.
3 Thy hair where it is falling off, and with the roots is torn away,
I wet and sprinkle with the Plant, the remedy for all disease.

HYMN CXXXVII.

THE Plant which Jamadagni dug to make his daughter's locks grow long,

---

A priest's fulmination against an enemy.

A charm to promote the growth of hair.

1 *Nitatnī:* an unidentified plant with deep roots, and therefore supposed to strengthen the roots of the hair.

Translated by Zimmer, Altindisches Leben, p. 68, and by Grill, Hundert Lieder, pp. 50, 176.

A charm to promote the growth of hair.

1 *The Plant:* Nitatni; see VI. 136. 1. *Jamadagni:* see II. 32. 3 *Vītahavya:* an ancient Rishi, the seer of Rigveda VI. 15, here regarded as a magician as Virgil was in the Middle Ages. *Asita:* see I. 14. 4

This same hath Vîtahavya brought to us from Asita's abode.

2 They might be measured with a rein, meted with both extended arms.
Let the black locks spring thick and strong and grow like reeds upon thy head.

3 Strengthen the roots, prolong the points, lengthen the middle part, O Plant.
Let the black locks spring thick and strong and grow like reeds upon thy head.

HYMN CXXXVIII.

O PLANT, thy fame is spread abroad as best of all the herbs that grow.
Unman for me to-day this man that he may wear the horn of hair.

2 Make him a eunuch with a horn, set thou the crest upon his head.
Let Indra with two pressing-stones deprive him of his manly strength.

3 I have unmanned thee, eunuch! yea, impotent! made thee impotent, and robbed thee, weakling! of thy strength.
Upon his head we set the horn, we set the branching ornament.

---

2 *They:* the lady's locks.

Translated by Ludwig, Der Rigveda, III. p. 512, by Zimmer, Altindisches Leben, p. 68, and by Grill, Hundert Lieder, pp. 50, 176.

A woman's imprecation on her unfaithful lover.

1 *The horn of hair:* the *opaśá*, meaning a horn-like arrangement or ornament of the hair: here regarded as a mark of effeminacy.

2 *The crest: kurîra;* apparently the same as the *opaśá.* See V. 31. 2.

3 *The horn: kúmba*; another word with the same meaning as *opaśá* and *kurîra.* See Geldner, Vedische Studien, pp. 130—132.

For stanzas 4 and 5 see Appendix.

The hymn has been translated by Weber, Indische Studien, V. p. 246, and by Ludwig, Der Rigveda, III. p. 470.

HYMN CXXXIX.

Thou hast grown up, a source of joy to bless me with prosperity.
A hundred are thy tendrils, three-and-thirty thy descending shoots.
With this that bears a thousand leaves I dry thy heart and wither it.

2 Let thy heart wither for my love and let thy mouth be dry for me.
Parch and dry up with longing, go with lips that love of me hath dried.

3 Drive us together, tawny! fair! a go-between who wakens love.
Drive us together, him and me, and give us both one heart and mind.

4 Even as his mouth is parched who finds no water for his burning thirst,
So parch and burn with longing, go with lips that love of me hath dried.

5 Even as the Mungoose bites and rends and then restores the wounded snake,
So do thou, mighty one, restore the fracture of our severed love.

HYMN CXL.

Two tigers have grown up who long to eat the mother and the sire:

A woman's love-charm.

1 *A source of joy: nyastikā́*; the meaning of the word is unknown.

5 *Restores the wounded snake:* the mungoose [Viverra Ichneumon] is popularly believed to protect itself, and cure its wounds received in encounters with snakes, by means of a medicinal plant; but it is not now credited with the chivalrous generosity here ascribed to it.

Translated by Weber, Indische Studien, V. p. 247, and by Ludwig, Der Rigveda, III. p. 515.

A blessing on a child's first two teeth.

Translated by Grill, Hundert Lieder, pp. 49, 176, and by Zimmer, A. I. L. p. 321.

Soothe, Brahmaṇaspati, and thou, O Jâtavedas, both these teeth.

2 Let rice and barley be your food, eat also beans and sesamum.
This is the share allotted you, to be your portion, ye two Teeth. Harm not your mother and your sire.

3 Both fellow teeth have been invoked, gentle and bringing happiness.
Elsewhither let the fierceness of your nature turn away, O Teeth! Harm not your mother or your sire.

HYMN CXLI.

VÂYU collected these: to find their sustenance be Tvashṭar's care:
May Indra bless and comfort them, and Rudra look that they increase.

2 Take thou the iron axe and make a pair by marks upon their ears.
This sign the Asvins have impressed: let these increase and multiply.

3 Even as Gods and Asuras, even as mortal men have done,
Do ye, that these may multiply in thousands, Asvins! make the mark.

HYMN CXLII.

SPRING high, O Barley, and become much through thine own magnificence:

A blessing on cattle.

1 *Vâyu collected these:* cf. II. 26. 1. *Tvashṭar's:* as the God who multiplies cattle.

Translated by Ludwig, Der Rigveda, III. p. 469.

A prayer for a plentiful harvest.

1 *Burst all the vessels:* fill all the large earthen jars in which the grain is stored till they burst with the weight.

Translated by Ludwig, Der Rigveda, III. p. 463, by Zimmer, Altindisches Leben, p. 237, and by Grill, Hundert Lieder, pp. 66, 177.

Burst all the vessels; let the bolt from heaven forbear to strike thee down.

2 As we invite and call to thee, Barley, a God who heareth us,
Raise thyself up like heaven on high and be exhaustless as the sea.

3 Exhaustless let thine out-turns be, exhaustless be thy gathered heaps,
Exhaustless be thy givers, and exhaustless those who eat of thee.

BOOK VII.

HYMN I.

THEY who by thought have guided all that Speech hath best, or they who with their heart have uttered words of truth,
Made stronger by the strength which the third prayer bestows, have by the fourth prayer learned the nature of the Cow.

2 Well knows this son his sire, he knows his mother well: he hath been son, and he hath been illiberal.
He hath encompassed heaven, and air's mid-realm, and sky: he hath become this All; he hath come nigh to us.

This introductory hymn is a glorification of the power of prayer and of Agni.

1 *Or:* not disjunctive here, both clauses referring to the same persons. *Third . . . . . fourth prayer:* 'mystic formulas of heavenly Prayer.'—Victor Henry. *The nature of the Cow: nā́ma* (name) meaning here mystic character, essence, or nature. The Cow is Vâk, Voice, Speech, especially Prayer. Cf. 'The Milch-cow's earliest name they comprehended' (Ṛigveda IV. 1. 16).

2 *This son:* Agni, the offspring of Heaven and Earth. *Illiberal:* this is the meaning of the word *púnarmaghaḥ* in the only other Vedic hymn (Atharva-veda V. 11. 2) in which it occurs, and it may refer to Agni's flight from his sacrificial duties (ṚV. I. 65. 1; X. 46. 2. 3) and general reluctance to appear, that is, the difficulty of obtaining fire by means of the wooden drill. The St. Petersburg Dictionary gives an opposite meaning to the word in this place, explaining it, in accordance with an Indian commentator, not as 'illiberal,' but as 'repeatedly granting gifts,' which is Agni's usual character.

The hymns of this Book have been translated and commented by M. Victor Henry (J. Maisonneuve: Paris. 1892). Professor Ludwig has translated some thirty-five hymns in Der Rigveda, III., and Dr. Grill fifteen in his Hundert Lieder des Atharva-veda.

HYMN II.

INVOKE for us, proclaim in sundry places, the kinsman of the Gods, our sire Atharvan,
His mother's germ, his father's breath, the youthful, who with his mind hath noticed this oblation.

HYMN III.

HE, in this manner showing forth his exploits—for he, bright God, is our broad way for choosing—
Rose up to meet his stay, the mead's best portion: of his own self he sent his body forward.

HYMN IV.

WITH thine eleven teams, to aid our wishes, yea, with thy two-and-twenty teams, O Vâyu,
With all thy three-and-thirty teams for drawing, here loose these teams, thou who art prompt to listen!

Praise of Atharvan.

1 *Atharvan:* cf. IV. 1. 7. Atharvan, as the discoverer of fire and the earliest fire-priest, is the father of Agni, and in this place is identified with him. *The youthful:* a frequently occurring epithet of Agni as being continually reproduced.

Praise of Agni as the Sun.

1 *His stay:* Soma is called the most 'excellent pillar of the heavens,' and 'sustainer of the sky' (Ṛigveda IX. 108. 16, and 109. 6).

According to the Kauṣika-Sûtra, XV. 11, the stanza is to be employed in a charm for victory in battle, the King and his charioteer being mounted on a new car.

A hymn to Vâyu the God of the Wind.

1 *Teams: viyúgbhis;* used instead of (according to the St. P. Dictionary a false reading for) *niyúdbhis* the usual word in the Ṛigveda for the horses of Vâyu, 'the viewless coursers of the wind.' *To aid our wishes:* to help us to success. The recitation of the stanza three times concludes the ceremony of blessing the horses (Kauṣika-Sûtra XLI. 26). See Victor Henry's note.

HYMN V.

THE Gods adored the Sacrifice with worship: these were the statutes of primeval ages.
Those mighty ones attained the cope of heaven, there where the Sâdhyas, Gods of old, are dwelling.

2 Sacrifice was, was manifest among us: it sprang to life and then in time grew stronger.
Then it became the deities' lord and ruler: may it bestow on us abundant riches.

3 Where the Gods worshipped Gods with their oblation, worshipped immortals with immortal spirit,
There in the loftiest heaven may we be happy, and look upon that light when Sûrya rises.

4 With their oblation, Purusha, the Gods performed a sacrifice.
A sacrifice more potent still they paid with the invoking hymn.

5 With dog the Gods, perplexed, have paid oblation, and with cow's limbs in sundry sacrifices.
Invoke for us, in many a place declare him who with his mind hath noticed this our worship.

The hymn is a glorification of Sacrifice.

1 The stanza is taken, with a change in the meaning, from Ṛigveda I. 164. 50. It appears also in ṚV. X. 90. 16. *Sâdhyas:* meaning probably, 'those who are to be propitiated.' According to Yâska 'the Gods whose dwelling-place is the sky.' In the *Amarakosha* they are named among the minor deities, but they seem rather to be the most ancient of the Gods.

4 *With their oblation, Purusha:* see Ṛigveda X. 90, the Purusha-Sûkta or hymn which describes the sacrifice of Purusha, embodied spirit, or Man personified and regarded as the soul and original source of the universe, the personal and life-giving principle in all animated beings; a pantheistic hymn which appears to be an attempt to harmonize the two ideas of sacrifice and creation.

5 *With dog:* no legend referring to this extraordinary sacrifice has survived. *Perplexed:* it seems impossible that *mugdhâs* (perplexed,

HYMN VI.

Aditi is the sky, and air's mid-region, Aditi is the father, son, and mother,
Aditi all the Gods and the Five Nations, Aditi what is now and what is future.

2 We call for help the Queen of Law and Order, great mother of all those whose ways are righteous,
Far-spread, unwasting, strong in her dominion, Aditi wisely leading, well protecting.

3 Sinless may we ascend, for weal, the vessel, rowed with good oars, divine, that never leaketh,
Earth, our strong guard, incomparable Heaven, Aditi wisely leading, well protecting.

4 Let us bring hither, in pursuit of riches, Aditi with our word, the mighty mother,
Her in whose lap the spacious air is lying: may she afford us triply-guarding shelter!

---

infatuated) can be the right reading here. A substantive in the instrumental case is required by the context. M. Victor Henry reads *mûrdhnâ*, with the head,' that is, with the horse's head given to Dadhyach, which, according to M. Bergaigne (Religion Védique, II. p. 458) symbolizes Agni or Soma. 'That mighty deed of yours, for gain, O heroes, as thunder heraldeth the rain, I publish, when by the horse's head Atharvan's offspring Dadhyach made known to you the Soma's sweetness' (Ṛigveda I. 116. 12). According to M. Victor Henry's suggested reading the translation would be: With head, with dog the Gods have paid oblation; but the meaning of the line is still obscure. *Him:* probably Agni.

A prayer to Aditi for help and protection.

1 *Aditi*: Infinity personified. See I. 9. 1, note. The stanza, taken from Ṛigveda I. 89. 10, is used in the ritual and in charms and incantations.

2 The stanza is employed in the benediction of boats, in the preparation of the domestic fire, in blessing the marriage bed, in funerals, and in other ceremonies. See M. Victor Henry's note.

3 Taken, with a variant, from Ṛigveda X. 63. 10. According to Sâyaṇa, the divine vessel is a metaphorical expression for sacrifice; but Aditi, including heaven and earth, is intended.

The hymn has been translated by Ludwig, Der Rigveda, III. p. 533.

HYMN VII.

I HAVE sung praise to Diti's sons and Aditi's, those very lofty and invulnerable Gods.

For far within the depths of ocean is their home, and in the worship paid them none excelleth these.

HYMN VIII.

Go forward on thy way from good to better: Bṛihaspati precede thy steps and guide thee!

Place this man here, within this earth's enclosure, afar from foes with all his men about him.

Praise of the Âdityas.

1 The poet gives two mothers, Diti and Aditi, to the Âdityas. The former is a personification, distinguished by no special character, and unknown to the poets of the Ṛigveda. She is mentioned again in XI. 3. 4; XV. 6. 7, and 18. 4. The name is evolved from Aditi in the same way as Sura, a God, is from Asura, a demon. *Those:* I omit to notice *áva* which in this place is unintelligible. M. Victor Henry suggests *náva*, nine, although the number of the Âdityas is at most eight. *Invulnerable:* I can make nothing of the *anarmáṇâm* of the text which, read *an-armáṇâm*, would mean 'free from ophthalmia.' M. Henry divides the word *a-narmáṇâm*, a word of his own coinage, which might signify 'who do not sport and trifle.' I think one may as well change the word into *anarváṇâm* (unscathed, unassailed, invulnerable) which is frequently applied to the Gods in the Ṛigveda. *Ocean:* the sea of air. M. Henry translates: 'for their mysterious essence is that of the celestial Ocean.'

Godspeed to a departing traveller.

1 *Place:* addressed to Bṛihaspati.

The hymn appears, with variations, in the Aitareya-Brâhmaṇa, 1. 3. 13, as an address by the Hotar to the sacrificer, the words 'from good to better' meaning from this world to heaven. By the second line the Hotar makes the Soma remain in the sacrificial court, and expels the enemy who would injure the sacrificer.

Translated by Ludwig, Der Rigveda, III. p. 431.

HYMN IX.

PÛSHAN was born to move on distant pathways, on roads remote from earth, remote from heaven.
To both most lovely places of assembly he travels and returns with perfect knowledge.

2 Pûshan knows all these realms: may he conduct us by ways that are most free from fear and danger.
Giver of blessings, glowing, all heroic, may he the wise and watchful go before us.

3 We are thy praisers here, O Pûshan: never let us be injured under thy protection.

4 From out the distance, far and wide, may Pûshan stretch his right hand forth.
Let him drive back our lost to us, let us return with what is lost.

HYMN X.

THAT breast of thine, exhaustless and delightful, good to invoke, beneficent, free giver,
Wherewith thou feedest all things that are choicest, bring that, Sarasvatî, that we may drain it.

A prayer for protection and recovery of lost property.

1 *Pûshan:* as the Sun, all-seeing, guide of travellers, and guardian of cattle and property in general. *Both places of assembly:* heaven and earth. Stanzas 1 and 2 are taken from Rigveda X. 17. 6, 5.

3 *Protection:* or dominion. This and the following stanza are taken from Ṛigveda VI. 54, 9, 10.

A prayer for the favour of Sarasvatî.

Exhaustless: *ṣaṣayúr*, pursuing the hare, is unintelligible here, and I translate the reading *ṣaṣayó* of the Ṛigveda hymn. But see M. Henry's note.

The stanza, taken, with this variant, from Ṛigveda I. 164. 49, is used to soothe an infant seized by Jambha, that is, probably, when teething. See II. 4. 2, and note.

HYMN XI.

THAT far-spread thunder, sent from thee, which cometh on all this world, a high celestial signal—
Strike not, O God, our growing corn with lightning, nor kill it with the burning rays of Sûrya.

HYMN XII.

IN concord may Prajâpati's two daughters, Gathering and Assembly, both protect me.
May every man I meet respect and aid me. Fair be my words, O Fathers, at the meetings.

2 We know thy name, O Conference: thy name is interchange of talk.
Let all the company who join the Conference agree with me.

3 Of these men seated here I make the splendour and the lore mine own.
Indra, make me conspicuous in all this gathered company.

4 Whether your thoughts are turned away, or bound and fastened here or there,
We draw them hitherward again: let your mind firmly rest on me.

A prayer to protect corn from lightning and drought.

O God: addressed to Indra.

Translated by Ludwig, III. 463, and by Grill, 66, 178.

A prayer or charm for influence at deliberative and religious meetings.

1 *Gathering: sabhā́;* meeting of the people of a village. *Assembly: sámitis;* a congregation for sacrificial and religious purposes.

2 *Conference:* or Gathering.

Translated by Muir, O. S. Texts, V. 439, by Ludwig, III. 253, and by Grill, 15, 178. See also Zimmer, Altindisches Leben, p. 173.

HYMN XIII.

As the Sun, rising, taketh to himself the brightness of the stars,
So I assume the glory of women and men mine enemies.

2 All ye among my rivals who behold me as I come to you,
I seize the glory of my foes as the Sun, rising, theirs who sleep.

HYMNS XIV.

I PRAISE this God, parent of heaven and earth, exceeding wise, possessed of real energy, giver of treasure, thinker dear to all,

2 Whose splendour is sublime, whose light shone brilliant in creation, who, wise, and golden-handed, in his beauty made the sky.

3 As thou, God! quickening, for our ancient father, sentest him height above and room about him,
So unto us, O Savitar, send treasures, abundant, day by day, in shape of cattle.

A charm to win superiority over foes and rivals.

2 *Theirs who sleep:* the comparison or illustration is vague. The meaning is, probably, as M. Henry says: I have surprised my rivals by taking their glory to myself in the same manner as the sun surprises late sleepers.

Translated by Ludwig, III. p. 241, and by Grill, Hundert Lieder, pp. 23, 179.

A prayer, for prosperity, to Savitar as the Vivifier or Generator.

1 Stanzas 1 and 2 are taken from Sâmaveda I. V. ii. 3. 8. *This God:* Savitar, the Sun. *Parent: savitdram. Of heaven and earth: oṇyos = oṇíos;* literally, two bowls used in the preparation of the Soma juice, and, figuratively, heaven and earth regarded as two hemispheres. *In his beauty: kṛipd,* as suggested in Prof. Whitney's Index Verborum, must be read instead of the *kṛipdt* of the text.

4 Savitar, God, our household friend, most precious, hath sent our fathers life and power and riches.
Let him drink Soma and rejoice when worshipped. Under his law even the Wanderer travels.

HYMN XV.

I CHOOSE, O Savitar, that glorious favour, with fruitful energy and every blessing,
Even this one's teeming cow, erst milked by Kaṇva, thousand-streamed, milked for happiness by the mighty.

HYMN XVI.

INCREASE this man Bṛihaspati! Illume him, O Savitar, for high and happy fortune.
Sharpen him throughly though already sharpened: with glad acclaim let all the Gods receive him.

HYMN XVII.

MAY the Ordainer give us wealth, Lord, ruler of the world of life: with full hand may he give to us.

---

4 *The Wanderer:* the Sun who journeys round the sky.

The hymn abounds in plays upon the root *su*, from which Savitar, and *sávîman* (creation) are formed, and which means 'to press or pour out (Soma juice)' as well as 'to send.' Hence in the ritual of the Atharvans the two stanzas are recited, during the purification of the Soma juice, by a priest who holds gold in his hand or wears a gold ring with reference to the *golden-handed* of the text.

A charm for divine favour and felicity.

1 *This one's:* Savitar's. *Cow:* the emblem of plenty. *Kaṇva:* the famous Ṛishi of the Ṛigveda.

A prayer for prosperity.

The stanza is employed in various incantations, and also in the ritual to wake the sleeping priests: *bṛihaspate savitariti svapato bodhayet.* Vaitâna-Sûtra V. 9. In the latter case *this man, enam* (hunc) will be 'this God,' that is, Agni. See M. Henry's note.

A prayer for wealth and children.

1 *The Ordainer:* Dhâtar regarded in this hymn more especially as the Upholder of the sacrament of marriage (see II. 36. 2, and note), and the giver of children.

2 May Dhâtar grant the worshipper henceforth imperishable life.
May we obtain the favour of the God who giveth every boon.

3 To him may Dhâtar grant all kinds of blessings who, craving children, serves him in his dwelling.
Him may the Gods invest with life eternal, yea, all the Gods and Aditi accordant.

4 May this our gift please Savitar, Râti, Dhâtar, Prajâpati, and Agni Lord of Treasures.
May Tvashṭar, Vishṇu, blessing him with children, give store of riches to the sacrificer.

HYMN XVIII.

Burst open, Pṛithivî, and cleave asunder this celestial cloud.
Untie, O Dhâtar—for thou canst—the bottle of the breast of heaven.

2 Let not the Sun's heat burn, nor cold destroy her. Let Earth with all her quickening drops burst open.
Even for her the waters flow, and fatness: where Soma is even there is bliss for ever.

---

4 *Râti:* gift; the Oblation personified as a Goddess.

A prayer for rain.

1 *Pṛithivî:* meaning here not Earth personified, but a deity of the middle air or firmament: *dvirûpâ pṛithivî*, says Sâyaṇa: Pṛithivî has two forms. 'Thou, of a truth, O Pṛithivî, bearest the tool that rends the hills: Thou rich in torrents who with might quickenest earth, O mighty one' (Ṛigveda V. 84. 1). *The bottle of the breast of heaven:* 'Who can number the clouds in wisdom? Or who can stay the bottles of heaven?' (Job, 38. 37.)

2 *Her:* Earth.

The hymn is employed also in charms to avert inundations. See Kauṣika-Sûtra CIII. 3, and Weber's Omina und Portenta, p. 366.

HYMN XIX.

PRAJÂPATI engenders earthly creatures: may the benevolent Ordainer form them,
Having one common womb, and mind, and spirit. He who is Lord of Plenty give me plenty!

HYMN XX.

ANUMATI approve to-day our sacrifice among the Gods!
May Agni bear mine offerings away for me the worshipper.

2 Do thou, Anumati! approve, and grant us health and happiness.
Accept the offered sacrifice, and, Goddess, give us progeny.

3 May he approving in return accord us wealth inexhaustible with store of children.
Never may we be subject to his anger, but rest in his benevolence and mercy.

4 Thy name is easy to invoke, good leader! approved, Anumati! and rich in bounty.
Source of all boons! fill up therewith our worship, and, Blest One! grant us wealth with goodly heroes.

A prayer for prosperity.

1 *Having one common womb:* or, One common womb (or source) have they: the adjective *sáyonayas* being in the nominative case.

A prayer for prosperity and happiness.

1 *Anumati:* Favour, or divine Grace personified. See I. 18. 2, note. According to the ritualists Anumati is also the personification of the fifteenth day of the Moon's age, and sometimes the New Moon.

3 *He:* Rudra.

As Anumati is a deity connected with procreation the hymn is used in charms to remove sterility in cows.

5 Anumati hath come to this our worship well-formed to give good lands and valiant heroes:
For her kind care hath blessed us. God-protected, may she assist the sacrifice we offer.

6 Anumati became this All, whatever standeth or walketh, everything that moveth.
May we enjoy thy gracious love, O Goddess. Regard us, O Anumati, with favour.

HYMN XXI.

WITH prayer come all together to the Lord of Heaven: he is the peerless one, far-reaching, guest of men.
He, God of ancient time, hath gained a recent thrall: to him alone is turned the path which all must tread.

HYMN XXII.

UNTO a thousand sages he hath given sight: thought, light is he in ranging all.

2 The Bright One hath sent forth the Dawns, a closely gathered band,
Immaculate, unanimous, brightly refulgent in their homes.

HYMN XXIII.

THE fearful dream, and indigence, the monster, the malignant hags,
All female fiends of evil name and wicked tongue we drive afar.

A stanza to be recited at a funeral.

1 *The Lord of heaven;* here Yama must be meant *A recent thrall:* the man whose funeral rites are being performed.

To Savitar, or to Yama invested with some of Savitar's attributes.

1 If, as M. Victor Henry thinks, Yama is the God of the hymn, *sight* means life in the world of the departed. The hymn is very difficult, and no sense can be made of it without alterations of the text. I have adopted those proposed by M. Henry, Le Livre VII de l' Atharva-veda, p. 62.

A charm to banish fiends and troubles.

HYMN XXIV.

WHAT treasure hath been dug for us by Indra, by Agni, Visvedevas, tuneful Maruts,
On us may Savitar whose laws are faithful, Prajâpati, and Heavenly Grace bestow it.

HYMN XXV.

THE early morning prayer hath come to Vishṇu and Varuṇa, Lords through might, whom none hath equalled,
Gods by whose power the realms of air were stablished, strongest and most heroic in their vigour.

2 The early prayer hath ever come to Vishṇu and Varuṇa by that God's high power and statute
In whose control is all this world that shineth, all that hath powers to see and all that breatheth.

HYMN XXVI.

I WILL declare the mighty deeds of Vishṇu, of him who measured out the earthly regions,
Who propped the highest place of congregation, thrice setting down his footstep, widely striding.

2 Loud boast doth Vishṇu make of this achievement, like some wild beast, dread, prowling, mountain-roaming.
May he approach us from the farthest distance.

A prayer for riches.

Tuneful: alluding to the wild music of the winds, the 'thunder-psalm' of the Storm-Gods.

A prayer of praise to Vishṇu and Varuṇa.

2 *That God's:* Sûrya the Sun-God is intended.

Translated by Ludwig, Der Rigveda, III. p. 429.

In praise of Vishṇu.

1 The stanza is found in Ṛigveda I. 154. 1. *The highest place of congregation:* heaven, where the Gods are assembled. *Thrice:* at rising, culmination, and setting; Vishṇu being the Sun.

2 The stanza is a combination, with variants, of Ṛigveda I. 154. 2 and X. 180. 2.

3 Thou within whose three wide-extended paces all worlds and creatures have their habitation,
Drink oil, thou homed in oil! promote the sacrificer more and more.

4 Through all this world strode Vishṇu: thrice his foot he planted, and the whole
Was gathered in his footstep's dust.

5 Vishṇu the guardian, he whom none deceiveth, made three steps, thenceforth
Establishing these high decrees.

6 Look ye on Vishṇu's works, whereby the friend of Indra, close-allied,
Hath let his holy ways be seen.

7 The princes evermore behold that loftiest place where Vishṇu is,
Like an extended eye in heaven.

8 From heaven, O Vishṇu, or from earth, O Vishṇu, or from the great far-spreading air's mid-region,
Fill both thy hands full of abundant treasures, and from the right and left bestow them freely.

---

3 The first line occurs in Ṛigveda I. 154. 2. *Homed in oil:* dwelling in the molten butter used in sacrifice.

4 This stanza and the three that follow it are found in Ṛigveda I. 22. 17—20. *In his footstep's dust:* so mighty was Vishṇu that the dust raised by his footsteps enveloped the whole world, or the earth was formed from the dust of his strides.

7 *The princes:* Sûris, wealthy householders who institute sacrifices and remunerate the officiating priests.

See Muir, O. S. Texts, IV. 63, 68, where stanzas 1—7 are translated and thoroughly discussed.

HYMN XXVII.

May Iḍâ with her statute dwell beside us, she in whose place the pious purge and cleanse them.
She, mighty, Soma-decked, whose foot drops fatness, meet for All-Gods, hath come to aid our worship.

HYMN XXVIII.

Blest be the Broom, may the Mace bring a blessing, and may the Altar and the Hatchet bless us.
Worshipful Gods, may they accept this worship, lovers of sacrifice, and sacrificers.

HYMN XXIX.

This is your glorious might, Agni and Vishṇu! Ye drink the essence of the mystic butter,
Placing in every home seven costly treasures. Let your tongue stretch to take the offered fatness.

2 Ye love the great law, Agni Vishṇu! joying, ye feast on mystic essences of butter,
Exalted in each house with fair laudation. Let your tongue stretch to take the offered fatness.

A prayer to Iḍâ, Goddess of Devotion.

1 *Iḍâ:* also Iḷâ and Ilâ, usually mentioned in connexion with Sarasvatî, and Bhâratî or Mahî, all being deities of sacred speech, prayer, and praise. See V. 12. 8.

Her *place* is the sanctuary or chapel in which libations and sacrifices are offered.

Translated by Ludwig, III. p. 433.

In praise of the sacrificial utensils.

Broom: vedás; a bunch of stiff grass tied up for sweeping the place of sacrifice.

Mace: to keep off improper visitants. *Gods:* the sacrificial implements, deified.

A hymn to Agni and Vishṇu.

1 *Seven:* used indefinitely for a great number. *Your tongue;* the sacrificial fire.

HYMN XXX.

HEAVEN, Earth, and Mitra here have caused mine eyes to be anointed well,
Savitar, Brahmaṇaspati take care that they be duly balmed!

HYMN XXXI.

ROUSE us to-day O Indra, Maghavan, hero, with thy best possible and varied succours.
May he who hateth us fall low beneath us, and him whom we detest let life abandon.

HYMN XXXII.

WE bringing homage have approached the friend who seeks our wondering praise,
Young, strengthener of the sacrifice. May he bestow long life on me.

HYMN XXXIII.

LET Pûshan, let the Maruts, let Bṛihaspati pour forth on me;
This present Agni pour on me children and riches in a stream!
May he bestow long life on me.

A charm accompanying the anointing of eyes.

The stanza is used in anointing the Yûpa or sacrificial post (Vaitâna-Sûtra X. 5); and in the Godânam ceremony (A. V. II. 13), when the youth's eyes are anointed as part of the procedure (Kauṣika-Sûtra LIV. 6).

A prayer for the overthrow of enemies.

The stanza is taken, with variants, from Rigveda III. 53. 21.

A prayer for long life, addressed to Agni.

The stanza is taken, excepting the final pâda, from Ṛigveda IX. 67. 29.

A prayer for long life, children, and riches.

HYMN XXXIV.

Agni, drive off my rivals born and living, repel those yet unborn, O Jâtavedas.
Cast down beneath my feet mine adversaries. In Aditi's regard may we be sinless.

HYMN XXXV.

Subdue with conquering might his other rivals, those yet unborn repel, O Jâtavedas.
For great felicity protect this kingdom, and in this man let all the Gods be joyful.

HYMN XXXVI.

Sweet are the glances of our eyes, our faces are as smooth as balm.
Within thy bosom harbour me; one spirit dwell in both of us!

HYMN XXXVII.

With this my robe, inherited from Manu, I envelop thee,
So that thou mayst be all mine own and give no thought to other dames.

A prayer for freedom from sin, and the overthrow of enemies.

A prayer for the prosperity of a King and his kingdom.

Stanzas 2 and 3 have a totally different object. See Appendix.

A charm to be pronounced by bride and bridegroom.

Smooth as balm: the pair anoint each other's eyes as part of the marriage ceremony (Kauṣika-Sûtra LXXIX. 2).

Translated by Grill, pp. 55, 179.

A nuptial charm, spoken by the bride.

From Manu: the father of mankind, Man, the Old German Mannus, with reference to the great antiquity of the custom. See M. Henry's note.

HYMN XXXVIII.

I DIG this Healing Herb that makes my lover look on me and weep;
That bids the parting friend return and kindly greets him as he comes.

2 This Herb wherewith the Âsurî drew Indra downward from the Gods,
With this same Herb I draw thee close that I may be most dear to thee.

3 Thou art the peer of Soma, yea, thou art the equal of the Sun,
The peer of all the Gods art thou: therefore we call thee hitherward.

4 I am the speaker here, not thou: speak thou where the assembly meets.
Thou shalt be mine and only mine, and never mention other dames.

5 If thou art far away beyond the rivers, far away from men,
This Herb shall seem to bind thee fast and bring thee back my prisoner.

HYMN XXXIX.

MAY he establish in our home the master of riches, gladdening with rain in season,
Mighty, strong-winged, celestial, dropping moisture, Bull of the plants and embryo of waters.

A maiden's love-charm.

2 *The Âsurî:* a female fiend, named Vilistengâ according to the legend. See Weber, Indische Studien, V. p. 250.

3 *Thou:* addressed to the plant.

4 Addressed to the man she loves.

Translated by Weber, I. S. V. 249, by Ludwig, III. 515, and by Grill, pp. 59, 179.

A sacrificial charm for rain and prosperity.

1 *Home: goshthé;* literally, fold or pen for cattle. *Master of riches:* or, wealthy possessor. *In season: abhîpatás;* the meaning of the

HYMN XL.

We call Sarasvân, under whose protection all cattle wander, to preserve and aid us,
Him in whose ordinance abide the waters, to whose command the Lord of Plenty listens.

2 Abiding here let us invoke Sarasvân, the seat of riches, glorious, wealth-increaser,
Him who inclines and gives to him who worships, the rich possessor and the Lord of Fulness.

HYMN XLI.

Observing men, and viewing home, the Falcon hath cleft his swift way over wastes and waters.

---

word is uncertain. Prof. Ludwig translates it by 'aus der nähe, 'from near at hand;' Prof. Grassmann by 'vom Wolkenraume,' 'from the region of cloud,' and M. Henry changes it to *abhîyatás* 'those who come to him.' *Dropping moisture:* or, milk-exuding: *payasám* being another obscure word, occurring in only one other passage (A. V. IV. 14. 6) where it is applied to a slaughtered victim, and appears to mean 'full of juices.' According to the St. Petersburg Dictionary the word is a corruption of *vâyasám*, great bird, of the Rigveda stanza. *Bull:* 'He (Parjanya) is the Bull of all (the plants) and their impregner' (R. V. VII. 101. 6). Nearly the whole stanza is taken from Rigveda I. 164. 52: 'The bird celestial, vast, with noble pinion, the lovely germ of plants, the germ of waters, Him who delighteth us with rain in season, Sarasvân I invoke that he may help us.' Sarasvân in this place is not the River-God, consort of Sarasvatî, but may be taken as an epithet (rich in water) of Parjanya, or any God who sends the rain.

According to the Kausika-Sûtra, XXIV. 9, the stanza is to be recited at the sacrifice of the omentum of a bull to Indra. The sacrificed bull (*he* of the first line) is to establish the Rain-God, who is also called a bull or chief, in the home or cow-pen of the worshipper.

A prayer for prosperity. Sequel to Hymn XXXIX.

1 *Sarasvân:* rich in water; the God who sends the rain; Parjanya. *Lord of Plenty:* here, probably, Pûshan, the nourisher and increaser of cattle and property in general.

A prayer for prosperity.

1 *The Falcon:* the swift Sun; with allusion also to the falcon who brought the Soma from heaven. See Hymns of the Rigveda, General Index. *Hath cleft his swift way:* M. Henry translates this pâda differently: 'hath pierced the arid deserts and made the waters spring forth.'

May he, with Indra for a friend, auspicious, traversing all air's lower realms, come hither.

2 The heavenly Falcon, viewing men, well-pinioned, strength-giver, hundred-footed, hundred-nested,
Shall give us treasure which was taken from us. May it be rich in food among our Fathers.

HYMN XLII.

Scatter and drive away, Soma and Rudra, the sickness that hath come within our dwelling.
Afar into the distance chase Destruction, and even from committed sin release us.

2 Lay on our bodies, O ye twain, O Soma and Rudra, all those balms that heal diseases.
Set free and draw away the sin committed, which we have still inherent in our persons.

HYMN XLIII.

Some of thy words bode weal and some misfortune: thou scatterest them all with friendly feeling.

---

2 *Hundred-footed:* exceedingly swift. *Hundred-nested:* visiting and resting for a while in countless places. *Rich in food:* supplying the means of offering libations to the Manes of our ancestors.

On the strength of the word *home* or house in the first line, the hymn is used in the ceremony of blessing the construction of a new house (Kauṣika-Sûtra XLIII. 3), and purifying the ground on which it is to stand. See M. Henry's note.

A prayer for delivery from sin and sickness.

1 The hymn is taken, with variations, from Ṛigveda VI. 74. 2, 3. *And even from committed sin release us:* taken from Ṛigveda I. 24. 9:—the original hymn (VI. 74. 2) has: 'may ours be excellent and happy glories.'

A charm against lightning, addressed to Parjanya.

Words: mutterings of the thunder-cloud. *Weal:* in the shape of rain. *Misfortune:* in the shape of destructive lightning. *Within this:* or, him: the cloud or the God. *Three words:* denoting thunder, rain, lightning. Cf. the hymn to Parjanya (R. V. VII. 101. 1) where three words are said to draw down the nectar from the cloud. *One hath flown off:* a mere clap of thunder has been heard, which passed away without rain or lightning.

According to Kauṣika-Sûtra XLVI. 1, the stanza is to be recited as a charm to rebut a calumnious accusation.

Deep within this three words are laid : among them
one hath flown off even as the sound was uttered.

HYMN XLIV.

Ye twain have conquered, and have not been vanquished : not either of the pair hath been defeated.
Ye, Indra Vishṇu, when ye fought your battle; produced this infinite with three divisions.

HYMN XLV.

Brought hitherward from Sindhu, from a folk of every mingled race,
Fetched from afar, thou art I deem, a balm that cureth jealousy.

2 As one with water quencheth fire, so calm this lover's jealousy,
Like heat of fire that burneth here, or flame that rageth through the wood.

HYMN XLVI.

O broad-tressed Sinîvâlî, thou who art the sister of the Gods,
Accept the offered sacrifice, and, Goddess, grant us progeny.

In praise of Indra and Vishṇu.

This infinite with three divisions: the vast world with all its creatures; the three divisions are heaven, firmament, and earth.

The stanza, taken with variants from Ṛ. V. VI. 69. 8, is, according to Kauṣika-Sûtra XLII. 6, to be used as a charm to reconcile two enemies.

A charm against Jealousy.

1 *Sindhu:* the Indus. *From afar:* obtained with difficulty, and therefore more efficacious.

Translated by Weber, Indische Studien, V. p. 250, by Ludwig, III. 514, and by Grill, Hundert Lieder, pp. 29, 180.

A charm for offspring and prosperity.

1 Stanzas 1 and 2 are taken from Ṛigveda II. 32. 6. 7. *Sinîvâlî:* a lunar Goddess, the day of New Moon personified, who aids the birth of children. See II. 26. 2.

2 Present the sacrifice to her, to Sinîvâlî, Queen of men, Beautiful-fingered, lovely-armed, prolific, bearing many a child.

3 Thou who as Queen of men art Indra's equal, a Goddess coming with a thousand tresses,
To thee our sacrifices are performed, O Consort of Vishṇu: Goddess, urge thy Lord to bounty!

HYMN XLVII.

Oft in this sacrifice with favoured cry I call Kuhû, beneficent Goddess, skilled in all her works.
May she vouchsafe us wealth with every boon, and give a hero meet for praise who gives a hundred gifts.

2 Kuhû, the Queen of Gods and immortality, called to assist, enjoy this sacrifice of ours!
Let her, desirous of our worship, hear to-day: may she, intelligent, give increase of our wealth.

HYMN XLVIII.

I call on Râkâ with fair laud and reverent cry: may she, auspicious, hear us and herself observe.
With never-breaking needle may she sew her work, and send a glorious man who gives a hundred gifts.

2 All thy kind favours, Râkâ! lovely in their form, wherewith thou grantest treasures to the man who gives,
With these come thou to us this day benevolent, O blessèd one, bestowing wealth of thousand sorts.

A prayer for wealth and the birth of a son.

1 *Kuhû:* the Goddess of the Waning Moon, presiding over childbirth. The phases of the Moon represented by Kuhû and other lunar Goddesses vary considerably, as they were not precisely determined till more recent times.

A prayer for prosperity and the birth of a son.

1 The hymn is taken, with variations, from Rigveda II. 32. 4. 5. *Râkâ:* a Goddess associated with childbirth and presiding over the actual day of full moon, Anumati (see II. 26. 2) being strictly the Goddess of the preceding day when the moon rises one digit less than full.

HYMN XLIX.

MAY the Gods' Consorts aid us of their own free will, help us to offspring and the winning of the spoil.
May Goddesses who quickly listen shelter us, both those on earth and they within the waters' realm.

2 May the Dames, wives of Gods, enjoy our presents, Râṭ, Asvinî, Indrâṇî, and Agnâyî;
May Rodasî and Varuṇânî hear us, and Goddesses come at the matrons' season.

HYMN L.

As evermore the lightning flash strikes, irresistible, the tree,
So, irresistible, may I conquer the gamblers with the dice.

2 From every side, from hale and sick, impotent to defend themselves,
May all the fortune of the folk as winnings pass into my hands.

3 I pray to Agni, him who guards his treasure: here, won by homage, may he pile our winnings.
As 'twere with racing cars I bring my presents: duly with reverence, let me laud the Maruts.

A prayer for children and booty.

1 *Râṭ:* the name of a Goddess, the Bright One, Clara; or the word may be an adjective qualifying *Asvinî:* 'Asvinî the sovereign:'—Henry. *Asvinî* is the consort of the Asvins, *Agnâyî* of Agni, *Rodasî* of Rudra.

The hymn is taken from Ṛigveda V. 46. 7, 8.

A gambler's prayer for success in gaming.

2 *From hale and sick:* or, from quick and slow; from players both good and bad alike.

3 Taken, with a variant, from Ṛigveda V. 60. 1. *Duly, with reverence: pradakshiṇâm:* literally, turned rightward; making reverential salutation by circumambulation from left to right; the Gaelic *deasil.*

4 With thee to aid us may we win the treasure: do thou assist our side in every battle.
Give us wide room and easy way, O Indra; break down, O Maghavan, the foemen's valour.

5 I have completely cleaned thee out, won from thee what thou keptest back.
As a wolf tears and rends a sheep, so do I tear thy stake away.

6 Yea, by superior play one gains advantage: in time he piles his spoil as doth a gambler.
He overwhelms with wealth's inherent powers the devotee who keeps not back his riches.

7 May we all, much-invoked! repel with cattle want that brings sin, hunger with store of barley.
May we uninjured, first among the princes, obtain possessions by our own exertions.

8 My right hand holds my winnings fast, and in my left is victory.
I would that I were winner of cattle and horses, wealth and gold.

9 Dice, give me play that bringeth fruit as 'twere a cow with flowing milk!
And, as the bowstring binds the bow, unite me with a stream of gains.

---

4 Taken from Ṛigveda I. 102. 4.

5 *I have completely cleaned thee out:* a conjectural translation of this line is all that can be given; the precise meaning of *sâmlikhitam* and *samrúdham*, probably technical or slang expressions, being undiscoverable.

6 This and the following stanza are taken, with variants, from Ṛ. V. X. 42. 9, 10. *He:* the die. See Ludwig, III. 455, and Grill, pp. 71, 180.

HYMN LI.

Bṛihaspati protect us from the sinner, from rearward, from above, and from below us!
May Indra from the front and from the centre, as friend to friends, vouchsafe us room and freedom.

HYMN LII.

Give us agreement with our own, with strangers give us unity:
Do ye, O Aṣvins, in this place join us in sympathy and love.

2 May we agree in mind, agree in purpose: let us not fight against the heavenly spirit.
Around us rise no din of frequent slaughter, nor Indra's arrow fly, for day is present!

HYMN LIII.

As thou, Bṛihaspati, from the curse hast saved us, from dwelling yonder in the realm of Yama,
The Aṣvins, leeches of the Gods, O Agni, have chased Death far from us with mighty powers.

2 Move both together; do not leave the body. Let both the breathings stay for thee united.

A prayer for protection.

The stanza is taken, with a variant, from Ṛigveda X. 42. 11.

A prayer for peace and concord.

2 *The heavenly spirit:* which inspires concord. See M. Henry's note. *For day is present:* we are no longer exposed to danger from nocturnal fiends, and can enjoy the safety and blessings of daylight.

Translated by Ludwig, Der Rigveda, III. p. 428, and by Grill, Hundert Lieder, pp. 31, 181.

A charm to recover a sick man at the point of death, or to restore animation to one apparently dead.

1 *Bṛihaspati:* as Lord of Prayer including incantations. *Leeches of the Gods:* 'And may the Aṣvins, the divine pair of physicians, send us health' (Ṛ. V. VIII. 18. 8).

2 *Move both together:* the two breathings, inspiration and expiration, are addressed.

Waxing in strength live thou a hundred autumns. Thy noblest guardian and thy lord is Agni.

3 Return, thy life now vanished into distance! Return, the breath thou drawest and exhalest!

Agni hath snatched it from Destruction's bosom: into thyself again I introduce it.

4 Let not the vital breath he draws forsake him, let not his expiration part and leave him.

I give him over to the Seven Ṛishis: let them conduct him to old age in safety.

5 Enter him, both ye breaths, like two draught-oxen entering their stall.

Let him, the treasure of old age, still wax in strength, uninjured, here.

6 I send thee back thy vital breath; I drive Consumption far from thee.

May Agni here, most excellent, sustain our life on every side.

7 From out the depth of darkness, we, ascending to the highest heaven,

Have come to the sublimest light, to Sûrya, God among the Gods.

HYMN LIV.

We worship holy Verse and Song, by which they carry out their acts.

Shining in Order's seat these twain present the sacrifice to Gods.

---

4 *Seven Ṛishis:* Bharadvâja, Kaṣyapa, Gotama, Atri, Vasishtha, Viṣvâmitra, and Jamadagni, represented by the seven stars of the Great Bear.

Translated by Muir, O. S. Texts, V. p. 443, and by Grill, Hundert Lieder, pp. 15, 182.

A charm to obtain knowledge of the Veda.

1 *Verse: ṛícham;* recited verse or hymn of praise, contained in the Ṛigveda. *Song: sấma;* sung or chanted hymn, contained in the Sâmaveda. *They carry out their acts:* men perform the rites of divine worship. *In Order's seat:* in the place of sacrifice. The text has only *sádasi*, in the seat; meaning, specially, a certain shed erected in the sacrificial enclosure.

2 As I have asked about Verse, Song, Sacrifice, strength, force, Yajus-text,
So never let this lore that I have sought forsake me, Lord of Might!

HYMN LV.

THY downward paths from heaven, whereby thou hast raised all the world to life,
Give us in gracious love, good Lord!

HYMN LVI.

WHETHER it came from viper, from black snake or snake with transverse stripes,
Or Kankaparvan's bite, this herb hath made the poison powerless.

2 Honey-born, honey-dropping, rich in honey, honey-sweet, this herb
Is medicine that heals the wound and kills the gnat that bites and stings.

3 Whatever bit, or sucked thy blood, we summon thence away from thee
The ineffectual poison of the little sharply-stinging gnat.

---

2 *Asked:* my teacher. *Sacrifice, strength:* sacrifice which is strength or makes the sacrificer powerful. *Yajus-text:* sacrificial formula, contained in the Yajur-Veda, which gives force to him who employs it. *Lord of Might: çachîpate;* Lord of *çáchî*, power, afterwards personified as the spouse of Indra. *Lore: vedáḥ;* (from *vid*, to know) science, especially sacred knowledge, ritual and theological lore.

A charm to ensure a prosperous journey.

Thy: the stanza is addressed to the Sun. In the third *pâda* the *tébhiḥ* of the text is superfluous. It mars the metre, and appears to have been inserted to correspond to *yébhir*, whereby, of the second *pâda*.

A charm against poisonous bites and stings.

1 *Kankaparvan:* apparently the name of some species of poisonous snake.

2 *The gnat: mashâka;* Latin, musca; mosquito; Hindi, machchhar.

4 Thou here who crookest wicked jaws, thou tortuous, jointless, limbless thing,
These jaws thou, Brahmaṇaspati! shalt bend together like a reed.

5 This scorpion here that creeps along, low on the ground and powerless—
I have removed his poison and then utterly demolished him.

6 No strength in thy two arms hast thou, nor in thy head, nor in thy waist:
Then what is that small thing thou so viciously bearest in thy tail?

7 The emmets make a meal of thee and peahens tear and mangle thee:
All ye are crying out, In sooth the scorpion's poison hath no strength.

8 Thou creature who inflictest wounds both with thy mouth and with thy tail,
No poison in thy mouth hast thou: what at thy tail's root will there be?

HYMN LVII.

WHATEVER trouble hath disturbed and shaken me—I speak with hope, I move, imploring, 'mid the folk—
What harm my body in myself hath suffered, now let Sarasvatî relieve with fatness.

---

4 *Crookest wicked jaws:* according to M. Henry, twistest the faces (of men) askew. *Brahmaṇaspati:* as the God of charms and prayer. *Shall bend together:* according to M. Henry, to restore them (men's faces) to their natural shape.

7 *Peahens:* the inveterate enemies of snakes. *The scorpion's poison hath no strength:* taken from Ṛigveda I. 191. 16.

Translated by Ludwig, Der Rigveda, III. p. 502, and by Grill, Hundert Lieder, pp. 5, 153.

A charm for some physical disorder.

1 *Trouble:* disorder of the body. *Imploring:* asking help. *Relieve:* literally, fill up.

2 Seven flow for him, the youth on whom the Maruts wait: the sons have taught the Father everlasting laws.
Both worlds are his: both shine belonging unto him. Both move together: both, as his possession, thrive.

HYMN LVIII.

True to laws, Indra Varuṇa, drinkers of the juice, quaff this pressed Soma which shall give you rapturous joy!
Let sacrifice, your car, to entertain the Gods, approach its resting-place that they may drink thereof.

2 O Indra Varuṇa, drink your fill, ye heroes, of this effectual and sweetest Soma.
This juice was shed by us that ye might quaff it. On this trimmed grass be seated and rejoice you.

HYMN LIX.

Like a tree struck by lightning may the man be withered from the root,
Who curseth us who curse not him, or, when we curse him, curseth us.

---

2 Taken, with variants, from Ṛigveda X. 13. 5. *Seven:* rivers, understood. *The youth:* Indra. *The sons:* the Maruts. *The Father:* Indra. *Everlasting laws:* which inculcate liberality. The flow of the full rivers symbolizes generosity, and the Gods of storm and rain are represented as having taught Indra the divine law of liberality, and induced him to shatter the cloud and pour down the treasures of the sky. See M. Henry's note.

Translated by Ludwig, Der Rigveda, III. p. 446.

An invitation addressed to Indra and Varuṇa.

1 The hymn is taken, with variants, from Ṛigveda VI. 68. 10. 11. *Indra Varuṇa: indrâvaruṇâ:* a compound in the dual number to signify the dual deity.

An imprecation.

Cf. VI. 37. 3.

HYMN LX.

I, PRUDENT, bringing power, a treasure-winner, with amicable eye that strikes no terror,
Come, praising and kind-thoughted, to these houses: be not afraid of me, be glad and joyful.

2 Let these delightful Houses that are rich in power and store of milk,
Replete with wealth and standing firm, become aware of our approach.

3 These Houses we invoke, whereon the distant exile sets his thought,
Wherein dwells many a friendly heart: let them be ware of our approach.

4 Thus greeted, ye of ample wealth, friends who enjoy delightful sweets,
Be ever free from hunger, free from thirst! Ye Houses, fear us not.

5 Kind greeting to the cattle here, kind greeting to the goats and sheep!
Then, of the food within our homes, kind greeting to the pleasant drink!

6 Full of refreshment, full of charms, of laughter and felicity,
Be ever free from hunger, free from thirst! Ye Houses, fear us not.

7 Stay here, and come not after me: prosper in every form and shape.
With happy fortune will I come. Grow more abundant still through me!

A parting traveller's address to the houses of his village.

2 *Become aware of our approach:* that is, recognize and welcome us when we return.

4 *Fear us not:* gladly welcome us.

The hymn is used as a charm to inaugurate the construction of a house, and on starting on a journey.

HYMN LXI.

SINCE, Agni, with our fervent zeal we undergo austerity,
May we be dear to Sacred Lore, may we be wise and live long lives.

2 Agni, we practise acts austere, we undergo austerity.
So listening to Holy Lore may we grow wise and full of days.

HYMN LXII.

LIKE a car-warrior, Agni here, grown mighty, Lord of the brave, Chief Priest, hath conquered footmen.
Laid on earth's centre he hath flashed and glittered. Low may he lay our enemies beneath us.

HYMN LXIII.

WE call with lauds from his most lofty dwelling victorious Agni, conqueror in battles.
May he convey us over all distresses, may the God Agni bear us past our troubles.

HYMN LXIV.

From all that woe and trouble may the Waters save and rescue me,

---

A prayer for the acquisition of sacred knowledge and its fruits.

1 M. Henry translates the first line differently, taking *tápas* as a verb: 'Since, O Agni, thou hast warmed (the world) by (thy) heat, (we also) we practise austerity.'

The stanza is employed in the religious initiation (*upanayanam*) of a novice, and in the ceremony called *godânam* (see II. 13. 1).

A prayer for the overthrow of adversaries.

Chief Priest: puróhitaḥ; usually, the domestic chaplain and counsellor of a prince. *Earth's centre:* literally, on the centre, on the earth; meaning the fire-receptacle or altar.

The stanza is employed at the preparation of the domestic fire.

A prayer for deliverance from affliction.

The stanza is employed at the preparation of the domestic fire.

Whate'er the Raven, black of hue, flying out hitherward, hath dropped.

2 May Agni Gârhapatya save and set me free from all this guilt
Which the black Raven with thy mouth, O Nirṛiti, hath wiped away.

HYMN LXV.

With retroverted fruit hast thou, O Apâmârga, sprung and grown.
Hence into distance most remote drive every curse away from me.

2 Whatever evil we have done, whatever vile or sinful act,
With thee, O Apâmârga, who lookest all ways, we wipe it off.

3 If with the cripple we have lived, whose teeth are black and nails deformed,
With thee, O Apâmârga, we wipe all that ill away from us.

A charm to avert an evil omen.

1 *Raven: ṣakúnis;* a bird, especially a large carnivorous bird, vulture or the like. The epithet 'black' points to the raven or the carrion crow.

2 *Agni Gârhapatya:* the sacred fire of the householder. See V. 31. 5. *Thy mouth,* that is, the raven himself, the evil-boding herald of misfortune. *Hath wiped away:* on himself, and so still liable to fall upon the speaker. See M. Henry's note.

Translated by Grill, Hundert Lieder, pp. 41, 186.

A charm against imprecations and threatened evils.

1 *Apâmârga:* the plant Achyranthes Aspera. See IV. 17. 6.

2 *Lookest all ways:* the branches tending in one direction and the fruit in another, the plant is regarded as the symbol of vigilant circumspection.

3 *The cripple:* M. Henry observes: 'This lame and hideous personage, the incarnation of sin and disease, strongly resembles our popular devil.' *We wipe away:* with allusion to the derivation of Apâmârga from *mṛij,* to wipe, with the particles *apa* and *â* prefixed.

Translated by Grill, Hundert Lieder, pp. 38, 186.

HYMN LXVI.

If it was in the wind or air's mid-region, if it was in the trees or in the bushes,
To meet whose utterance forth streamed the cattle, may that Celestial Power again approach us.

HYMN LXVII.

May sense return to me again, and spirit, return my Sacred Power and my possessions!
Again let fires, aflame on lesser altars, each duly stationed, here succeed and prosper.

HYMN LXVIII.

Sarasvatî, in thy decrees, Goddess, in thy celestial laws,
Accept the offered sacrifice, and, Goddess, grant us progeny.

2 Here is, Sarasvatî, thy fat libation, this sacrifice passing to the mouth of Fathers.
These most auspicious offerings have ascended to thee: through these may we be full of sweetness.

3 Be kind and most auspicious, be gracious to us, Sarasvatî. May we be ever in thy sight.

A prayer to Vâk.

The *Celestial Power:* for whose return the poet prays is the first Word, the first emanation of the Eternal, the omnific Logos, the type of which is Vâk (see IV. 30. 7), in this place the voice of thunder which calls forth the cattle, the imprisoned waters in the cloud. See M. Henry's note.

A priest's prayer to the Agnayo Dhishṇyâḥ, the Agnis or fires on the side altars. *Sacred Power: brâhmaṇam;* 'the sacred formula.'—Henry.

A prayer for children and prosperity.

The hymn is employed, according to the Vaitâna-Sûtra, in oblation to the Full Moon and to the Viṣve Devâḥ, and, according to the Kauṣika-Sûtra, in the funeral ritual.

HYMN LXIX.

MAY the wind kindly breathe on us, may the Sun warm us pleasantly.

May days pass happily for us, may night draw near delightfully, may dawn break joyfully for us!

HYMN LXX.

WHATEVER sacrifice that man performeth with voice, mind, sacred formula, oblation,

May, in accord with Death, Destruction ruin his offering before it gain fulfilment.

2 For him may sorcerers, Destruction, demons strike and prevent fulfilment through their falsehood.

Let Gods, by Indra sent, destroy his butter, and let his sacrifice be ineffective.

3 Let the two Sovrans, swift to come, like falcons swooping on their prey,

Destroy the butter of the foe whoever plots to injure us.

4 I seize thine arms and draw them back, I bind a bandage on thy mouth.

I with the anger of the God Agni have killed thy sacrifice.

5 Behind thy back I tie thine arms, I bind a bandage on thy mouth:

With the terrific Agni's wrath have I destroyed thy sacrifice.

A prayer for prosperity.

A charm to frustrate and ruin the sacrifice offered by an enemy.

3 *The two Sovrans:* Death and Destruction, Mṛityu and Nirṛiti.

Translated by Ludwig, Der Rigveda, III. p. 374, and by Grill, Hundert Lieder. pp. 46, 187.

HYMN LXXI.

WE set thee round us as a fort, victorious Agni! thee a sage,
Bold in thy colour day by day, destroyer of the treacherous foe.

HYMN LXXII.

RISE up and look upon the share of Indra fixt by ritual use.
Whether ye poured libation dressed or took delight in it uncooked.

2 Libation is prepared. Come to us, Indra: the Sun hath travelled over half his journey.
Friends with their treasures sit around thee, waiting like heads of houses for their wandering chieftain.

3 Dressed in the udder and on fire, I fancy; well dressed, I fancy, is this new oblation.
Quaff thickened milk of noon's libation, Indra, well pleased, O Thunderer, famed for many an exploit!

HYMN LXXIII.

INFLAMED is Agni, Heroes! charioteer of heaven. The caldron boils: the meath is drained to be your food.

In praise of Agni.

The stanza is taken, with one variant, from Ṛigveda X. 87. 22.

The hymn is an invitation to Indra to drink the mid-day libation.

1 The whole hymn is a reproduction, with variants, of Ṛigveda X. 179. *Rise up:* the Hotar calls upon the Adhvaryu priests (see I. 11. 1) to rise and milk the cow for milk required for the libation. See Vaitâna-Sûtra XIV. 3.

3 *Dressed*: the milk is twice dressed or cooked; first matured in the cow's udder and then heated in a caldron on the fire.

An ivitation to the Asvins to come to the morning libation.

1 *Heroes:* the many mighty acts of the Asvins are recounted in Ṛigveda I. 112, 116, 117, 118, 119, 182; VII. 68; X. 39, 40. *The caldron:* in which the milk for the libation is heated. *Meath: mádhu*, the sweet fluid; milk.

For we, O Asvins, singers sprung from many a house, invite you to be present at our banquetings.

2 Asvins, the fire is all aglow: your caldron hath been heated; come!
Here, even now, O Heroes, are the milch-kine milked. The priests, ye mighty ones! rejoice.

3 Pure with the Gods is sacrifice with cry of Hail! That is the Asvins' cup whence Gods are wont to drink.
Yea, the Immortal Ones accept it, one and all, and come to kiss that cup with the Gandharva's mouth.

4 Milk, molten butter offered when the mornings break, —this is your portion, Asvins! Come ye hitherward.
Lords of the brave, balm-lovers, guards of sacrifice, drink ye the warm libation in the light of heaven.

5 Let the warm drink approach you with its Hotar-priest: let the Adhvaryu come to you with store of milk.
Come, O ye Asvins, taste the meath that hath been drained, drink of the milk provided by this radiant cow.

6 Come hither, quickly come, thou milker of the kine: into the caldron pour milk of the radiant cow.
Most precious Savitar hath looked upon the heaven. After Dawn's going-forth he sends his light abroad.

7 I invocate this milch-cow good for milking, so that the milker, deft of hand, may milk her.
May Savitar give goodliest stimulation. The caldron hath been warmed. Let him proclaim it.

---

3 *With the Gandharva's mouth:* that is, by means of Agni, the sacrificial fire which bears oblation to the Gods.

5 *With its Hotar priest:* whose duty it is to present the libation.

7 *I invocate this milch-cow:* this is recited by the Adhvaryu when the cow is to be milked. The stanza is taken, with variants, from Rigveda I. 164. 26. In the original hymn, which from beginning to end is a series of enigmas, the cow may, according to Sâyaṇa, be the rain, the milk being the rain and the milker Vâyu the God of Wind who causes it to flow.

8 She, sovran of all treasures, is come hither yearning in spirit for her calf, and lowing.
May this cow yield her milk for both the Asvins, and may she prosper to our great advantage.

9 As dear house-friend, guest welcome in the dwelling, to this our sacrifice come thou who knowest.
And, Agni, having scattered all assailants, bring to us the possessions of our foemen.

10 Show thyself strong for mighty bliss, O Agni! Most excellent be thine effulgent splendours!
Make easy to maintain our household lordship, and overcome the might of those who hate us.

11 Fortunate mayst thou be with goodly pasture, and may we also be exceeding wealthy.
Feed on the grass, O Cow, at every season, and, coming hither, drink the limpid water.

HYMN LXXIV.

Black is the mother, we have heard, from whom the red-hued Pustules sprang.
With the divine ascetic's root I pierce and penetrate them all.

2 I pierce the foremost one of these, I perforate the middlemost,
And here I cut the hindermost asunder like a lock of hair.

---

8 Taken, with variants, from Ṛigveda I. 164. 27. In the original hymn the calf is the world longing for the rain to fall.

9 Taken from Ṛigveda V. 4. 5.

10 Taken from Ṛigveda V. 28. 3. *Make easy to maintain our household lordship:* according to Sâyaṇa: Perfect the well-knit bond of wife and husband.

11 Taken from Ṛigveda I. 164. 40.

A charm to cure pustules or scrofulous tumours.

1 *Pustules: apachítas;* see VI. 25. 1. Scrofulous or inflammatory swellings affecting the glands of the neck, *gaṇḍamâlâ* or king's-evil, appear to be intended. *The divine ascetic's root:* there is no clue to the name of the root or of its divine discoverer.

3 With spell that Tvashṭar sent to us I have dispelled thy jealousy.
We mitigate and pacify the anger that thou feltest, Lord!

4 Lord of religious rites, by law, anointed, shine thou forth here for ever friendly-minded.
So may we all with children, Jâtavedas! worship and humbly wait on thee enkindled.

HYMN LXXV.

Let not a thief or wicked man possess you: let not the dart of Rudra come anear you,
Prolific, shining in the goodly pasture, drinking at pleasant pools the limpid water.

2 Ye know the place and rest content, close-gathered, called by many a name. Come to me, Goddesses, with Gods.
Bedew with streams of fatness us, this cattle-pen, and all this place.

HYMN LXXVI.

Rapidly dropping, quick to drop, more evil than the evil ones,
More sapless than a dried-up bone, swifter than salt to melt away:

A blessing on cows.

1 The stanza is taken, with variations, from Rigveda VI. 28. 7. *The dart of Rudra:* 'Far be thy dart that killeth men or cattle' (Ṛigveda I. 114. 10.)

2 *Goddesses:* so in the hymn from which stanza 1 is taken the cows are addressed as deified beings: 'Prosper my house, ye with auspicious voices. Your power is glorified in our assemblies;' and 'To me the cows seem Bhaga, they seem Indra, they seem a portion of the first-poured Soma.'

A charm to cure scrofulous pustules.

1 *Rapidly dropping, quick to drop:* *á susrásaḥ susráso;* the text appears to be corrupt. Prof. Bloomfield proposes to read *á susráso susrástarâ*, more swift to fall than what falls fast, which would restore

2 Pustules that rise upon the neck, Pustules upon the shoulder-joints,
Pustules that, falling of themselves, spring up on every twofold limb:

3 I have expelled and banished all Scrofula harboured in the head,
And that which bores the breast-bone through, and that which settles in the sole.

4 Scrofula flies borne on by wings: it penetrates and holds the man.
Here is the cure of either kind, the chronic and the transient.

5 We know thine origin, Scrofula! know whence thou, Scrofula, art born.
How hast thou then struck this man here, him in whose house we sacrifice?

---

the metre without, however, disposing of the superfluous *á*. M. Henry suggests a causative verb *asisraso*, thou (the remedy) hast caused to fall, with which the prefix *á* might be construed, instead of *susráso*. The drying and falling off of the pustules is a sign that the disease is yielding to the remedy. *More sapless than a dried-up bone: séhorarasátará*; the text is unintelligible and probably corrupt, *séhu* meaning, not bone, but some internal organ of the body, although the St. Petersburg Dictionary gives the word in this passage the meaning of 'a certain dry material.' M. Henry reads *arasád arasátará*, drier than the dry.

2 *On every twofold limb: vijámni*; on the legs and arms. 'Eruption that appears upon the twofold joints' (Ṛigveda VII. 50. 2).

3 *Scrofula*: '*jáyánya* appears to be the general scrofulous habit of which the *apachitas* or pustules are the external manifestation.'—Henry. I adopt M. Henry's reading *nír ásyaṃ* in place of *nírástaṃ* of the text.

4 *The chronic and the transient*: I read *súkshitasya* with Prof. Ludwig instead of *súkshatasya*.

5 *Scrofula, art born: jáyánya jáyase*; a play on the words, both from the root *jan*, to generate.

6 Boldly drink Soma from the beaker, Indra! hero in war for treasure! Vṛitra-slayer.
Fill thyself full at the mid-day libation: thyself possessing riches grant us riches.

HYMN LXXVII.

YE Maruts, full of fiery heat, accept this offering brought for you
To help us, ye who slay the foe.

2 Maruts, the man who filled with rage against us beyond our thoughts would harm us, O ye Vasus,
May he be tangled in the toils of Mischief: smite ye him down with your most flaming weapon.

3 Each year come, friends to man, the tuneful Maruts, dwelling in spacious mansions, trooped together.
Exhilarating, gladdening, full of fiery heat, may they deliver us from binding bonds of sin.

HYMN LXXVIII.

I FREE thee from the cord, I loose the bond, I loose the fastening.
Even here, perpetual, Agni, wax thou strong.

2 I with celestial prayer appoint thee, Agni, maintainer of this man in princely powers.
Here brightly shine for us with wealth: declare thou to Gods this favoured giver of oblations.

---

6 The stanza, taken from Ṛigveda VI. 47. 6, has no apparent connexion with the object of the charm.

Translated by Ludwig, Der Rigveda, III. p. 500. See also Zimmer, Altindisches Leben, p. 377.

An incantation against an enemy.

1 Stanzas 1 and 2 are taken, with variants, from Ṛigveda VII. 59. 9, 8.

2 *Mischief:* or one of the malicious spirits called Druhs.

A charm for a prince's prosperity.

1 *Thee:* according to the Vaitâna-Sûtra IV. 11 the stanza is recited when the symbolical band is removed from the sacrificer's wife.

HYMN LXXIX.

Night of the New-born Moon, whatever fortune the Gods who dwell with greatness have assigned thee,
Therewith fulfil our sacrifice, all-bounteous! Blessèd One, grant us wealth with manly offspring.

2 I am the New Moon's Night, the good and pious are my inhabitants, these dwell within me.
In me have Gods of both the spheres, and Sâdhyas, with Indra as their chief, all met together.

3 The Night hath come, the gatherer of treasures, bestowing strength, prosperity, and riches.
To New Moon's Night let us present oblation: pouring out strength, with milk hath she come hither.

4 Night of New Moon! ne'er hath been born another than thou embracing all these forms and natures.
May we have what we longed for when we brought thee oblations: may we be the lords of riches.

HYMN LXXX.

Full in the front, full rearward, from the middle the Full Moon's Night hath conquered in the battle.
In her may we, dwelling with Gods and greatness, feast in the height of heaven, on strengthening viands.

A hymn to the New Moon.

1 *Night of the New-born Moon: amâvâsyâ* (from *vas*, to dwell, and *amâ*, together, is the night during which the moon dwells together with or in the same quarter as the sun; Night of New Moon personified as a Goddess.

2 *Sâdhyas:* a class of ancient Gods. See VII. 5. 1.

4 Cf. stanza 3 of Hymn LXXX.

A hymn to the Full Moon.

1 *From the middle:* of the lunar month.

2 To him, the Full Moon's mighty Bull, we pay our solemn sacrifice.
May he bestow upon us wealth unwasting, inexhaustible.

3 No one but thou, Prajâpati, none beside thee, pervading, gave to all these forms their being.
Grant us our hearts' desire when we invoke thee: may we have store of riches in possession.

4 First was the Full Moon meet for adoration among the days and in the nights' deep darkness.
Into thy heaven, O Holy One, have entered those pious men who honour thee with worship.

HYMN LXXXI.

FORWARD and backward by their wondrous power move these two youths, disporting, round the ocean.
One views all living things, and thou, the other, art born again arranging times and seasons.

2 Thou art re-born for ever new: thou marchest, ensign of days, in forefront of the mornings.
Marching thou dealest to the Gods their portion. Thou lengthenest, Moon! the days of man's existence.

3 O spray of Soma, Lord of Wars! all-perfect verily art thou.
Make me all-perfect, Beauteous One! in riches and in progeny.

---

2 *Bull:* the God of the Moon.

3 Taken, with variants, from Ṛigveda X. 121. 10, which appears to be a later addition to the original hymn.

A hymn to the New Moon.

1 The introductory stanzas 1 and 2 are taken, with variations, from Ṛigveda X. 85. 18, 19. *Two youths:* Sûrya and Soma, or Sun and Moon. *Ocean:* of air.

2 *Ensign of days:* referring to the waning moon which precedes the dawn.

3 *O spray of Soma:* Soma the Moon identified with Soma the plant. *Lord of Wars:* probably because the first quarter of the moon was considered a favourable time for predatory excursions.

4 Thou art the New Moon, fair to see, thou art complete in every part.
May I be perfect, fully blest in every way in steeds and kine, in children, cattle, home, and wealth.

5 Inflate thee with his vital breath who hates us and whom we detest.
May we grow rich in steeds and kine, in children, cattle, houses, wealth.

6 With that unwasting stalk which Gods, unwasting Gods, increase and eat,
May Varuṇa, Bṛihaspati, and Indra, the Lords and Guardians of the world, increase us.

HYMN LXXXII.

Sing with fair laud the combat for the cattle. Bestow upon us excellent possessions.
Lead to the Gods the sacrifice we offer: let streams of oil flow pure and full of sweetness.

2 Agni I first appropriate with power, with splendour, and with might.
I give myself children and lengthened life, with Hail! take Agni to myself.

---

4 *New Moon: darṣás. Fair to see: darṣatás. Thou art complete:* said euphemistically and proleptically.

6 *Stalk:* the Soma plant, identified with the Moon. *Increase: âpyâyáyanti;* this verb, here in the indicative and in the second line in the imperative, is used with a quibbling reference to *âpyâyana* (causing to swell or increase), a technical word for a part of the procedure followed in preparing Soma juice. See M. Henry's note.

According to the Kauṣika-Sûtra XXIV. 18, the hymn is to be recited on return from a journey.

A hymn in praise of Agni.

1 The stanza is taken, with variants, from Ṛigveda IV. 58. 10. *Sing: abhyàrchata;* addressed to the singers. The Ṛigveda has *abhyàrshata*, addressed to the Gods: 'Send to our eulogy a herd of cattle,' according to Sâyaṇa. *Bestow:* addressed to the Gods. *Oil:* molten butter.

2 *With Hail!:* that is, while I offer sacrifice and utter the prescribed exclamation Svâhâ, Ave, or Hail!

3 Even here do thou, O Agni, stablish wealth : let not oppressors injure thee by thinking of thee first.
Light be thy task of ruling, Agni, with thy power : may he who worships thee wax strong, invincible.

4 Agni hath looked upon the spring of Mornings, looked on the days, the earliest Jâtavedas.
So, following the gleams of Morning, Sûrya hath entered heaven and earth as his possession.

5 Agni hath looked upon the spring of Mornings, looked on the days, the earliest Jâtavedas.
So he in countless places hath extended, full against heaven and earth, the beams of Sûrya.

6 Butter to thee in heaven thy home, O Agni! Manu this day hath kindled thee with butter.
Let the Celestial Daughters bring thee butter : let cows pour butter forth for thee, O Agni.

HYMN LXXXIII.

Stablished amid the waters is, King Varuṇa, thy golden home.
Thence let the Sovran who maintains the statutes loose all binding cords.

2 Hence free thou us, King Varuṇa, from each successive bond and tie.

---

3 *Let not oppressors:* let not the wicked, anticipating our worship, secure thy attention before us, and, as unworthy adorers, insult and degrade thy majesty.

4 *Sûrya:* that is, Agni as the Sun.

6 *Manu:* the priest as representative of Manu regarded as the first institutor of religious ceremonies. *Celestial Daughters:* the heavenly Waters.

Translated by Ludwig, Der Rigveda, III. p. 428.

A prayer for deliverance from sin and other evils.

1 *Amid the waters:* Varuṇa, God of the starry firmament and the celestial ocean, presiding also over the waters of earth. See Muir, O. S. Texts, V. pp. 72—74. *The Sovran:* Varuṇa.

As we have cried, O Varuṇa! have said, The Waters, they are kine, thence set us free, O Varuṇa.

3 Loosen the bonds, O Varuṇa, that hold us, loosen the bond above, between, and under.
So before Aditi may we be sinless under thy favouring auspices, Âditya!

4 Varuṇa, free us from all snares that bind us, Varuṇa's bonds, the upper and the lower.
Drive from us evil dream, drive off misfortune: then let us pass into the world of virtue.

HYMN LXXXIV.

Holder of sway, shine here refulgent, Agni! invincible, immortal Jâtavedas.
With succours friendly to mankind, auspicious, driving away all maladies, guard our dwelling.

2 Thou, Indra, lord and leader of the people, wast born for lovely strength and high dominion.
Thou dravest off the folk who were unfriendly, and madest for the Gods wide room and freedom.

---

2 *Have cried, O Varuṇa!:* have invoked thy name. *The Waters, they are kine:* have glorified the waters in which thou dwellest by likening them to beneficent and sacred cows.

3 The stanza is taken from Ṛigveda I. 24. 15.

4 Repeated, with variants, from A. V. VI, 121. 1.

According to the Kauṣika-Sûtra CXXVII. 4, the hymn is to be recited together with other verses of the Atharva-veda at a propitiatory sacrifice when a comet has darkened the constellation of the Seven Ṛishis or Ursa Major. See Weber's Omina und Portenta, p. 387. Parts of the hymn are also to be recited in incantations against dropsy, a disease especially attributed to the displeasure of Varuṇa. See Ṛigveda VII. 89.

A prayer for protection.

1 *Succours:* or, perhaps, Goddesses, the Waters or the Dawns. The adjectives stand, in the feminine gender, without a substantive.

2 This and the following stanza are taken from Ṛigveda X. 180. 3, 2. Stanza 2 was recited at the coronation of a King.

3 Like a dread wild beast roaming on the mountain, may he approach us from the farthest distance.
Whetting thy bolt and thy sharp blade, O Indra, crush down our foes and scatter those who hate us.

HYMN LXXXV.

THIS very mighty one whom Gods urge onward, the conqueror of cars, ever triumphant,
Swift, fleet to battle, with uninjured fellies, even Târkshya for our weal will we call hither.

HYMN LXXXVI.

INDRA the rescuer, Indra the helper, Indra the brave who hears each invocation,
Ṣakra I call, Indra invoked of many. May Indra Maghavan prosper and bless us.

HYMN LXXXVII.

To Rudra in the fire, to him who dwells in floods, to Rudra who hath entered into herbs and plants,
To him who formed and fashioned all these worlds, to him this Rudra, yea, to Agni, reverence be paid!

A charm to ensure success in battle.

The stanza is taken from Ṛigveda X, 178. 1. *Târkshya:* a personification of the Sun, usually described as a kind of celestial horse.

A prayer to ensure success in battle.

The stanza is taken from Ṛigveda VI. 47. 11.

A prayer to Rudra as Agni.

Rudra: here, as in other passages, regarded as a form of Agni.

In floods: as lightning, in the watery clouds, the waters of the ocean of air. *Herbs and plants:* which Agni enters in the form of lightning descending with the rain. *All these worlds:* all living creatures.

HYMN LXXXVIII.

DEPART! thou art a foe, a foe. Poison with poison hast thou mixt. Yea, verily poison hast thou mixt.
Go to the serpent: strike him dead.

HYMN LXXXIX.

THE heavenly Waters have I ranged: we have been sated with their dew.
Here, Agni, bearing milk, am I. Endow me with the gift of strength.

2 Endow me with the gift of strength, with children, and a lengthened life.
May the Gods mark this prayer of mine, may Indra with the Ṛishis mark.

3 Ye Waters, wash away this stain and whatsoever taint be here,
Each sinful wrong that I have done and every harmless curse of mine.

4 Thou art the wood, may I succeed! fuel, may I be glorified! splendour, give splendour unto me.

A charm to cure a snake-bite.

The stanza is apparently addressed to the poison in the wound. *Poison with poison:* thou hast made thyself doubly strong. According to M. Henry, who considers the literal meaning to be very vague and inapplicable to the procedure prescribed in Kausika-Sûtra XXIX. 6, the words are addressed to the blade of grass, used in the charm, which has become impregnated with the poison which by its means has been extracted from the wound. M. Henry accordingly translates: 'In the poison thou hast filled thyself with poison.'

Translated by Ludwig, Der Rigveda, III. p. 511.

A prayer for purification and prosperity.

The hymn is recited in the ceremony of purification with holy water.

HYMN XC.

TEAR thou asunder, as of old, like tangles of a creeping plant. Demolish thou the Dâsa's might.

2 May we with Indra's help divide the gathered treasure of the foe.
I, by the law of Varuṇa, bring down thy pride and wantonness.

HYMN XCI.

MAY Indra with his help, Lord of all treasures, be unto us a careful good protector,
Drive off our foes and give us peace and safety. May we be lords of goodly store of heroes.

HYMN XCII.

MAY this rich Indra as our good protector keep even far away the men who hate us.
May we enjoy his favour, his the holy: may we enjoy his blessèd loving-kindness.

HYMN XCIII.

WITH Indra's and with Manyu's aid may we subdue our enemies, resistlessly destroying foes.

A charm to prevent the success of a rival in love.

Stanzas 1 and 2 are taken, with variations, from Ṛigveda VIII. 40. 6, and are originally part of a prayer to Indra and Agni for victory over hostile natives of the land. According to the Kauṣika-Sûtra, XXXVI. 35 sqq., the hymn is to be used, with certain prescribed ceremonies, as a charm against a rival. For stanza 3 see Appendix.

A prayer for protection.

The stanza occurs, with variants, in Ṛigveda VI. 47. 12, and X. 131. 6.

A prayer for protection.

The stanza occurs, with variants, in Ṛigveda VI. 47. 13, and X. 131. 7.

A prayer for success in battle.

Manyu's aid: the aid of warlike Anger or Rage personified. See IV. 31.

HYMN XCIV.

WE lead the constant Soma on with constant sacrificial gift,
That Indra may make all the tribes unanimous and only ours.

HYMM XCV.

To heaven, as 'twere, have soared this man's two vultures, staggering, dusky hued,
The Parcher and the Drier-up, the pair who parch and dry his heart.

2 I verily have stirred them up like oxen resting after toil,
Like two loud-snarling curs, or like two wolves who watch to make their spring:

3 Like two that thrust, like two that pierce, like two that strike with mutual blows.
I bind the conduit of the man or dame who hence hath taken aught.

A charm to ensure the obedience of subjects.

The stanza is taken, with variants, from Ṛigveda X. 173. 6, the subject of the original hymn being the benediction of a newly elected King.

An incantation against an undiscovered thief.

1 The stanza is unintelligible.

2 *Stirred them up:* M. Henry strikes out *úd* which mars the metre, and translates: 'I have reduced them to immobility.'

3 *Two that thrust:* perhaps bulls.

The procedure prescribed in connexion with this hymn in the Kauṣika-Sûtra XLVIII. 40—43, which consists in tying two threads, one black and one red, to a striped frog and plunging the animal into hot water, does not throw much light on this very obscure incantation. See M. Henry's note.

The hymn has been translated by Ludwig, Der Rigveda, III. p. 517.

HYMN XCVI.

The kine are resting in the stall, home to her nest hath flown the bird,
The hills are firmly rooted: I have fixed the kidneys in their place.

HYMN XCVII.

As we have here elected thee, skilled Hotar! to-day as this our sacrifice proceedeth,
Come to the firm place, mightiest! yea, come firmly. Knowing the sacrifice, approach the Soma.

2 With kine connect us, and with spirit, Indra! Lord of Bay Steeds, with princes and with favour,
With the God-destined portion of the Brahmans, and the good-will of Gods who merit worship.

3 The willing Gods whom, God, thou hast brought hither, send thou to their own dwelling-place, O Agni.
When ye have eaten and have drunk sweet juices, endow this man with precious wealth, ye Vasus.

4 Gods, we have made your seats of easy access, who, pleased with me, have come to my libation.
Bearing and bringing hitherward your treasures, after the rich warm beverage mount to heaven.

5 Go to the sacrifice, go to its master, Sacrifice! To thy birth-place go with Svâhâ.

An incantation against an undiscovered thief.

The stanza is a sequel to Hymn XCV.

The hymn consists of a series of sacrificial formulas.

1 The stanza is taken, with variations, from Ṛigveda III. 29. 16. *To the firm place:* the sanctuary. Or the translation may be: Come firmly, O most mighty! yea, come firmly.

2 Taken, with variations, from Ṛigveda V. 42. 4.

4 *Easy of access:* that is, 'we have kindled Agni in order that he may show us the way to heaven.'—Henry.

5 Stanzas 5—8 are non-metrical in the original.

6 This is thy sacrifice with holy hymnal, Lord of the Rite, Svâhâ! and fraught with vigour.

7 Vashaṭ to paid and yet unpaid oblations! Ye Gods who know the way, find and pursue it!

8 Lord of the Mind, lay this our sacrifice in heaven among the Gods. Svâhâ in heaven! Svâhâ on earth!
Svâhâ in air! In wind have I paid offerings. Hail!

HYMN XCVIII.

Balmed is the Grass with butter and libation, with Indra gracious Lord, and with the Maruts.
Hail! let the sacrifice go forth anointed to Indra with the Gods and Viṣve Devas.

HYMN XCIX

Strew thou the Grass, and spread it on the Altar: rob not the sister who is lying yonder.
The Hotar's seat is green and golden: these are gold necklets in the place of him who worships.

---

6 *Fraught with vigour:* bringing us the strength of heroes.

7 *To paid and yet unpaid oblations!:* or, to those (Gods) who have been worshipped, and to those who have not (yet) been worshipped, with oblations.

8 *Lord of the Mind:* Lord of the mental powers and life of men; here, Agni.

Translated by Ludwig, Der Rigveda, III. p. 429.

The subject is the anointing of the Sacred Grass.

1 *With Indra:* graced by the presence of Indra.

The subject is the preparation of the Altar.

Strew: on the floor of the sacrificial chamber for the Gods to sit on. *The sister:* the altar, regarded as closely connected with the priest. *Green and golden:* being strewn with fresh bright grass. *These:* the tufts of grass. *In the place of him who worships:* in the sanctuary or place of sacrifice. See M. Henry's note for an exhaustive discussion of the stanza.

Translated by Ludwig, Der Rigveda, III. p. 434.

HYMN C.

I TURN away from evil dream, from dream of sin, from indigence.
I make the prayer mine inmost friend. Hence! torturing dreamy phantasies!

HYMN CI.

THE food that in a dream I eat is not perceived at early morn.
May all that food be blest to me because it is not seen by day.

HYMN CII.

WHEN I have worshipped Heaven and Earth, reverenced Firmament and Death,
I will make water standing up. Let not the Sovrans injure me.

HYMN CIII.

WHAT princely warrior, seeking higher fortune, will free us from this shameful fiend of mischief?
What friend of sacrifice? what guerdon-lover? Who winneth 'mid the Gods a long existence?

A charm against nightmare.

I turn away: and lie on my other side. *Mine inmost friend:* cf. I. 19.4. Translated by Ludwig, Der Rigveda, III. p. 498.

A charm against nightmare.

The food: dreaming of eaten food is unlucky, and requires a purification.

A charm to obtain pardon for an indecent act.

The stanza is considered to be one of the *svastyayanas* or charms to ensure success. See Kauṣika-Sûtra LII. 15.

The cry of an unemployed priest.

Princely warrior: or Kshatriya. *Fiend of mischief:* here, apparently, meaning the demon of poverty. *A long existence:* a long life in heaven as the reward of the sacrifices which I am ready to perform for any employer. See Ludwig, Der Rigveda, III. p. 269.

HYMN CIV.

Who will prepare the dappled Cow, good milker, ne'er without calf, whom Varuṇa gave Atharvan,
And, joying in Bṛihaspati's alliance, arrange according to his will her body?

HYMN CV.

Leaving humanity behind, making the heavenly word thy choice,
With all thy friends address thyself to furthering and guiding men.

HYMN CVI.

Each thoughtless ill that we have done, O Agni, all error in our conduct, Jâtavedas!
Therefrom do thou, O sapient God, preserve us. May we thy friends, for bliss, have life eternal.

HYMN CVII.

The seven bright beams of Sûrya bring the waters downward from the sky,
The streams of ocean: these have made the sting that pained thee drop away.

A prayer for prosperity.

Who: what God. *The dappled Cow:* the symbol of Plenty. *Whom Varuṇa gave Atharvan:* see V. 11.

An initiation formula.

The stanza is spoken by the Âchârya or spiritual teacher in the *upanayana* ceremony, when he invests the religious student with the sacrificial thread, instructs him in the Veda, and gives him authority to teach.

A prayer for pardon.

Agni is entreated to preserve the priests from the consequences of any error in conducting divine worship.

A charm against cough.

The sunbeams may be said to cause the waters to descend in-asmuch as they have first drawn them up in the shape of vapour. The water is to be used in rinsing the mouth of the patient. *The sting:* the pricking or tickling sensation in the throat.

HYMN CVIII.

WHOSO by stealth or openly would harm us, a friend who knows us, or a stranger, Agni!
May the strange she-fiend armed with teeth attack them: O Agni, theirs be neither home nor children!

2 Whoso oppresseth us, O Jâtavedas, asleep or waking, standing still or moving,
Accordant with Vaiṣvânara thy comrade, O Jâtavedas, meet them and consume them.

HYMN CIX.

MY homage to the strong, the brown, the sovran lord among the dice!
Butter on Kali I bestow: may he be kind to one like me.

2 Bear butter to the Apsarases, O Agni, and to the Dice bear dust and sand and water.
The Gods delight in both oblations, joying in sacrificial gifts apportioned duly.

3 The Apsarases take pleasure in the banquet between the Sun and the libation-holder.
With butter let them fill my hands, and give me, to be my prey, the man who plays against me.

4 Evil be mine opponent's luck! Sprinkle thou butter over us.

A prayer for protection.

2 *With Vaiṣvânara:* Agni in another character being here regarded as a separate deity.

Translated by Ludwig, Der Rigveda, III. p. 517.

A prayer to ensure success in gambling.

1 *The brown:* the nuts of the Vibhidaka, or, later, Vibhîtaka, tree (Terminalia Bellerica) were used as dice in early times. See Rigveda X. 34. 1. *Kali:* the die, or side of a die, which is marked with one point; the ace (personified as an evil genius in the poem of Nala). Kali is propitiated with sacrificial butter on account of his ruinous power as the worst throw.

2 *To the Apsarases:* who preside over dice and influence the gambler's luck. See II. 2. 5; IV. 38. 1—4; VI. 118. 1. *Dust:* apparently, the dice, after being dipped in butter, were dried in sand, and then washed with water. See M. Henry's note.

3 *Between the Sun and the libation-holder:* that is, in mid-air.

Strike, as a tree with lightning flash, mine adversary in the game.

5 The God who found for us this wealth for gambling, to cast the dice and count the winning number,
May he accept the sacrifice we offer, and with Gandharvas revel in the banquet.

6 Fellow-inhabitants, such is your title, for Dice with looks of power support dominion.
As such with offerings may we serve you, Indus! May we have riches in our own possession.

7 As I invoke the Gods at need, as I have lived in chastity,
May these, when I have grasped the Dice, the brown, be kind to one like me.

HYMN CX.

Resistless, Agni, Indra, smite his foemen for the worshipper,
For best foe-slayers are ye both.

2 Agni I call, and Indra, foe-destroyers, swift moving, heroes, Gods who wield the thunder,
Through whom they won the light in the beginning, these who have made all worlds their habitation.

3 The God Bṛihaspati hath won thy friendly favour with the cup.
With hymns, O Indra, enter us for the juice-pouring worshipper.

---

5 *Gandharvas:* as the husbands of the dice-loving Apsarases.

6 *Fellow-inhabitants: sáṃvasavas;* equivalent, according to M. Henry, to the Etrusco-Roman Dii Consentes. According to Prof. Ludwig 'Containers of all wealth.' *Indus:* drops of Soma juice. M. Henry would read *devâ*, Gods!

7 *Lived in chastity:* led the chaste life of the Brahmachârî or religious student.

Translated by Ludwig, Der Rigveda, III. p. 456.

A prayer for success in battle.

2 *They won the light:* the Gods obtained the light of heaven.

HYMN CXI.

BELLY of Indra art thou, Soma-holder! the very soul of Gods and human beings.
Here be the sire of offspring, thine here present! Here be they glad in thee who now are elsewhere.

HYMN CXII.

RADIANT with light are Heaven and Earth, whose grace is nigh, whose sway is vast.
Seven Goddesses have flowed to us: may they deliver us from woe;
2 Release me from the curse's bond and plague that comes from Varuṇa;
Free me from Yama's fetter and from every sin against the Gods.

HYMN CXIII.

ROUGH Plant, thou rough rude parasite, cut thou that man, O Rough and Rude,
That thou mayst hinder from his act that man in all his manly strength.
2 Thou, rugged Plant, art rude and rough, Vishâ, Vishâtakî art thou,

---

A prayer for progeny.

Soma-holder: the reservoir containing the clarified Soma juice is addressed as the representative of the deity. *Here present*: *átra*, here, instead of *âsú*, in these females. The reading of the text may be traced to the employment of the stanza at a *vṛishotsarga*, the liberation of a bull (according to some authorities, with four heifers) on the occasion of a sacrifice or as a religious observance generally. See M. Henry's note. *Elsewhere*: in the other world.

A prayer for protection and freedom from sin.

1 *Seven Goddesses*: the Seven Rivers. See IV. 6. 2. *Âpas*: a gloss that mars the metre: *á* should be read. See M. Henry's note.

2 This stanza, taken from Ṛigveda X. 97. 16, occurs also in A. V. VI. 96. 2.

A woman's incantation against a rival.

1 The woman appears to address some anti-aphrodisiac plant.

2 *Vishá, Vishátakí*: some unknown herbs: 'Poison and Poison-draught' according to Prof. Weber. The second line is addressed to the absent rival. *A barren cow*: on account of great age.

The hymn has been translated by Weber, Indische Studien, V. p. 252.

That thou mayst be cast off by him, as by a bull a barren cow.

HYMN CXIV.

I HAVE extracted from thy sides, I have extracted from thy heart,
I have extracted from thy face the strength and splendour that were thine.

2 Let pain and suffering pass away, let cares and curses vanish hence.
Let Agni slay the fiendish hags, Soma kill hags who trouble us.

HYMN CXV.

HENCE, Evil Fortune! fly away, vanish from this place and from that.
We fix thee with an iron hook unto the man who hateth us.

2 Granting us riches, Savitar! golden-handed, send thou away from us to other regions
That Fortune who, flying, abominable, hath, as a creeper climbs a tree, assailed me.

3 One and a hundred Fortunes all together are at his birth born with a mortal's body.
Of these we send away the most unlucky: keep lucky ones for us, O Jâtavedas.

Conclusion of the incantation in Hymn CXIII.

1 Addressed to the bewitched rival.

2 *Fiendish hags*: said with reference to the woman who has been her rival.

A charm against Misfortune.

1 *Evil Fortune*: Lakshmî; more usually the Goddess of good luck. See I. 18. 1.

3 *One and a hundred*: see V. 18. 12.

According to the procedure prescribed in the Kauṣika-Sûtra, XVIII. 16—18, a hook is to be attached to the left leg of a black bird (explained by Dàrila as a crow), a rice-cake is to be hung on the hook, and the bird is to be let fly as the first stanza is recited.

Translated by Muir, O. S. Texts, V. p. 348; Ludwig, Der Rigveda, III. p. 499.; and Grill, Hundert Lieder, pp. 41, 187.

4 I have disparted these and those like cows who stray on common land.

Here let auspicious Fortunes stay: hence have I banished evil ones.

HYMN CXVI.

Homage to him the burning one, shaker, exciter, violent!

Homage to him the cold who acts according to his ancient will!

2 May he, the lawless one, who comes alternate or two following days, pass over and possess the frog.

HYMN CXVII.

Come hither, Indra, with bay steeds, joyous, with tails like peacock plumes.

Let none impede thy way as fowlers stay the bird: pass o'er them as o'er desert lands.

HYMN CXVIII.

Thy vital parts I cover with thine armour: with immortality King Soma clothe thee!

Varuṇa give thee what is more than ample, and in thy triumph let the Gods be joyful.

A charm against Fever.

1 *Homage:* Takman or Fever is addressed as a *devá*, a supernatural being or God to whose influence the disease may be attributed. See note on I. 25. 1. Similarly 'pest or fever was formerly, and is still among the superstitious Slaves, held to be a female deity or spirit of evil.'—Baring-Gould, Strange Survivals, p. 47.

2 *The frog:* which occupies an important place in the attendant procedure prescribed in the Kauṣika-Sûtra, XXXII. 17. The frog, which has two different coloured strings tied round it, relieves the patient of his disease. See VII. 95. 3, note.

An auspicious formula to ensure prosperity.

The stanza is taken from Ṛigveda III. 45. 1, found also in Sâmaveda I. iii. ii. 1. 4, and II. viii. iii. 1.

A benediction on a warrior.

The stanza is taken from Ṛigveda VI. 75. 18, the deified objects of the original hymn being armour and warlike weapons, charioteer, chariot, horses, and tutelary deities. It occurs also in Sâmaveda II. ix. iii. 8. 1. *Armour:* the *vârman* or coat of mail protected the shoulders, back, chest, and lower parts of the body. If not made of metal, it was strengthened and adorned with metal of some kind.

BOOK VIII.

HYMN I.

HOMAGE to Death the Ender! May thy breathings, inward and outward, still remain within thee.
Here stay this man united with his spirit in the Sun's realm, the world of life eternal!

2 Bhaga hath lifted up this man, and Soma with his filaments,
Indra and Agni, and the Gods the Maruts, raised him up to health.

3 Here is thy spirit, here thy breath, here is thy life, here is thy soul:
By a celestial utterance we raise thee from Destruction's bonds.

4 Up from this place, O man, rise! sink not downward, casting away the bonds of Death that hold thee.
Be not thou parted from this world, from sight of Agni and the Sun.

5 Purely for thee breathe Wind and Mâtariṣvan, and let the Waters rain on thee their nectar.
The Sun shall shine with healing on thy body; Death shall have mercy on thee: do not leave us!

6 Upward must be thy way, O man, not downward: with life and mental vigour I endow thee.
Ascend this car eternal, lightly rolling; then full of years shalt thou address the meeting.

The hymn is a charm or incantation designed to recover a man who is at the point of death, or even to recall the departed spirit.

5 *Mâtariṣvan:* here a name of Vâyu or Wind. See V. 17. 1.

6 *Ascend this car:* be borne back to life by our incantation.

7 Let not thy soul go thither, nor be lost to us: slight not the living, go not where the Fathers are.
Let all the Gods retain thee here in safety.

8 Yearn not for the departed ones, for those who lead men far away.
Rise up from darkness into light: come, both thy hands we clasp in ours.

9 Let not the black dog and the brindled seize thee, two warders of the way sent forth by Yama.
Come hither; do not hesitate: with mind averted stay not there.

10 Forbear to tread this path, for it is awful: that path I speak of which thou hast not travelled.
Enter it not, O man; this way is darkness: forward is danger, hitherward is safety.

11 Thy guardians be the Fires within the Waters, thy guardian be the Fire which men enkindle.
Thy guardian be Vaiṣvânara Jâtavedas: let not celestial Fire with lightning burn thee.

12 Let not the Flesh-Consumer plot against thee: depart thou far away from the Destroyer.
Be Heaven and Earth and Sun and Moon thy keepers, and from the dart of Gods may Air protect thee.

13 May Vigilance and Watchfulness protect thee, Sleepless and Slumberless keep guard above thee!
Let Guardian and let Wakeful be thy warders.

14 Let these be thy preservers, these thy keepers. All hail to these, to these be lowly worship!

15 May saving Savitar, Vâyu, Indra, Dhâtar restore thee to communion with the living.
Let not thy vigour or thy breath forsake thee: we recall thy life.

---

9 *Two warders:* see V. 30. 6.

12 *The Flesh-Consumer:* Agni Kravyâd, the fire of the funeral pile. Cf. III. 21. 9.

13 *Vigilance, Watchfulness*, and the others are the Genii of living men.

16 Let not the fiend with snapping jaws, nor darkness find thee: tongue, holy grass: how shouldst thou perish?
May the Âdityas and the Vasus, Indra and Agni raise thee and to health restore thee.

17 The Sky hath raised thee, and the Earth, Prajâpati hath raised thee up.
The Plants and Herbs with Soma as their King have rescued thee from Death.

18 Here let this man, O Gods, remain: let him not go to yonder world.
We rescue him from Mṛityu with a charm that hath a thousand powers.

19 I have delivered thee from Death. Strength-givers smelt and fashion thee!
Let not she-fiends with wild loose locks, or fearful howlers yell at thee.

20 I have attained and captured thee: thou hast returned restored to youth,
Perfect in body: so have I found all thy sight and all thy life.

21 Life hath breathed on thee; light hath come: darkness hath past away from thee.
Far from thee we have buried Death, buried Destruction and Decline.

---

16 *The fiend with snapping jaws: jambháḥ sáṁhanus;* see II. 4. 2. *Tongue, holy grass:* the construction and meaning are obscure. Prof. Ludwig suggests *ábarhíḥ* instead of *barhíḥ*, and translates 'nicht die zunge au sich reiszen.'

19 *Strength-givers smelt and fashion thee:* 'may the vigorous breathe upon thee.'—Muir. See VIII. 2. 4.

21 *Decline: yákshma*, pulmonary consumption.

Translated by Muir, O. S. Texts, V. 444, and Ludwig, Der Rigveda, III. p. 495

HYMN II.

SEIZE to thyself this trust of life for ever : thine be longevity which nothing shortens.
Thy spirit and thy life again I bring thee : die not, nor vanish into mist and darkness.

2 Come to the light of living men, come hither : I draw thee to a life of hundred autumns.
Loosing the bonds of Death, the curse that holds thee, I give thee age of very long duration.

3 Thy breath have I recovered from the Wind, thy vision from the Sun.
Thy mind I stablish and secure within thee : feel in thy members, use thy tongue, conversing.

4 I blow upon thee with the breath of bipeds and quadrupeds, as on a fire new-kindled.
To thee, O Death, and to thy sight and breath have I paid reverence.

5 Let this man live, let him not die : we raise him, we recover him.
I make for him a healing balm. O Death, forbear to slay this man.

6 Here for sound health I invocate a living animating plant,
Preserving, queller of disease, victorious, full of power and might.

7 Seize him not, but encourage and elease him : here let him stay, though thine, in all his vigour.
Bhava and Sarva, pity and protect him : give him full life and drive away misfortunes.

A charm or incantation designed to recover a man who is at the point of death, or even to recall the departed spirit.

3 *Thy breath :* at death, like goes to like : 'The sun receive thine eye (or thy sight), the wind thy spirit' (Rigveda X. 16. 3). Cf. also A.V. XI. 8. 31.

7 *Bhava and Sarva :* see note on IV. 28. 1.

8 Comfort him, Death, and pity him: let him arise and pass away.
Unharmed, with all his members, hearing well, with eld, may he through hundred years win profit with his soul.

9 May the Gods' missile pass thee by. I bring thee safe from the mist: from death have I preserved thee.
Far have I banished flesh-consuming Agni: I place a rampart for thy life's protection.

10 Saving him from that misty path of thine which cannot be defied,
From that descent of thine, O Death, we make for him a shield of prayer.

11 I give thee both the acts of breath, health, lengthened life, and death by age.
All Yama's messengers who roam around, sent by Vaivasvata, I chase away.

12 Far off we drive Malignity, Destruction, Piṣâchas banqueters on flesh, and Grâhî.
And all the demon kind, the brood of sin, like darkness, we dispel.

13 I win thy life from Agni, from the living everlasting Jâtavedas.
This I procure for thee, that thou, undying, mayst not suffer harm, that thou mayst be content, that all be well with thee.

14 Gracious to thee be Heaven and Earth, bringing no grief, and drawing nigh!

---

9 *Flesh-consuming Agni:* the fire of the funeral pile. *A rampart:* cf. 'Here I erect this rampart for the living' (Ṛigveda X. 18. 4); a line of demarcation limiting the jurisdiction of Death until the natural time for his approach.

11 *Vaivasvata:* Vivasvân's son, Yama.

12 *Piṣâchas:* see I. 16. 3. *Grâhî:* see II. 9. 1.

Pleasantly shine the Sun for thee, the Wind blow sweetly to thy heart!
Let the celestial Waters full of milk flow happily for thee.

15 Auspicious be the Plants to thee! I have upraised thee, borne thee from the lower to the upper earth:
Let the two Sons of Aditi, the Sun and Moon, protect thee there.

16 Whatever robe to cover thee or zone thou makest for thyself,
We make it pleasant to thy frame: may it be soft and smooth to touch.

17 When, with a very keen and cleansing razor, our hair and beards thou shavest as a barber,
Smoothing our face steal not our vital forces.

18 Auspicious unto thee be rice and barley, causing no painful sickness or consumption.
These two expel consumption, these deliver from calamity.

19 Thy food, thy drink, whate'er they be, corn grown by cultivation, milk,—
Food eatable, uneatable, I make all poisonless for thee.

20 We give thee over as a charge to Day and Night, in trust to both.
Keep him for me from stingy fiends, from those who fain would feed on him.

21 A hundred, yea, ten thousand years we give thee, ages two, three, four.
May Indra, Agni, all the Gods, with willing favour look on thee.

---

15 *Moon:* 'The Moon is not in the Vedas generally reckoned among the Âdityas'.—Muir.

17 *Thou shavest:* causest us to shave as a sign of mourning.

21 *Ages: yugas* here meaning probably generations.

22 To Autumn we deliver thee, to Winter, Spring, and Summer's care.
We trust thee with auspicious years wherein the plants and herbs grow up.

23 Death is the lord of bipeds, Death is sovran lord of quadrupeds.
Away I bear thee from that Death the ruler: be not thou afraid.

24 Thou, still uninjured, shalt not die: be not afraid; thou shalt not die.
Here where I am men do not die or go to lowest depths of gloom.

25 Here verily all creatures live, the cow, the horse, the man, the beast,
Here where this holy prayer is used, a rampart that protecteth life.
Let it preserve thee from thy peers, from incantation, from thy friends.

26 Live very long, be healthy, be immortal: let not the vital breath forsake thy body.

27 One and a hundred modes of death, dangers that may be overcome,—
May Gods deliver thee from this when Agni, dear to all men, bids.

28 Body of Agni prompt to save, slayer of fiends and foes art thou,
Yea, banisher of malady, the healing balm called Pûtudru.

---

27 *One and a hundred modes of death:* see note on V. 18. 12.

28 *Pûtudru:* the Khadira (Acacia Catechu), or, according to others, the Devadâru (Pinus Deodar). Muir and Zimmer write 'Pûtadru,' which is said to be a name of the Palâsa (Butea Frondosa).

Translated by Muir, O. S. Texts, V. p. 447, and by Ludwig, Der Rigveda, III. p. 496.

HYMN III.

I BALM with oil the mighty demon-slayer, to the most famous friend I come for shelter.

Enkindled, sharpened by our rites, may Agni protect us in the day and night from evil.

2 O Jâtavedas, armed with teeth of iron, enkindled with thy flame, attack the demons.

Seize with thy tongue the foolish gods' adorers: rend, put within thy mouth the raw-flesh-eaters.

3 Apply thy teeth, the upper and the lower, thou who hast both, enkindled and destroying.

Roam also in the air, O King, around us, and with thy jaws assail the wicked spirits.

4 Pierce through the Yâtudhâna's skin, O Agni; let the destroying dart with fire consume him.

Rend his joints, Jâtavedas! let the eater of raw flesh, seeking flesh, tear and destroy him.

5 Where now thou seest, Agni Jâtavedas! a Yâtudhâna, standing still or roaming,

Or one that flieth through the air's mid-region, kindled to fury as an archer pierce him.

6 Bending thy shafts through sacrifices, Agni! dipping thine arrows in the hymn to point them,

Pierce to the heart therewith the Yâtudhânas, and break their arms uplifted to attack thee.

The hymn is a prayer for the destruction of demons.

1 Stanzas 1—23 are taken, with transpositions and other variations, from Ṛigveda X. 87. 1—23, ascribed to the Ṛishi Pâyu and addressed to Agni Rakshohâ, the Slayer of Râkshasas.

2 *Demons:* Yâtudhânas (see I. 7. 1) explained by Sâyaṇa as Râkshasas. *Foolish gods' adorers: mûradevân:* according to Sâyaṇa = *mâraṇakrîḍân*, 'sporting in destruction,' an epithet of a particular class of demons.

4 *The eater of raw flesh:* the wolf or other carnivorous wild beast.

7 Rescue the captives also, Jâtavedas! yea, those whom Yâtudhânas' spears have captured.
Strike down that fiend, blazing before him, Agni! Let spotted carrion-eating kites devour him.

8 Here tell this forth, O Agni: whosoever is, he himself, or acteth as, a demon,
Grasp him, O thou most youthful, with thy fuel: to the Man-Seer's eye give him as booty.

9 With keen glance guard the sacrifice, O Agni: thou Sage, conduct it onward to the Vasus.
Let not the fiends, O Man-Beholder, harm thee burning against the Râkshasas to slay them.

10 Look on the fiend, 'mid men, as Man-Beholder: rend thou his three extremities in pieces.
Demolish with thy flame his ribs, O Agni: the Yâtudhâna's root destroy thou triply.

11 Thrice, Agni, let thy noose surround the demon who with his falsehood injures holy Order.
Loud roaring with thy flame, O Jâtavedas, fetter him in the presence of the singer.

12 Agni, what curse the pair this day may utter, what rude rough word the worshippers have spoken,

---

7 I translate the first line in accordance with Prof. Ludwig's suggestion (Der Rigveda, IV. p. 415) that *yâtudhânân* stands for *yâtudhânânâm*. The Ṛigveda reading is simpler: 'Tear from the Yâtudhâna, Jâtavedas! what he hath seized and with his spears hath captured.'

8 *To the Man-Seer's eye:* the Man-Seer, the Viewer of all Mankind, is Agni himself.

9 *To the Vasus:* to the Gods to whom the oblations are made. Sâyaṇa explains *vásubhyaḥ* by *vasûnâmarthâya:* 'to (the acquisition of) riches.'—Wilson.

10 *His three extremities:* his three heads, according to Sâyaṇa. His head and shoulders, according to Prof. Grassmann. *Root:* his feet. *Triply:* used vaguely, to correspond with the three upper extremities.

12 *The pair:* the married pair; perhaps the sacrificer and his wife. The Ṛishi prays that every hasty word that may have been uttered by pious people in their anger may be used as a weapon to wound the Yâtudhâna.

Each arrowy taunt sped from the angry spirit,—
pierce to the heart therewith the Yâtudhânas.

13 With fervent heat exterminate the demons: destroy
the fiends with glow and flame, O Agni.
Destroy with fire the foolish gods' adorers: destroy
the insatiate fiercely-burning creatures.

14 May Gods destroy to-day the evil-doer: may uttered
curses turn again and strike him.
Let arrows pierce the liar in his vitals, and Viṣva's
net enclose the Yâtudhâna.

15 The fiend who smears himself with flesh of cattle,
with flesh of horses and of human bodies,
Who steals the milch-cow's milk away, O Agni,—
tear off the heads of such with fiery fury.

16 Let the fiends steal the poison of the cattle: may
Aditi cast off the evil-doers.
May the God Savitar give them up to ruin, and be
their share of herbs and plants denied them.

17 The cow gives milk each year, O Man-Beholder:
let not the Yâtudhâna ever taste it.
Agni, if one should glut him with the biestings,
pierce with thy flame his vitals as he meets thee.

18 Agni, from days of old thou slayest demons: never
have Râkshasas in fight o'ercome thee.
Burn up the foolish ones, the flesh-devourers: let
none of them escape thy heavenly arrow.

19 Guard us, O Agni, from above and under, protect us
from behind and from before us;
And may thy flames, most fierce and never wasting,
glowing with fervent heat, consume the sinner.

---

14 *Viṣva's net:* the noose of all-pervading Agni.

16 *Steal the poison of the cattle:* if they take the milk and drink it, let it poison them. According to Sâyaṇa: let them drink (the Ṛigveda has *pibantu*) the poison of the cattle (which is kept in the house), perhaps some poisonous ointment used for external application only.

20 From rear, from front, from under, from above us,
Agni, protect us as a sage with wisdom.
Guard to old age thy friend as friend eternal:
O Agni, as immortal, guard us mortals.

21 Lend thou the worshipper that eye, O Agni, wherewith thou lookest on the hoof-armed demons.
With light celestial in Atharvan's manner burn up the fool who ruins truth with falsehood.

22 We set thee round us as a fort, victorious Agni! thee, a sage,
In conquering colour day by day, destroyer of the treacherous foe.

23 With deadly poison strike thou back the treacherous brood of Râkshasas,
O Agni, with thy sharpened glow, with rays that flash with points of flame.

24 Agni shines far and wide with lofty splendour, and by his greatness makes all things apparent.
He conquers godless and malign enchantments, and sharpens both his horns to gore the ogres.

25 Thy two unwasting horns, O Jâtavedas, keen-pointed weapons, sharpened by devotion—
With these transfix the wicked-souled Kimîdin, with fierce flame, Jâtavedas! when he meets thee.

26 Bright, radiant, meet to be adored, immortal with refulgent glow,
Agni drives Râkshasas away.

---

21 *Hoof-armed:* striking with the hoof. According to Sâyaṇa, 'having nails like hoofs.' *In Atharvan's manner:* like Atharvan the ancient priest who is said to have been the first who obtained fire and offered burnt oblations.

22 This Anushṭup stanza is found also in VII. 71.

24 Taken from Ṛigveda V. 2. 9.

25 *Kimîdin:* see I. VII. 1.

26 Taken from Ṛigveda VII. 15. 10.

HYMN IV.

INDRA and Soma, burn, destroy the demon foe! Send downward, O ye Bulls, those who add gloom to gloom.
Annihilate the fools, slay them and burn them up: chase them away from us, pierce the voracious fiends.

2 Let sin, Indra and Soma! round the wicked boil, like as a caldron set amid the flames of fire.
Against the foe of prayer, eater of gory flesh, the fearful-eyed Kimîdin, keep perpetual hate.

3 Indra and Soma, plunge the wicked in the depth, yea, cast them into darkness that hath no support,
So that not one of them may ever thence return: so may your wrathful might prevail and conquer them.

4 Indra and Soma, hurl your deadly crushing bolt down on the wicked fiend from heaven and from the earth.
Yea, fashion from the big clouds your celestial dart wherewith ye burn to death the waxing demon race.

5 Indra and Soma, cast ye downward from the sky your deadly bolts of stone burning with fiery flame,
Eternal, scorching darts. Plunge the voracious fiends within the depth, and let them pass without a sound.

The hymn consists mainly of a series of imprecations directed against demons and evil spirits, Râkshasas and Yâtudhânas.

1 The whole hymn is taken, with unimportant variants, from Ṛig-veda VII. 104, attributed to the famous Ṛishi Vasishṭha. *Indra and Soma: índrâsomâ;* addressed as a dual deity. *The demon foe:* Râkshasas, fiends, demons, who wander about at night, disturbing sacrifices and devout men, ensnaring and even devouring human beings, and generally hostile to the human race.

1 *Kimîdin:* see I. 7. 1.

5 *Without a sound:* so suddenly that they have not time to cry out.

6 Indra and Soma, let this hymn control you both, even as the girth encompasses two vigorous steeds—
The song of praise which I with wisdom offer you. Do ye, as Lords of men, animate these my prayers.

7 In your impetuous manner think ye both thereon: destroy those evil spirits, kill the treacherous fiends.
Indra and Soma, let the wicked have no bliss whoso at any time attacks and injures us.

8 Whoso accuses me with words of falsehood when I pursue my way with guileless spirit,
May he, the speaker of untruth, be, Indra! like water which the hollowed hand compresses.

9 Those who destroy, as is their wont, the simple, and with their evil natures harm the righteous,
May Soma give them over to the serpent, or to the lap of Nirṛiti consign them.

10 O Agni, whosoever seeks to injure the essence of our food, kine, steeds, or bodies,
May he, the adversary, thief, and robber, sink to destruction, both himself and offspring.

11 May he be swept away, himself and children; may all the three earths press him down beneath them.
May his fair glory, O ye Gods, be blighted, who in the day or night would fain destroy us.

12 The prudent finds it easy to distinguish the true and false: their words oppose each other.
Of these two that which is the true and honest Soma protects, and brings the false to nothing.

---

8 *Whoso accuses me:* Vasishṭha himself had been accused of demoniacal practices. See note on stanza 13.

9 *To the serpent:* that is, to death by serpents' bites. *Nirṛiti:* Destruction, personified.

13 Never doth Soma aid and guide the wicked or him who falsely claims the Warrior's title.
He slays the fiend and him who speaks untruly: both lie entangled in the noose of Indra.

14 As if I worshipped deities of falsehood, or thought vain thoughts about the Gods, O Agni!
Why art thou angry with us, Jâtavedas? Destruction fall on those who lie against thee!

15 So may I die this day if I have harassed any man's life, or if I be a demon.
Yea, may he lose all his ten sons together who with false tongue hath called me Yâtudhâna.

16 May Indra slay him with a mighty weapon, and let the vilest of all creatures perish,
The fiend who says that he is pure, who calls me a demon though devoid of demon nature.

17 She too who wanders like an owl at night-time, hiding her body in her guile and malice,
May she fall downward into endless caverns. May press-stones with loud ring destroy the demons.

---

13 *The Warrior's title:* the rank of a Kshatriya or prince of the military order. The first eleven verses 'are considered to be a malediction on the *Rákshasas* by the *Ṛishi.* To account for the change of tone [in 12—16] *Sáyaṇa* gives an unusual version of the legend told in the *Mahábhárata* of king *Kalmáshapáda* being transformed to a *Rákshasa,* and devouring the 100 sons of *Vasishṭha:* here it is said that a *Rákshasa,* having devoured the *Ṛishi's* sons, assumed his shape, and said to him, "I am Vasishṭha, thou art the *Rákshasa;*" to which Vasishṭha replied by repeating this verse [stanza 12] declaratory of his discriminating between truth and falsehood.'—Wilson.

'The verses may, as Professor Max Müller supposes, have arisen out of Vasishṭha's contest with Viṣvāmitra, and it may have been the latter personage who brought those charges of heresy, and of murderous and demoniacal character against his rival.'—Muir, O. S. Texts, I. p. 327.

17 Here the malediction on evil spirits in general is resumed and continued to the end of the hymn. *She too:* the Râkshasi or female fiend.

18 Spread out, ye Maruts, search among the people: seize ye and grind the Râkshasas to pieces,
Who fly abroad, transformed to birds, at night-time, and sully and pollute our holy worship.

19 Hurl down from heaven thy bolt of stone, O Indra: sharpen it, Maghavan, made keen by Soma.
Forward, behind, and from above and under, smite down the demons with thy rocky weapon.

20 They fly, the demon dogs, and, bent on mischief, fain would they harm indomitable Indra.
Ṣakra makes sharp his weapon for the wicked: now let him cast his bolt at fiendish wizards.

21 Indra hath ever been the fiends' destroyer who spoil oblations of the Gods' invokers.
Yea, Ṣakra, like an axe that splits the timber, assails and smashes them like earthen vessels.

22 Destroy the fiend shaped like an owl or owlet, destroy him in the form of dog or cuckoo.
Destroy him shaped as eagle or as vulture: as with a stone, O Indra, crush the demon.

23 Let not the fiend of witchcraft-workers reach us: may Dawn drive off the couples of Kimîdins.
Earth keep us safe from earthly woe and trouble! From grief that comes from heaven Mid-air preserve us!

24 Indra destroy the demon, male and female, joying and triumphing in arts of magic!
Let the fools' gods with bent necks fall and perish, and see no more the Sun when he arises.

25 Look, each one, hither, look around. Indra and Soma, watch ye well.
Cast forth your weapon at the fiends: against the sorcerers hurl your bolt.

HYMN V.

UPON the strong is bound the strong, this magic cord, this Amulet,
Potent, foe-slayer, served by valiant heroes, happy and fortunate defence.

2 This Charm, foe-slayer, served by many heroes, strong, powerful, victorious, and mighty, goes bravely forth to meet and ruin witchcraft.

3 With this same Amulet wise Indra routed the Asuras, with this he slaughtered Vṛitra,
With this he won this pair, both Earth and Heaven, and made the sky's four regions his possession.

4 May this encircling magic cord, this Amulet of Srâktya wood,
Mighty, subduing enemies, keep us secure on every side.

5 This Agni hath declared, Soma declared it, Bṛihaspati, and Savitar, and Indra.
So may these Gods whom I have set before me oppose with saving charms and banish witchcraft.

6 Whoever for his armour takes an amulet of the Sraktya tree,
Like the Sun risen up to heaven, quells witchcraft with superior might.

7 With Amulet of Srâktya wood, as with a thoughtful Ṛishi's aid,
In every fight have I prevailed; I smite the foes and Râkshasas.

The hymn is a charm to accompany investiture with an Amulet of Srâktya wood.

1 *Upon the strong:* the man who is to be invested being a Kshatriya or man of the military and princely order.

3 *Routed the Asuras:* cf. IX. 2. 17. In the Ṛigveda Indra is armed only with thunderbolt, arrows, and hook.

4 *Srâktya wood:* wood of the Sraktya tree. See II. 11. 2.

8 All witchcraft of Angirases, all witchcraft wrought by Asuras,
All witchcraft self-originate, and all that others have prepared,
May these depart to both remotest spaces, past ninety ample water-floods.

9 May the Gods bind the Charm on him for armour, Indra, and Vishṇu, Savitar, Rudra, Agni,
Prajâpati, sublimest Parameshṭhin, Virâj, Vaiṣvânara, and all the Ṛishis.

10 Thou art the chief of all the plants, even as a bull among the beasts,
A tiger of the beasts of prey. Him whom we sought for have we found, him lying near in wait for us.

11 A tiger verily is he, he is a lion, and a bull,
Subduer of his foes is he, the man who wears this Amulet.

12 No mortal beings slay him, no Gandharvas, no Apsarases;
O'er all the regions he is king, the man who wears this Amulet.

---

8 *Angirases:* magical powers were ascribed to this ancient family of Ṛishis as Solomon was regarded by the Jewish Rabbis as the great master of all arts of enchantment. *Both remotest spaces:* places beyond the limits of heaven and earth. Cf. VI. 75. 3. *Ninety ample water-floods:* or, literally, navigable streams, the waters of the ocean of air. 'Far over ninety spacious floods thy thunderbolts were cast abroad' (R. V. I. 80. 8): 'Casting them forth beyond the ninety rivers, thou dravest down into the pit the godless' (R. V. I. 121. 13). In other places (R. V. I. 32. 14; X. 104. 8) ninety-nine rivers of the air are spoken of, both numbers being used indefinitely.

9 *Parameshṭhin:* standing in the highest place, supreme; here an epithet of Prajâpati, the Lord of Life, the Creator. *Virâj:* a divine being, evolved by speculation, identified with Purusha, Prajâpati, Agni, and, later, Vishṇu. See VIII. 10. 1, note.

10 *Thou:* the Sraktya tree of whose wood the amulet is made.

14 Kaṣyapa formed and fashioned thee, Kaṣyapa raised and sent thee forth.
Indra wore thee, and, wearing thee, won in the wrestling-match with man.
The Amulet of boundless might the Gods have made a coat of mail.

15 Whoever would destroy thee with Dîkshâ-rites, sacrifices, spells,
Meet him and smite him, Indra! with thy hundred-knotted thunderbolt.

16 Verily let this Amulet, circular, potent, conquering,
Happy and fortunate defence, preserve thy children and thy wealth.

17 Brave Indra, set before us light, peace and security from below,
Peace and security from above, peace and security from behind.

18 My coat of mail is Heaven and Earth, my coat of mail is Day and Sun:
A coat of mail may Indra and Agni and Dhâtar grant to me.

19 Not all the Gods may pierce, all leagued together, the vast strong shield which Indra gives, and Agni.
May that great shield on all sides guard my body, that to full eld my life may be extended.

20 Let the Gods' Charm be bound on me to keep me safe from every ill.
Come ye and enter all within this pillar, the safeguard of the body, thrice-defended.

---

14 *Kaṣyapa:* cf. I. 14. 4, and II. 33. 7.

15 *Dîkshâ-rites:* religious observances designed to consecrate a person for some special purpose.

16 Addressed to the recipient of the amulet.

19 This and the following stanza are spoken by the recipient of the charm.

21 In this let Indra lay a store of valour: approach ye Gods, and enter it together,
For his long life, to last a hundred autumns, that to full age his days may be extended.

22 Lord of the clan who brings us bliss, fiend-slayer, queller of the foe,
May he, the conqueror, ne'er subdued, may Indra bind the Charm on thee,
Bull, Soma-drinker, he who gives us peace.
May he protect thee round about, by night and day on every side.

HYMN VI.

Let neither fiend of evil name, Aliṅṣa, Vatsapa, desire
Thy pair of husband-wooers which thy mother cleansed when thou wast born.

2 Palâla, Anupalâla, Ṣarku, Koka, Malimlucha, Palîjaka,
Vavrivâsas and Âṣresha, Ṛikshagrîva and Pramîlin.

3 Approach not, come not hitherward: creep not thou in between her thighs.

---

21 *This pillar:* this protective amulet.

22 Portions of this stanza are taken from Ṛigveda X. 152. 2.

The hymn is an incantation designed to exorcise various evil spirits who beset women.

1 *Aliṅṣa:* the meaning of this demon's name is unknown. *Vatsapa:* meaning, probably, as Prof. Weber suggests, 'drinking like a calf,' the name of a demon who robs the young mother of her milk. *Husband-wooers:* the dainties which attract the future husband; the breasts. *Cleansed:* squeezed dry.

2 The meaning of some of these demons' names is obscure; and where the meaning is obvious as in the case of *Palâla* (Straw), *Malimlucha* (Robber), *Koka* (Wolf), *Ṛikshagrîva* (Bear-necked), the special suitability of the name is not apparent. They stand in the accusative case, and must be governed by some verb as 'I banish,' understood.

I set, to guard her, Baja, that which chases him of evil name.

4 Durnâmâ and Sunâmâ both are eager to converse with her.
We drive away Arâyas: let Sunâmâ seek the women-folk.

5 The black and hairy Asura, and Stambaja and Tuṇḍika,
Arâyas from this girl we drive, from bosom, waist, and parts below.

6 Sniffer, and Feeler, him who eats raw flesh, and him who licks his lips,
Arâyas with the tails of dogs, the yellow Baja hath destroyed.

7 Whoever, in thy brother's shape or father's comes to thee in sleep,—
Let Baja rout and chase them like eunuchs with woman's head-dress on.

8 Whoever steals to thee asleep or thinks to harm thee when awake,—
These hath it banished, as the Sun travelling round drives shade away.

---

3 *Baja:* apparently some strong-smelling herb (see stanza 10), by whose scent the demon is chased away as was Asmodeus by 'the fishy fume, That drove him, though enamoured, from the spouse Of Tobit's son' (Paradise Lost, IV. 168). See Apocrypha. Tobit, VIII. 3.

4 *Durnâmâ and Sunâmâ:* Ill-named and Well-named. The latter is apparently a good genius who protects women, whereas the former injures them. *Arâyas:* a class of malevolent spirits, the female fiends being called Arâyîs. See I. 28. 4.

5 *Stambaja:* growing in a clump or bush, or in a pillar. *Tuṇḍika:* furnished with a snout.

6 *Him who licks his lips: rerihâm;* so Vilediî, Licker, is the name of a sorceress, witch, or female fiend in I. 18. 4.

8 *These hath it banished:* the purpose of the charm being regarded as already effected.

9 Whoever causeth her to lose her child or bear untimely fruit,—
Destroy him, O thou Plant, destroy the slippery fiend who lusts for her.

10 Those who at evening, with the bray of asses, dance around the house, Kukshilas, and Kusûlas, and Kakubhas, Srimas, Karumas,
These with thine odour, O thou Plant, drive far away to every side.

11 Kukundhas and Kukûrabhas who dress themselves in hides and skins,
Who dance about like eunuchs, who raise a wild clamour in the wood, all these we banish far away.

12 All those who cannot bear the Sun who warms us yonder from the sky,
Arâyas with the smell of goats, malodorous, with bloody mouths, the Makakas we drive afar.

13 All those who on their shoulders bear a head of monstrous magnitude,
Who pierce the women's loins with pain,—those demons, Indra! drive away!

14 Those, bearing horns upon their hands, who first of all approach the brides;
Standing in ovens, laughing loud, those who in bushes flash forth light, all these we banish hence away.

15 Those who have retroverted toes, and heels and faces in the front,

---

10 *Kukshilas:* big-bellied fiends. *Kusûlas:* the meaning is uncertain. *Kakubhas:* humpbacks. *Srimas:* the meaning is unknown. *Karumas:* dissonant.

11 *Kukundhas:* the meaning is unknown. *Kukûrabhas:* perhaps, howlers.

12 *Makakas:* the meaning is unknown.

Khalajas Ṣakadhûmajas, Uruṇḍas, all the Maṭmaṭas, impotent Kumbhamushkas, these,
Drive thou, O Brahmaṇaspati, far from this girl with vigilance.

16 Sightless and with distorted eyes, impotent, womanless be they.
O Healing Plant, cast each away who, not her husband, would approach this woman wedded to her lord.

17 The Bristly-haired, the Maniac-haired, the Biter, and the Groper-fiend,
The Creeper-near, the Copper-hued, the Snouty, and the Ṣâluḍa,
With foot and heel kick over, as a hasty cow her milking-pan.

18 If one should touch thy coming babe or kill thine infant newly born,
The yellow Plant with mighty bow shall pierce him even to the heart.

19 Those who kill infants unawares, and near the new-made mothers lie,—
Let Piṅga chase the amorous Gandharvas as wind chases cloud.

20 Let it maintain the genial seed: let the laid embryo rest secure.
Let both strong Healers, to be worn within the girdle, guard the babe.

---

15 *Khalajas:* produced on threshing-floors. *Ṣakadhûmajas:* produced from the smoke of cow-dung. *Kumbhamushkas:* urceis similes testiculos habentes. The meaning of *Uruṇḍas* and *Maṭmaṭas* is unknown, and that of *ayaṣávas* (impotent) is uncertain.

19 *Piṅga:* yellow; another name of Baja. *Amorous Gandharvas:* See IV. 37. 11.

20 *It:* Baja. *Both strong Healers:* Piṅga and Baja regarded as two separate plants.

21 From the Kimîdin, for thy lord and children, Piṅga shield thee well,
From Ṣâyaka, and Nagnaka, Tangalva, and Pavînasa.

22 From the five-footed, fingerless, from the four-eyed, the double-faced,
From the Close-creeper, from the Worm, from the Quick-roller guard her well.

23 Those who eat flesh uncooked, and those who eat the bleeding flesh of men,
Feeders on babes unborn, long-haired, far from this place we banish these.

24 Shy slinkers from the Sun, as slinks a woman from her husband's sire,—
Deep down into the heart of these let Baja and let Piṅga pierce.

25 Piṅga, preserve the babe at birth, make not the boy a female child.
Let not Egg-eaters mar the germs: drive the Kimîdins far away.

26 Sterility, and infants' death, and weeping that announceth woe,—
Dear! lay them on the fiend as thou wouldst pluck a garland from a tree.

---

21 *Nagnaka:* naked. *Pavînasa:* having a nose like a spear-head. The meanings of *Sâyaka* and *Tangalva* are unknown.

24 *As slinks a woman from her husband's sire:* the timid reverence of a daughter-in-law for her father-in-law was proverbial. See Zimmer, Altindisches Leben, p. 327.

25 *Egg-eaters:* fiends who devour the unborn babe. Cf. II. 25. 4.

26 *Dear!:* the plant Baja is addressed.

The belief in Incubi was common among the Jews and the Latins. 'Such pretty pranks,' says Burton, 'can love play with birds, fishes, beasts, and if all be certain that is credibly reported, with the spirits of the air, and devils of hell themselves, who are as much enamoured and dote (if I may use that word) as any other creatures whatsoever. For if those stories be true that are written of incubus and succubus, of nymphs, lascivious fauns, satyrs, and those heathen gods which were

HYMN VII.

THE tawny-coloured, and the pale, the variegated, and the red,
The dusky-tinted, and the black,—all Plants we summon hitherward.

2 This man let them deliver from Consumption which the Gods have sent.
The father of these Herbs was Heaven, their mother Earth, the Sea their root.

3 The Waters are the best, and heavenly Plants:
From every limb of thine have they removed Consumption caused by sin.

4 I speak to Healing Herbs spreading, and bushy, to creepers, and to those whose sheath is single,
I call for thee the fibrous and the reed-like, and branching Plants, dear to the Viṣve Devas, powerful, giving life to men.

5 The conquering strength, the power and might which ye, victorious Plants, possess,
Therewith deliver this man here from this Consumption, O ye Plants: so I prepare the remedy.

6 The living Plant that giveth life, that driveth malady away,

---

devils, those lascivious Telchines, of whom the Platonists tell so many fables; or those familiar meetings in our days, and company of witches and devils, there is some probability for it.'—Anatomy of Melancholy, Part 3, Sect. 2, Memb. I. Subs. I. Prof. Weber refers to the Incubones of the Romans (Preller, Roman Mythology, p. 337), and to the German Alpdrücken and Teufelsbuhlschaft.

The hymn has been translated, with an exhaustive commentary, by Weber, Indische Studien, V. pp. 252—261, and, without commentary, by Ludwig, Der Rigveda, III. pp. 523—525.

The hymn, which extols the excellence of medicinal herbs, is an incantation designed to restore a sick man to health.

2 *The Sea*: the ocean of the air.

Arundhatî, the rescuer, strengthening, rich in sweets
I call, to free this man from scath and harm.

7 Hitherward let the sapient come, the friendly sharers of my speech,
That we may give this man relief and raise him from his evil plight.

8 Germ of the Waters, Agni's food, Plants ever growing fresh and new,
Sure, healing, bearing thousand names, let them be all collected here.

9 Let Plants whose soul is water, girt with Avakâs, piercing with their sharp horns expel the malady.

10 Strong, antidotes of poison, those releasers, free from Varuṇa,
And those that drive away Catarrh, and those that frustrate magic arts, let all those Plants come hitherward.

11 Let purchased Plants of mightier power, Plants that are praised for excellence,
Here in this village safely keep cattle and horses, man and beast.

12 Sweet is their root, sweet are these Plants' top branches, sweet also is their intermediate portion;
Sweet is their foliage, and sweet their blossom, combined with sweetness is their taste of Amrit: food, fatness let them yield, with kine preceding.

---

6 *Arundhatî:* a creeping plant used in medicine; called also Silâchî. See IV. 12. 1; V. 5; VI. 59. 1.

7 *The sapient:* the plants which understand the cure of disease.

9 *Avakâs:* Avakâ is a grassy plant growing in marshy land (Blyxa Octandra). See IV. 37. 8.

10 *Free from Varuṇa:* independent of his power, and able to ward off the diseases which he sends. *Catarrh*: *balâsaḥ;* the exact nature of the disease is somewhat uncertain. See IV. 9. 8.

13 These Plants that grow upon the earth, whate'er their number and their size,—
Let these with all their thousand leaves free me from Death and misery.

14 May the Plants' Tiger-amulet, protective, guardian from the curse,
Beat off the brood of demons, drive all maladies afar from us.

15 Before the gathered Plants they fly and scatter, as though a lion's roar or fire dismayed them.
Expelled by Plants, let men's and kine's Consumption pass from us to the navigable rivers.

16 Emancipated from the sway of Agni, of Vaiṣvânara, go, covering the earth, ye Plants whose ruler is Vanaspati.

17 May these be pleasant to our heart, auspicious, rich in store of milk,
These Plants of the Angirases which grow on mountains and on plains.

18 The Plants I know myself, the plants that with mine eye I look upon,
Plants yet unknown, and those we know, wherein we find that power is stored,

19 Let all the congregated Plants attend and mark mine utterance,
That we may rescue this man here and save him from severe distress.

20 Aṣvattha, Darbha, King of Plants, is Soma, deathless sacrifice:
Barley and Rice are healing balms, the sons of Heaven who never die.

---

14 *Tiger-amulet:* an exceedingly potent charm.

16 *Vanaspati:* lord of the wood; here the Soma Plant.

20 *Aṣvattha:* Ficus Religiosa; the Sacred Fig-tree. *Darbha:* Sacrificial Grass. See VI. 43. 1.

21 Lift yourselves up, ye Healing Plants, loud is the thunder's crash and roar
When with full flow Parjanya, ye Children of Pṛiṣni! blesseth you.

22 We give the essence of that stream of nectar to this man to drink:
So I prepare a remedy that he may live a hundred years.

23 Well doth the wild boar know a Plant, the mungoose knows the Healing Herb.
I call, to aid this man, the Plants which Serpents and Gandharvas know.

24 Plants of Angirases which hawks, celestial Plants which eagles know;
Plants known to swans and lesser fowl, Plants known to all the birds that fly,
Plants that are known to sylvan beasts,—I call them all to aid this man.

25 The multitude of herbs whereon the Cows whom none may slaughter feed, all that are food for goats and sheep,
So many Plants, brought hitherward, give shelter and defence to thee!

26 Hitherward unto thee I bring the Plants that cure all maladies,
All Plants wherein physicians have discovered health-bestowing power.

27 Let Plants with flower and Plants with bud, the fruitful and the fruitless, all,
Like children of one mother, yield their stores for this man's perfect health.

---

21 *Pṛiṣni:* here meaning Earth, the mother of plants. *Parjanya:* the deity of the rain-cloud. See I. 2. 1.

23 *Wild boar:* cf. II. 27. 2, and V. 14. 1. Wild pigs are extraordinarily quick at discovering and unearthing potatoes and all sorts of edible roots. *The mungoose:* cf. VI. 139. 5.

28 From the Five-arrowed, from the Ten-arrowed have I delivered thee,
Freed thee from Yama's fetter and from all offence against the Gods.

HYMN VIII.

INDRA the Shaker shake them up, brave, hero, fort-demolisher,
That into thousand fragments we may strike the armies of our foes!

2 Let Pûtirajju with her breath corrupt and putrefy that host,
And terror smite our foemen's heart when fire and smoke are seen afar.

3 Asvattha, rend those men; do thou devour them quickly, Khadira!
Like reeds let them be broken through, down-smitten by a lifted rush.

4 Let Parushâhva make them reeds, and let the bulrush strike them down;
Bound in a mighty net let them break quickly like an arrow's shaft.

---

28 *Five-arrowed:* this and *Ten-arrowed* appear to be fanciful epithets of fever or other severe disease personified.

With this hymn may be compared Rigveda X. 97, Praise of Herbs. Translated by Ludwig, Der Rigveda, III. p. 504.

The hymn consists of a series of imprecations directed against a hostile army.

2 *Pûtirajju:* some unidentifiable malodorous plant. According to Prof. Ludwig, a species of serpent.

3 *Rend:* the Asvattha or Ficus Religiosa is called Burster or Render because it splits asunder the wood, masonry, or stone in whose crevices its seed has germinated and grown. See III. 6. 2, 3. *Devour them . . . Khadira!: khâda khadira;* a play upon the words. The Khadira is the Acacia Catechu, a tree with solid hard wood.

4 *Parushâhva:* a kind of reed or rush. *Reeds:* weak and fragile as reeds. Prof. Ludwig translates differently: 'diser rauhen feinde schlachtruf mache er heiser.'—Der Rigveda, III. p. 527.

5 Air was the net; the poles thereof were the great quarters of the sky:
Ṣakra therewith enveloped and cast on the ground the Dasyus' host.

6 Verily mighty is the net of mighty Ṣakra rich in wealth:
Therewith press all the foemen down so that not one of them escape!

7 Great is thy net, brave Indra, thine the mighty, match for a thousand, Lord of Hundred Powers!
Holding them, with his host, therewith hath Indra slaughtered Dasyus a hundred, thousand, myriad, hundred millions.

8 This world so mighty was the net of Ṣakra, of the Mighty One:
With this, the net of Indra, I envelop all those men with gloom.

9 Great weakness and misfortune, pain which words can never charm away,
Languor, fatigue, bewilderment, with these I compass all the foes.

10 I give those foemen up to Death: bound in the bonds of Death are they.
I bind and carry them away to meet Death's wicked messengers.

11 Bear them away, Death's messengers! envoys of Yama! bind them fast.
More than a thousand be their slain: the club of Bhava pierce them through!

---

5 *Ṣakra:* the powerful Indra. *The Dasyus' host:* demons who fought against the Gods.

8 *Net of Indra: indrajâlá* is, in the Mahâbhârata, the name of a wonderful weapon wielded by the hero Arjuna, and in later Sanskrit means incantation, magic, trickery, and delusion in general.

11 *Bhava:* see note on IV. 28. 1.

12 Forth go the Sâdhyas in their might bearing one net-pole raised aloft.
One pole the Rudras carry, one the Vasus, and the Âdityas one.

13 The Visve Devas from above shall come depressing it with might,
And in the midst the Angirases, slaying the mighty host, shall go.

14 Trees of the forest, trees that bear flower and fruit, and herbs and plants,
Quadruped, biped send I forth that they may strike this army dead.

15 Gandharvas, and Apsarases, Gods, Serpents, Fathers, Holy Men,
Seen and unseen, I send them forth that they may strike this army dead.

16 Here spread are snares of Death wherefrom thou, once within them, ne'er art freed:
Full many a thousand of the host yonder this horn shall smite and slay.

17 The Gharma hath been warmed with fire: this Homa slays a thousand men.
Let Bhava, Pṛiṣnibâhu, and Ṣarva destroy that armament.

18 Their portion be the fire of Death, hunger, exhaustion, slaughter, fear.

---

12 *Sâdhyas:* see VII. 5. 1.

15 *Seen and unseen:* 'According to the Mahābhārata, Sabhāparvan, 461, there are seven groups of Pitṛis or Fathers, four embodied (*mūrttimantaḥ*) and three bodiless (*aśarīriṇaḥ*).'—Muir, O. S. Texts, V. p. 296.

16 *Horn:* the symbol of power.

17 *Gharma:* the libation of hot milk offered especially to the Aṣvins. *Homa:* an oblation poured into the fire; a burnt-offering. *Pṛiṣnibâhu:* having speckled arms; the name of a mythical being, not mentioned elsewhere. *Ṣarva:* see note on IV. 28. 1.

With your entangling snares and nets, Ṣarva and Indra! slay that host.

19 Fly, conquered, in alarm, ye foes, run driven by the spell away!
Let not one man escape of those when routed by Bṛihaspati.

20 Down fall their weapons on the ground: no strength be theirs to point a shaft:
Then in their dreadful terror let their arrows wound their vital parts.

21 Let Heaven and Earth roar out in wrath against them, and Air with all the Deities in concert.
Let them not find a surety or a refuge, but torn away go down to Death together.

22 The mules of the Gods' car are heaven's four quarters; their hooves are sacred cakes, the air its body.
Its sides are Heaven and Earth, its reins the Seasons, Voice is its hood, its grooms are sky's mid-regions.

23 Year is the car, Full Year the seat for driving, Virâj the pole, the chariot's front is Agni, Indra the warrior, and the Moon the driver.

24 Hence conquer, conquer, Hail! be thou the victor! Let these be conquerors and those be conquered.
Good luck to these, ill luck to those men yonder! With the dark-blue-and-red our foes I cover.

---

21 The second line occurs also in VI. 32. 2.

22 *Voice:* or Vâk; see IV. 1. 2.

23 *Virâj:* or Virâṭ; a mystical being, evolved by speculation. See VIII. 10. 1, note.

24 *With the dark-blue-and-red:* that is, with two strings or threads of these colours which are to be used in the incantation. See Kauṣika-Sûtra, XVI. 19.

HYMN IX.

WHENCE were these two produced? which was that region? From what world, from which earth had they their being?
Calves of Virâj, these two arose from water. I ask thee of these twain, who was their milker.

2 He who prepared a threefold home, and lying there made the water bellow through his greatness,
Calf of Virâj, giving each wish fulfilment, made bodies for himself far off, in secret.

3 Which are the three, the mighty three, whereof the fourth divides the voice,
This may the Brahman know by prayer and fervour, whereto belongs the one, whereto the other.

4 Out of the Bṛihat as the sixth five Sâmans have been fashioned forth:
From Bṛihatî was Bṛihat formed: whence was the Bṛihatî composed?

The hymn, which is a kind of Brahmodyam (see note at the end of V. 1), consists of a series of purposely enigmatical questions and dark answers on cosmogonical, ritual, and metrical doctrine. It is obscure throughout, and in many parts I find it absolutely unintelligible.

1 *These two:* perhaps the Sun and Lightning. *Virâj:* a mysterious Divine Being or Abstraction, evolved by speculation, endowed with creative and other miraculous powers, and the subject of many fanciful allegories. See the following hymn.

2 *Threefold home:* heaven, firmament, and earth, wherein Agni dwells as Sun, lightning, and fire.

3 *The mighty three:* or, the three Bṛihats; a mystical power is represented as residing in the metres which are regarded as divine beings.

4 *Bṛihat:* the name of various Sâmans or chanted songs in the Bṛihatî metre which consists of thirty-six syllables in four Pâdas, 8 + 8 + 12 + 8.

5 On measure Bṛihatî is based, and measure on the measurer:
From magic might came magic might, from magic might came Mâtalî.

6 Vaiṣvânara's image is the sky above us, so far as Agni forced both spheres asunder.
Thence from that region as the sixth come praise-songs, and every sixth day hence again go upward.

7 We, Kaṣyapa! six present Ṛishis, ask thee—for thou hast proved things tried and meet for trial—
They call Virâj the father of Devotion: tell her to us thy friends in all her figures.

8 She whom, advancing, sacrifices follow, and when she takes her station stand beside her,
By whose control and hest the spirit moveth, she is Virâj, in highest heaven, O Ṛishis.

9 Breathless, she moves by breath of living creatures. Svarâj precedes, Virâj comes closely after.
Some men behold her not, and some behold her, Virâj meet-shaped, who thinks of all existence.

---

5 *Mâtalî*: the name of a divine being associated wtih Yama and the Fathers. But the meaning here is uncertain, the name being, perhaps, introduced with punning reference to the *mâ* in *mâtrâyâḥ*, measure, *mâtúr*, measurer, in the preceding, and *mâyấ*, *mâyấyâḥ*, magic power, in the same line, and intended, as Ludwig suggests, to signify *mâtar*, a measurer.

6 *Every sixth day*: in ceremonies performed on each sixth day of the lunar fortnight.

7 *Kaṣyapa*: the celebrated Ṛishi of the Ṛigveda. See Index of Names, Etc. *Father . . . . her*: Virâj, or Virâṭ, appears sometimes as a male being, identified with Purusha, Prajâpati, and Agni, sometimes as a female, the daughter of one of these deities. See the following hymn.

9 *Svarâj*: or Svarâṭ, self-luminous; the Supreme Being.

10 Who hath perceived Virâj's duplication, perceived her seasons and her rule and practice?
Who knows her steps, how oft, how far extended, who knows her home and number of her dawnings?

11 She here who first of all sent forth her lustre moves onward resting on these lower creatures.
Exalted power and might are stored within her: the woman hath prevailed, the new-come mother.

12 Both Dawns on wings of song, with rich adornment, move on together to their common dwelling.
Sûrya's two wives, unwasting, most prolific, knowing their way, move, rich in light, together.

13 The three have passed along the path of Order— three warm libations have regarded offspring—
One quickens progeny, one strengthens vigour, and one protects the kingdom of the pious.

14 She who was fourth was made by Agni, Soma, and Ṛishis as they formed both halves of worship,
Gâyatrî, Trishṭup, Jagatî, Anushṭup, Bṛihadarkî lightening the sacrificer.

15 Five milkings answer to the fivefold dawning, five seasons to the cow who bears five titles.
The five sky-regions made fifteen in number, one head have these to one sole world directed.

16 Six Elements arose, first-born of Order: the six-day time is carried by six Sâmans.

---

12 *Both Dawns:* Morning and her sister Night.

13 *The three:* Dawn, Sunlight, and Night.

14 *Bṛihadarkî:* containing or forming the great or best hymn of praise. *Lightening:* winning the light of heaven for.

15 *Five seasons:* instead of the more usual six; the Dewy and the Cold seasons being counted together as one. *Made fifteen:* by the addition of intermediate spaces, or multiplication by three.

16 *Six elements:* earth, air, fire, water, ether, and the subtile element. *Both broad ones:* heaven and earth, each of which is regarded as threefold.

Six-yoked the plough is, as each trace is numbered: they call both broad ones six; six, Earth and Heaven.

17 They call the cold months six, and six the hot ones. Which, tell us, of the seasons is redundant?
Seven sages, eagles, have sat down together: seven metres match the seven Consecrations.

18 Seven are the Homas, seven the logs for burning, seven are the streams of mead, and seven the seasons.
Into the world have come seven streams of butter: those we have heard of as the Seven Vultures.

19 Seven metres, by four syllables increasing, each of the seven founded upon another—
How are the hymns of praise on these supported, and how are these imposed upon the praise-songs?

20 How hath the Gâyatri filled out three triads? On the fifteen how is the Trishṭup moulded,
Jagatî fashioned on the three-and-thirty? How is Anushṭup formed? how Ekavinṡa?

---

17 *Seven sages:* the Seven Ṛishis. See V. 17. 6. *Seven metres:* the seven generic metres of the Veda. *Consecrations: dîkshâs;* solemn initiatory or preparatory ceremonies.

18 *Homas:* oblations of clarified butter poured into the fire. *Seven Vultures:* this literal translation is unintelligible. Professor Ludwig suggests that the meaning is: as (men) eager after everything that is sevenfold, or wishing to turn all things into sevens.

20 *Triads:* or triplets. 'The Sâman consists of two verses only, it is first to be made to consist of three by repetition of some part of the two principal verses before it can be used as a chant at a Soma sacrifice. After a triplet of verses has been thus obtained, it is to be chanted in three turns, each turn containing in three subdivisions a certain number of repetitions.' Haug, Aitareya Brâhmaṇa, Translation, Book III. 2. 17, note. These questions on the formation of the metres are not easily explained or answered, nor are they of any general importance. *Ekavinṡa:* a Stoma or hymn consisting of twenty-one parts.

21 Eight Elements sprang up, first born of Order: the Priests divine are eight in number, Indra!
Eight are the wombs of Aditi, eight her children: for the eighth night is the libation destined.

22 So planning bliss for you have I come hither to win your friendship: kind am I, and gracious.
Born from one source, propitious is your wisdom: knowing full well to all of you it cometh.

23 To Indra eight, to Yama six, seven to the Ṛishis, seven to each:
The number five accompanies waters and men and healing herbs.

24 The Heifer, all his own, poured forth for Indra control and milk at her first time of milking;
And he then satisfied the four divisions, the Gods and men and Asuras and Ṛishis.

25 Who is the Cow? Who is the Single Ṛishi? What is the law, what are the benedictions?
What on the earth is the one only Spirit? Which of the number is the Single Season?

---

21 *Eight elements:* apparently the six of stanza 16 with Intellect and Mind added. *Eight her children:* the Âdityas or sons of Aditi (see I. 9. 1, note) are in the Ṛigveda (IX. 114. 3) said to be seven. In the period of the Brâhmaṇas they were twelve, as representing the sun in the twelve months of the year. *Eighth night:* the Ashṭami or eighth lunar day in each half-month.

22 *I:* Virâj may be meant.

23 *Waters:* with reference to the five rivers of the Panjâb. *Men:* referring to the Five Nations, or Races of Âryans.

24 *The Heifer:* perhaps the rain-cloud, the *milk* being the rain, and *control* the power which Indra derives from the sacrifices which the fertilizing rain enables men to offer to him.

25 *The Single Ṛishi:* meaning the first or chief sage. *Single Spirit: yakshám,* here rendered by spirit, means a living supernatural being deserving worship. Professor Ludwig here and elsewhere renders the word by Fest, feast or festival. *The Single Season:* the intercalary month. These questions of the Ṛishis and Kasyapa's replies are unintelligible. The hymn has been translated by Ludwig, Der Rigveda, III. p. 439.

26 One is the Cow, one is the Single Spirit, one is the law, single are benedictions.
The Spirit dwelling on the earth is single: the Single Season never is transcended.

HYMN X.

VIRÂJ at first was This. At birth all feared her; the thought, She will become this All, struck terror.

2 She rose, the Gârhapatya fire she entered. He who knows this becomes lord of a household, performer of domestic sacrifices.

3 She mounted up, the Eastward fire she entered. He who knows this becomes the Gods' belovèd, and to his call they come when he invokes them.

4 She mounted up, the Southward fire she entered. He who knows this becomes a fit performer of sacrifice, meet for honour, shelter-giver.

5 She mounted up, she entered the Assembly. He who knows this becomes polite and courtly, and people come as guests to hisassembly.

The hymn is a glorification of the mystical abstraction Virâj.

1 *Virâj*: in Rigveda X. 90. 5. Virâj is said to have been born from Purusha (the Primeval Male from whom the universe was evolved). In A. V. IX. 2. 5, she is identified with Vâk, the Word, and, in IX. 10. 24, with Vâk, Air, Earth, Prajâpati the Creator, with Death, and the Regent of the Sâdhyas. In XI. 4. 12 she is identified with Prâṇa or Vital Spirit. Virâj is also the personified forty-syllable metre of that name to which miraculous powers were attributed. In some Vedic passages *virâj* is an epithet (radiant, splendid) applied to Indra, Prajâpati, and Parameshṭhin the Supreme. See Muir, O. S. Texts, V., pp. 369, 370. *This*: the universe.

2 *The Gârhapatya fire she entered*: here Virâj is a mysterious divine influence completing the sanctity and efficacy of the western sacred fire which it is the householder's privilege and duty to maintain.

5 *The Assembly*: of the people of the village or hamlet.

6 She mounted up, she passed within the meeting. He who knows this becomes fit for the meeting, and to his hall of meeting come the people.

7 She mounted up, she entered Consultation. Whoso knows this is fit to be consulted, and to his consultation come the people.

8 She mounted up, and, into four divided, she took her station in the air's mid-region.

9 Of her the Gods and men said, This she knoweth. That we may both have life let us invoke her.

10 Thus did they cry to her :

11 Come, Strength! come, Food! come, Charmer! come, Free-giver!

12 Her calf, her well-belovèd calf, was Indra: Gâyatrî was her rope, the cloud her udder.

13 Two teats she had, Rathantara and Bṛihat, two, Yajñâyajñiya and Vâmadevya.

14 With the Rathantara the Gods milked from her the Plants, and all the wide expanse with Bṛihat.

---

6 *The meeting:* of the people of the district. On *sabhā́*, assembly, and *sámiti*, meeting or congress, see Zimmer, Altindisches Leben, pp. 172—175.

11 *Food!: svádhe;* 'But svadhā́ means also food, lit. one's own portion, the sacrificial portion due to each god, and lastly, food in general.'—Max Müller, Vedic Hymns, Part I. p. 35.

12 *Her calf:* Virâj, identified with Vâk, is in A. V. IX. 2. 5 called the Cow, representing the creative power of Nature like the Cow Audhumbla in Teutonic mythology. See Simrock, Handbuch der Deutschen Mythologie, pp. 18, 215.

13 *Rathantara:* the name of various Sâmans or chanted Vedic verses. *Bṛihat:* the name of chanted verses in the Bṛihatî metre of thirty-six syllables. See IV. 34. 1, note.

Yajñâyajñiya: a Sâman so called after the beginning (Yajñā́-yajñâ) of Ṛigveda I. 168. 1. *Vâmadevya:* the name of various Sâmans. See IV. 34. 1, note.

15 They drew the Waters forth with Vâmadevya, with Yajñâyajñiya they milked out worship.

16 For him who knoweth this, Rathantara poureth out Plants, and Bṛihat yieldeth wide expansion.

17 Waters from Vâmadevya come, from Yajñayajñiya sacrifice.

18 She rose, she came unto the trees: they killed her. A year went by and she again existed.
Hence in a year the wounds of trees heal over. He who knows this sees his loathed rival wounded.

19 She mounted up, she came unto the Fathers: they killed her: in a month she re-existed.
Hence men give monthly offerings to the Fathers: who knows this, knows the path which they have trodden.

20 She rose, she came unto the Gods: they killed her; but in a fortnight she again was living.
Fortnightly, hence, men serve the Gods with Vashaṭ! Who knows this knows the way which Gods pass over.

21 She mounted up, she came to men: they killed her. Presently she regained her life and being.
Hence on both days to men they bring aud offer—whoso knows this—near-seated in the dwelling.

22 She rose, approached the Asuras: they called her: their cry was, Come, O Mâyâ, come thou hither.

---

18 Proper recognition of the power of Virâj, as renovating Nature, to repair the injuries which trees may have suffered will be rewarded by triumph over a suffering enemy.

19 *Monthly offerings:* oblations presented on the day of full moon. *The path which they have trodden:* and, consequently, how to reach heaven themselves.

21 *Both days:* meaning two consecutive days.

22 *The Asuras:* the fiends who fought against the Gods. *Mâyâ:* Miraculous Power, Might of Gods, personified. *Virochana Prâhrâdi:* a chief of the Asuras, son of Prahrâda. *Dvimûrdhâ Ârtvya:* the name of a two-headed Asura. *A fit supporter: upajîvanîyaḥ;* a wealthy man, on whom others can depend for their livelihood.

Her dear calf was Virochana Prâhrâdi: her milking-vessel was a pan of iron.
Dvimûrdhâ Ârtvya milked her, yea, this Mâyâ. The Asuras depend for life on Mâyâ. He who knows this becomes a fit supporter.

23 She mounted up, she came unto the Fathers. The Fathers called to her, O Food, come hither.
King Yama was her calf, her pail was silvern. Antaka, Mṛityu's son, milked her, this Svadhâ.
This Food the Fathers make their lives' sustainer. He who knows this becomes a meet supporter.

24 She mounted up, she came to men. They called her, Come unto us, come hither thou Free-giver!
Earth was her milking-pail, the calf beside her Manu Vaivasvata, Vivasvân's offspring.

---

23 *O Food:* see note on stanza 11. *Antaka:* the Ender; generally a name of Death himself, as in VI, 46. 2, and VIII. 1. 1. *Their lives' sustainer:* the Manes depend for their existence on the oblations presented to them by their relations on earth. A somewhat similar idea led the Greeks and Romans to visit the tombs of their relatives at certain periods, and to offer to them sacrifices, food, and various gifts. 'The parkin cakes baked in Yorkshire in November, the simnel or soul-mass cakes of Lancashire, the *gauffres* baked at All Souls-tide in Belgium, are all reminiscences of the food prepared and offered to the dead at All Souls, the great day of commemoration of the departed . . . . In the north of England all idea as to the connection between these cakes and the dead is lost, but the cakes are still made. This custom is a transformation under Christian influence of the still earlier usage of putting food on the graves.'—S. Baring-Gould, Strange Survivals, p. 272.

24 *Manu Vaivasvata:* the seventh Manu, son of Vivasvân or the Sun, regarded as the progenitor of the present race of human beings. *Prithî:* called Vainya or son of Vena (see ṚV. VIII. 9. 10), said to have been the first anointed sovereign of men, and to have introduced the arts of husbandry into the world. He is also called Prithu, and is counted among the Ṛishis, Ṛigveda X. 148 having been revealed to him.

Prithî the son of Vena was her milker: he milked forth husbandry and grain for sowing.
These men depend for life on corn and tillage. He who knows this becomes a meet supporter, successful in the culture of his corn-land.

25 She rose, she came unto the Seven Rishis. They called her, Come, Rich in Devotion! hither.
King Soma was her calf, the Moon her milk-pail. Brihaspati Ângirasa, her milker,
Drew from her udder Prayer and Holy Fervour. Fervour and Prayer maintain the Seven Rishis.
He who knows this becomes a meet supporter, a priest illustrious for his sacred knowledge.

26 She rose, she came unto the Gods. They called her, crying, O Vigour, come to us, come hither!
God Savitar milked her, he milked forth Vigour. The Gods depend for life upon that Vigour. He who knows this becomes a meet supporter.

27 She rose, approached the Apsarases and Gandharvas. They called her, Come to us, O Fragrant-scented!
The son of Sûryavarchas, Chitraratha, was her dear calf, her pail a lotus-petal.
The son of Sûryavarchas, Vasuruchi, milked and drew from her most delightful fragrance.
That scent supports Apsarases and Gandharvas. He who knows this becomes a meet supporter, and round him ever breathes delicious odour.

---

25 *The Seven Rishis:* Bharadvâja, Kasyapa, Gotama, Atri, Vasishtha, Visvâmitra, and Jamadagni. *Ângirasa:* closely connected with Angiras or his descendants.

27 *Sûryavarchas:* Sun-bright. *Chitraratha:* Borne on a brilliant car; the King of the Gandharvas. *Vasuruchi:* Radiant as a God; one of the chief Gandharvas. *That scent supports:* the names of four of the Apsarases mentioned in IV. 37. 3 are derived from fragrant plants or sweet scents, and the word Gandharva is supposed to be connected with *gandha*, scent.

28 She mounted up, she came to Other People. They called her, crying, Come, Concealment! hither.
Her dear calf was Vaiṣravaṇa Kubera, a vessel never tempered was her milk-pail.
Rajatanâbhi, offspring of Kubera, milked her, and from her udder drew concealment.
By that concealment live the Other People. He who knows this becomes a meet supporter, and makes all evil disappear and vanish.

29 She mounted up, she came unto the Serpents. The Serpents called her, Venomous! come hither.
Her calf was Takshaka, Viṣâla's offspring: a bottle-gourd supplied a milking-vessel.
Irâvân's offspring, Dhṛitarâshṭra milked her, and from her udder drew forth only poison.
That poison quickens and supports the Serpents: He who knows this becomes a meet supporter.

30 One would ward off, for him who hath this knowledge, if with a bottle-gourd he sprinkled water.

31 And did he not repel, if in his spirit he said, I drive thee back, he would repel it.

32 The poison that it drives away, that poison verily repels.

33 The man who hath this knowledge pours its venom on his hated foe.

---

28 *Other People:* a euphemistic expression for certain beings who appear to be considered as spirits of darkness. So in England fairies are called folk, people, neighbours; in Germany, little folk; and in Switzerland hill people, and earth people. *Vaiṣravaṇa Kubera:* in later Sanskrit, Kuvera, son of Viṣravas, chief of the spirits of darkness and afterwards the God of riches and treasure.

29 *Takshaka:* one of the principal Nâgas or Serpents of Pâtâla or the under-world. *Dhṛitarâshṭra:* a chief Nâga, called Airâvata or son of Irâvân.

31 The knowledge and the mere wish or thought without any external action would be sufficient to counteract the deadliest poison.

33 The same knowledge enables a man to poison his enemy secretly.

BOOK IX.

HYMN I.

THE Asvins' Honey-whip was born from heaven and earth, from middle air, and ocean, and from fire and wind.
All living creatures welcome it with joyful hearts, fraught with the store of Amrit it hath gathered up.

2 They call thee earth's great strength in every form, they call thee too the ocean's genial seed.
Whence comes the Honey-whip bestowing bounty, there Vital Spirit is, and Amrit treasured.

3 In sundry spots, repeatedly reflecting, men view upon the earth her course and action;
For she, the first-born daughter of the Maruts, derives her origin from Wind and Agni.

4 Daughter of Vasus, mother of Âdityas, centre of Amrit, breath of living creatures,
The Honey-whip, gold-coloured, dropping fatness, moves as a mighty embryo 'mid mortals.

5 The deities begat the Whip of Honey: her embryo assumed all forms and fashions.

The hymn is a glorification of the Whip of the Asvins, and a prayer for the gift of sweetness, splendour, and strength from them and other deities.

1 *Honey-whip: madhukaśá = káśá mádhumatí* (R. V. I. 22. 3), with which the Asvins are prayed to 'sprinkle the sacrifice.' It signifies, perhaps, the early stimulating and life-giving morning breeze which accompanies the first appearance of the Asvins, the Lords of Light, who precede the Dawn, and represents in this hymn all creative, vivifying, and sustaining power.

3 *Her course and action:* the coming and operation of the wondrous Honey-whip.

5 *The Whip of Honey: mádhoḥ káśám.*

The mother nourishes that tender infant which at its birth looks on all worlds and beings.

6 Who understandeth well, who hath perceived it, her heart's uninjured Soma-holding beaker?
Let the wise Brahman priest therein be joyful.

7 He understandeth them, he hath perceived them, her breasts that pour a thousand streams, uninjured:
They unreluctantly yield strength and vigour.

8 She who with voice upraised in constant clamour, mighty, life-giving, goes unto her function,
Bellowing to the heated three libations, suckles with streams of milk, and still is lowing.

9 On whom, well-fed, the Waters wait in worship, and steers and self-refulgent bulls attend her.
For thee, for one like thee down pour the Waters, and cause desire and strength to rain upon thee.

10 The thunder is thy voice, O Lord of Creatures: a Bull, thou castest on the earth thy vigour.
The Honey-whip, the Maruts' first-born daughter, derives her origin from Wind and Agni.

11 As at the morning sacrifice the Asvins twain love Soma well,
Even so may both the Asvins lay splendour and strength within my soul.

12 As at the second sacrifice Indra and Agni love him well,
Let the pair, Indra Agni, lay splendour and strength within my soul.

13 As at third sacrifice Soma is the Ribhus' well-belovèd one,
Even so may they, the Ribhus, store splendour and strength within my soul.

---

10 *Lord of Creatures*: Prajâpati. Thunder is his voice inasmuch as it heralds the seasonable rain which sustains the life of his creatures. *Thy vigour*: thy generative power from which living beings are produced.

13 *Ribhus*: the three renowned artists who by their excellent work obtained divinity, exercised superhuman powers, and became entitled

14 Fain would I bring forth sweetness, fain would make it mine.
Bringing milk, Agni! have I come: splendour and strength bestow on me!

15 Grant me, O Agni, splendid strength, and progeny, and lengthened life.
May the Gods know me as I am, may Indra with the Rishis know.

16 As honey-bees collect and add fresh honey to their honey store,
Even so may both the Asvins lay splendour and strength within my soul.

17 As over honey flies besmear this honey which the bees have made,
So may both Asvins lay in me splendour and strength and power and might.

18 May all the sweetness that is found in hills and mountains, steeds and kine,
And wine that floweth from the cup,—may all that sweetness be in me.

19 May both the Asvins, Lords of Light, balm me with honey of the bees,
That I may speak among the folk words full of splendour and of strength.

20 The thunder is thy voice, O Lord of Creatures: a Bull, thou castest strength on earth and heaven.
To that all cattle look for their existence: with this she nourishes their force and vigour.

---

to worship. They are called collectively Ribhus from Ribhu the eldest of the three brothers, the others being named separately Vibhvan and Vâja. Several hymns of the Rigveda are addressed to these deities.

---

15 The stanza is taken from Rigveda I. 23, 24.

20 See stanza 11. *She*: the Whip of the Asvins.

21 The Whip itself is Heaven, Earth is the handle, the point of juncture is the Air's mid-region.
The lash is lightning, and the tip is golden.
22 Whoever knows the Whip's seven kinds of honey, becomes himself a man endowed with sweetness.
Brâhman and King, the draught-ox and the milch-cow, barley and rice, and honey is the seventh.
23 Sweet is the man, sweet are his goods and chattels: he who knows this conquers the worlds of sweetness.
24 The thundering of Prajâpati in heaven is verily manifest to living creatures.
Therefore I stand from right to left invested, and, O Prajâpati, I cry, regard me!
The man who hath this knowledge is regarded by living beings and the Lord of Creatures.

HYMN II.

KÂMA the Bull, slayer of foes, I worship with molten butter, sacrifice, oblation.
Beneath my feet cast down mine adversaries, with thy great manly power, when I have praised thee.
2 That which is hateful to mine eye and spirit, that harasses and robs me of enjoyment,
The evil dream I loose upon my foemen. May I rend him when I have lauded Kâma.
3 Kâma, do thou, a mighty Lord and Ruler, let loose ill dream, misfortune, want of children,

---

21 *The point of juncture:* *gárbhaḥ* (from *grabh* = *grah*, to take, to conceive); the receptacle, meaning here the place where the thong is attached to the whip-stock.

23 *Conquers the worlds of sweetness:* gains admittance into heaven.

24 *From right to left invested:* *prâchînopavîtâḥ;* wearing the sacrificial cord over the right shoulder and passed under the left arm.

The hymn is a glorification of Kâma or Love, the God of general desire of all that is good.

1 *The Bull:* or, the strong; the hero.

Homelessness, Kâma! utter destitution, upon the sinner who designs my ruin.

4 Drive them away, drive them afar, O Kâma; indigence fall on those who are my foemen!
When they have been cast down to deepest darkness, consume their dwellings with thy fire, O Agni.

5 She, Kâma! she is called the Cow, thy daughter, she who is named Vâk and Virâj by sages.
By her drive thou my foemen to a distance. May cattle, vital breath, and life forsake them.

6 By Kâma's might, King Varuṇa's and Indra's, by Vishṇu's strength, and Savitar's instigation,
I chase my foes with sacrifice to Agni, as a deft steersman drives his boat through waters.

7 May Kâma, mighty one, my potent warder, give me full freedom from mine adversaries.
May all the Deities be my protection, all Gods come nigh to this mine invocation.

8 Accepting this oblation rich with fatness, be joyful here, ye Gods whose chief is Kâma,
Giving me freedom from mine adversaries.

9 Ye, Indra, Agni, Kâma! come together and cast mine adversaries down beneath me.
When they have sunk into the deepest darkness, O Agni, with thy fire consume their dwellings.

10 Slay those who are mine enemies, O Kâma: headlong to depth of blinding darkness hurl them.
Reft be they all of manly strength and vigour! Let them not have a single day's existence.

---

5 *The Cow*: *kâmadhuk* or *kâmadhenu*; the Cow of Plenty who yields every thing that is desired. *Vâk*: Goddess of Speech; the Creative Word. *Virâj*: here, apparently, the productive power of Nature. See VIII. 10.

6 *Savitar's instigation*: *savitúḥ savéna*; a play upon the words, as though it were 'Savitar's saving guidance.'

11 Kâma hath slain those who were mine opponents, and given me ample room to grow and prosper.
Let the four regions bow them down before me, and let the six expanses bring me fatness.

12 Let them drift downward like a boat torn from the rope that held it fast.
There is no turning back for those whom our keen arrows have repelled.

13 Agni averts, Indra averts, and Soma: may the averting Gods avert this foeman.

14 To be avoided by his friends, detested, repelled, with few men round him, let him wander.
Yea, on the earth descend the lightning-flashes: may the strong God destroy your adversaries.

15 This potent lightning nourishes things shaken, and things unshaken yet, and all the thunders.
May the Sun, rising with his wealth and splendour, drive in victorious might my foemen downward.

16 Thy firm and triply-barred protection, Kâma! thy spell, made weapon-proof extended armour—
With that drive thou my foemen to a distance. May cattle, vital breath, and life forsake them.

17 Far from the world wherein we live, O Kâma, drive thou my foemen with that selfsame weapon
Wherewith the Gods repelled the fiends, and Indra cast down the Dasyus into deepest darkness.

18 As Gods repelled the Asuras, and Indra down to the lowest darkness drove the demons,
So, Kâma, from this world, to distant places, drive thou the men who are mine adversaries.

---

11 *Six expanses:* the four cardinal points, and the upper and lower spaces; or, according to another account, Heaven, Earth, Day, Night, Water, and Plants.

12 The stanza is repeated, with a variation, from III. 6. 7.

15 *Shaken . . . . unshaken:* perishable and imperishable; all nature.

17 *With that selfsame weapon:* the text has merely *téna*, with that. See VIII. 5. 3; 8. 5 sqq.

19 First before all sprang Kâma into being. Gods, Fathers, mortal men have never matched him.
Stronger than these art thou, and great for ever. Kâma, to thee, to thee I offer worship.

20 Wide as the space which heaven and earth encompass, far as the flow of waters, far as Agni,
Stronger than these art thou, and great for ever. Kâma, to thee, to thee I offer worship.

21 Vast as the quarters of the sky and regions that lie between them spread in all directions, vast as celestial tracts and views of heaven,
Stronger than these art thou, and great for ever. Kâma, to thee, to thee I offer worship.

22 Many as are the bees, and bats, and reptiles, and female serpents of the trees, and beetles,
Stronger art thou than these, and great for ever. Kâma, to thee, to thee I offer worship.

23 Stronger art thou than aught that stands or twinkles, stronger art thou than ocean, Kâma! Manyu!
Stronger than these art thou, and great for ever. Kâma, to thee, to thee I offer worship.

---

19 *First before all:* 'Thereafter rose Desire in the beginning, Desire, the primal seed and germ of Spirit' (Ṛigveda X. 129. 4). Similarly, in Greek mythology Erôs or Love is said to have been the first of all the Gods. See the passage from Plato (Symposium, section 6), quoted and translated by Muir, O. S. Texts, V., 406.

20 *Far as Agni:* shines, or, extends.

22 *Beetles:* the meaning of *vágdḥ* is obscure. By comparison with *vághâpate* (VI. 50. 3) noxious or troublesome insects of some kind appear to be meant.

23 *Stands or twinkles:* inanimate and animate nature. All that stands without the power of moving away, as trees and plants, and all creatures that open and shut their eyelids, as men, beasts, and birds. *Manyu:* Passion or Ardour personified. See Ṛigveda X. 83, 2—6, where Manyu is addressed as a mighty God, identified with Indra, Varuṇa, and Agni.

24 Not even Vâta is the peer of Kâma, not Agni, Chandramas the Moon, nor Sûrya.
Stronger than these art thou, and great for ever. Kâma, to thee, to thee I offer worship.

25 Thy lovely and auspicious forms, O Kâma, whereby the thing thou wilt becometh real,
With these come thou and make thy home among us, and make malignant thoughts inhabit elsewhere.

HYMN III.

We loose the ties and fastenings of the house that holds all precious things,
The bands of pillars and of stays, the ties of beams that form the roof.

2 All-wealthy House! each knot and band, each cord that is attached to thee
I with my spell untie, as erst Bṛihaspati disclosed the cave.

3 He drew them close, he pressed them fast, he made thy knotted bands secure:

---

25 *The thing thou wilt:* or, choosest. Kâma, the God of Desire, is the fulfiller, as well as the inspirer, of his worshippers' wishes.

The hymn has been translated by Muir, O. S. Texts, V. 404, and by Ludwig, Der Rigveda, III. p. 519.

The occasion of the hymn is the consecration of a newly built house.

1 *We loose the ties:* symbolizing the removal by prayer of all malignant spells and charms by which the various parts of the house are tied and bound. Prof. Ludwig understands the words literally as signifying the actual dismantling of a dwelling-house. *Pillars:* the corner-posts. *Stays:* the slanting poles which strengthen the pillars.

2 *As erst Bṛihaspati:* with prayer, or with my spell, as Bṛihaspati, Lord of Prayer, opened therewith the hiding-place of the demon of drought. See Ṛigveda I. 62. 3; II. 23. 18; 24. 2; IV. 50. 5; VI. 73. 1.

3 *He:* the hostile enchanter. *Slaughterer:* the Immolator, who understands the important work of deftly cutting up the victim whose

With Indra's help we loose them as a skilful Slaughterer severs joints.

4 We loose the bands of thy bamboos, of bolts, of fastening, of thatch,
We loose the ties of thy side-posts, O House that holdest all we prize.

5 We loosen here the ties and bands of straw in bundles, and of clamps,
Of all that compasses and binds the Lady Genius of the Home.

6 We loose the loops which men have bound within thee, loops to tie and hold.
Be gracious, when erected, to our bodies, Lady of the Home!

7 Store-house of Soma, Agni's hall, the ladies' bower, the residence,
The seat of Gods art thou, O Goddess House.

8 We with our incantation loose the net that hath a thousand eyes,
The diadem, securely tied and laid upon the central beam.

9 The man who takes thee as his own, and he who was thy builder, House!
Both these, O Lady of the Home, shall live to long-extended years.

---

joints are to be carefully apportioned to the several Gods to whom the offering is made.

5 *Straw in bundles:* with which the house is thatched, or which line the walls.

7 *Store-house of Soma:* a chamber in which bundles of Soma plants, ready for pressing, were kept; secondarily, a pantry or store-room in general. *Agni's hall:* the chamber in which the domestic fire is kept up. *The residence:* the men's general living-room. Dr. Grill omits this 'schlechte Vers' as being an interpolation.

8 *The net that hath a thousand eyes:* probably a coarse reed mat, serving as a ceiling-cloth.

10 There let her come to meet this man. Firm, strongly fastened, and prepared
Art thou whose several limbs and joints we part and loosen one by one.

11 He who collected timber for the work and built thee up, O House,
Made thee for coming progeny, Prajâpati, the Lord Supreme.

12 Homage to him! We worship too the giver and the Mansion's lord:
Homage to Agni! to the man who serves at holy rites for thee.

13 Homage to kine and steeds! to all that shall be born within the house!
We loose the bonds that fasten thee, mother of multitudes to come!

14 Agni thou shelterest within, and people with domestic beasts.
We loose the bonds that fasten thee, mother of multitudes to come!

15 All space that lies between the earth and heaven, therewith I take this house for thy possession,
And all that measures out the air's mid-region I make a hollow to contain thy treasures. Therewith I take the house for his possession.

16 Rich in prosperity, rich in milk, founded and built upon the earth,
Injure not thy receivers, House who holdest food of every sort!

---

10 *This man:* the owner of the house.

11 *Prajâpati:* the builder is a second Prajâpati or Lord of Life as he built thee for the sake of *prajâ* or progeny.

12 *The giver:* the institutor of the sacrifice which the hymn accompanies.

17 Grass-covered, clad with straw, the house, like Night, gives rest to man and beast.
Thou standest, built upon the earth, like a she-elephant, borne on feet.

18 I loosen and remove from thee thy covering formed by mats of reed.
What Varuṇa hath firmly closed Mitra shall ope at early morn.

19 May Indra, Agni, deathless Gods, protect the house where Soma dwells,
House that was founded with the prayer, built and erected by the wise.

20 Nest upon nest hath been imposed, compartment on compartment laid :
There man shall propagate his kind, and there shall everything be born.

21 Within the house constructed with two side-posts, or with four, or six,
Built with eight side-posts, or with ten, lies Agni like a babe unborn.

22 Turned to thee, House! I come to thee, innocent, turned to welcome me :
For Fire and Water are within, the first chief door of sacrifice.

23 Water that kills Consumption, free from all Consumption, here I bring.
With Agni, the immortal one, I enter and possess the house.

---

17 *Borne on feet:* the four corner pillars representing the elephant's legs.

18 *Varuṇa:* God of the starry firmament; the heaven at night, that is, night. *Mitra:* God of day; the morning sun.

20 *Compartment:* it is difficult to decide which of its many meanings *kóśaḥ* has here. Ludwig renders it by 'korb,' basket, Zimmer by 'Behâlter,' receptacle, and Grill by 'Fachwerk,' panelling.

23 This stanza is repeated from III. 12. 9.

24 Lay thou no cord or noose on us: a weighty burthen, still be light!
Withersoever be our will, O House, we bear thee like a bride.

25 Now from the east side of the house to the Great Power be homage paid!
Hail to the Gods whose due is Hail!

26 Now from the south side of the house, etc.

27 Now from the west side of the house, etc.

28 Now from the north side of the house, etc.

29 So from the mansion's every side to the Great Power be homage paid!
Hail to the Gods whose due is Hail!

HYMN IV.

THE Bull, fierce, thousandfold, filled full of vigour, bearing within his flanks all forms and natures,
Bṛihaspati's Steer, hath stretched the thread, bestowing bliss on the worshipper, the liberal giver.

2 He who at first became the Waters' model, a match for everyone, like Earth the Goddess;
The husband of the cows, the young calves' father, may he secure us thousandfold abundance.

---

24 The stanza appears to point to the future removal of the house, built entirely of timber, bamboos, reeds, and straw, to some other situation. According to Grill the meaning is merely, We intend to make the house useful as a young married woman ought to be.

The hymn has been translated by Ludwig, Der Rigveda, III. p. 464; by Zimmer, Altindisches Leben, p. 151; and by Grill, Hundert Lieder, pp. 60, 188.

The hymn is a glorification in mystical language of the typical Sacrificial Bull.

1 *Stretched the thread:* a figurative expression, frequently occurring in the Veda, for, commenced the uninterrupted course of sacrifice. *Giver:* of guerdon or fees to the officiating priests.

3 Masculine, pregnant, stedfast, full of vigour, the Bull sustains a trunk of goodly treasure.
May Agni Jâtavedas bear him offered, on pathways traversed by the Gods, to Indra.

4 The husband of the cows, the young calves' father, father is he of mighty water-eddies.
Calf, after-birth, new milk drawn hot, and biestings, curds, butter, that is his best genial humour.

5 He is the Gods' allotted share and bundle, essence of waters, and of plants, and butter.
Ṣakra elected him, the draught of Soma. What was his body was a lofty mountain.

6 A beaker filled with Soma juice thou bearest, framer of forms, begetter of the cattle.
Kindly to us be these thy wombs here present, and stay for us, O Axe, those that are yonder.

7 He bears oblation, and his seed is butter. Thousand-fold plenty; sacrifice they call him.
May he, the Bull, wearing the shape of Indra, come unto us, O Gods, bestowed, with blessing.

8 Both arms of Varuṇa, and Indra's vigour, the Maruts' hump is he, the Asvins' shoulders.
They who are sages, bards endowed with wisdom, call him Bṛihaspati compact and heightened.

---

3 *Pregnant:* laden with blessings.

4 All that the cow produces originates from him.

6 *Kindly to us:* meaning, apparently: May the sacrificial axe of the typical immolator of the victim secure to us blessings both present and future.

8 *The Maruts' hump:* in Ṛigveda VIII. 20. 20 the Maruts are likened to 'bright-shining bulls.' *Bṛihaspati:* that is, the embodiment of sacerdotal rank and dignity, Bṛihaspati being the prototype of the priestly order.

9 Thou, vigorous, reachest to the tribes of heaven. Thee they call Indra, thee they call Sarasvân.
Turned to one aim, that Brâhman gives a thousand who offers up the Bull as his oblation.

10 Bṛihaspati, Savitar gave thee vital vigour: thy breath was brought from Tvashṭar and from Vâyu.
In thought I offer thee in air's mid-region. Thy sacrificial grass be Earth and Heaven!

11 Let the priest joyfully extol the limbs and members of the Bull
Who moved and roared among the kine as Indra moves among the Gods.

12 The sides must be Anumati's, and both rib-pieces Bhaga's share.
Of the knee-bones hath Mitra said, Both these are mine, and only mine.

13 The Âdityas claim the hinder parts, the loins must be Bṛihaspati's.
Vâta, the God, receives the tail: he stirs the plants and herbs therewith.

14 To Sûryâ they assigned the skin, to Sinîvâlî inward parts.
The Slaughterer hath the feet, they said, when they distributed the Bull.

---

9 *Sarasvân*: a divinity of the upper region, guardian of the heavenly waters (cf. 'father is he of mighty water-eddies' in stanza 4), and bestower of fertility.

11 *Let the priest joyfully extol*: in animal sacrifices the carvers or dissectors of the victim are to call out the names of the several parts of the carcase as they divide them, each portion being assigned to a separate divinity. See Ṛigveda I. 162. 18.

12 *Anumati's*: the portion of Divine Favour personified. See I. 18. 2, note.

14 *Sûryâ*: the daughter of the Sun. *They*: the Gods who portioned out the ideal archetypal Bull. *Sinîvâlî*: Goddess of the New Moon.

15 They made a jest of kindred's curse : a jar of Soma juice was set,
What time the deities, convened, assigned the Bull's divided parts.

16 They gave the hooves to tortoises, to Saramâ scraps of the feet :
His undigested food they gave to worms and things that creep and crawl.

17 That Bull, the husband of the kine, pierces the demons with his horns,
Banishes famine with his eye, and hears good tidings with his ears.

18 With hundred sacrifices he worships : the fires consume him not :
All Gods promote the Brâhman who offers the Bull in sacrifice.

19 He who hath given away the Bull to Brâhmans frees and cheers his soul.
In his own cattle-pen he sees the growth and increase of his cows.

20 Let there be cattle, let there be bodily strength and progeny :
All this may the Gods kindly grant to him who gives away the Bull.

21 Indra here verily hath rejoiced : let him bestow conspicuous wealth.
May he draw forth at will from yonder side of heaven a deft cow, good to milk, whose calf is never wanting.

---

15 *They made a jest :* they made light of the angry imprecations of the Gods who were dissatisfied with the portions assigned to them.

16 *To tortoises :* that they might renovate their shells with the horny material. *Saramâ :* the hound of Indra, represented in Ṛigveda X. 14. 10 as the mother of Yama's two brindled four-eyed dogs. See V. 30. 6. *Scraps of the feet : kúshṭhikâḥ ;* according to Sâyaṇa, the contents of the entrails. Cf. IX. 7. 10 ; X. 9. 23.

22 With close connexion mingle with the cows in this our cattle-pen :
Mingle, the Bull's prolific flow, and, Indra! thine heroic strength!

23 Here we restore this Bull, your youthful leader: sporting with him, go, wander at your pleasure.
Ne'er, wealthy ones! may he be reft of offspring; and do ye favour us with growth of riches.

HYMN V.

SEIZE him and bring him hither. Let him travel, foreknowing, to the regions of the pious.
Crossing in many a place the mighty darkness, let the Goat mount to the third heaven above us.

2 I bring thee hither as a share for Indra; prince, at this sacrifice, for him who worships.
Grasp firmly from behind all those who hate us: so let the sacrificer's men be sinless.

---

22 This stanza is taken, with variations, from Ṛigveda VI. 28. 8. The impregnation of the cows is the object of the wish.

23 The stanza is addressed to the cows.

The hymn is a glorification, partly in mystical language, of the Sacrificial Goat.

1 *Him:* the victim; the Goat. *Regions of the pious:* the victim sacrificed to the Gods goes immediately to heaven. So, of the sacrificed Horse: 'The Steed is come unto the noblest mansion, is come unto his father and his mother (Heaven and Earth). This day shall he approach the Gods, most welcome: then he declares good gifts to him who offers' (Ṛigveda I. 163. 13). *Third heaven:* cf. A. V. XVIII. 2. 48, where three heavens are mentioned, the lowest, the intermediate and the third in which the Fathers dwell.

2 *Prince:* the Sûri is the prince, noble, or wealthy householder who institutes the sacrifice and rewards the officiating priests; and the goat when sacrificed is to be the prince who brings a reward to the sacrificer in the shape of blessings from the God to whom the offering is presented.

3 Wash from his feet all trace of evil-doing: fore-
knowing, with cleansed hooves let him go upward.
Gazing on many a spot, crossing the darkness, let
the Goat mount to the third heaven above us.

4 Cut up this skin with the grey knife, Dissector!
dividing joint from joint, and mangle nothing.
Do him no injury: limb by limb arrange him, and
send him up to the third cope of heaven.

5 With verse upon the fire I set the caldron: pour in
the water; lay him down within it!
Encompass him with fire, ye Immolators. Cooked,
let him reach the world where dwell the righteous.

6 Hence come thou forth, vexed by no pain or torment.
Mount to the third heaven from the heated vessel.
As fire out of the fire hast thou arisen. Conquer and
win this lucid world of splendour.

7 The Goat is Agni: light they call him, saying that
living man must give him to the Brahman.
Given in this world by a devout believer, the Goat
dispels and drives afar the darkness.

8 Let the Pañchaudana Goat, about to visit the three
lights, pass away in five divisions.

---

4 The carcase is to be most carefully cut up and the joints neatly divided. 'Let not a greedy clumsy Immolator, missing the joints, mangle thy limbs unduly' (Ṛigveda I. 162. 20).

5 *With verse:* reciting a *ṛich*, a sacred verse or hymn of praise, distinguished from the *sâman* which is sung or chanted, and from the *yajus* or sacrificial formula.

6 *As fire out of the fire:* or, As Agni out of fire. See stanza 6.

7 *The Goat is Agni:* somewhat similar is the old Scandinavian belief that a victim offered to a god became incorporate in the god and obtained a portion of his divine power. *Brahman:* the chief priest who directs the sacrifice.

8 *Pañchaudana:* offered with a fivefold mess, or five messes, of boiled rice, or grain mashed and cooked with milk. *Three lights:* three luminous heavens. See stanza 1. *In five divisions:* one for each *odana* or mess of boiled rice. *Parted:* referring to the goat, divided into five.

Go midst the pious who have paid their worship, and, parted, dwell on the third cope of heaven.

9 Rise to that world, O Goat, where dwell the righteous: pass, like a Ṣarabha veiled, all difficult places.
The Goat Pañchaudana, given to a Brahman, shall with all fulness satisfy the giver.

10 The Goat Pañchaudana, given to a Brahman, sets the bestower on the pitch of heaven,
In the third vault, third sky, third ridge. One only Cow omniform art thou, that yields all wishes.

11 That is the third light that is yours, ye Fathers. He gives the Goat Pañchaudana to the Brahman.
Given in this world by the devout believer, the Goat dispels and drives afar the darkness.

12 Seeking the world of good men who have worshipped, he gives the Goat Pañchaudana to the Brahman.
Win thou this world as thy complete possession. Auspicious unto us be he, accepted!

13 Truly the Goat sprang from the glow of Agni, inspired as sage with all a sage's power.
Sacrifice, filled, filled full, offered with Vashaṭ—this let the Gods arrange at proper seasons.

14 Home-woven raiment let him give, and gold as guerdon to the priests.
So he obtains completely all celestial and terrestrial worlds.

---

9 *Ṣarabha:* probably some kind of deer; according to Mahîdhara an eight-legged animal, a dangerous enemy of the lion.

10 *One only Cow:* the Cow of Plenty.

11 *The third light:* the highest heaven. See note on stanza 1. *He:* the sacrificer.

12 *He:* the sacrificed goat. *Accepted:* by the God.

13 *Filled, filled full:* instead of *pûrtám abhípûrtam* Prof. Ludwig would read *gûrtam abhigûrtam*, approved, accepted.

15 Near to thee, Goat! approach these streams of Soma, divine, distilling meath, bedecked with butter!
Stay thou the earth and sky and fix them firmly up on the seven-rayed pitch and height of heaven.

16 Unborn art thou, O Goat: to heaven thou goest. Through thee Angirases knew that radiant region. So may I know that holy world.

17 Convey our sacrifice to heaven, that it may reach the Gods, with that
Whereby thou, Agni, bearest wealth in thousands, and all precious things.

18 The Goat Pañchaudana, when cooked, transporteth, repelling Nirṛiti, to the world of Svarga.
By him may we win worlds which Sûrya brightens.

19 The droppings of the Odanas attending the Goat which I have lodged with priest or people—
May all this know us in the world of virtue, O Agni, at the meeting of the pathways.

20 This Unborn cleft apart in the beginning: his breast became the earth, his back was heaven.
His middle was the air, his sides the regions; the hollows of his belly formed both oceans.

---

16 *Unborn art thou, O Goat:* the goat (*ajá*) is identified, mystically, with the Unborn Spirit (*ajá*), and in sacrificial hymns the two meanings are sometimes difficult to distinguish. In Ṛigveda X. 16. 4, it is not absolutely certain whether *ajáḥ*) means 'goat' or 'unborn (soul);' and in stanza 7 of this hymn the word which I have translated by 'Goat' is rendered by 'unborn' in the St. Petersburg Dictionary. See Muir's note, O. S. Texts, V. p. 304.

17 *With that:* power understood.

18 *Transporteth:* removes the sacrificer after death.

19 *May all this know us:* may the whole sacrifice, even the particles fallen on the ground from the messes of boiled rice, recognize us in heaven as the originators or performers of the ceremony.

21 His eyes were Truth and Right. The whole together was Truth: Virâj his head, and Faith his breathing.
This Goat Pañchaudana was indeed a sacrifice unlimited.

22 A boundless sacrifice he performs, he wins himself a boundless world
Who gives the Goat Pañchaudana illumined with a priestly fee.

23 Let him not break the victim's bones, let him not suck the marrow out.
Let the man, taking him entire, here, even here deposit him.

24 This, even this is his true form: the man uniteth him therewith.
Food, greatness, strength he bringeth him who giveth the Goat Pañchaudana illumed with guerdon.

25 The five gold pieces, and the five new garments, and the five milch-kine yield him all his wishes
Who gives the Goat Pañchaudana illumined with a priestly fee.

26 The five gold pieces are a light to light him, robes become armour to defend his body;
He winneth Svarga as his home who giveth the Goat Pañchaudana illumed with bounty.

27 When she who hath been wedded finds a second husband afterward,
The twain shall not be parted if they give the Goat Pañchaudana.

---

21 *Virâj:* see VIII. 10.

22 *Illumined:* enhanced in value.

25 *Gold pieces: rukmá*; or gold necklets. These and the other presents mentioned are the *dakshiṇâ* or honorarium bestowed on the priests by the institutor of the sacrifice.

27 *A second husband:* after the death of the first.

28 One world with the re-wedded wife becomes the second husband's home
Who gives the Goat Pañchaudana illumined with the priestly fee.

29 They who have given a cow who drops a calf each season, or an ox,
A coverlet, a robe, or gold, go to the loftiest sphere of heaven.

30 Himself, the father and the son, the grandson, and the father's sire,
Mother, wife, her who bore his babes, all the belovèd ones I call.

31 The man who knows the season named the Scorching —the Goat Pañchaudana is this scorching season—
He lives himself, he verily burns up his hated rival's fame,
Who gives the Goat Pañchaudana illumined with the priestly fee.

32 The man who knows the season called the Working takes to himself the active fame, his hated rival's active fame.
The Goat Pañchaudana is this Working season.
He lives himself, etc.

33 The man who knows the season called the Meeting takes to himself the gathering fame, his hated rival's gathering fame.
The Goat Pañchaudana is this Meeting season.

34 The man who knows the season called the Swelling takes to himself the swelling fame, his hated rival's swelling fame.

---

28 *One world:* heaven after death.

31 *The Scorching: naidâgha*; summer, the hot weather before the Rains.

32 *The Working:* the cold weather. The other divisions of the year in stanzas 33—36 are probably fanciful and variable.

The Goat Pañchaudana is this Swelling season.
He lives himself, etc.

35 The man who knows the season called the Rising takes to himself the rising fame, his hated rival's rising fame.
The Goat Pañchaudana is this Rising season.

36 The man who knows the season called Surpassing takes to himself the conquering fame, his hated rival's conquering fame.
The Goat Pañchaudana is this Conquering season.
He lives himself, he verily burns up his hated rival's fame
Who gives the Goat Pañchaudana illumined with a priestly fee.

37 He cooks the Goat and the five boiled rice messes. May the united Quarters, all accordant, and intermediate points, accept him from thee.

38 May these preserve him for thee. Here I offer to these the molten butter as oblation.

HYMN VI.

Whoso will know Prayer with immediate knowledge, whose members are the stuff, whose spine the verses:

---

38 *These:* the Quarters of the sky, with the intermediate points.
The hymn has been translated by Ludwig, Der Rigveda, III. p. 435.

The hymn is a glorification of the hospitable reception of guests, regarded as identical with sacrifice offered to the Gods. Stanzas 3—62 are in prose.

1 *With immediate knowledge: pratyáksham;* literally, before the eyes, face to face; meaning here, embodied in practice. Cf. 'laborare est orare.' *The stuff:* the material of which the sacred verses are composed. *The verses: ṛíchas;* the holy verses of prayer and praise in the form in which they have been revealed.

2 Whose hairs are psalms, whose heart is called the Yajus, whose coverlet is verily oblation—

3 Verily when a host looks at his guests he looks at the place of sacrifice to the Gods. 4 When he salutes them reverently he undergoes preparation for a religious ceremony: when he calls for water, he solemnly brings sacrificial water. 5 The water that is solemnly brought at a sacrifice is this same water. 6 The libation which they bring, the sacrificial victim dedicated to Agni and Soma which is tied to the post, that, verily, is this man. 7 When they arrange dwelling-rooms they arrange the sacred chamber and the shed for housing the Soma cars. 8 What they spread upon the floor is just Sacrificial Grass. 9 With the couch that the men bring, he wins for himself the world of Svarga. 10 The pillow-coverings that they bring are the green sticks that surround the sacrificial altar. 11 The ointment that they bring for inunction is just clarified liquid butter. 12 The food they bring before the general distribution represents the two sacrificial cakes of rice meal. 13 When they call the man who prepares food they summon the preparer of oblation. 14 The grains of rice and barley that are selected are just filaments of the Soma plant. 15 The pestle and mortar are really the stones of the Soma press. 16 The winnowing-basket is the filter, the chaff the Soma dregs,

---

2 *Psalms: sâmâni;* chanted hymns or songs. *The Yajus:* sacrificial text or formula. The sense of the two stanzas is incomplete should hear what follows, or something similar, may be understood.

3 *Preparation for a religious ceremony:* the initiatory or preparatory rite called Dikshâ or Consecration. 7 *Sacred chamber: sâdas;* literally, seat (of the Gods); a shed erected in the sacrificial court or enclosure to the east of the Prâchînavaṅṣa chamber, which has its supporting beam turned towards the east. *Soma cars:* light carts in which the plants are brought to be pressed. 10 *Green sticks:* which

the water the pressing-gear. 17 Spoon, ladle, fork,
stirring-prong are the wooden Soma tubs; the
earthen cooking-pots are the mortar-shaped Soma
vessels; this earth is just the black-antelope's skin.
18 Or the host acts in this way to a Yajamâna's
Brâhman: when he looks at the furniture and utensils
he says, More here! Yet more here. 19 When
he says, Bring out more, he lengthens his life thereby.
20 He brings oblations: he makes the men sit down.
21 As the guest of the seated company he himself
offers up sacrifice. 22 With ladle, with hand, in life,
at the sacrificial post, with cry of Ladle! with exclamation
of Vashaṭ! 23 Now these guests, as
priests beloved or not beloved, bring one to the world
of Svarga. 24 He who hath this knowledge should
not eat hating, should not eat the food of one who
hates him, nor of one who is doubtful, nor of one
who is undecided. 25 This man whose food they eat
hath all his wickedness blotted out. 26 All that man's
sin whose food they do not eat remains unblotted out.
27 The man who supplies food hath always pressing
stones adjusted, a wet Soma filter, well prepared
religious rites, and mental power to complete the
arranged sacrifice. 28 The arranged sacrifice of the
man who offers food is a sacrifice to Prajâpati.
29 The man who offers food follows the steps of
Prajâpati. 30 The fire of the guests is the Âhavanîya,
the fire in the dwelling is the Gârhapatya, that
whereon they cook food is the Southern Sacrificial Fire.

---

serve as a fence to restrict the range of the fire. 17 *Wooden Soma tubs: dronakalaśâḥ*; large vessels that receive and hold the Soma juice as it flows from the press. *Black-antelope's skin:* which is to be spread on the floor.

18 *Yajamâna:* a wealthy householder who institutes sacrifices and defrays all the expenses. 22 *Ladle!... Vashaṭ!:* exclamations of the officiating priest as he offers the libation. 25 *Blotted out:* literally, burnt up. 30 *Âhavanîya:* the eastern sacrificial fire. *Gârhaptya:* the householder's western sacred fire. *Southern:* the Dakshiṇâgni.

31 Now that man who eats before the guest eats up the sacrifice and the merit of the house. 32 He devours the milk and the sap: 33 And the vigour and prosperity: 34 And the progeny and the cattle: 35 And the fame and reputation. 36 The man who eats before the guest eats up the glory and the understanding of the house. 37 The man should not eat before the guest who is a Brâhman versed in holy lore. 38 When the guest hath eaten he should eat. This is the rule for the animation of the sacrifice and the preservation of its continuity. 39 Now the sweetest portion, the produce of the cow, milk, or flesh, that verily he should not eat.

40 The man who having this knowledge pours out milk and offers it wins for himself as much thereby as he gains by the performance of a very successful Agnishṭoma sacrifice. 41 The man who having this knowledge pours out clarified butter and offers it wins for himself thereby as much as he gains by the performance of a very successful Atirâtra sacrifice. 42 He who pours out mead and offers it wins for himself thereby as much as he gains by the performance of a very successful Sattrasadya sacrifice. 43 He who having this knowledge besprinkles flesh and offers it wins for himself thereby as much as he gains by the performance of a very successful Twelve-Day sacrifice. 44 The man who having this knowledge pours out water and offers it obtains a resting-place for the procreation of living beings and becomes

---

31 *The merit:* of good works that will be rewarded in heaven.

40 *Agnishṭoma:* (praise of Agni), a protracted ceremony, extending over several days, and forming an essential part of the Jyotishṭoma which, consisting of four or seven divisions, is considered as the typical form of a whole class of Soma ceremonies. 41 *Atirâtra:* an optional part of the Jyotishṭoma sacrifice. 42 *Sattrasadya:* a long sacrifice, sacrificial session, or Soma ceremony, conducted by many officiating priests, and lasting, according to some authorities, from thirteen to a hundred days. See note on I. 30. 4.

dear to living beings, even the man who having this knowledge pours out water and offers it.

45 For him Dawn murmurs, and Savitar sings the prelude; Bṛihaspati chants with vigour, and Tvashṭar joins in with increase; the Visve Devâḥ take up the conclusion. He who hath this knowledge is the abiding-place of welfare, of progeny, and of cattle. 46 For him the rising Sun murmurs, and Early Morning sings the prelude; Noon chants the psalm, Afternoon joins in; the setting Sun takes up the conclusion. He who hath this knowledge is the abiding place of welfare, of progeny, and of cattle. 47 For him the Rain-cloud murmurs when present, sings the prelude when thundering, joins in when lightening, chants the psalm when raining, and takes up the conclusion when it stays the downpour. He who hath this knowledge is the abiding-place of welfare, of progeny, and of cattle. 48 He looks at the guests, he utters a gentle sound; he speaks, he sings the prelude; he calls for water, he chants the psalm; he offers the residue of the sacrifice, he takes up the conclusion.

49 When he summons the door-keeper he gives instruction. 50 He (the door-keeper) pronounces the sacrificial formula in his answer to what he hears. 51 When the attendants with vessels in their hands, foremost and hindmost, come in, they are just the priests who manage the Soma cups. 52 Not one of

---

45 The Gods themselves form a choir for the liberal host, and chant for him a song of praise. *Dawn murmurs:* utters a low sound, introducing, or giving the key-note of, the hymn. *Sings the prelude:* acts as Prastotar, or precentor. *Chants:* acts as Udgâtar. *Joins in:* acts as Pratihartar, or assistant of the Udgâtar, and joins in the chanting of the last Pâda of the verse. 48 Not only do the Gods, the Sun in his divers stages, and the Rain-cloud form the host's priestly chorus, but each hospitable act of his represents a portion of the choral service.

51 *Priests who manage the Soma cups: chamasâdhvaryavaḥ:* the Adhvaryus or priests in charge of the vessels out of which the Soma

them is incompetent to sacrifice. 53 Or if the host, having offered food to his guest, goes up to the house, he virtually enters the bath of purification. 54 When he distributes food he distributes priestly fees; what he performs he asks as favour. 55 He, having been invited on earth, regales, invited, in that which wears all various forms on earth. 56 He, having been invited in air, regales, invited, in that which wears all various forms in air. 57 He having been invited in the sky, regales, invited, in that which wears all various forms in the sky. 58 He, having been invited among the Gods, regales, invited, in that which wears all various forms among the Gods. 59 He, having been invited in the worlds, regales, invited, in that which wears all various forms in the worlds. 60 He, having been invited, hath been invited. 61 He gains this world and the world yonder. 62 He who hath this knowledge wins the luminous spheres.

HYMN VII.

PRAJÂPATI and Parameshṭhin are the two horns, Indra is the head, Agni the forehead, Yama the joint of the neck. 2 King Soma is the brain, Sky is the upper jaw, Earth is the lower jaw. 3 Lightning is the tongue, the Maruts are the teeth, Revatî is the neck, the Kṛittikâs are the shoulders, the Gharma is

---

juice is drunk. 53 *The bath of purification:* the *avabhṛitha*, water for the purification of the sacrificer and the sacrificial vessels at the conclusion of the ceremony. 54 *Priestly fees: dakshiṇâ;* meaning originally a good milch-cow, which in the earliest times was the usual honorarium.

The hymn, which is entirely prose, is a glorification of the typical Bull and Cow.

1 *Parameshṭhin:* Lord Supreme. In I. 7. 2, Jâtavedas (Agni) is so called; in IX. 3. 11, the title is given to Prajâpati. 3 *Revatî:* one of the Lunar Mansions. *The Kṛittikâs:* the Pleiades (a Lunar Mansion) personified as the nurses of Skanda or Kumâra the War-God, who is

the shoulder-bar. 4 His universe is Vâyu, Svarga is his world, Kṛishṇadram is the tendons and vertebrae. 5 The Ṣyena ceremony is the breast, Air is the region of the belly, Bṛihaspati is the hump, Bṛihatî the breast-bone and cartilages of the ribs. 6 The consorts of the Gods are the ribs, the attendants are ribs. 7 Mitra and Varuṇa are the shoulder-blades, Tvashṭar and Aryaman the fore-arms, Mahâdeva is the arms. 8 Indrâṇî is the hinder parts, Vâyu the tail, Pavamâna the hair. 9 Priestly rank and princely power are the hips, and strength is the thigh. 10 Dhâtar and Savitar are the two knee-bones, the Gandharvas are the legs, the Apsarases are bits of the feet, Aditi is the hooves. 11 Thought is the heart, intelligence is the liver, law the pericardium. 12 Hunger is the belly, refreshing drink is the rectum, mountains are the inward parts. 13 Wrath is the kidneys, anger the testes, offspring the generative organ. 14 The river is the womb, the Lords of the Rain are the breasts, the thunder is the udder. 15 The All-embracing (Aditi) is the hide, the herbs are her hair, and the Lunar Mansions her form. 16 The hosts of Gods are her entrails, men are her bowels, and demons her abdomen. 17 Râkshasas are the blood, the Other Folk are the contents of the stomach. 18 The rain-cloud is her fat, her resting-place her marrow. 19 Sitting he is Agni, when he hath stood up he is the Asvins. 20 Standing eastwards he is Indra, standing southwards, Yama.

---

hence called Kârttikeya. 4 *Kṛishṇadram:* the word is unintelligible. 5 *Ṣyena:* a kind of Ekâha or Soma sacrifice lasting one day. 7 *Mahâdeva:* Great God, an appellation usually given to Rudra or one of the Gods connected with him. In classical Sanskrit, and at the present time, the title is applied to Ṣiva, Mahâdeo. 8 *Indrâṇî:* the Consort of Indra. *Pavamâna:* the deified Soma juice. 10 *Dhâtar:* the Ordainer. 14 The Cow is now the subject of glorification. 17 *Other Folk:* a euphemistic expression for certain beings considered to be spirits of darkness. Cf. VIII. 10. 28. 19 The Bull is again the subject. *Sitting:* Agni as Sacrificial Fire being stationary. 20 *Indra:*

21 Standing westwards he is Dhâtar, standing northwards Savitar. 22 When he hath got his grass he is King Soma. 23 He is Mitra when he looks about him, and when he hath turned round he is joy. 24 When he is yoking he belongs to the All-Gods, when yoked he is Prajâpati, when unyoked he is All. 25 This verily is omniform, wearing all forms, bovine-formed. 26 Upon him wait omniform beasts, wearing every shape, each one who hath this knowledge.

HYMN VIII.

EACH pain and ache that racks the head, earache, and erysipelas,
All malady that wrings thy brow we charm away with this our spell.

2 From both thine ears, from parts thereof, thine earache, and the throbbing pain,
All malady that wrings thy brow we charm away with this our spell.

3 So that Consumption may depart forth from thine ears and from thy mouth,
All malady that wrings thy brow we charm away with this our spell.

---

regarded as Warder of the East. 23 *Mitra:* the all-surveying Sun.

The hymn is a charm for the cure of various diseases and pains more or less connected, or supposed to be connected, with Consumption.

1 *Erysipelas: vilohitáḥ* (dark-red, or purple); apparently an inflammatory disease attacking the head; probably erysipelas. See Wise, Hindu System of Medicine, p. 270.

2 *From parts thereof: káṅkûshebhyaḥ;* what these *káṅkûshas* are is unknown. *Throbbing pain:* or the disease that causes throbbing or piercing pains in various parts of the body, called *visályaka.* Cf. VI. 127. 1.

4 The malady that makes one deaf, the malady that makes one blind,
All malady that wrings thy brow we charm away with this our spell.

5 The throbbing pain in all thy limbs that rends thy frame with fever-throes,
All malady that wrings thy brow we charm away with this our spell.

6 The malady whose awful look makes a man quiver with alarm,
Fever whom every Autumn brings we charm away with this our spell.

7 Disease that creeps about the thighs and, after, reaches both the groins,
Consumption from thine inward parts we charm away with this our spell.

8 If the disease originates from love, from hatred, from the heart,
Forth from the heart and from the limbs we charm the wasting malady.

9 The yellow Jaundice from thy limbs, and Colic from the parts within,
And Phthisis from thine inward soul we charm away with this our spell.

10 Let wasting malady turn to dust, become the water of disease.
I have evoked the poison-taint of all Consumptions out of thee.

---

4 *Deaf: pramótam*, explained in the St. Petersburg Dictionary as a certain disease, must be an adjective like *andhám*, blind, and means probably either deaf, or dumb. See Zimmer's note, Altindisches Leben, p. 378.

6 *Whom every Autumn brings:* malarial fever begins to be prevalent at the commencement of the Rains, and frequently becomes epidemic when the Rains are over and the Autumn sun begins to dry up the deposits left by the swollen rivers, tanks, and inundations. Cf. note on I. 25. 1.

11 Forth from the hollow let it run, and rumbling sounds from thine inside.
I have evoked the poison-taint of all Consumptions out of thee.

12 Forth from thy belly and thy lungs, forth from thy navel and thy heart
I have evoked the poison-taint of all Consumptions out of thee.

13 The penetrating stabs of pain which rend asunder crown and head,
Let them depart and pass away, free from disease and harming not.

14 The pangs that stab the heart and reach the breast-bone and connected parts,
Let them depart and pass away, free from disease and harming not.

15 The stabs that penetrate the sides and pierce their way along the ribs,
Let them depart and pass away, free from disease and harming not.

16 The penetrating pangs that pierce thy stomach as they shoot across,
Let them depart and pass away, free from disease and harming not.

17 The pains that through the bowels creep, disordering the inward parts,
Let them depart and pass away, free from disease and harming not.

18 The pains that suck the marrow out, and rend and tear the bones apart,
May they speed forth and pass away, free from disease and harming not.

19 Consumptions with their Colic pains which make thy limbs insensible—
I have evoked the poison-taint of all Consumptions out of thee.

20 Of piercing pain, of abscesses, rheumatic ache, ophthalmia—
I have evoked the poison-taint of all Consumptions out of thee.

21 I have dispelled the piercing pains from feet, knees, hips, and hinder parts,
And spine, and from the neck and nape the malady that racked the head.

22 Sound are the skull-bones of thy head and thy heart's beat is regular.
Thou, Sun, arising with thy beams hast chased away the head's disease, hast stilled the pain that racked the limbs.

HYMN IX.

The second brother of this lovely Hotar, hoary with eld, is the voracious Lightning.
The third is he whose back is balmed with butter. Here have I seen the King with seven male children.

---

20 *Ophthalmia: alaji;* more precisely, disease of the eye attended with the appearance of small red pimples at the juncture of the cornea and sclerotica. See Wise, Hindu System of Medicine, p. 296.

22 *Hast chased away the head's disease:* cf. 'Sûrya, remove my heart's disease' (Ṛigveda I. 50. 11).

The hymn has been translated by Zimmer, Altindisches Leben, p. 378, whose work may be consulted for further information regarding the pains and diseases mentioned in the text.

The hymn, which is taken with variations and transpositions, from stanzas 1—22 of Ṛigveda I. 164—one of the most abstruse and difficult of that Collection—consists mainly of questions and enigmatical enunciations of doctrine on mystico-theological and cosmogonical subjects.

1 *This lovely Hotar:* or gracious and benign Priest, is Agni in his celestial form as the Sun. *Lightning:* the secondary form of Agni. The text has *áśnaḥ*, voracious, that is, destructive, without a substantive expressed. *The third:* brother, or form, of Agni is the Gârhapatya or sacred fire maintained by each householder and fed with oblations of clarified butter. *The King with seven male children:* Agni or Sacrificial Fire with the attendant priests.

2 The seven make the one-wheeled chariot ready:
bearing seven names the single Courser draws it.
The wheel, three-naved, is sound and undecaying:
thereon these worlds of life are all dependent.

3 The seven who on this seven-wheeled car are mounted
have horses, seven in tale, who draw them onward.
Seven sisters utter songs of praise together, in whom
the Cows' seven names are held and treasured.

4 Who hath beheld at birth the Primal Being, when
She who hath no bone supports the bony?
Where is the blood of earth, the life, the spirit?
Who may approach the man who knows, to ask it?

---

2 *The Seven:* priests, according to Prof. Grassmann. Perhaps the Maruts are meant, who appear in Ṛigveda I. 6. 1 to be the harnessers of the bright red steed the Sun. In Ṛigveda VIII. 28. 5, 'The Seven' are the Maruts, generally represented as seven times nine in number. *The one-wheeled chariot:* the Sun. *Seven names:* perhaps the seven rays of Agni or the Sun. *Three-naved:* with reference, probably, to the three seasons, the hot weather, the rains, and the cold weather; or to morning, noon, and evening. On this wheel of the Sun all living creatures depend.

3 *The seven:* according to Sâyaṇa, the seven solar rays, or the seven divisions of the year, solstice, season, month, fortnight, day, night, hour. The seven wheels of the chariot, and the seven horses may also, according to Sâyaṇa, be solar rays. According to Dr. Haug, *the seven-wheeled car* is the Jyotishṭoma sacrifice with its seven divisions, and Prof. Ludwig thinks that the six pairs of months and the intercalary month are meant. *Seven sisters:* probably the seven celestial rivers, counterparts of the Seven Rivers of earth. These, as emblems of fertility, may be said to bear *the names of the seven cows*, that is, each may be called a cow, symbolizing the abundance which they produce on earth. Sâyaṇa explains the *seven sisters* as the solar rays, or the six seasons and the year, or the six pairs of months with the intercalary month, and the *seven cows* as the seven notes of music as employed in chanting the praises of the Sun.

4 *She who hath no bone:* the boneless female is probably Prakṛiti or Nature, the original source of the bony or substantial one, that is, the material and visible world. Or Earth and Man may be intended.

5 Let him who knoweth presently declare it, this lovely Bird's securely-founded station.
Forth from his head the Cows draw milk, and wearing his vesture with their foot have drunk the water.

6 Unripe in mind, in spirit undiscerning, I ask of these the Gods' established places.
High up above the yearling Calf the sages, to form a web, their own seven threads have woven.

7 Here, ignorant, I ask the wise who know it, as one who knows not, for the sake of knowledge,
What is That One, who in the Unborn's image hath stablished and fixed firm this world's six regions.

8 The Mother gave the Sire his share of Order. With thought at first she wedded him in spirit.
She, coyly loth, was filled with dew prolific. With adoration men approached to praise her.

---

5 *This lovely Bird's securely-founded station:* the place of the Sun, and how he stands in heaven secure although apparently unsupported. *The Cows:* the rays of the Sun which draw light and vivifying power from his head or crown, and reabsorb from earth the water which they send down in rain.

6 *The yearling Calf:* probably the Sun, in reference to his yearly course. What the *seven threads* are is uncertain. Sâyaṇa says they are the seven forms or divisions of a Soma sacrifice (the Jyotishṭoma), or the seven metres of the Veda. Prof. Ludwig thinks that the general meaning of the stanza is: I (the poet) content myself with asking information regarding the places or traces of the Gods in our world; but the sages talk about matters which are beyond my power of comprehension. According to Prof. Grassmann, *the sages* here are the wise Gods, and the *seven threads* are the seven year-sacrifices of a sacrificial cycle.

7 *In the Unborn's image:* in the form of the Sun, the main type and agent of generation, who as being the first of created things is represented as Aja the Unborn, the Creator. Cf. 'He (Agni), like the Unborn, holds the broad earth up, and with effective utterance fixed the sky' (Ṛigveda I. 67. 3).

8 *The Mother:* Earth. *The Sire:* Heaven. *Of Order:* that is, in the great work of cosmical production or creation. *Dew prolific:* in the shape of fertilizing rain.

9 Yoked was the Mother to the boon Cow's car-pole:
in humid folds of cloud the infant rested.
Then the Calf lowed and looked upon the Mother,
the Cow who wears all shapes in three directions.

10 Bearing three mothers and three fathers, single he
stood erect: they never made him weary.
On yonder heaven's high ridge they speak together
in speech not known to all, themselves all-knowing.

11 Upon the five-spoked wheel revolving ever, whereon
all creatures rest and are dependent,
The axle, heavy-laden, is not heated: the nave from
ancient time remains unheated.

12 They call him in the farther half of heaven the Sire
five-footed, of twelve forms, wealthy in watery
store.
These others, later still, say that he takes his stand
upon a seven-wheeled car, six-spoked, whose sight
is clear.

---

9 *Yoked was the mother:* Earth undertook the functions of the cow who supplies milk for sacrificial purposes. *The infant:* the young Sun. *Three directions:* heaven, mid-air, and earth.

10 *Three mothers and three fathers:* the three earths and the three heavens. The world is divided into heaven, sky or air, and earth, and each of these, again, is sometimes spoken of as threefold. Cf. 'Now clear the triple region of the air' (Marlowe's Tamburlaine the Great, Act I. Scene II. Part I.) *He:* the Sun. *They:* the Gods. *Speak together:* converse about the Sun, says Sâyaṇa. The reading of the Atharva-veda in the last páda is decidedly better than that of the Ṛigveda, 'in speech all-knowing but not all-impelling.'

11 *The five-spoked wheel:* the year with five seasons, elsewhere said to be six, or seven, in number. See stanza 12.

12 *Five-footed:* the five feet of the Sire or Sun are according to Sâyaṇa, the five seasons, the dewy and the cold seasons being counted as one. The *twelve forms* are the twelve months. The seven wheels are said to be the solar rays, and the six spokes of each wheel are the six seasons, Vasanta or Spring, Grîshma or Summer, Varshâḥ or the Rains, Sarad or Autumn, Hemanta or Winter, and Ṣiṣira or the Cool or Dewy Season. *Whose sight is clear:* instead of *vichakshaṇé*, qualifying *ráthe*, the car, the Ṛigveda has *vichakshaṇám*, referring to the Sun.

13 Formed with twelve spokes, too strong for age to weaken, this wheel of during Order rolls round heaven.
Herein established, joined in pairs together, seven hundred sons and twenty stand, O Agni.

14 The wheel revolves, unwasting, with its felly: ten draw it, yoked to the far-stretching car-pole.
Girt by the region moves the eye of Sûrya, on whom dependent rest all living creatures.

15 They told me these were males, though truly females. He who hath eyes sees this, the blind discerns not.
The son who is a sage hath comprehended: who knows this rightly is his father's father.

16 Of the co-born they call the seventh single-born: the six twin pairs are called the Ṛishis, sons of Gods.
Their good gifts sought of men are ranged in order due, and, various, form by form, move for their guiding Lord.

---

14 *Ten:* probably the ten regions of space, the four cardinal and the four intermediate points, with the zenith and the nadir. *The region:* mid-air, the firmament between heaven and earth.

15 *They told me these were males:* Prof. Wilson observes: 'This is a piece of grammatical mysticism; *raṣmi*, a ray of the sun, here personified as a female, is properly a noun masculine.' But this is just the reverse of the explanation that is required. Prof. Grassmann suggests that the meaning may be that Night and Morning, both feminine, have received the name of Day. *The son who is a sage:* an intelligent son may be called the parent of an ignorant father as being his superior in knowledge.

16 *The co-born:* the six pairs of months, or six seasons of two months each. The *single-born* is the thirteenth and intercalary month of the luni-solar year: 'the moon of later birth' (Ṛigveda I. 25. 8). *The Ṛishis:* according to Sâyaṇa, *ṛishayaḥ* here means *gantâraḥ*, goers, but in what sense is uncertain. *Guiding Lord:* their controller, the Sun.

17 Beneath the upper realm, above this lower, bearing her Calf at foot, the Cow hath risen.
Whitherward, to what place hath she departed? Where doth she calve? Not in this herd of cattle.

18 Who, that the father of this Calf discerneth beneath the upper realm, above the lower,
Showing himself a sage, may here declare him? Whence hath the godlike spirit had its rising?

19 Those that come hitherward they call departing, those that depart they call directed hither.
Whatever ye have made, Indra and Soma! steeds draw, as 'twere, yoked to the region's car-pole.

20 Two Birds with fair wings, knit with bonds of friendship, in the same sheltering tree have found a refuge.
One of the twain eats the sweet Fig-tree's berry: the other, eating not, regardeth only.

21 The tree whereon the fine Birds eat the sweetness, where they all rest and procreate their offspring—
Upon the top, they say, the fruit is luscious: none gaineth it who knoweth not the Father.

---

17 Ushas or Dawn has risen between heaven and earth, carrying with her the young Sun her offspring. *Where doth she calve?*: Where does she bring forth the Sun? *This herd of cattle:* the visible world wherein we live.

18 Ushas is the mother, but who can say who the father of the Sun is? *The godlike spirit:* the Sun.

19 This stanza refers to the planets which change their relative position as they revolve. Indra is here the Sun, and Soma the Moon.

20 *Two Birds with fair wings:* according to Sâyaṇa, the vital and the Supreme Spirit dwelling in one body. The vital spirit enjoys the fruit or reward of actions while the Supreme Spirit is merely a passive spectator.

21 In this stanza the *fine Birds* are perhaps the Fathers or Spirits of the Departed who enjoy in heaven the reward of their actions on earth. *Procreate their offspring:* see Ṛigveda X. 64. 14, where the

22 Where the fine birds hymn ceaselessly their portion
of life eternal, and the sacred synods.
There is the Universe's Guard and Keeper who, wise
hath entered into me the simple.

HYMN X.

How on the Gâyatrî the Gâyatrî was based; how
from the Trishṭup they fashioned the Trishṭup forth;
How on the Jagatî was based the Jagatî—they who
know this have won themselves immortal life.

Fathers are represented as the cause of the fruitfulness of the mothers, Heaven and Earth, who give birth to Gods and men. *None gaineth it:* this enjoyment in heaven is not obtained by meritorious actions only, but knowledge of the Father, the great Primal Cause of being, is also necessary. Sâyaṇa explains *suparṇấḥ*, 'having beautiful wings,' 'fine birds,' in this and the following stanza as 'smooth-gliding (rays).' *Their offspring* is, he says, the light, and *the Father* is the cherishing and protecting Sun. Prof. Ludwig thinks that stanzas 23—22 are originally unconnected fragments inserted together in this hymn merely because the word *suparṇấḥ* (used, apparently, in various senses) has a prominent place in each verse. *Suparṇấḥ* has been explained by various scholars as two species of souls; rays of light; metres; Spirits of the Dead; priests; Day and Night; and the tree on which they rest is the body; the orb or region of the Sun; the Sacrificial Post; the world; the mythical World-Tree. A generally satisfactory explanation of the three stanzas is hardly to be hoped for.

22 *The fine birds* here are perhaps the priests, and *the Universe's Guard and Keeper* may be the deified Soma, the inspirer of the poet.

The hymn, which is a continuation of Hymn IX., is taken, with variations, transpositions, omissions, and additions, from Ṛigveda I. 164. 23—47.

1 Prof. Wilson, following Sâyaṇa, paraphrases this stanza as follows: 'They who know the station of Agni upon the earth; the station of Vâyu that was fabricated from the firmament, and that station of the Sun which is placed in heaven, obtain immortality.' He observes that the purport of the phraseology, borrowed from the several metres Gâyatrî, Trishṭubh, and Jagatî, is not very clear, and that it may be merely an obscure and mystic reference to the text of the Veda, a knowledge of which is essential to final felicity. The meaning seems to be that those who are thoroughly acquainted with the appropriate rewards that follow the due employment of each of the sacred metres named are on the right road to immortal life and happiness in heaven.

2 With Gâyatrî he measures out the praise-song, Sâman with praise-song, triplet with the Trishṭup,
The triplet with the two or four-foot measure, and with the syllable they form seven metres.

3 With Jagatî the flood in heaven he stablished, and saw the Sun in the Rathantara Sâman.
Gâyatrî hath, they say, three logs for burning: hence it excels in majesty and vigour.

4 I invocate this Milch-cow good at milking, so that the Milker, deft of hand, may milk her.
May Savitar give goodliest stimulation. The caldron is made hot: he will proclaim it.

5 She, Lady of all treasures, hath come hither, yearning in spirit for her calf, and lowing.
May this Cow yield her milk for both the Asvins, and may she prosper to our high advantage.

---

2 The Gâyatrî metre consists of three pâdas or divisions, and the Sâman or chanted hymn is generally composed of three ṛichas or verses of praise. *Triplet:* the word *vâkú* in the text is said to mean either two or three connected stanzas, that is, a short hymn. *Two or four-foot measure:* consisting of two or four pâdas, divisions, or hemistichs. The meaning is not clear. *With the syllable:* they form the seven generic metres of the Veda with the syllable, which is the chief element of metre, the Gâyatrî consisting of eight syllables in a pâda, the Trishṭup of eleven, and the Jagatî of twelve.

3 *With Jagatî:* through the power of this metre. *He:* the Creator; Brahmâ, according to Sâyaṇa. *The flood:* the celestial ocean; the waters above the firmament. *Rathantara:* a name of various Sâmans. *Three logs:* the three pâdas or divisions of the stanza being fancifully likened to pieces of fuel used for the sacrificial fire.

4 The Milch-cow in this and the two following stanzas may be the Cow who supplies milk for the sacrifice. According to Sâyaṇa, the cow may be the rain-cloud, her milk being the rain, and her milker Vâyu, the God of Wind, who causes it to flow. The calf, Sâyaṇa says, is the world longing for the rain to fall. *The caldron:* in which the milk that is to be offered as a libation is heated.

5 *Lady of all Treasures:* as supplying the milk used in the sacrifice which brings prosperity to the worshipper. *The Asvins:* who are especially worshipped with the Gharma or libation of hot milk.

6 The Cow hath lowed after her blinking youngling: she licks his forehead as she lows, to form it.
His mouth she fondly calls to her warm udder, and suckles him with milk while gently lowing.

7 He also snorts, by whom encompassed round the Cow lows as she closely clings to him who sheds the rain.
She with her shrilling cries hath humbled mortal men, and, turned to lightning, hath stripped off her covering robe.

8 That which hath breath and life and speed and motion lies firmly stablished in the midst of houses.
The living moves by powers of the departed: the immortal is the brother of the mortal.

9 The old hath waked the young Moon from his slumber, who runs his circling course with many round him.
Behold the God's high wisdom in its greatness: he who died yesterday to-day is living.

10 He who hath made him doth not comprehend him: from him who saw him surely he is hidden.

---

7 *He:* probably Parjanya, the God of the rain-cloud. *The Cow:* the cloud. *To form it:* or, in order to low: 'sie brült ihr Gebrüll.'—Grassmann. *Shrilling cries:* the whizzing sound supposed to be made by lightning.

8 The subject of the first line is apparently Agni. *By powers:* or, after the manner. *Brother of:* or, sharer of one dwelling with. Living man follows the steps of, or is supported by those who have gone before, and finally enjoys a home with them in heaven. Prof. Wilson, following Sâyaṇa, translates the second line differently: 'the life of the mortal body, cognate with the mortal frame, endures immortal, (sustained) by (obsequial) offerings.' The stanza is very obscure.

9 This stanza is taken from Rigveda X. 55. 5. Sâyaṇa explains it differently, making Indra, identified with Time, the subject. I follow Prof. Ludwig's interpretation which is simpler and more rational. *Many round him:* stars of the asterisms through which the Moon passes.

10 Lightning, regarded as the immediate cause of rain, appears to be the subject of the stanza. He springs from the bosom of his mother, the cloud, with his countless offspring in the shape of fertilizing rain-drops, appears for a moment and then is lost to sight.

He, yet enveloped in his mother's bosom, source of much life, hath sunk into destruction.

11 I saw the Herdsman, him who never stumbles, approaching by his pathways and departing.
He, clothed with gathered and diffusive splendours, within the worlds continually travels.

12 Dyaus is our father, our begetter: kinship is here. This great Earth is our kin and mother.
Between the wide-spread world-halves is the birth-place. The Father laid the Daughter's germ within it.

13 I bid thee tell me earth's extremest limit, about the Stallion's genial flow I ask thee;
I ask about the universe's centre, and touching highest heaven where Speech abideth.

14 The earth's most distant limit is this altar: this Soma is the Stallion's genial humour;
This sacrifice the universe's centre: this Brahman highest heaven where Speech abideth.

15 What thing I truly am I know not clearly: mysterious, fettered in my mind I wander.
When the first-born of holy Law approached me, then of this Speech I first obtain a portion.

---

11 *The Herdsman:* the Sun who surveys and guards the world.

12 *Dyaus:* Heaven. *World-halves:* literally two bowls or vessels into which the Soma juice is poured, or the upper and the lower board of the Soma press, and figuratively an expression for heaven and earth. The firmament or space between these two is, as the region of the rain, the womb of all beings. The Father is Dyaus, and the Daughter is Earth whose fertility depends upon the germ of rain laid in the firmament.

14 *This altar:* as the place nearest to heaven, the place where Gods visit men. *Soma:* regarded as the principle of life and fertility. *The Stallion* is Dyaus or Father Heaven who impregnates the clouds and Earth. *Speech:* personified as the Goddess Vâk.

15 *The first-born of holy Law:* according to Sâyaṇa, the first-born (perceptions) of the truth.

16 Back, forward goes he, grasped by power inherent, immortal born the brother of the mortal.
Ceaseless they move in opposite directions: men mark the one and fail to mark the other.

17 Seven germs unripened yet are Heaven's prolific seed: their functions they maintain by Vishṇu's ordinance.
Endued with wisdom through intelligence and thought, present on every side they compass us about.

18 Upon what syllable of holy praise-hymn, as 'twere their highest heaven, the Gods repose them—
Who knows not this, what will he do with praise-hymn? But they who know it well sit here assembled.

19 They, ordering the verse's foot by measure, with the half-verse arranged each thing that moveth.
Prayer was diffused in many forms three-footed: thereby the world's four regions have their being.

20 Fortunate mayst thou be with goodly pasture, and may we also be exceeding wealthy.
Feed on the grass, O Cow, through all the seasons, and coming hitherward drink limpid water.

---

16 This stanza appears to refer to the Sun in his daily course from east to west and his nightly return to the east, the former visible to men and the latter invisible. *They*, in this case, would mean the Sun by day and the invisible Sun at night.

17 This stanza, as Prof. Ludwig remarks, is one of the most unintelligible in the whole Veda. *The seven*, according to Sâyaṇa, are the solar rays, and Vishṇu is said to be the Sun.

18 The *syllable* is probably the *Praṇava*, the mystical sacred syllable Om. This syllable is set forth in the Upanishads as the object of profound religious meditation, and the highest spiritual efficacy is attributed to it.

19 *They:* the *bhûtakṛitas* or creative Ṛishis. See III. 28. 1. *Three-footed:* expressed in the Gâyatrî metre of three pâdas or divisions. *Have their being:* the whole world is supported and kept alive by prayer. This stanza is not taken from the Ṛigveda.

20 Addressed to the cow who supplies milk for the libations, when she is let loose.

21 Forming the water-floods the Cow herself hath lowed, one-footed or two-footed or four-footed, she,
Who hath become eight-footed or acquired nine feet, the universe's thousand-syllabled Pankti. From her descend in streams the seas of water.

22 Dark the descent: the birds are golden-coloured. Robed in the floods they fly aloft to heaven.
Again from Order's seat have they descended, and inundated all the earth with fatness.

23 The footless Maid precedeth footed creatures. Who marketh, Mitra Varuṇa! this your doing?
The Babe unborn supporteth this world's burthen, supporteth Right and watcheth Wrong and Falsehood.

24 Virâj is Speech, and Earth, and Air's mid-region. He is Prajâpati, and he is Mṛityu.

---

21 *The Cow herself hath lowed:* the great rain-cloud, regarded as Vâk, Speech or Sound, has thundered. Sâyaṇa explains *one-footed* as sounding from the cloud; *two-footed*, from cloud and sky; *four-footed*, from the four cardinal points; *eight-footed*, from the four points and the four intermediate points; the *nine feet* being these eight and the zenith. The Ṛigveda has *gaurī́h*, female buffalo, instead of *gaúh*, cow. *Pankti:* a fivefold metre consisting of five pâdas of eight syllables each, here representing the long roll of the thunder.

22 *Dark the descent:* the rays of light descend into the darkness of the earth when wrapped in night, and rise again to heaven with the moisture which they have absorbed to descend again in the form of fertilizing rain. See Ludwig.

23 This stanza is taken, with an unimportant variant, from Ṛigveda I. 152. 3. *The footless Maid:* Ushas or Dawn, who moves unsupported in the sky: Cf. 'First, Indra Agni! hath this Maid come footless unto those with feet' (Ṛigveda VI. 59. 6). *The Babe unborn:* the Sun before his appearance in heaven.

24 *Virâj:* see. A. V. VIII. 10. 1, note. *Sâdhyas:* said by Yâska to be 'Gods whose dwelling-place is the sky.' They are named among the minor divinities in the Amarakosha, and, as Wilson observes, it would seem that in Sâyaṇa's day the purport of the designation had become uncertain.' See VII. 5. 1; 79. 2; VIII. 8. 12. The stanza is not taken from the Ṛigveda.

He is the Lord Imperial of the Sâdhyas. He rules what is and what shall be hereafter. May he make me lord of what is and shall be.

25 I saw from far away the smoke of fuel with spires that rose on high o'er that beneath it.
The heroes cooked and dressed the spotted bullock. These were the customs in the days aforetime.

26 Three with long tresses show in ordered season. One of them sheareth when the year is ended.
One with his powers the universe regardeth. Of one the sweep is seen, but not the figure.

27 Speech hath been measured out in four divisions: the Brâhmans who have wisdom comprehend them.
Three, kept in close concealment, cause no motion. Of Speech men speak the fourth division only.

28 They call him Indra, Mitra, Varuṇa, Agni; and he is heavenly nobly-winged Garutmân.
That which is One bards call by many a title: they call It Agni, Yama, Mâtariṣvan.

---

25 *The smoke of fuel:* arising from burning cow-dung. *The heroes:* the Gods. This is, perhaps, a figurative description of the gathering of the rain-clouds.

26 The three are Agni who burns up the vegetation, the all-seeing Sun, and Vâyu the invisible wind.

27 *Three* might, apparently, mean the three Vedas; but these cannot be said to be *kept in close concealment.* *The fourth division:* ordinary language. See Wilson's Translation of the Rigveda-Sanhitâ for Sâyaṇa's elaborate explanation of the stanza as interpreted by the scholars of his time.

28 *Garutmân:* the celestial Bird; the Sun. All these names, says the poet, are names of one and the same Divine Being, the One Supreme Spirit under various manifestations.

The original Rigveda hymn contains five stanzas more. A very full commentary—to which I am indebted for much valuable assistance—will be found in Vol. V. of Ludwig's Der Rigveda, pp. 445—457. The hymn has been discussed also by Dr. Haug, Sitz. ber. der philos. philol. Classe der k. bayer Akademie der Wiszenschaften, bd. II. heft 3. 1875.

APPENDICES.

I. Latin version of Hymns and Stanzas omitted in the English Translation.

II. Index of Hymns.

III. Index of Names, etc.

I. APPENDIX.

OMITTED HYMNS AND VERSES.

Book I. 11. 3—6.

3 Puerpera (infantem) detegat : nos uterum aperimus. Laxa teipsam, puerpera. Tu, parturiens! emitte eum non carni, non adipi, non medullae adhaerentem.

4 Descendat viscosa placenta, cani comedenda placenta; decidat placenta.

5 Diffindo tuum urinae ductum, diffindo vaginam, diffindo inguina. Matrem natumque divido, puerum a placenta divido : decidat placenta.

6 Sicut ventus, sicut mens, sicut alites volant, sic, decem mensium puer, cum placenta descende : descendat placenta.

Book IV. 4. 3—9.

3 Sicut tui surgentis (membrum virile) tanquam inflammatum palpitat, hoc illud tui ardentius haec herba faciat.

4 Sursum (estote) herbarum vires, taurorum vigor. Tu, Indra, corporis potens, virorum masculum robur in hoc homine depone.

5 Ros aquarum primigenitus atque arborum, Somae etiam frater es, vatum sacrorum masculus vigor es.

6 Hodie, Agnis! hodie Savitar! hodie dea Sarasvatis! hodie Brahmanaspatis! hujus fascinum velut arcum extende.

7 Velut nervum in arcu ego tuum fascinum extendo. Aggredere (mulierem) semper indefessus velut cervus damam.

8 Quae sunt equi vires, muli, capri, arietis, atque tauri, illas, corporis potens! in hoc homine depone.

---

3 *Puerpera : sûshấ = sûshaṇâ*, from the root *sû*, to bring forth; one desiring to bring forth; a parturient.

6 Cf. Rigveda V. 78. 8.

The hymn has been translated by Ludwig, Der Rigveda, III. p. 478.

Book VI. 72.

1 Sicut anguis niger ad voluntatem se extendit, Asurarum arte magica formas novas efficiens, sic fascinum tuum, partem cum parte, conjunctum, hic hymnus efficiat.

2 Velut penis (tayadarus) quem ventus permagnum fecit, quantus est onagri penis, tantus penis tuus increscat.

3 Quantum est onagri membrum masculinum, elephanti, asinique, quantum est fortis equi, tantus penis tuus increscat.

Book VI. 101.

1 Taurum age, palpita, incresce et teipsum extende: per totum membrum increscat penis: hoc tu caede feminam.

2 Quo debilem stimulant, quo aegrum excitant (homines), hoc, O Brahmanaspatis, hujus penem in arcus modum extende.

3 Velut nervum in arcu ego tuum fascinum extendo. Aggredere (mulierem) semper indefessus velut cervus damam.

Book VI. 138.

4 Duas tuas venas, a Diis factas, in quibus stat vigor virilis, paxillo ligneo in testiculis ob istam mulierem tibi findo.

5 Ut mulieres mattam (tegetem) facturae arundinem lapide findunt, sic fascinum tuum cum testiculis ob istam mulierem findo.

---

2 *Tayadarus:* the meaning of the word *tâyâdarám* in the text is not discoverable. *Onagri : párasvataḥ;* the animal called Parasvân is probably, as conjectured by von Roth, the wild ass or Onager found on the banks of the Indus, and in former times even in Southern India. The animal is mentioned in Ṛigveda X. 86. 18, and again in Atharvaveda XX. 131. 22.

---

2 *Hoc:* that is, by virtue of this charm, or with this drug.

3 The stanza is repeated from IV. 4. 7.

Book VII. 35.

2 Hae quot tibi sunt venae atque arteriae harum omnium os tibi lapide occlusi.

3 Uteri tui summam partem inferam facio : ne tibi soboles neque filius eveniat. Sterilem et infecundam te facio : lapidem tuum operimentum facio.

Book VII. 90.

3 Ut virga abeat et feminis innocua fiat, (virga) membri humidi, membri quod verberat penetratque, id quod tentum est laxa, id quod sursum tentum est deorsum tende.

Innocua : inoffensive. 'C'est pour *ánāvayās* le seul sens possible, indiqué par l'esprit du morceau, et d'ailleurs la dérivation par *áva yā* (P. W.) n'explique pas la longue. Je conjecture un composé, à coup sûr récent et très exceptionel (mais aussi est-ce un ἅπαξ) fait sur *āvdyati* "il devore," cf. le rapport *cétati : acheták̄s* (l' accentuation importe peu pour une formation aussi hystérogène et arbitraire). L'assimilation du membre viril à une bête féroce qui assaille les femmes est de tous les temps et de tous les lieux.'—M. Victor Henry, whose version of the obscure stanza I have put into the Latin above.

INDEX OF HYMNS.

BOOK I.

BOOK II.

BOOK III.

BOOK IV.

BOOK V.

BOOK VI.

BOOK VIII.

BOOK IX.

INDEX OF NAMES, ETC.